Feminism and the Early Frankfurt School

Studies in Critical Social Sciences Book Series

Haymarket Books is proud to be working with Brill Academic Publishers (www.brill.nl) to republish the *Studies in Critical Social Sciences* book series in paperback editions. This peer-reviewed book series offers insights into our current reality by exploring the content and consequences of power relationships under capitalism, and by considering the spaces of opposition and resistance to these changes that have been defining our new age. Our full catalog of *SCSS* volumes can be viewed at https://www.haymarketbooks.org/series_collections/4-studies-in-critical-social-sciences.

FEMINISM AND THE EARLY FRANKFURT SCHOOL

EDITED BY
CHRISTINE A. PAYNE
JEREMIAH MORELOCK

Haymarket Books
Chicago, IL

First published in 2023 by Brill Academic Publishers, The Netherlands
© 2023 Koninklijke Brill NV, Leiden, The Netherlands

Published in paperback in 2024 by
Haymarket Books
P.O. Box 180165
Chicago, IL 60618
773-583-7884
www.haymarketbooks.org

ISBN: 979-8-88890-343-8

Distributed to the trade in the US through Consortium Book Sales and
Distribution (www.cbsd.com) and internationally through Ingram Publisher
Services International (www.ingramcontent.com).

This book was published with the generous support of Lannan Foundation,
Wallace Action Fund, and the Marguerite Casey Foundation.

Special discounts are available for bulk purchases by organizations and
institutions. Please call 773-583-7884 or email info@haymarketbooks.org for more
information.

Cover design by Jamie Kerry and Ragina Johnson.

Printed in the United States.

Library of Congress Cataloging-in-Publication data is available.

Contents

Preface

1   Why This, Why Now?

On June 24th, 2022, the Supreme Court of the United States overturned Roe vs. Wade. By a 5-4 margin, the constitutional right to abortion established in 1973 was struck down, effectively instituting a ban or very severe restrictions on abortion in approximately half of the fifty states in the nation. Warnings of future court rulings that would overturn the constitutional rights to contraception, same-sex marriage, and interracial marriage have been sounded. Violent threats, actions, and policies against the safety, medical care, bodily autonomy, and very lives of transgender individuals are occurring with horrifying frequency. Cynically manufactured moral panics about queer 'groomers' are repeatedly taken up with deadly seriousness. Under the rhetorical banners of 'Western' or 'Cultural' Marxism and 'critical race theory,' school boards and college review committees are gaining alarming ground in their efforts to scrub K-12 and higher education of 'woke' curricula and careers that have the audacity to identify and explain histories and current relations of racial, gendered, and capitalist inequalities and unfreedoms. White supremacist terrorism is overt. Christian fascist nationalism is increasingly embraced and explicitly declared as the goal of a growing number of fundamentalists. So-called 'traditional' marriage, gender roles, sexuality, and family structures are declared to be 'under attack' and in need of both personal defense and government enforcement. Screeds decrying declining birth rates couched in explicitly eugenical rhetoric about racial 'replacement' are widely broadcast and taken seriously as a threat to the literal and symbolic health and strength of nations. 'Men's Rights' mouthpieces, misogynistic 'incel' culture, right-wing and 'libertarian' militia movements, and near-constant mass shootings proliferate. Paeons to technocratic culture and near hagiographical renderings of autocratic heads of state and heads of corporations ring out. Military and police brutality, mass incarceration, and surveillance technologies abound. Anti-democratic 'populist' leaders have amassed power and leadership positions across scores of countries.

The status of truth is itself a central ideological weapon, with cynical and nihilistic intellectual relativism and 'radical' skepticism serving as seemingly sophisticated battering rams against all facts and norms that center on collective freedom and flourishing. At the same time, *the* Truth of the world – the reified 'truth' of political, cultural, and economic repression and domination – is not only embraced but violently imposed as the normal, necessary, even natural way that the world is and must be. All of this in the context of a climate crisis that rages exponentially, a staggeringly deadly and disabling global pandemic that has been normalized in political, media, and many everyday circles, and an ongoing accumulation crisis in global capitalism that, by design, means acute and chronic misery for the masses in concert with nearly untouchable profit and power for the few. The decades-long fusion of neoliberal market fundamentalism and neoconservative 'family values' fundamentalism has long been a symptom of, and has predictably resulted in, the current situation of authoritarian modern society.

This brief accounting is of course not exhaustive – though it is exhausting and overwhelming. This compounding reality feels like a series of infinitely nested dolls of despair and death. The current moment requires an immediacy of very critical collective action. Many and frequent have been the voices sounding alarm bells about this literally lethal series of situations. Varied and ongoing social movements, protests, and refusals of the fatally repressive status quo exist and gain strength across admittedly fractured fault lines of class, race, gender, sexuality, and nationality. Mass labor unionization from service industries to higher education, serious discussions about police and prison abolition, student and medical debt cancellation, environmental justice, reproductive rights and justice, bodily safety, integrity, and autonomy: these and related movements and their associated demands are growing in number and in explicit support. Such urgent and connected fights for liberation are very much reason for more than cautious optimism.

At the same time and in tandem with social movement organizing, careful critical reflection is necessary to make sense of and to meet the urgency of the current moment. The collection of writings presented in this volume were born out of a desire to address significant components and relations tied to the troubling situations of our times. Addressing the contemporary social-cultural and political-economic landscape requires an 'all-hands-on-deck' approach spanning critical scholarship, practical policy and legislation, and large-scale popular activism; within the realm of critical scholarship, the moment likewise requires varied but overlapping disciplinary lenses and analyses. It is our aim and hope that this volume fruitfully contributes to just such an overarching project of scholarship in solidarity with many others. In particular, the chapters in this edited volume address historical and ongoing ideas, values, practices, and relations related to gender, sex, and sexuality in light of the alarming amplification and acceleration of inequality and unfreedom impacting our lives. To this end, two central threads of critical analysis and emancipatory world-building are brought together: key elements of feminist scholarship and the scholarship of members of the early Frankfurt School. With these key elements and prior to an outline of the specific thinkers and works addressed in this volume as provided in the 'Chapter Summaries' section below, a brief outline of the volume's major themes and central analytic throughlines will serve as a helpful overarching roadmap.

2   Motivating Questions and Guiding Frameworks

Members of the early Frankfurt School including Theodor Adorno, Max Horkheimer, Walter Benjamin, Eric Fromm, and Herbert Marcuse were pioneers of interdisciplinary social science, bringing together ideas from philosophy, sociology, and psychoanalysis to examine the woes of capitalist society in an expansive and integrated way, bridging micro and macro levels of analysis. In the same broad theories, they addressed capital accumulation, dialectics, epistemology, alienation, the social psychology of fascism, popular culture, and the liberatory potentials of aesthetic experience, among other things. Prolific and innovative, the Frankfurt School continues to inspire many among the political Left, and they remain well worth consulting even 90 years later.

Yet in the contemporary period, Leftist theory must dialogue meaningfully with issues of sex, gender, sexuality, and feminism. The Frankfurt School is not well-known for doing this, and in this respect, they often fall out of – or fail to win – the favor of thinkers who are specifically concerned about questions of sex, gender, sexuality, and feminist thought. For this reason, scholars of the Frankfurt School and scholars of feminist theory tend to be different scholars, and their academic clusters of affiliation are typically distinct from one another.

In the interests of building genuine and productive academic dialogue, as well as in the interests of practically building a more informed, comprehensive, unified Left, this divide is very problematic. It is also unnecessary. While the Frankfurt School did not centrally and systematically focus on issues of sex, gender, and feminism, they very much did write on these issues, and when they did, their allegiances were clearly marked with many key feminist precepts. In other of their theories, the extension beyond their focus to issues of feminist concern is a very small, very easy stretch. In other cases, their ideas, insightful as they were, would benefit from the insights of feminist analysis. Reciprocally, the power of the early Frankfurt School could be an enormous intellectual asset to understanding sex and gender relations and serving movements for feminist empowerment – if they are productively and critically synthesized with current feminist theories and insights.

This edited volume presents an original collection of precisely such over-due syntheses of scholarship. Chapters included in our volume articulate and explore ideas from the early Frankfurt School that were explicitly focused on sex, gender, sexuality, and feminism, apply ideas from the early Frankfurt School to a new focus on sex, gender, sexuality, and feminism, and bring ideas from the early Frankfurt School into productive dialogue with historical and contemporary feminist theory.

In order to treat these key elements, we have divided this edited volume into four parts. The first part examines a series of analyses concerning questions of power and the stubborn persistence of authoritarianism in both its explicitly political formations as well as its insidious presence in nominally private areas of life – including the family. Processes of socialization and their subsequent internalization with respect to normative gender and sex roles, ideals, and relationships are examined, alongside the proliferation of explicitly fascist and authoritarian political ideologies and movements that serve as both reflections and reinforcements of relations of domination.

The analyses below concerning the cultural politics of authoritarianism pivot around the dynamics between capitalist class politics and the politics of culture. Historical and contemporary forms of authoritarianism are seen to be strongly rooted in assumptions and expectations regarding relations of domination and repression within particular family structures which are themselves predicated upon assumptions and expectations concerning gender and sexuality. The structure and character of bourgeois family formations hinge in no small part upon presumed lines of authority and submission – lines of authority that reflect and reinforce broader political-economic forms of domination and unfreedom. As concerns gender, sexuality, and, arguably, age, particular roles and associated 'responsibilities' are rendered prescriptively normal, functionally necessary, and natural (in either or both the theological or biological sense). Certain 'kinds' or 'types' of gendered and sexual selves *ought* to – because they seemingly simply *have* to – adhere to pregiven/unquestion(ed/able) positions and practices. The bourgeois nuclear family appears as a model of society in miniature, complete with all the trappings of gender naturalization common to similarly naturalized accounts of "The Market." In its current neoliberal instantiation, the naturalized market, shorn increasingly of any state supports serving as a social wage, works to lock in so-called traditional family roles and values. To the extent that gendered reproductive labor in a wide sense is bereft of public safety nets, such unwaged labor falls to the family, reinforcing the apparently natural and necessary dichotomy between public vs. private and associated masculine vs. feminine spheres. Second and third shifts of labor for women (particularly working-class women and women of color) working outside the home are rendered practically necessary, while at the same time, calls for 'traditional' family structures aiming to restrict women to the 'private' home are common.

Naturalistic fallacies – what ought to be the case presumed to follow from what naturally is the case – are doing at least double work in such frameworks: what is 'naturally' the case in terms of gender, sexuality, and family as well as what is 'naturally' the case vis-à-vis capitalist markets and class relations more broadly. However, these cases are *not* natural kinds or cases to begin with. Such compounding layers of reified assumptions in both the public and putatively private spheres act back upon one another, solidifying and justifying both family and class repressions in a stubborn loop. Forms of public and private life seem to support the fatalist position that 'it just is what it is.' Those in positions of power take for granted the seemingly natural and thereby correct submission of others to their will and whims. Additionally, such apparently natural/necessary and normal/good demands for submission and repression affect those in positions of power and authority as well; in the interests of securing a relative sense of security and order, the viciousness of authoritarianism perversely attracts and attacks its own purveyors and perpetrators.

The doubly false naturalistic fallacy undergirding patriarchal authoritarianism finds a supremely stubborn anchor in biological determinist accounts of gender and sexuality. The second part of this volume addresses questions concerning personal and group identity. The chapters in this part focus on the liberatory potentials of challenging or subverting taken-for-granted gender, sex, and sexuality identity categories and roles, including their intersections with racial, ethnic, and class-based identities.

From a biological determinist standpoint, social relations, including all manner of social inequalities, ultimately reduce down to and serve as reflections of biological differences, where differences – real or imagined – by extension explain and justify inherent inequalities.[1] Insofar as biological determinist accounts falsely presume gender and associated gender roles to be synonymous with a falsely presumed biological sex binary – which is then/also falsely presumed to be synonymous with heterosexuality – the naturalness and normalcy of heteropatriarchy appears beyond dispute.

---

1 It is worth noting that putatively biological/secular claims regarding the 'inherent' nature of gender, sex, sexuality, and associated inequalities and unfreedoms can and do merge with religious claims concerning the necessity of heteropatriarchy. Whether couched in secular or sacred frameworks, the always-already denigrated status of those who are not cisgender, not straight, not men proves stubbornly persistent.

Within this ideological loop, and often in concert with fundamentalist – indeed theocratic – religious imperatives, patriarchy is justified by recourse to apparently essential (and unequal) biological features and functions, while such features and functions are made to explain the how and why of patriarchy. On such an account, to argue against heteropatriarchy would be to argue against nature – a feat seemingly both practically futile as well as morally suspect. Coupled with a falsely naturalized and often teleological conceptualization of capitalist economic relations, the possibility for critique and transformation of the existing socio-cultural and political-economic states of affairs are falsely and unnecessarily foreclosed.

That the entire chain of reasoning relied upon in such determinist accounts is factually inaccurate seems not to dissuade those committed to the rationalization of the social status quo by recourse to 'nature.' The concrete consequences of assuming a biological determinist or essentialist approach vis-à-vis gender, sex, and sexuality are clear and dire. The assignation and expectation of 'properly' masculine and feminine gender expressions are maintained. Entire groups of human beings are rendered 'unnatural,' 'immoral,' or 'nonexistent.' Forced assimilation to the social and sexual status quo, as well as calls for outright genocidal eradication occur. Authoritarian force in the name of natural/necessary/normal heteropatriarchy also underwrites ideologies and practices concerning divisions of labor – in particular, reproductive labor. Insofar as women are understood to be essentially and primarily the bearers and raisers of children, demands to equitably share reproductive labor face resistance. The human right to decide if and under what conditions pregnancy is desired remains insecure when not stripped away entirely. Indeed, forced pregnancy and childbirth are the necessary consequences (one suspects the explicit or implicit goals) that result when the freedom and right to abortion and contraception are restricted or revoked.

Analyses in this volume bring feminist and early Frankfurt School work to bear on the myriad aspects of individual and collective life falsely biologized and/or falsely essentialized – in other words, rendered static and 'stuck.' Gender, sex, and sexuality are unconflated and understood as layered but distinct components of self, identity, and social relations. The empirically false and ethically – indeed existentially – harmful assumptions of gender, sexuality, and sex binaries are demonstrated, while the social and historical mediations of such identities are centered; this, in order to demand radical reconceptualizations and radically different – liberatory – experiences. Beyond such critiques of reductive determinism, several chapters also consider the usefulness of the concept of 'non-identity' in the technical sense of inherent contradiction and necessary incompleteness in comparison to senses of self (and other selves) anchored in seamless synthesis or completion.

In addition to its central role in the critiques of biological determinism vis-à-vis gender, sex, and sexuality, questions concerning essentialism recur in several chapters below that are centrally concerned with questions of knowledge. In the third part, the significance of standpoint and intersectional analyses are taken up, with a focus on the real and potentially emancipatory role that imagination, desire, and creative expression serve in relation to the repressive, exploitative, and alienating social structures, identity schema, and political ideologies identified and challenged in the volume's adjacent parts. Alongside analyses of political economy, social and natural scientific schemata, and constructions of modern subjects, this series of reflections on the power and necessity of standpoint and intersectional analyses gesture towards projects guided by cautious optimism – critically-grounded hope for new understandings and practices of self and society amid the all-too-common contexts of modern repressions and dominations.

In order to identify, critique, and transform reified conceptions, beliefs, and practices, it is necessary that the perspectives of particular individuals and groups be taken seriously; specifically, those perspectives that are grounded in particular lived experiences of domination, exclusion, and unfreedom must be shifted from their economic, social, and political positions of marginalization to the center of accounts and analyses of truth. This political-epistemic shift is partially captured in a turn towards feminist and other forms of standpoint theory; with such an approach, the standpoints of variously and multiply marginalized people are recognized as potentially providing more objective understandings and accounts of reality, insofar as said reality is suffused with unequal relations and experiences of power. Those individuals and groups who experience oppressive forms of power as a brute fact of their everyday existence are potentially well-positioned to know and to critique such facts of power relations. Such epistemic vantage points born of lived experience are rarely singular in character, meaning that intersectionality as theoretical approach and as lived reality is crucial. As demonstrated in a number of chapters in this volume, the multiple and compounding forms of unfreedom across gender, sex, sexuality, race, ethnicity, class, disability, etc. allow for both specific critiques of particular oppressions as well as more general assessments of the systemic failures and harms at work in the contemporary world.

Crucially, such intersectional standpoints neither rely upon nor seek any sort of 'return' to essentialized selves. To be sure, standpoint and intersectional analyses and critiques of social reality are grounded in the specific experiences of gendered, racialized, and classed selves; nevertheless, such selves and associated situations and standpoints demand that the historical and material conditions of (im)possibility from which such selves emerge and coalesce in the first place be located front and center in analyses. That there are essentialized assumptions regarding different groups of people, and that such essentialized assumptions have and continue to repeatedly serve as grounds and justification for unequal and oppressive lives, precisely inform and motivate many intersectional standpoint analyses. To the extent that different groups are 'essentially' different from other groups in society as concerns lived experiences, the marshalling of said experiences as epistemic warrants for critique ultimately serve as emancipatory tools against the essential(izing) experiences of unfreedom themselves. Simply put – there is no 'essence' to, for example, femininity or womanhood that grants women special access to truths. It is rather that unique experiences grounded in historical material reality provide relatively unique and useful perspectives from which to see and challenge seemingly universal or hegemonic truths and relations.

A word of caution is in order in light of standpoint and intersectional frameworks; namely, that the burden of doing epistemological, practical, and political-ethical work should not be shouldered solely by those most marginalized in society. The use of intersectional standpoint theories as necessary tools for enhancing the objectivity of accounts and critiques of society should not result in assumptions or calls for the most unfree people and groups to do the most or heaviest lifting with respect to transforming society. The demands made, and made possible through, specifically situated standpoints require – both practically and ethically – that broad-based collective actions be undertaken.

The fourth and final part of this volume offers a series of reflections on the real, the presumed, and the potential relationships between the spheres of culture and nature, as well as the gendered typologies frequently associated with these respective spheres. Drawing on early Frankfurt School thought, feminist theory, and potent interdisciplinary scholarship in the field of science and technology studies, the chapters in this part variously highlight and challenge a pair of frequently intertwined assumptions concerning the dualistic relationship of nature and culture, as well as the gendered traits and characteristics assigned to these seemingly distinct areas of life.

Authors in this and preceding parts draw attention to the ongoing significance of one of the early Frankfurt School's most enduring series of analyses – those concerning the dialectic of Enlightenment and the domination of nature via one-dimensional instrumental reasoning and technological rationality. Spanning the analytic spheres of political-economy, culture, epistemology, and

ontology, Frankfurt School and feminist work is brought into particularly fruitful dialogue as concerns the long-standing associations in the modern West
between women and/as nature and men's mastery of nature. Predicated upon
figurations of nature – including non-humans – as essentially brute matter that
is nonetheless prone to 'irrational' or 'violent' dynamics in need of taming by
humans/culture, centuries-long efforts to not only schematize, order, and predict but to also dominate nature are taken to be the prerogatives of our own –
somehow related, somehow different, but also superior—human nature. The
radical separation presumed to exist between humanity and the natural (and,
ironically, often the social) contexts, in and by which humans take and have
their existence, supports demands for the ever-increasing scope and scale of
scientific and technological progress; 'progress,' here understood in part as
bringing the natural world increasingly under the direct command of humans.

To be sure, it is not scientific or technological progress as such that claims
the critical attention of early Frankfurt School or feminist thinkers. Rather,
what gives pause are the underlying ideologies and subsequent practices that
presume seamless or total human knowledge and control are either possible
or necessary. More centrally and alarming is that mastery over nature – even
if not 'yet' total – increasingly serves as a taken-for-granted 'end' rather than
'means' towards liberatory human ends. Horkheimer and Adorno's 'Dialectic of
Enlightenment,' in part, names the historical dynamic whereby human desires
for safety and security through mastery of the world necessarily pivot around
scientific positivism and technological rationality as ends-in-themselves,
which reign supreme in a myth-like fashion. In seeking to escape superstition,
illusion, chaos, and lack of control, modern Western science and technology
ironically function increasingly as reified ideological projects that humanity
must submit to regardless of substantive content, practices, and goals. The
repression of nature in the service of humanity acts back in a repressive fashion upon humans insofar as the human elements (themselves, of course, part
of nature) lose significance vis-à-vis fixations on brute positive facts, calculating and predictive logic, and increasingly refined scientific and social methods rigorously employed for their own sake. Or, not simply for their own sake;
such reified conceptions and practices serve ends or goals beyond themselves,
namely, the ends and goals of capitalism (often couched in the language of
'pragmatism'): profit, productivity, efficiency, competition, and thus better
lives for all. The reified dynamics of capitalism, in combination with the reification of instrumental rationality leads to (a one-sided form of) human progress eating its own tail.

As many members of the early Frankfurt School as well as feminist and other
critical thinkers have and continue to stress, such a conception and series of

practices of humans vis-à-vis nature is neither necessary nor desirable. The radical separations made between humanity and nature, the reification of science and technology as ends-in-themselves (shorn of their actually critical and emancipatory potential), and the desire to dominate rather than understand and work with the world around us are historically specific ways of being in the world that can be critiqued and transformed. Of particular interest in many chapters collected here is the radical potential of technology to help rather than hinder our collective desire for freedom and flourishing. Eschewing reactionary pulls 'back to nature' as well as pragmatism-as-progress pushes towards 'technoscience as salvation,' contributors to this volume use early Frankfurt School and feminist thought to stake out alternative visions and ways forward. Rather than assert false naturalizations of what are in fact social relations, and rather than engineer and enforce social unfreedom and inequalities, we can instead seek to cultivate human – humane – ways of being in the world within and across the natural-social contexts that are our lives. In the absence of smooth seamless selves or reassuring security via total knowledge and control, what are desperately needed and what must be insisted upon now and moving forward are second 'natures.' The near and distant futures are not yet realized; radical desires for radically different selves, societies, and social relations demand our attention.

Within and across each of the four parts, central concepts and arguments developed by both early Frankfurt School scholars as well as feminist theorists are provided, along with ample historical and contemporary examples serving as concrete touchstones and illustrative elaborations. Readers will encounter ideas from critical race theory, queer theory, science and technology studies, and cultural studies, in conversation with the volume's two central strands of scholarship. Taken as a whole, this volume serves as a timely and fruitful illustration of the significance of reading and thinking with feminist and Frankfurt School analyses, together.

3   Chapter Summaries

This volume is organized into four parts, each investigating a central area of intersection between the work of the early Frankfurt School and critical feminist scholarship. The first part explores relationships between class politics and the politics of culture, with a particular focus on the cultural politics of authoritarianism. The second part examines characteristics and instantiations of power in relation to the creation, reproduction, and transformation of identity – identity in terms of personal and group identities, as well as identity thinking vis-à-vis concepts, categories, and classification schema. The third part considers the centrality of intersectional analyses for critical theory, highlighting the significance of analyzing gender, sex, and sexuality in relation with race and class in particular. The fourth part turns to a series of ontological, epistemological, and political-ethical concerns in the domain of science and technology studies regarding the concept/category of 'the feminine;' the authors in this final part consider the creation of conditions of possibility for thinking and experiencing 'human nature' in radically different ways.

Part 1: Culture and Class: the Libidinal Politics of Authoritarianism opens with Kristin Lawler's *Sex, Hope, and Rock and Roll: Radical Feminism and the Freudian Left*. Lawler revisits the Freudian Marxism of Wilhelm Reich and Herbert Marcuse, in connection with the radical feminist thought exemplified by Shulamith Firestone and Ellen Willis, to demonstrate the 'explosive' potential present in taking seriously the biological-libidinal bases of our human desires for freedom, creativity, and pleasure. Against approaches that would identify, explain, and seek to transform social relations under modern capitalism by way of a singular focus upon class exploitation, Lawler reminds us of the centrality of repressive authoritarianism present in the institution of the nuclear family and associated cultural roles, norms, and values related to gender and sexuality. Noting that cultural conservatism, expressed as unquestioned support for productivist work ethics and 'family values,' persistently permeates the political right *and* many politically left projects otherwise aimed at critiquing capitalist alienation and exploitation, Lawler contends that those seeking truly liberatory ways of being in the world instead revisit and revive an historical materialist, psychoanalytically-informed radical feminist approach that aims to rip out the foundational roots of repression; namely, the taken-for-granted sexual division of labor (and labor in general) and all associated social relations that radically restrict our basic libidinal drives for pleasure, gratification, and autonomy. The repression and authoritarian structures nurtured within the family both reflect and reproduce the repression and authoritarianism of the culture of modern capitalism writ large.

Lawler fuses anti-authoritarian Critical Theory and radical feminism in order to imagine and demand a truly 'libidinal morality' cut free from the ideologies of material scarcity and sexual asceticism. She follows early Frankfurt School analyses in demonstrating that the rifts presumed to exist naturally and necessarily between sexuality and civilization, pleasure and responsibility, are in fact false dichotomies that need no longer be mistaken as transhistorical truths against which human life and desire must contort to find a semblance of security and connection. The desire for freedom is a universal human need – a need that has been repeatedly stamped out historically by way of reference to

a series of naturalized, normalized, reality principles. Universal human emancipation surely requires that capitalism and class exploitation be overcome;
more fundamentally still, so too must sexual repression in its myriad manifestations be uprooted in the most radical – both biological and cultural – fashion. The stakes Lawler identifies are clear: "In the culture wars, half measures,
then, are political suicide ... a little liberation without full liberation sends
people running for cover in authoritarianism ... As we continue to be engaged
in the political battles around working class cultural and economic emancipation that both the early Frankfurt School and women's liberation feminists
analyzed, and as the left continues to eat itself alive in battles over the universal vs. the particular, class vs. identity, mainstream vs. radical, we would do well
to take their counsel to heart."

Ryan Moore likewise draws attention to the central role played by the patri-
archal family in priming individuals for the acceptance and perpetuation
of repressive authoritarian social relations. In *Fascism and the Patriarchal
Family: the Studies of Authoritarianism at the Institute for Social Research*,
Moore traces the series of arguments put forth by Wilhelm Reich in *The Mass
Psychology of Fascism*, as well as the collection of essays by Max Horkheimer,
Eric Fromm, and Herbert Marcuse in *Studien über Autorität und Familie*
(Studies on Authority and the Family). Across these works, Moore identifies
a common concern to understand the "subjective factor(s)" at work in the
formation of character types and personality-structures amenable to fascism.
Recognizing the inadequacy of a strictly class-based analysis, these early
Frankfurt School thinkers sought to identify the social psychological components partially responsible for the stubborn reproduction of authoritarian
political, economic, and social relations in modern society. Fusing Marx's
critiques of the inherent contradictions of capitalism with Freud's insights
into the libidinal economic theory of drives, Reich, Horkheimer, Fromm, and
Marcuse each attempted to pinpoint exactly how and why fascism, Nazism,
and authoritarianism in a broad sense had been able to secure the alarming
foothold they had. Individual and collective desires for at least relative security
and certainty, coupled with the cultivation of unquestioned respect-qua-fear
of authority secured – in the context of modern capitalism and its inherently
exploitative dynamics – a fatal basis for both submission to domination and
wielding domination over others.

In contrast to the reductive analyses provided by orthodox Marxists focused
on 'objective' economic factors, Reich and members of the early Frankfurt
School took equally seriously the 'subjective factor' of ideology; a comprehensive explanation of nationalism, fascism, and Nazi race 'science' required careful attention to the everyday structures of power incubated within patriarchal

family and sexual relations. Failure to recognize or reckon with the role that gender, sexuality, and the family play vis-à-vis the creation and reproduction of authoritarian-primed personalities, is to be left wondering, with Reich, why so many who are exploited fail to resist their exploitation – or, more troubling still, actively support economic, political, and social structures of domination and repression. In concert with Lawler, Moore makes clear the connections between Critical Theory and feminist theory. His unflinching focus on the patriarchal family's gendered and sexual structure demonstrates 'internal' dynamics of authority-obedience, fear-aggression, and desire-repression that mimic and make ready in fatally repetitive fashion the 'external' realities of fascism. Moore's concluding insights drive home the connections between and continuing relevance of both the thought of the early Frankfurt School and critical feminist theory in the present moment: "The theoretical analyses and empirical studies from the early years of Nazism have much to offer for contemporary critics of fascism. However, their categories and methods cannot simply be replicated in our present context, especially in light of the changing social relationships of gender, sexuality, and family. Horkheimer, Fromm, and Marcuse all observed that the classic ideal of the bourgeois family was deteriorating under the conditions of postliberal monopoly capitalism. The pressing challenge for anti-fascist scholars today is to understand how the changing landscapes of gender, sexuality, and family continue to create authoritarian personalities in an age of digital media and commodified data science [...] Just as we need a typology of the Authoritarian Personality 2.0 upgraded for our new media and niche markets that have made theories of mass society obsolete, current mutations of patriarchy and misogyny demand updated models for understanding how fascism continues to spawn in this diversifying, increasingly "unconventional" landscape of gender, sexuality, and family."

Such a contemporary investigation is taken up in *Family and Authoritarianism* by Caio Vasconcellos and Rafaela N. Pannain. Here, Horkheimer's essay in *Studien über Autorität und Familie* (Studies on Authority and the Family) is analyzed alongside Melinda Cooper's *Family Values: Between Neoliberalism and the New Social Conservatism* in order to bring into focus the continuities of authoritarian familial and social relations across distinct historical and political contexts. Pivoting from Horkheimer's analysis of the role of the bourgeois patriarchal family in the context of the rise of fascism and Nazism towards Cooper's investigations into the ideological overlaps between more recent neoliberal and neoconservative political-economic projects, Vasconcellos and Pannain make clear that contemporary Critical and feminist work must continue to focus explicitly upon the family and its associated roles, norms, and values when aiming to make sense of and challenge broader social patterns of exploitation and domination.

As Vasconcellos and Pannain remind us, Horkheimer's analyses of the patriarchal family demonstrated that "misogyny is the anteroom of fascism" – a succinct and sobering summation of material-psychical dynamics that have, in different but deeply related fashions, survived and taken hold with fervor in the wake of neoliberalism's rise to global dominance. Indeed, the authors' inclusion of Cooper's strikingly insightful account detailing the history and current forms of both neoliberalism and neoconservatism leave little doubt regarding the deeply intertwined – "Janus-face" – relations between 'free-market' economic dynamics and 'family values' cultural imperatives. Vasconcellos and Pannain persuasively demonstrate the forgotten (repressed?) interdependencies at play between economic elites' promotion of unregulated market competition and cultural conservatives' promotion of traditional family – and by extension gender and sexuality – roles and functions. Free market ideology, premised upon the idealized presumption of atomized and autonomous individuals exchanging goods and services absent public/government intervention of any sort, quires a very deeply regulated entity in the form of the bourgeois family as its support. 'Free' individuals are able to 'choose' if and how they will act vis-à-vis the market, all the while shouldering full personal responsibility for their good or bad lot in life. At the same time, in the absence of any social wage or safety net, the family unit serves as a hit-or-miss substitution for material and emotional support. Neoliberalism's free market fundamentalism and neoconservatism's traditional family values fundamentalism serve individual ends and work in reciprocity to reinforce each other at the expense of actual human freedom and flourishing.

Of particular note throughout Vasconcellos' and Pannain's analysis is the clear recognition that the radical unfreedom cultivated in the superficially disavowed alliance between neoliberalism and neoconservatism has repeatedly found support across seemingly stark left-right political divides. The authors trace the trajectories of a number of policies implemented in the United States and elsewhere beginning in the late 1960's and early 1970's with the decline of the Fordist 'family wage.' This historical narrative brings into sharp relief the bipartisan character of the neoliberal/conservative agenda as witnessed in pro-work, pro-marriage platforms and policies. Neither incidentally, nor unintentionally, continuing bipartisan efforts to force work and force family upon all has had the effect of reinscribing and reproducing hierarchies of gender, sexuality, race, and class. That such reinforcements of radically unfree and radically hierarchical social relations have proven 'successful' across political parties allows us to grasp the broader patterns and parallels across time and space

identified by Vasconcellos and Pannain. "In both democracies and dictatorships, the reproduction of the capitalist social order restores patterns of gender domination to preserve economic exploitation between classes – and vice
versa. In addition to its theoretical interest, the dialogue between Horkheimer
and Cooper can shed light on misogyny as a crucial element for understanding
the current rise of far-right leaders and movements – as well as the antagonism
and conflicts that characterize periods of democratic normality in capitalism."

Karyn Ball's *Rethinking "Toxic" Sovereignty? On Horkheimer and Adorno's
"Second Nature" between Nietzsche's "Bad Conscience" and Freud's "Death Drive"*
tracks a provocative genealogical account of the character trait/type that is
'toxic masculinity.' Ball charts an intellectual history of this increasingly
remarked-upon concept by way of Horkheimer and Adorno's analyses of 'second nature' and reification, Friedrich Nietzsche's insights on guilt and bad conscience, and Freud's accounts of the death drive. These interlocking strands
are woven together in order to provide historical specificity – and by extension
explanatory precision – to accounts drawing attention to such dangerous and
destructive gendered expressions of rage and *ressentiment*.

What is often referred to today as 'toxic masculinity' can perhaps be better
understood (which is not to say excused) by situating it within the long durée
context of heteropatriarchal capitalism. The internal dynamics of capitalism
necessarily impose relations and realities of unfreedom, exploitation, and
hierarchy upon the vast majority in society. In addition, capitalism supports
and is supported by cultural expectations, roles, and values that encourage, to
the point of enforcing, rational-instrumental calculation/calculability, ascetic
renunciation of spontaneity, creativity, and emotion, and mastery over nature,
social processes, and other people. In a final protraction of such alienating and
disenchanting logic, the material and cultural imperatives of modern capitalism simultaneously instill and insist upon repeated rituals of repressive 'self-
sovereignty' – 'sovereignty' here in the troubling sense of mastery over one's
basic libidinal drives in the service of a ceaseless, single-minded focus on repetitive capitalist productivity. Crucially, the structural contexts in which such
impossible imperatives of mastery arise and gain potency are all-too-frequently
taken as simple, brute givens. In other words, social relations are reified – taken
for granted as static immutable facts of the matter. If the basic contours of
social reality appear as beyond questioning or transformation, then it falls to
individuals to adjust themselves to that reality as best they can. Such adjustments to reified reality can and do result in the formation of 'second' natures –
human natures that are 'hardened' to themselves and others. Such hardened
second natures serve as defensive adaptation mechanisms, shielding individuals' inner selves and drives from the systematic pain of existence in relations

of radical unfreedom and domination. Insofar as such self-mastery is at base an impossible imperative, so-called 'lapses' in sovereignty lead with predictable frequency to feelings of guilt, fear, and aggression towards self and others. Intersecting across such toxic milieu is patriarchy in its many and multifaceted instantiations. Those in positions of relative or absolute power and privilege, vis-à-vis gender and sexuality, exhibit particularly dangerous levels of *ressentiment* and associated expressions of sadomasochistic aggression when faced with threats – real or imagined – to their status in social hierarchies. Ball's analysis suggests that what we frequently denote as 'toxic masculinity' gestures towards not only this second, hardened, sadomasochistic nature, but to a *third* nature beginning to take revenge on itself in its misery.

"If the will to power is perceived as an expropriated entitlement, then its domestication generates self-loathing, paranoia, and *ressentiment*. At the same time, when Freud portrays the deadening of a primal organism's cortical layer as a "sacrifice" made on behalf of the system's capacity for work, this sacrifice loses its presumed nobility when it re-emerges as a death-driven repetition geared toward leveling out the trauma of life itself. To the extent that Horkheimer and Adorno's critique of bourgeois stoicism lambasts internal hardening as a regression into mimicry in an increasingly automated world, a seething performance of emotional containment might strike us as outmoded, if not also as an uncanny return of the repressed. *In its exaggerated campaign against vulnerability and compassion, toxic masculinity potentially attests to the rise of a third nature taking revenge on a death-driven society that no longer venerates the sovereignty of the sacrifice it requires.*"

Part 2: Power, Truth, and (Non)Identity begins with Mary Caputi's *Marcuse's "Feminine Principle" and Non-binary Subversions*. Caputi brings into conversation Marcuse's conceptualization of a 'feminine principle' and Adorno's negative dialectical approach with contemporary expressions and experiences of gender and sexuality in order to reflect upon the latent and manifest possibilities of living life in and as expressions characterized by an 'aesthetic' manner – one of playful 'polymorphous perversities' absent the suffocating and unnecessary surplus-repressions of our current capitalistic confinements. In approaching such possibilities, Caputi recounts the second excursus in Horkheimer and Adorno's *Dialectic of Enlightenment – Juliette or Enlightenment and Morality*. In this essay, Horkheimer and Adorno bring their powerful concept of the dialectic of Enlightenment to bear on Marquis de Sade's (in)famous Juliette character. In what may be at least partially likened to today's 'power feminism,' de Sade's Juliette is characterized by a cultivation and brazen deployment of 'manly' as opposed to 'feminine' traits. Juliette's narrative sees her coldly calculating, using people by – and as – any means necessary to achieve her desired ends. Determined to game and win within a system set against her in terms of class, upbringing, and her gendered position as a woman, Juliette can and has been read as an exemplar of gritty, liberated feminist determination and empowerment – taking up the master's tools against the master(s) in order to craft a place for oneself against the master's world. Caputi's analysis of Juliette contests such a reading, asking if it is not rather that in taking up the master's tools – exploitation, domination, ruthless cunning, 'clever' calculation, and using others as means to one's own self-protective ends – one in fact remains within and reinforces the very systems of power that one 'pragmatically' seeks to subvert. She asks further: is it the case that Juliette's gritty libertine actions serve as an *assimilation to* – as opposed to a *subversion of* – class and gender hierarchies?

Caputi's excursus through Horkheimer and Adorno's own excursuses (the first of which, concerning Odysseus is also examined in contrast to Juliette's) leads back to the essay's central considerations – if and to what extent challenges to traditional Western gender and sexuality do or can radically subvert identitarian, binary, and heterosexist roles and norms. Can the limitations of taken for granted gender and sexual identities – including their conceptualization as binary, static, and essentialized 'facts' to be calculated and catalogued in the interests of capitalist-laden contexts of conformity – be truly subverted and transcended such that Marcuse's oft-invoked demand for an aesthetic rationality grounded in Eros may yet be at least partially realized? Caputi contends that there are increasing signs of, and grounds for, hope. "Much work has been done in terms of rethinking these categories both in the realm of social movements and legislation as well as in the area of gender and sexuality studies. Indeed, by any standard our society's interpretation of gender and sexuality has undergone considerable change, often moving in the direction of the negative fluidity promoted by Marcuse's aesthetic, "feminine principle" and Adorno's negative dialectics [...] In its eschewal of formal, identitarian logic, such a "post-identity" politics surely resonates with Marcuse's feminine principle and its embodied optimism. It surely foreshadows the undoing of gender in ways that open up categories of human identity in ways that allow for the joy and generosity that Marcuse envisages. For if something as integral to the human experience as gender and sexuality demand not the use of instrumental rationality, but of its aesthetic counterpart, then a liberationist politics undergoes assimilation into our everyday lives where it can truly have an effect."

The theme of identity is reprised in the context of identity politics in Tivadar Vervoort's *Towards a Critical Identity Politics: Butler, Adorno, and the Force of Non-identity*. In this chapter, Vervoort reads in concert the work of Judith

Butler and Theodor Adorno as concerns (non)identity thinking to highlight both the frequent points of convergence between the two theorists, as well as to champion a form of critical identity politics that recognizes and actively aims to repeatedly work through an otherwise paradoxical puzzle at the core of identity thinking more broadly. Vervoort succinctly presents said paradox: "subordinated social groups need to affirm the identity upon which they are subordinated to question their oppression." The question: how to affirm one's identit(y/ies) and one's recognition without reinscribing and reifying said identit(y/ies) as essentialized, and often naturalized, static brute facts of the matter? Butler's work on performativity and Adorno's critiques of identity thinking, respectively, assist Vervoort in gesturing towards a *reflexive* and *critical* identity politics as a possible way through the risks and paradoxes of identity politics and theorizing.

Adorno's critique of identity thinking rests upon the recognition that universal (and universalizing) concepts are never adequate to the particularities of the objects to which they refer. The multiplicity and fluidity of material lives, bodies, experiences, meanings, and social relations do not admit of seamless – let alone static universal – capture by way of concepts and categories. Nonetheless, Adorno is quite clear that there is no moving beyond concepts or conceptual thinking; instead, what is needed is persistent reflexivity vis-à-vis our attempts to capture, pin down, and organize the material and meaningful multitude that is human life. Adorno's critique of identity thinking (here, expressed by attempts to seamlessly and comprehensively capture life via adequate universal concepts, leaving no remainder un-catalogued/-contained) gestures towards the ultimately *aporic* character of thought in relation to life. To avoid the pitfalls of reification constitutive of identity thinking, Adorno offers as an alternative the practice of thinking in constellations; within constellations there are no central positions from which to deduce strict and universal covering laws or categories. Rather, constellations demonstrate the relational and non-identical character of concepts to life. Crucially, the poetics of constellations invite us to a relatively open-ended process of resignification, as needed or desired, as contexts and conditions change across historical times and social spaces. In their accounts of performativity, Butler also calls attention to the necessity of reflexive resignification in relation to social identities, paying particular attention to identities of gender and sexuality. Echoing Adorno, Butler likewise recognizes the ultimately inescapable character of thinking, speaking, and acting relative to social identities. Rather than argue for the abolition of identities, Butler maintains that said identities remain open-ended and subject to change as needed or desired. The risk of the original paradox does indeed remain, but now with a significant and hopeful qualifier: "Insofar as all reification is a forgetting ... the tendency from resignification towards reification demands any form of identity politics to place its categories under constant critical scrutiny." Critical identity politics can and do recognize and affirm us in our individual and group specificity without succumbing to the trappings of reification and associated desires for representational-only politics – precisely those trappings that critical identity politics seek to critique and subvert.

In *Adorno, Foucault, and Feminist Theory: the Politics of Truth*, Lambert Zuidervaart considers how feminist critical theory fruitfully utilizes the analyses of power and truth found across the work of Foucault and Adorno, while also gesturing towards the necessity of feminist critical theory to go beyond these two theorists in developing a new conception of truth and truth's relation to forms of power – this, in service to critiques of domination and ongoing emancipatory social transformations. In a fashion analogous to Vervoort's discussion of Adorno and Butler, and in conversation with the critical feminist thought of both Amy Allen and Deborah Cook, Zuidervaart demonstrates a series of parallels in the thought of Adorno and Foucault, highlighting in particular their distinct but overlapping projects of connecting truth to power (and vice versa). Foucault's focus upon disciplinary and biopolitical forms of power is placed into productive tension with Adorno's focus upon a 'discontinuous continuity' of domination across historical epochs. Likewise, Foucault's focus upon regimes of truth and Adorno's focus upon negative dialectical and non-identitarian thinking highlight the possibilities for different truths and, by extension, different forms of subjectivity: cracks in seemingly all-encompassing power/truth regimes appear possible (if not always immediately probable), leading both Foucault and Adorno to posit alternative ways of knowing and being in the world. Crucially, neither thinker posits an 'objective' 'outside' to either truth or power relations. Instead, they gesture towards resistant-subversive desubjection and non-identical concepts and truths, respectively.

To Zuidervaart's assessment, what remains to be accomplished in these analyses, and what Zuidervaart sees to be a crucial task for contemporary critical feminist theory, is the development of a sufficiently normative grounding of critiques of power and domination, coupled with the development of a more robust and concrete conception of truth – concepts of power and truth and their interrelations robust, normatively grounded, and dynamic enough to posit productive/positive, non-speculative, and non-counterfactual utopian projects of social transformation and liberation. "Like Foucault and Adorno, feminist critical theorists have offered sophisticated critiques of power. But we have run stuck, it seems to me, because we have not developed a sufficiently normative critique of power. To do that, I have suggested, feminist critical theorists need to reexamine Foucault's genealogy and Adorno's negative dialectics to ask what forms of power these have ignored or overlooked. And, given the prominence of truth for both Foucault and Adorno, that will also require a new conception of truth, one that neither restricts truth to science nor treats it as a counterfactual idea, but locates it instead in the historically emergent and malleable social domains of power."

Frida Sandström's chapter *The Disintegration of Autonomy: Jill Johnston's Anti-criticism* concludes Part 2 of the volume. In this piece, Sandström takes up questions of identity in relation to self and social movements from the vantage point of Jill Johnston's art criticism. Her proposal "is that Johnston's anti-criticism is a social critique of her own practice ... Johnston's 'overlap' of subjectivities not only questions formal art criticism as a practice, but also the subjectivation of the critic as part of the mediation of the work of art, aesthetically and socially: as autonomous and social fact."

Sandström draws fruitful connections between Johnston's formal art criticism and biographical writings and Adorno's investigations into negative dialectics and the non-identical. Throughout the chapter, a series of reflections concerning the characteristics and the status of identity are layered in such a fashion that stability vis-à-vis one's sense of self is increasingly troubled – though perhaps troubled in such a fashion as to reach a kind of actual liberating transcendence beyond formal and only apparent postures of transcendence in the figure of the art critic. To the extent that Johnston's position as a formal art critic required that she establish distance from her own lived experiences – particularly concerning her sexuality – as well as from the larger social context of the labor of art criticism qua labor and the larger social contexts in which art is performed and assessed in terms of substantive content, then Johnston's increasingly explicit practices of 'anti-criticism' gain clarity. Sandström illustrates Johnston performing a sophisticated series of immanent meta-reflections concerning self-identity, culminating in a radical self-critique – 'self-objectivation' – that both reflects as well as reverberates back 'out' towards the social world conditioning her sense of subjectivity. The conceptual abstractions as well as the abstractions away from material subjectivities and social contexts seemingly required of the art critic are increasingly identified and challenged in Johnston's work. The apparent dichotomy between subject and object, theory and practice, as well as form and content (i.e., between art critic and art criticism, art critic and art; art and social context, and self and social context) seem to at least partially dissolve – to 'disintegrate.'

"If Johnston's sexual subjectivity emerges *in negation* to her art critical subjectivity, which is what in the first place gives it its form as art criticism, then she is not only immersing her critical autonomy into the social heteronomy in which she lives and works. Her writing also takes form *against* this context, as an opposing social reality residing within the 'artform' of her writing. It is from the perspective of the act of giving form to her individuation that Johnston also reflects the social objectivity of her art critical subjectivity, which here in itself becomes an object for her criticism. Yet different from Johnston's art critical judgment, her anti-criticism is historically specific. By negating the form of her art critical subjectivity *from within* the autonomy that it presupposes, her 'praxis' restructures meaning by figuring an individuation that *negates* the social objectivity of Johnston-as-critic." A complexly mediated liberation from absolute, alienated/alienating identification – in a sense partially in tune with Adorno's analyses and critiques of identity thinking – results.

Part 3: Intersectional Investigations begins with Jana McAuliffe's *Historical Traumas in the Critiques of Theodor Adorno and Joy James*. In this poignant analysis, McAuliffe reflects upon how and why engagements with historical traumas are undertaken, particularly in light of a commitment to intersectional feminist theory and activism today. McAuliffe traces James' analyses of 'Captive Maternal' – those groups of individuals who, in light of their racial and gendered subject positions, have and continue to bear the brunt of reproductive and productive labor (continuous, often violent, theft of time, labor, and care) in relation to the development of the wealth of nations (specifically in this reading, the United States). The historical and ongoing founding trauma of slavery in the United States is examined in its continuing assumptions and effects using an intersectional feminist framework. As a point of comparison and instructive contrast, McAuliffe subsequently traces Adorno's analyses of the historical trauma of Auschwitz. While Adorno does of course treat this trauma at the level of the particular-concrete (i.e., in terms of the all-too-real concentration camps, sufferings, and deaths of millions of human beings), Adorno also treats the trauma of Auschwitz from a broader metaphysical perspective. For Adorno, the horrors of Auschwitz are such that an inescapable, existential condition of guilt necessarily haunts humanity: a guilt that must be – and is repeatedly – forgotten such that human life may continue in the wake of such extreme historical trauma. One takes from Adorno's accounts that Auschwitz stands for a (the?) singular historical trauma of modern humanity.

McAuliffe is clear that a very great deal can and ought to be taken from Adorno's piercing and poignant reflections on historical trauma. At the same time, throughout the chapter McAuliffe demonstrates that intersectional frameworks are indispensable in their attention to the concrete particularities of multiple and compounding subject positions (e.g., race, gender, class, sexuality, disability, nationality, etc.) relative to ideologies, practices, and institutions of domination and exploitation. McAuliffe's attention to James' treatment of gendered racial oppression in the context of U.S. slavery, when placed into conversation with Adorno's metaphysical treatment of the horrors of Auschwitz, leads McAuliffe to a powerful overarching assessment of the how and the why of engaging with historical trauma. McAuliffe recognizes in her analysis of James' thought "at least four implications for understanding the need for feminist social theory that engages historical trauma [...] Intersectionally informed feminist engagements with historical trauma should, first, not represent any one historical trauma as a singular, paradigmatic event; second, engage a raced and gendered attention to historical traumas and their contemporary impact; third, prioritize the agency and action (not just the subordination) of oppressed peoples, especially those most disempowered by Western democracies; and fourth, contest the ways that Western theory has diminished the theoretical contributions of diverse thinkers." In such attention to historical and subject specificity, analyses of trauma, such as those of James, provide a welcome concrete analytical approach for more nuanced understandings of, and possible (only ever partial) reckonings/responses to, the ongoing traumatic past. Simply put: "Feminist engagements with historical violence must expand what theory means in meaningful ways that engender plurality."

In *Beyond One-Dimensional Theory and Praxis: a Marcusean Alliance with Black Feminism*, Nicole Yokum takes up the thread of intersectional feminist analysis along with the early Frankfurt School by demonstrating the fruitful affinities to be found between Marcusean Critical Theory and Black Feminism. Taking cues from radical Black feminist thinkers such as Angela Davis, bell hooks, Patricia Hill Collins, Audre Lorde, Kimberlé Crenshaw, and Brittany Cooper, Yokum makes a powerful case for the necessity of intersectional analyses in the search for objective truths about, and liberatory paths forward through, the social world. Drawing inspiration in particular from Crenshaw's formulation of intersectionality, Hill Collins' concept of the 'outsider within,' and Lorde and Coopers' examination of the emancipatory potential of Black feminist anger, Yokum contends that knowledge of exploitation, domination, and oppression are strengthened – achieving greater levels of objectivity – through the inclusion and centering of those individuals and groups who are multiply-marginalized in society. As Yokum is careful to caution, such 'strong objectivity' does not arise due to any essentialized or a priori epistemological privilege on the part of society's most marginalized individuals and groups; rather, the specific experiences of multiply-marginalized groups afford certain subject-positions particular standpoints or perspectives that, in turn, generate insights on the uses of power that at least partially elide other subject-standpoints who may fail to recognize the full truth of the dynamics of domination due to their relatively privileged (and therefore relatively partial) experiences of oppression. As Yokum explains in relation to Crenshaw's formulation of the intersecting oppressions of race and gender experienced by Black women: it "is not that more oppression equals more knowledge, in a kind of additive view of how experience of various forms of structurally-based oppression leads to epistemological insight; rather, it's that Black women don't suffer the same illusions as white women with respect to their relationship to white male power, for they can't find comfort in their white privilege to balance out or cover over the pains associated with their gendered subordination. Being subject to oppression along the lines of both gender and race also enables Black Feminists to better understand the links among various systems of oppression, since they are actually all interconnected [...] which sets them up to potentially be more astute critical social theorists."

In addition to reflections on the significance of centering intersectional approaches in the search for more robust, accurate, and useful analyses of domination and exploitation, Yokum also traces a series of instructive examples in the Black feminist tradition that insist upon a fusion of rigorous theoretical work with concrete practical actions and activism. Rejecting 'one-dimensional' or one-sided approaches to interrogations of oppression, Yokum draws inspiration from the ongoing tradition of radical Black feminist work that explicitly demands and delivers on the 'both/and' of theory and practice. Eschewing a focus that rests exclusively upon one of the two poles of praxis – theory without action or action without theory – Yokum instead demonstrates that both components are necessary (insufficient by themselves in isolation) for radical emancipatory projects. The terminology of 'one-dimensionality' is, of course, that of Marcuse, and Yokum's chapter is bookended by a series of key links between the praxis of the Frankfurt School scholar and the intersectionally-oriented praxis of Black Feminism. Reminding us that Marcuse himself explicitly identified those marginalized in terms of race and gender as potentially best-positioned to grasp the full truths of oppressive systems of power, Yokum traces a biographical and conceptual genealogy between Marcusean Critical Theory and Black Feminism, indicating that such an alliance has and will continue to prove particularly helpful in thinking through and acting against domination with productively rage-informed hope for liberated ways of being in the world.

Sergio Bedoya Cortés' *Herbert Marcuse and Intersectional (Marxist) Feminism* echoes certain of Yokum's reflections, noting that "the search of the political subject for revolution was the principal commitment of Marcuse in his late decades." Bedoya Cortés further notes that Marcuse saw in those communities forcibly kept at the margins of an otherwise pessimism-provoking, one-dimensional mass industrial society reason for optimism: resistance in the form of a Great Refusal was present and poised to achieve still greater strength via the urgency of multiple, compounding, immediate, and ongoing experiences of suffering. Despite sharing these and additional similarities with several authors in the present volume, Bedoya Cortés maintains that Marcuse's analyses remain fundamentally rooted in a Marxist paradigm that ultimately emphasizes the primary centrality of a united working class as the force necessary for truly revolutionary transformations in the present social relations and dynamics of capitalism.

Traces of Moore's earlier examination of the 'subjective factor(s)' either hindering or helping in the development of revolutionary social consciousness, Bedoya Cortés sees in Marcuse's reflections on the radical refusals and resistances of marginalized groups – people of color, women, and students serving as key examples – a hopeful cultivation of radical forms of social consciousness increasingly well-positioned to 'trigger' transformations in the 'objective' coordinates and processes of capitalism. In the apparent absence of a sufficiently revolutionary and unified working class – the proletariat as the key traditional Marxist subject positioned to effect the most fundamental, most thoroughgoing radical change – additional-adjacent social liberation movements such as the Women's Liberation Movement may serve as 'pre-revolutionary' sparks set to ignite a broader revolutionary movement challenging the capitalist world to its core. As Yokum indicated, the experiences and associated knowledge born by multiply marginalized groups may indeed be better positioned than Orthodox Marxism's rarified proletarian subject to recognize, resist, and actively work towards transformation of the ideological and practical relations of modern capitalist society. Against the grain of previous chapters in this collection, Bedoya Cortés contends that, in the last instance, total social transformation is unlikely to arise from particular social movements aimed at securing recognition, representation, or equal rights within the current system for historically marginalized groups. For Bedoya Cortés, the emancipation of particular groups ultimately hinges upon the emancipation of the social totality. "Marcuse finds the category of class to be the transversal axis for contemporary intersectionality [...] Marcuse finds that the principle of intersectionality must be represented in what he called a "united front", where the manifestations of exploitation, as evidenced in the sexual and racial divisions of labour, mobilize the irruption of objective conditions in people's consciousness,' thus generating the possibility for radical transformation."

Part 3 concludes with Jennifer L. Eagan's reflections on Adorno and astrology in *Rethinking Astrology as Feminist Re-enchantment: a Reading of Adorno's "The Stars Down to Earth."* Eagan invites us to examine Adorno's oft-overlooked essay 'The Stars Down to Earth' against his broader theoretical oeuvre. Eagan notes that in comparison with the majority of Adorno's analyses concerning modern culture and its relations to monopoly capitalism, "Stars" is relatively lacking in conceptual and methodological nuance. Moreover, Eagan finds in Adorno's content analysis of a 1950s *Los Angeles Times* horoscope column a series of surprisingly derogatory statements about women. In uncharacteristic fashion, Adorno in "Stars" appears to rely upon hackneyed gender stereotypes to arrive at his conclusions concerning the allures, illusions, and dangers of astrology in general. Eagan also asks us to consider how concepts such as reason, rationality, truth, and nature are positioned and functioning in "Stars" relative to Adorno's treatments of the same concepts elsewhere in his works. As part of his scathing indictment and dismissal of astrology – both in the immediate context of his content analysis of the *LA Times* horoscope column, as well as in the broader context of pseudoscientific occult ideologies – Adorno nonetheless shines perceptive light upon a series of material and psychological symptoms and sicknesses rooted in modern capitalist societies. Taking up the tools of Freudian psychoanalysis (themselves also critically addressed in Eagan's chapter) in his reading of the newspaper column, Adorno recognizes in the astrological advice series a recurring pattern of assumptions/imperatives pertaining to 'making it/getting ahead,': that is, cultivating one's individual self (in the context of societal standards of status), cleverly maneuvering through personal/private conflicts so as to maintain domestic peace in the service of productive professional life, and repetitively fitting one's apparently uniquely cultivated self into the 'system' in the hopes of reposing in a lifetime's worth of deferred gratification (assuming one lives long enough to get 'out' of said system at the end of one's life).

Adorno's critiques of the culture of late capitalism are as sharp here as elsewhere, and Eagan uses precisely these insights to ground her 'counternarrative' of astrology vis-à-vis Adorno's exasperated account in "Stars." Against Adorno and Adorno's use of reason against astrology, Eagan contends that contemporary women, BIPOC, and queer astrologers gesture towards the possibility of a 're-enchantment' between humans and nature as well as our own human natures. In contrast to astrology as anti-Enlightenment in the sense of complacent acquiescence to soothing illusions or pseudo-individualized practices of self-cultivation in the service of submission to the standardized status quo, Eagan instead invites the possibility of an anti-Enlightenment astrology in the emancipatory sense of a critique of instrumental reason, alienation, and domination of nature, others, and self. Eagan poses the questions: "Could astrology in this new register be a constructive coping mechanism for women and femmes under patriarchy? Could it perhaps be a way of claiming outsider status and resisting patriarchal views of nature? Astrology is anti-Enlightenment in the sense that it is against the domination of nature. The contemporary feminist/ BIPOC/queer astrologers are trying to recoup something lost from an ancient practice and remake it differently ... Astrology could be seen as a way of releasing our desire for domination over nature as well as the desire to control our own nature – to be in tune and in touch with the universe as a larger structure than the material world which has been co-opted by capitalism ... Astrology can provide a powerful counter narrative to break through that hegemony, even if some regard it as fake or flakey."

Part 4: Socialized Nature: Essential Categorical Questions in Science leads off with Simon Reiners' *Negative Dialectics and the Force of Matter: Theodor W. Adorno and Karen Barad: towards a New-Material Feminism for Thinking Contemporary Crises*. Reiner provides a careful tracing of Adorno's analysis between knowing subjects, mediating concepts, and objective material-objects together with Karan Barad's account of agential realism and the ontological primacy of phenomena in order to suggest a productive, if incomplete, overlap between the concerns of the early Frankfurt School and feminist new materialism in the context of questions of responsibility in the age of the crisis-ridden 'not-so-Anthropocene.' Highlighting the partial parallels across Adorno's negative dialectical critiques of identitarian thinking and Barad's performativity-based critiques of dualistic subject-object (human-nature) presuppositions prevalent in traditional Western science and philosophy, Reiner makes a case for an updated critical historical materialism that takes seriously the de-centering of human subjects in analyses of natural-social relations. In their respective focus upon Being as Becoming, Adorno and Barad each provide compelling frameworks for thinking the subject-object relation as foundationally relational; such a processual understanding of thought and matter shine much needed light on the openings of possibility for thinking and being other than what currently is the case.

Still, Reiner contends that Barad's feminist new materialism does not (yet) fully account for the normative grounding necessary for subjective critique and emancipatory practices in the face of modern human-nature crises. Adorno's ultimate grounding of critique in the ongoing immediacy of suffering in domination may serve as a bridge between the non-essentialist historical and feminist new materialist accounts. "'Western' rationality must be taken seriously as a real agential, praxeological-historical cut in the phenomenon 'world.' It causes exclusions, hierarchies, and suffering, qua its real existence. And yet, this present must be read not as a stable whole but as contingent, conditioned by material-discursive practices. Only such a perspective opens a view upon contemporary relations and entailed crises that go beyond solemn human means – as relational. Thus, even if we are incapable of comprehending and unable to succeed, we must take up the infinitely abandoned task of reading the present for what these constitutive, material-discursive practices are that close off the space of the possibility of another becoming. This is a task, which therefore cannot succeed through our solemn actions as human subjects, but also cannot succeed without us."

In *Theorizing beyond the Man: the Frankfurt School and Post-humanist Feminism*, Mario Mikhail identifies and weaves together additional complementary threads across the work of the early Frankfurt School and posthumanist feminism, focusing particular attention on the writings of Horkheimer, Adorno, and Marcuse together with the writings of Donna Haraway and Rosi Braidotti. Mikhail reminds us of the central role questions concerning relationships between humans and nature play across much of the early Frankfurt School's oeuvre. The repeated connections drawn in these accounts between the domination of nature and the domination of women are outlined in order to assert that questions of gender, sex, and sexuality are – albeit in sometimes scattered, fragmentary form – clearly present throughout the thought of the early Frankfurt School. The stress laid upon nature in the work of Horkheimer, Adorno, and Marcuse (as well as in Benjamin's many reflections upon the mediating role of technology), holds a crucial clue for understanding the early Frankfurt School's analyses of gender. The oft-remarked upon link between the domination of nature and the heteropatriarchal domination of (supposedly 'closer to nature') women, is taken up in Mikhail's chapter to demonstrate the fabricated 'nature' of gender classifications and the relations of unfreedom enacted onto and through such supposedly essential categories of life. In critiquing the interconnected dominations of nature, of humans in general, and of ourselves individually, the early Frankfurt School is read in alliance with radical feminist and queer thought and practice.

Mikhail finds in the early Frankfurt School's deconstruction of gender and sexuality categories, as well as in their critiques of domination across forms of life, a strong resonance with work taking place within posthumanist feminist thought. In particular, feminist posthumanist examinations of human-nature-technology matrices, material-discursive practices, and the complexly irreducible entanglements of living and non-living subjects and objects share important affinities with the early Frankfurt School's critiques of reified hierarchical practices and identitarian thinking. In both approaches, the place of humans vis-à-vis the life world is radically reconstructed to make conceptual and practical space for non-essentialized, non-dualistic, non-hierarchical difference – towards playfully perverse reconfigurations of self in relation to other selves and our collective natural-social worlds. Absent assumptions of, or aspirations towards, seamless syntheses or unifying reconciliations, both schools of thought demonstrate the necessity of ontological and epistemological humility on the part of Enlightenment-saturated modern humanity in the service of humane political, ethical, and libidinal life. Mikhail concludes by contending that such a "radical attitude towards humanity and nature predicated posthumanist feminist thought. The key motifs articulated by posthumanist feminist scholars such as Braidotti and Haraway are found in the thought of Adorno, Horkheimer, Marcuse, and Benjamin. The destruction of the centrality of man, abolishing the demarcation between humanity and other creatures in the world, and liberating marginalized humans and animals from the instrumental reason of heteropatriarchy were the underlying themes in their thought, despite the variations in their philosophical reflections."

Exploring further the rich line of thought concerning ontological matters of (human) 'nature,' Cristian Arão's *The New Man Is a Woman: Marcuse and the Question of the New Anthropology* recounts Marcuse's still-provocative discussions concerning the prospects of 'feminizing society.' Drawing upon a series of insights developed by his student Angela Davis, Marcuse (in)famously called for the feminization of humans – men in particular – and of society more broadly. In doing so, Marcuse was building upon and refining earlier formulations in *Eros and Civilization* concerning the overcoming of surplus-repression and aggression, instrumental forms of domination, and the capitalist-cultivated performance principle in favor of liberated erotic drives and desires. Taking key cues from Davis and from the Women's Liberation Movement of his time, Marcuse increasingly emphasized the significance of feminist socialism in his analyses of radical transformation. Arão contends that, for Marcuse, "ending patriarchy becomes ... as important as taking over the means of production [...] Paraphrasing the author of *Das Kapital*, Marcuse compares the formation of the proletariat in capitalism with the formation of the feminine in patriarchy."

Patriarchy and capitalism will not – cannot – successfully be rejected and overcome in isolation from one another. As Lawler's lead chapter in this volume makes abundantly clear, the patriarchy and the capitalist system are deeply interdependent, and a truly radical critique and challenge to one necessitates by definition a radical critique and challenge to the other. In coming to a greater appreciation of these structural and cultural truths, Marcuse came to conceptualize a 'feminized man' and 'feminized society' as the antithesis and antidote to 'masculine' traits and values cultivated and commanded by patriarchal capitalist existence. As Kangussu and Barroso's chapter in this volume recounts, Marcuse's notion of 'feminized society' did (and does) strike resonant chords and wary nerves alike – particularly among critical feminist scholars. Consternation in the wake of Marcuse's calls for a 'feminized society' are understandable. Insofar as 'feminine' is taken as a synonym for women, or as a proxy for an essentialized complex of traits, behaviors, or values onto-logically rooted in women qua women, Marcuse's choice of phrasing rightly results in charges of biological or cultural determinism. Likewise, assuming 'feminized society' to be a call for an inversion of traditional gendered power dynamics – as, for example, a call to matriarchy – one might again suspect the creep of essentialism and/or the reformism attendant with reversals of roles absent radical reorganizations of social relations writ large. Marcuse is very clear that his conception of 'feminized society' is precisely not a call to matri-archy, nor is it meant to imply the existence of any essentialized attributes to women (or anyone else). Instead, Marcuse's 'female' or 'feminized' society is one that cultivates traits and values expressive of care, emotion, and receptiv-ity – these, in place of the relentlessly hyper-rational, fatally aggressive, and unnecessarily productivist traits and values Marcuse labels 'masculine' in vir-tue of their preponderance within patriarchy-driven capitalist societies. What Marcuse envisions is precisely not a 'return to' any first natures, gendered or otherwise. To the contrary, Marcuse envisions the cultivation of a second nature – one he calls 'feminine' – amongst human beings in general. In relation to his other works and thought, we might read in this new formulation previ-ous formulations concerning the potential of Eros transcending (or at least significantly subduing) Thanatos.

Rather than elide historical and currently existing gendered roles, traits, and values, Marcuse indicates a way *out* of suffocating systems precisely *through* the re-purposed use of what are, at base, social constructions in the service of sys-tems of domination. As Arão posits: "It is not possible to deny that gender roles exist and are present in our reality. From there, what Marcuse does is to under-stand that patriarchy, by keeping many women away from the world of waged work and simultaneously making women responsible for reproductive and emotional care, ended up fostering an axiology antithetical to the performance principle and, therefore, may unintentionally create a risk to the perpetuation of patriarchy and capitalism [...] this is not about defending the assertion that women are feminine. For Marcuse, the important movement is the femi-nization of man. This means that men need to be guided by the gradual aban-donment of qualities linked to the performance principle, and recognize the importance of values such as passivity, tolerance, and care. Hence a kind of androgyny may arise. From the moment that men acquire feminine character-istics, the boundaries that mark gender divisions loosen." Arão is thus able to close with the provocative conclusion that, "When looking for the "new man", that is, this kind of figure that represents the denial of the *ethos* of capitalism,

Marcuse finds the image of the woman, because femininity is the antithesis of the performance principle. It is up to man to feminize himself to abandon the culture of brutalization, violence, and the death instinct."

Lea Gekle's *Reification and Forgetting: Thinking the Domination of Nature and of Women with and against Adorno* provides a partial counter-reading of the connections drawn in early Frankfurt School scholarship between the domination of nature and the domination of women, focusing upon Adorno's simultaneously productive and problematic application of the concept of reification to the historical oppressions born by women within patriarchal capitalist contexts. Beginning from a partial critique of Ynestra King's ecofeminist accounting of women's domination that sees in said domination a 'forgetting' of a primary 'first nature' relation of dependency between men and women (and humans and nature), Gekle goes on to assess the adequacy of Adorno's apparently more historically and socially specific account of women's contemporary domination. King's ecofeminist account (itself aiming to draw from Horkheimer and Adorno's analysis of reification and the domination of nature) seeks to widen explanations of the domination of women beyond a reductive economistic account – one that would attribute domination of women to the social relations of capitalism as a mode of production. Gekle demonstrates that this 'enlargement' of the scope of analysis results, unhelpfully, in both de-historization and the reinscription of biologically essentialized understandings of women – as naturally and primarily bearers of children whose vital role in the reproduction of life has been radically devalued to the point of having been forgotten.

Gekle's turn to Adorno's writing directly demonstrates that his are accounts of the domination of women that admirably avoid, indeed explicitly reject, essentialized understandings of gender specifically, and nature more broadly. In this sense, Adorno's analyses serve as a welcome antidote to those essentialized ecofeminist accounts that seek to draw inspiration from the early Frankfurt School. However, Gekle illustrates that Adorno's anti-essentialist account of the domination of women and of nature nevertheless runs into problems of its own – problems that are somewhat surprising given the emphasis Adorno places on the necessity of grounding analysis and critique in historical and social specificity. (One is reminded of Eagan's earlier reflections on Adorno's uncharacteristically less nuanced analysis of astrology, as well as McAuliffe's reflections of the perhaps too sweeping and singular claims made by Adorno in relation to the historical trauma of Auschwitz). Gekle proposes "that the process of reification developed by Adorno, which helps to criticize a primary form of essentialism, needs itself a historization and stronger confrontation in order to maintain its critical capacity." Gekle finds in Maria Mies' analyses of social reproduction and gendered divisions of labor – both of which exist within a larger historical horizon of patriarchy preceding modern capitalism – a more concrete and hence more productive line of approach for identifying and transforming the sources of women's domination. For Gekle, Mises' thought "allows a concrete analysis of female subjectivation in a materialist framework without neglecting a larger historical horizon and helps to think about contemporary forms of oppression as having simultaneously a specific historical configuration as well as a longer history than only the recent history of capital." Gekle concludes that "only under a critical backdrop to feminist authors analyzing in an empirically more precise way the reification and integration of women in late capitalist society, can one use Adorno's larger conception of a social theory in order to think about contemporary forms of social domination."

By way of this volume's conclusion, Imaculada Kangussu and Nathalia N. Barroso's *About Mules, Divas, and Other* Specifically Feminine *Characteristics* brings back discussions of Marcuse's concept of a feminized society and 'specifically feminine' traits and values. Reiterating that the concept of 'feminine' at play in Marcuse's thought refers to an historical and not a metaphysical or biological essence, we are reminded of the central place afforded the biological (in the sense of libidinally instinctual) throughout Marcuse's oeuvre. Human beings' collective "essence" is biological insofar as 'biological' is conceptualized here in terms of drives, desires, and creative expressions of life that are contained and variously channeled (constructed?) in relation to broader social relations. In other words, such a libidinal-biological "essence" is in fact always-already historical (subject to and changing across contexts) insofar as social relations, roles, and values structure – for better or worse – the capacities and even the desires of individuals. That particular human libidinal expressions (and forcible restriction and deadening of particular libidinal expressions) have historically come to be associated with particular genders is an effect of history and culture. The ascription of particular gendered roles and expressions to humans is likewise an effect of history and social relations: biology, in the Marcusean sense of libidinal drives and desires, is fundamental. What is not fundamental, necessary, or liberating are the impositions of static, unequal (often binary), categories and associated roles and traits upon differently situated individuals. As noted in Arão's chapter, Marcuse is directing us across his works to the possibility of a transformed collective human being – a radically new humanity in and through a radically new reality. Kangussu and Barroso are clear: "The confrontation of male reason and female sensibility is a cultural situation, and behind it is hidden the social necessity of harmony and consonance between them. This does not mean that men should become irrational, nor that women should turn themselves into walking brains. The solution is not to substitute reason for sensibility but to reconcile them in a non-hierarchical relationship [...] the abandonment of patriarchal and capitalist values would undermine the specific masculine characteristics, overcome the stereotypes of gender normativity, and the hierarchical differences between feminine and masculine characteristics [...] The end goal here is dissolution of essentialized/ naturalized divisions and distinctions in favor of humane ways of being in the world."

Kangussu and Barroso go on to consider the many connections drawn in Marcuse's work between the concept of the 'feminine' and his reflections on the vital role aesthetics can and must play in the construction of human ways of being and relating in the world. From a consideration of Marcuse's frequent stress upon the 'aesthetic dimension' relative to liberated life, the chapter moves to consider the historical and ongoing role of music as a vibrant tool of creative expression, pleasure, and subversion of dominant status quos. More specifically, Kangussu and Barroso turn to Angela Davis' analyses of the Black female Blues tradition; in giving both individual and collective expression to the particular sufferings, desires, and demands of Black women, this rich musical legacy in turn points towards the truths and power located in multiply marginalized subject-positions. In line with Yokum's explorations of intersectionality, particularly those Black feminist approaches that draw to the center the standpoints and experiences of 'outsiders within,' Kangussu and Barroso illustrate the already actual and future potential aesthetic and transformative power of Black female Blues. Here, "expressed desires are thus incorporated – they have a body in the songs – even though it is not yet possible to fulfill them. Notwithstanding that their expression happens in the aesthetic dimension, somehow it is in this dimension that the forbidden desires are lightened and become visible – or hearable, at least."

As noted in many chapters throughout this volume, Marcuse and other thinkers in the early Frankfurt School tradition stress the significance of the 'subjective' factor – the necessity of the coming to and changing of subjective consciousness in order to recognize and revolt against and beyond current reality. In repeatedly underscoring the revolutionary role of aesthetics in conjunction with his increasing conviction that individuals and groups falling outside orthodox conceptions of the proletariat as the obvious or necessary agent of revolutionary change, Marcuse arrives at conclusions shared and developed by Davis; namely, that the collective creative expressions of resistance and reimagining of reality born from the sufferings and the desires of marginalized groups contain the kernels of a truly explosive Great Refusal of current reality. From the standpoint of society's most marginalized, the truth of current reality as well as the necessary desire and power to transcend said reality are already prefiguring a radically different, radically liberated set of social relations – a set of social relations that requires as its base a radically different, radically liberated ('second nature') humanity. It is this radical 'qualitative leap' into liberated second natures that Marcuse and Davis see burgeoning in those social movements aimed at radical gender, sexual, racial, and class liberations.

Acknowledgements

The editors would like to thank Brill series editor, David Fasenfest, for his ongoing enthusiasm and patient support in seeing this volume to completion. We wish to acknowledge and thank each of the authors who have contributed their time, passion, and scholarship to this timely project. We also acknowledge and thank our readers – may we continue thinking and acting together in critically creative multi-dimensional fashions about gender, sexuality, liberated selves, and societies!

Notes on Contributors

Cristian Arão
holds a Ph.D. in philosophy from Universidade Federal da Bahia. He is affiliated to the group "Marx no século XXI" and develops research in Political Philosophy, Philosophy of Technology and Philosophy of Psychoanalysis, within the Critical Theory tradition, dialoguing more deeply with Marx, Marcuse, and Freud.

Karyn Ball
is a professor of English and Film Studies at the University of Alberta. Her articles have appeared in *Cultural Critique, Women in German Yearbook, Research in Political Economy, Differences, English Studies in Canada, New Literary History, Alif,* the open-access journal *Humanities,* the *Journal of Holocaust Studies, Angelaki, Law and Critique,* and *History and Theory.* She guest edited a special issue of *Cultural Critique* on "Trauma and Its Cultural Aftereffects" (2000); and a special issue of *Parallax* on the concept of "visceral reason" (2005); with Susanne Soederberg. Ball co-edited a special issue of *Cultural Critique* on "Cultures of Finance" (2007); with Melissa Haynes, a special issue of *ESC* on "The Global Animal" (2013); and, with Stefan Mattessich, a special issue of *Cultural Critique* on "pornocracy" (2018). Other representative publications include the edited collection *Traumatizing Theory: the Cultural Politics of Affect in and beyond Psychoanalysis* (Other Press, 2007) and the monograph *Disciplining the Holocaust* (State University of New York Press, 2008) (paperback: 2009).

Nathalia N. Barroso
is a student in Aesthetics and Philosophy of Art from the postgraduate Program in Philosophy at the Universidade Federal de Ouro Preto. She develops the research "The Power of Classic Female Blues evidenced by Angela Davis and Herbert Marcuse" with special interest in the concepts "new sensitivity" and "great refusal". She is co-author of *Angela Davis, as Mulas do Mundo e a Música: por um novo paradigma* (Angela Davis, The Mules of the World and Music: For a New Paradigm) published in the book *Filosófas* (2021).

Sergio Bedoya Cortés
obtained an undergraduate degree in Political Science from the Universidad de Los Andes, a master's degree from the Universidad Complutense de Madrid in Maps and Tools for a New Culture of Citizenship, and a master's degree in

Philosophy and Political Sciences from the Universidad de Los Andes. He currently teaches philosophy, logic and critical theory at the Faculty of Philosophy and Human Sciences of the Universidad Libre de Colombia and is a Ph.D. student in Politics at Manchester Metropolitan University. His research interests focus on Critical Theory, Marx and Marxism of the 20th and 21st centuries, Decolonial Theory, and the different forms of subjectivity (subjectivation) concerning the social movements of feminism and race. He is the Spanish translator of the *Herbert Marcuse Conferences Transvaluation of Values and Radical Social Change: Five New Lectures* (2021) and *Herbert Marcuse's 1974 Paris Lectures at Vincennes University* (2021) published by the International Herbert Marcuse Society. https://orcid.org/0000-0003-3606-7605.

Mary Caputi
is a professor of Political Science at California State University, Long Beach where she teaches courses in political theory, feminist thought, and critical thinking. Most recently, she published *Slow Culture and the American Dream: A Slow and Curvy Philosophy for the 21st Century* (Lexington Books, 2022). She is also the author of *Feminism and Power: the Need for Critical Theory* (Lexington Books, 2013), *A Kinder, Gentler America: Melancholia and the Mythical 1950s* (University of Minnesota Press, 2005), and *Voluptuous Yearnings: a Feminist Theory of the Obscene* (Rowman & Littlefield, 1994). With Amirhosein Khandizaji, she co-authored *David Riesman and Critical Theory: Autonomy versus Emancipation* (Palgrave MacMillan, 2021). She also co-edited and contributed to two collections of essays: *Teaching Marx and Critical Theory in the Twenty-First Century*, co-edited with Bryant Sculos (Brill, 2019), and *Jacques Derrida and the Future of the Liberal Arts*, co-edited with Vincent Del Casino (Bloomsbury, 2013). She is currently at work on the *Research Handbook on Feminist Political Thought*, co-edited with Patricia Moynagh and under contract with Edward Elgar Press. She also served as editor of *Politics & Gender* from 2016–2019. Caputi has taught abroad in Italy on three occasions, and in addition to her Ph.D. from Cornell, she holds a master's degree in Italian Studies from California State University, Long Beach.

Jennifer L. Eagan
is a professor of Philosophy and Public Affairs & Administration at California State University, East Bay. Working at the intersection of theory and praxis, she has published articles in the areas of feminist philosophy, critical theory, political philosophy, ethics, and the philosophy of public administration. Her ongoing research interests include organizing and activism and the works of Theodor Adorno, Herbert Marcuse, Michel Foucault, and Judith Butler.

Additionally, she has served on the editorial team of the journal *Administrative Theory & Praxis* and as a leader in her labor union, the California Faculty Association.

Lea Gekle

is currently writing a doctoral thesis on Adorno's critique of sociology as an epistemological project, at the University de Picardie Jules Verne and Goethe Universität Frankfurt. She also teaches philosophy at the University de Picardie Jules Verne. Having completed an MA in contemporary philosophy at the École Normale Supérieure and École des Hautes Études en Sciences Sociales, she passed the agrégation in German studies in 2018, before taking her position as a fully funded Ph.D. student in 2019. Since 2020, she is also a co-tutelle scholarship-holder of the DAAD. She is also associated at the Marc Bloch Center in Berlin. Her main research areas are epistemology of social theory, political philosophy, social philosophy, critical theory, and feminist theory.

Imaculada Kangussu

is a professor at the Instituto de Filosofia, Artes e Cultura of the Universidade Federal de Ouro Preto, Brasil. She is the author of *Sobre Eros* (About Eros, 2007), *Leis da Liberdade* (Laws of Freedom, 2008), and *A Fantasia e as Fantasias* (The Fantasy and the Fantasies, 2020). Among her edited volumes are *Katharsis* (2002), *Theoria Aesthetica* (2005), *O cômico e o trágico* (2008), and *Estéticas moderna e contemporânea* (2018). She serves on the board of the International Herbert Marcuse Society.

Kristin Lawler

is a professor of Sociology at the College of Mount Saint Vincent in New York City. Her first book, *The American Surfer: Radical Culture and Capitalism*, was published by Routledge in 2011, and her new book, co-edited with Michael Roberts and David Cline, entitled *Board Studies: the Political Ontology of Surfing and Skateboarding* is forthcoming from San Diego State University Press in 2023. Her work has been published in numerous edited collections, including, most recently, *Back to the 30s? Recurring Crises of Capitalism, Liberalism, and Democracy*; *Nietzsche and Critical Social Theory*; *Class: the Anthology*; and *The Critical Surf Studies Reader*. She is a contributing member of the editorial board of the journal, *Situations: Project of the Radical Imagination*, where her work has also been published, and a member of the board of directors of the Institute for the Radical Imagination.

Jana McAuliffe

is an assistant professor of Philosophy at the University of Arkansas at Little Rock, specializing in social-political philosophy and critical philosophies of gender, race, and class. Her research is interested in everyday politics as exemplified in cultural and aesthetic taste, including "She's Making Profit Now: Neoliberalism, Ethics, and Feminist Critique" in *philoSOPHIA* and "How to feminist affect: Feminist comedy and post-truth politics" in *Philosophy and Social Criticism*. She can be reached at jxmcauliffe@ualr.edu.

Mario Mikhail

is a writer and a researcher interested in political and social theory. He is currently a Euroculture Master's student at the Universities of Udine and Groningen and a recipient of an Erasmus Mundus scholarship. He has academic publications in the fields of political and social theory. His latest article is "A messianic life can be lived rightly: Democracy contra the capitalist-sovereign order" published in the *Central European Journal of Politics*. He also writes for the Development, Advocacy, and Media Center (DAM) and Masr360.

Ryan Moore

teaches sociology at San Francisco State University and is the author of *Sells like Teen Spirit: Music, Youth Culture, and Social Crisis* (NYU Press, 2010).

Jeremiah Morelock

is a postdoctoral researcher and instructor of sociology at Boston College. He is editor of two published volumes on the critical theory of the early Frankfurt School: *Critical Theory and Authoritarian Populism*, and *How to Critique Authoritarian Populism: Methodologies of the Frankfurt School*. He is also author of *Pandemics, Authoritarian Populism, and Science Fiction: Medicine, Military, and Morality in American Film*, and co-author with Felipe Ziotti Narita of *O Problema do Populismo* as well as *The Society of the Selfie: Social Media and the Crisis of Liberal Democracy*.

Rafaela N. Pannain

received a Ph.D. in Sociology from the University of São Paulo and a master's degree in Political Science from Sorbonne University. She is a postdoctoral researcher at the University of São Paulo and a member of the research group "Intersectional Dialogues and Latin American Epistemologies" (NUPEDELAS). She organized the book *The Consequences of Brazilian Social Movements in Historical Perspective* (Routledge, 2022).

Christine A. Payne

lectures in STS and Women's Studies at San Diego State University and Sociology at University of California, San Diego. Her teaching and research interests include social and political theory, science and technology studies, cultural studies, and the sociology of knowledge. She is co-editor, with Michael J. Roberts, of *Nietzsche and Critical Social Theory: Affirmation, Animosity, and Ambiguity*, as well as a special issue by the same name of the journal *Critical Sociology.*

Simon Reiners

is a research assistant at the Oswald von Nell Breuning Institute for social and economic ethics, Frankfurt am Main, Germany, where he teaches social philosophy. Currently, he is doing his doctorate at the Johann Wolfgang Goethe University Frankfurt, Department of Social Philosophy. His research focuses on the nature-culture relations and the role of the body in the writings of Friedrich Nietzsche, the Frankfurt School, and contemporary Material Feminism. The project he is working on is called *Embodied Knowledge. Material Feminism and Critical Theory*.

Frida Sandström

is a Ph.D. fellow in Modern Culture at the Department of Arts and Cultural Studies at the University of Copenhagen, supervised by Mikkel Bolt. She is currently working on the Ph.D. thesis, "Art criticism as social critique," focusing on the social critique of art criticism and of revolutionary subjectivity, undertaken by Carla Lonzi, (1931–1982) Jill Johnston (1931–2009) and Adrian Piper (1948–). As part of this research, Sandström is undertaking collective research together with Fredrik Svensk, James Day and Mikkel Bolt, on the "Promise and Compulsion of Art Criticism's Universalism", which during 2020–2021 was manifested in two symposia. Sandström is teaching in the fields of aesthetic philosophy, art theory and fine art practice, at the University of Copenhagen, and at The Royal Academy of Fine Arts, Copenhagen, and during 2021–22, she was a visiting research student at Center for Research in Modern European Philosophy, Kingston University, London, and supervised by Peter Osborne. Since 2015, Sandström is a contributing editor at *Paletten Art Journal* (SE). She writes recurrent essays and art criticism for *Artforum International* and other Swedish and international journals.

Caio Vasconcellos

is an Adjunct Professor at the Federal University of Triângulo Mineiro. He holds a Ph.D. in Sociology from the University of São Paulo and is a member of the

Critical Theory and Sociology research group from the University of Campinas. He also coordinates the Capitalism, Collapse and Utopia research group. He published the book *O Moloch do presente. Adorno e a crítica à Sociologia* (Alameda, 2012).

Tivadar Vervoort

studied philosophy in Amsterdam, Berlin, and Leuven. His current research project is entitled "The Revitalization of Political Subjectivity: Contesting Neoliberal Governmentality and the Reification of Social Life," and funded by a Ph.D.-Fellowship of the Research Foundation Flanders (FWO). Vervoort is part of the editorial collective of *Krisis: Journal for Contemporary Philosophy* and an editor for *The Dutch Review of Books* (De Nederlandse Boekengids).

Nicole Yokum

is a Visiting Assistant Professor of Philosophy at St. Olaf College. She specializes in Feminist Philosophy, Critical Philosophy of Race, and Social and Political Philosophy. She is currently working on her first book manuscript entitled *The Politics of Insecurity*, an investigation into affect, oppression, and political agency through the framework of attachment. Drawing on the concepts of Adornian coldness, Fanonian affective erethism, and Marcusean one-dimensionality, Yokum recuperates an "insecure" style of political engagement as an ethical and politically valuable response to longstanding oppressive conditions. Yokum's recent publications include work on Fanon and psychosexual neuroses, and Foucault on Sade's *Juliette*.

Lambert Zuidervaart

is Emeritus Professor of Philosophy at the Institute for Christian Studies and the University of Toronto, and a Visiting Scholar at Calvin University in Grand Rapids, Michigan, where he resides. An internationally recognized expert in Critical Theory, especially the work of Theodor Adorno, he is currently developing a comprehensive and transformative conception of truth for an allegedly post-truth society, in three volumes: *Truth in Husserl, Heidegger, and the Frankfurt School: Critical Retrieval* (The MIT Press, 2017), *Shattering Silos: Reimagining Knowledge, Politics, and Social Critique* (McGill-Queen's University Press, 2022), and *Social Domains of Truth: Science, Politics, Art, and Religion* (Routledge, 2023). His new book on Adorno, titled *Adorno, Heidegger, and the Politics of Truth* (SUNY Press) will appear in 2024.

PART 1

Culture and Class: the Libidinal Politics of Authoritarianism

∵

CHAPTER 1

Sex, Hope, and Rock and Roll

Radical Feminism and the Freudian Left

Kristin Lawler

At this writing, what is arguably the most important material gain of the women's liberation movement, safe, legal, accessible abortion, is very close to becoming a thing of the past in the United States. And yet sexual freedom and autonomy for women seems no longer the central concern for American feminists, nor does an explicit challenge to the nuclear family as the only state and culturally sanctioned structure in which to rear children.

This is a result of the right-wing cultural backlash to feminism and all the other anti-authoritarian liberationist currents for which "the sixties" serves as shorthand. Although full social and political subjectivity for women is simply impossible without the bodily autonomy that the right to abortion makes possible, the final nail in the coffin of American abortion rights may be nigh. The Supreme Court, the Democratic party, and professionalized women's organizations have not been equal to the long, relentless attack of the religious right. There is an important current of "social reproduction feminism," rooted in the Wages for Housework movement of the 1970s and its greatest theorists, Silvia Federici, Selma James, and Mariarosa Dalla Costa, which insists that reproduction in the family, and women's resistance to it, must be central to a full class struggle analysis, a "feminism for the 99%." But as this autonomist feminism gains ground among Marxists, some of its roots in the politics of desire are obscured. My goal in this chapter is to remember the argument that without a movement that explicitly and collectively rejects the guilt trips and shame delivered upon women who dare to live their lives in "selfish" ways not exclusively shaped by maternal sacrifice, rational claims to rights, privacy, fairness, and justice have simply no chance.

The intensification of capitalist class struggle in the wake of the sixties has played its part in this too. Postwar American affluence generated not the docility that elites had hoped to buy with televisions, dishwashers, pensions, and steady jobs, but instead fomented a new and intensified sense of entitlement on the part of women, racial minorities, workers, soldiers, homemakers, prisoners, and students. Capital and the state responded to these mass uprisings with the imposition of neoliberal austerity intended to reconnect noses with grindstones. It did.

Still, economic explanations only go so far.

1   The Tradition of Cultural Radicalism

Instead, I argue, in the tradition of the cultural radicals I discuss, that reactionary movements – economic and cultural – gain territory at the expense of a desire for freedom, pleasure, and autonomy that animates working class struggle in all its particularities. It was the Freudian Marxism of Frankfurt School theorists like Erich Fromm, Herbert Marcuse, and their major influence, Wilhelm Reich, that allowed them to properly analyze the relationship between the desire for freedom and the politics of class struggle. In inflecting a Marxist understanding of capitalism with a Freudian read of repression, they generated a comprehensive social theory that influenced the radical feminism of writers like Ellen Willis and Shulamith Firestone, as well as the broader make-love-not-war rock and roll counterculture of which this feminism was a part.

In particular, I argue that without a psychoanalytic reading of the sexual repressions of work and the family, any critique of capitalism will miss its productivist cultural logic and thus what is essential in it and what essentially opposes it. Many argue today that the artistic, utopian, transgressive cultural politics that emerged in the sixties are no longer relevant to those who would oppose capitalist exploitation, despoilation of the environment, and authoritarianism. Either because today's proto-fascist right loves to transgress civilized morality or because capital uses for its own purposes the countercultural impulse, this impulse is widely considered to be without contemporary political content. And yet – right-wing cultural conservatives can't stop talking about radical feminism, the sexual revolution, and, associated with both, "cultural Marxism."[1] They seem to sense the enduring and, from their perspective, dangerous appeal.

---

1   In 2021, Fox News host Mark Levin published the bestselling "American Marxism" in which he repeatedly and hilariously refers to the Freudian Marxism of the Frankfurt Institute for Social Research as the "Franklin School" and cites its location as having been in Berlin. This ignorance – of a piece with the contemporary right's misreading and conflation of critical theories of all varieties – does not change the fact that the Freudian left in general, and the Critical Theory of the Frankfurt School in particular, remain preoccupations of the proto-fascist American right, as of course does radical feminism.

What the right calls "cultural Marxism" is indeed linked to women's liberation; both combine a Freudian critique of capitalism to push a still socially explosive project of universal liberation. What unites them is a radical critique of repression, a critique that theorizes social unfreedom under capitalism as rooted in the repression of libido for the purpose of work. Marcuse's *Eros and Civilization* is probably the best example of the radical Freudian reading of class struggle and the dialectical, materialist reading of Freud that constitutes the theoretical perspective known broadly as the Frankfurt School.[2]

Marcuse's work refutes Freud's contention that repression is necessary for civilized social order by taking it seriously but also historicizing it. That is, what Freud referred to as a transhistorical "reality principle," Marcuse's historical materialism reframed in the specific terms of modern rational capitalism and the "surplus repression" necessitated not by the "reality principle" but by the "performance principle" – the specific, productivist cultural and economic logic of modern rational capitalism and the repressive Protestant work ethic without which it could never have gained dominance. And for Marcuse, as for Reich before him, sexual repression in the family is the basis of the reproduction of submission not just to authority but to the specifically bourgeois authority of the capitalist boss and the performance principle.

This move allows Marcuse to argue, on the basis of a dialectical reading of Freud's instinct theory, that a non-repressive social order is not only possible, but, in the face of the destructive aggressiveness progressively unleashed by a repressive society, necessary. The "fatal union of productivity and destruction" – the fact that the most productive and "developed" societies are also by far the most violent – can only be defused, overcome, by a cultural and class struggle in which the pleasure principle is to the performance principle as the working class is to capital. The dialectical nature of history has opened space for revolutionary struggle both because the fruits of technological progress can now be deployed toward liberation from authoritarian work relations and because the family itself is breaking down. If this struggle is victorious,

---

2   In this chapter, I focus on Marcuse's countercultural optimism in *Eros and Civilization*, in which he highlights the subterranean, anti-work explosiveness of libido and which is more resonant with radical feminism than is his later *One-Dimensional Man*'s analysis of the "repressive desublimation" whereby desire is not forbidden but instead satisfied in a controlled and ultimately, for the system, more effective way. It is worth remembering that Marcuse himself identified 1955's *Eros* as his most significant work. It is certainly the one that holds up better in the context of a pandemic-generated interruption in the machinations of the performance principle and the resulting breakdown of the work ethic in the U.S.

Marcuse argues that neither a free Eros nor a free Thanatos[3] would endanger social life, because Eros would self-sublimate and the death instinct, read as a desire for an end to the pain of alienated individuation, would "come to rest" in a free and peaceful society.

Orthodox Marxists as well as sixties and seventies leftists critical of a turn away from exclusive concern with the economic, rejected psychoanalytic Marxism and the radical feminism that invoked it. Christopher Lasch's best-selling *The Culture of Narcissism,* for instance, claimed that patriarchy was a 'pseudo-problem' that took attention away from 'real' problems like corporations, the state, industrialism, and consumerism. Like so many, then and now, he saw cultural radicalism's focus on pleasure as selfish, frivolous distractions from real politics.

Feminist journalist and cultural critic Ellen Willis disagreed. After a career of writing essays – in form and substance, still some of the sharpest writing out there – on politics, culture, feminism, and rock and roll (she was famously the *New Yorker*'s first rock critic and was a *Village Voice* columnist for years), she set out near the end of her life to write a full book on what she termed the "cultural unconscious in American political life." In it, Willis, like Marcuse, insists that we see pleasure in serious political terms: "by looking at American cultural conflict and its international context through a radical Freudian lens, I mean to revive a long-neglected question: suppose a radical democratic politics that affirms freedom and pleasure is not a summons to moral corruption, not dangerous utopian nonsense, not even simply an ethical or spiritual possibility, but an expression of needs anchored in the body and in the long run a condition of human survival?" (2014: 493).

Although Willis was a vocal critic of orthodox Marxists for whom economic determinants are all, she once referred to her politics during the height of the feminist movement as a "somewhat confused mix of cultural radicalism, populism, and Marxism." As a democrat with a small "d," she distanced herself from the authoritarian, ascetic, elitist, and mechanistic tendencies that have always been too closely associated with many variants of Marxism, but she was a radical critic of capitalism for whom Wilhelm Reich was a singularly powerful intellectual influence. In one of the chapters she was able to finish before she died, Willis summarizes the "Freudian left" tradition in which she situates her own work, laying out libido theory and its relationship with women's liberation

---

3   For Freud, Eros is the drive, in humans and in nature, toward pleasure, vitality, and creativity, and is the wellspring of human libido. Thanatos is its other – the death drive. When directed outwards, this regressive drive, originally toward the dissolution of the self, becomes aggressiveness.

and locating her work in the only Marxist tradition that refused to ignore the psychosexual aspects of politics.

Freud, of course, lays out how biologically-based libidinal desire is opposed to civilized social and sexual morality. But:

> Where Freud saw libido as inherently aggressive and antisocial, the Freudian radicals contended that the natural erotic impulse is benign, life-enhancing and self-regulating, while repression gives rise to sexual rage and therefore to the very aggressive and antisocial tendencies, including predatory and violent sexuality, that are then invoked to justify the repression that produced them in the first place. The twin psychic engines of authoritarian culture, Wilhelm Reich argued, are rebellious sadism and reactive, guilty, masochistic submission to authority: by appealing to these sadomasochistic impulses, Hitler had won over much of the German working class *despite a program inimical to its rational economic and political interests.* As for Russia, as Reich saw it the profound patriarchal conservatism of the population, shared by most of the communist leaders, had crushed efforts at radical sexual and educational reform [including the radical democracy of the original soviets, as well as the sexual liberation feminism of thinkers like Alexandra Kollontai] leading to the consolidation of dictatorship and ultimately to Stalinist terror. Thus, the clear lesson of the European crisis in the radical Freudian view was that no program for democratic social transformation can succeed without a social and cultural revolution.
>
> 2014: 488, emphasis mine

Marcuse and Reich both read Freud to claim that libido is the only force strong enough to contain the aggressive drive. For them, it is the unceasing productivity demanded of workers under capitalism and productivist communism,[4] (and not of humans under a transhistorical "reality principle") that necessitates modern society's intense and inherently unsustainable levels of libidinal repression and the institutions – the family, centrally – that reproduce it. Key to Willis' analysis and its resonance with the work of Reich and Marcuse is the

---

4   In the tradition of anti-Stalinist Marxism running from Frankfurt School co-founder Friedrich Pollock, through the Johnson-Forest tendency of the American Trotskyist movement, council communists, the influential French *Socialism ou Barbarie* group, and the Italian autonomist tradition, the 20th century Communist mode of production is referred to as "state capitalism" in acknowledgement of the centrality of this productivist ethic as well as accumulation and wage labor to both systems.

fact that she uncompromisingly roots the desire for freedom from all this in biological need.

2   Women's Liberation, Human Liberation

It may seem counterintuitive, but it is precisely this insistence on a biological imperative that ultimately makes this argument for sexual liberation a feminist one. The biological roots of libido are, in Freud's theory, characterized by "polymorphous perversity," so they are not at all the same as the much-narrowed "mature" sexuality that emerges within the family. This acknowledgment of the centrality of biological drives to a politics of freedom, a critique of the cultural analysis of "neo-Freudian revisionists" that she shares with Marcuse, is also profoundly humanist: "if there is no inherent human need for freedom – if all desire is purely a social construction – then a free society is, arguably, merely a matter of taste, one possibility among others" (2014: 489).

If, however, as she contends, the need for libidinal freedom and pleasure is a biological reality of human life, the principles of libidinal energy – drive, object, repression, rebellion, sublimation, return – are universally shared. (The fear of freedom and rage against it that fuels authoritarianism is then a perversion, a return of the repressed, of biological need). And if the need for freedom is common to all humans, the liberation of women from the shackles of the family and its function of controlling and repressing human sexuality by controlling and repressing women and children, is necessarily universal liberation too.

Shulamith Firestone was a comrade of Willis and together they co-founded the New York feminist group Redstockings; they were important political and intellectual leaders of the tradition of emancipatory feminism I am discussing here. The original back cover of Firestone's seminal 1970 book *The Dialectic of Sex* proclaimed in large block letters: "The missing link between Marx and Freud." In her chapter on the family entitled "Down with Childhood," she argues that the nuclear family and the retarding category of "childhood" it enforces puts all children into a state of economic and physical dependence, sexual repression, and stunted human development; this is the essence of family life, and it functions to prepare – "discipline" – those children for a life of servitude. Thus, if there is to be universal human freedom, the enslavement of "women and children" in the family must come to an end.

In other words, the liberation from the family to be gained by women and children flows to human emancipation overall. Universal and particular liberation do not diverge; universal liberation comes precisely *through* the liberation of the particular. In Firestone's words, "If early sexual repression is the basic mechanism by which character structures supporting political, ideological, and economic serfdom are produced ... the abolition of the family would have profound effects: sexuality would be released from its straitjacket to eroticize our whole culture, changing its very definition" (1970: 60).

Ellen Willis draws out the same connections between the family, sexual repression, and the imposition of work in more explicit terms: "But again, if it's impossible to understand women's condition without making a real critique of the family as an institution, the [so-called] radical feminist strategy of isolating male supremacy from other forms of domination breaks down. The family has more than one political dimension: besides subordinating women, it's also a vehicle for getting children of both sexes to submit to social authority and *actively embrace the values of the dominant culture*" (1992a: 127, emphasis mine).

3   Freud and Feminism

Freudianism, for Firestone, is, despite Freud's "wrong" ideas about women, essentially aligned with feminism. That is, until it devolved into the therapy of healthy adjustment. She categorically rejects therapeutic psychoanalysis, which she sees as Freud's theory evacuated of its socially explosive content to become just another method of domestication. Noting that feminism and psychoanalysis emerged "from the same soil," – a ferment around issues of women and sexuality that, she observes, was picked up best by novelists like D.H. Lawrence, Henry James, and Virginia Woolf as well as playwrights like Shaw and Ibsen – she argues that "essentially they are made of the same substance: the basic tenets of Freudianism ... are also the raw material of feminism. The difference lies only in that radical feminism does not accept the social context in which repression (and the resulting neurosis) must develop as immutable. If we dismantle the family, the subjection of 'pleasure' to 'reality,' i.e., sexual repression, has lost its function and is no longer necessary" (1970: 61). This defanged psychoanalysis came to subsume the place of feminism:

> As the lesser of two evils ... regroomed for its new function of 'social adjustment,' it was used to wipe up the feminist revolt ... Freudianism was the perfect foil for feminism because, though it struck the same nerve, it had a safety catch that feminism didn't – it never questioned the given reality. While both at their cores are explosive, Freudianism was gradually revised to suit the pragmatic needs of clinical therapy ... Thus Freudianism gained the ground that feminism lost: it flourished at the

expense of feminism, to the extent that it acted as a container of its shattering force.

1970: 70–71

Now, she says, women are waking up and finally a "therapy that has proven worse than useless" may be replaced with "the only thing that can do any good: political organization."

Marcuse's *Eros and Civilization* makes a similar critique of "revisionists" that, in his analysis as well, dampened the explosive content of psychoanalysis when they disavowed the biological basis of the desire for freedom and thus framed radical political organizing as pathologically anti-social maladjustment.[5] For Marcuse:

> Deep conformity holds sway over this psychology, which suspects all those who 'cut loose from their earlier moorings' and become 'radicals' as neurotic (the description fits all of them, from Jesus to Lenin, from Socrates to Giordano Bruno), and which almost automatically identifies 'the promise of a better world' with 'Utopia,' its substance with 'revery,' and mankind's sacred dream of justice for all with the personal resentment of maladjusted types. This 'operational' identification of mental health with 'adjustive success' and progress eliminates all the reservations with which Freud hedged the therapeutic objective of adjustment to an inhuman society and thus commits psychoanalysis to this society far more than Freud ever did.
>
> 1955: 256–7

Marcuse instead insists on a Freudianism that unleashes the repressed memory of libidinal gratification and is thus a potentially explosive process. In this formulation, psychoanalysis "liberates tabooed aspirations" denied by the mature ego. In his words:

> [Memory's] truth value lies in the specific function of memory to preserve promises and potentialities which are betrayed and even outlawed

---

5 Whether or not Marcuse's critique of the later Fromm and other "neo-Freudian revisionists" is justified is beyond the scope of this chapter to consider. (Ellen Willis, for instance, thought that Marcuse was oversimplifying Fromm.) The historical fact remains that overall, the mainstream of psychoanalysis did become a therapy of "healthy" adjustment and that both Marcuse and Firestone rejected this defanging of the political potential of psychoanalysis, sharing a sense that the move from biological drive to cultural transmission was largely responsible.

by the mature, civilized individual, but which had once been fulfilled in his dim past and which are never entirely forgotten … the … liberation of memory explodes the rationality of the repressed individual. As cognition gives way to re-cognition, the forbidden images and impulses of childhood begin to tell the truth that reason denies. Regression assumes a progressive function. The rediscovered past yields critical standards which are tabooed by the present. Moreover, the restoration of memory is accompanied by the restoration of the cognitive content of phantasy. Psychoanalytic theory removes these mental faculties from the non-committal sphere of daydreaming and fiction and recaptures their strict truths. The weight of these discoveries must eventually shatter the framework in which they were made and confined.

> 1955: 19

Also similar to Marcuse, Firestone's reading of Freud is explicitly infused with an anti-authoritarian form of historical materialism that refuses to either hypostatize social reality or to ignore the material substratum of social life. Of Marx and Engels, she says:

They saw the world as process, a natural flux of action and reaction, of opposites yet inseparable and interpenetrating. Because they were able to perceive history as a movie rather than as snapshot, they attempted to avoid falling into the stagnant 'metaphysical' view that had trapped so many other great minds. They combined this view of the dynamic interplay of historical forces with a materialist one, that is, they attempted for the first time to put historical and cultural change on a real basis, to trace the development of economic classes to organic causes.

> 1970: 2–3

In contrast to the pure economism she saw in Marx and Engels, though, Firestone looks to develop a materialist view of history "based on sex itself." In this she says we must do to orthodox Marxism what the physics of relativity did to Newtonian physics – not to invalidate it, but to understand that it applies only to a limited part of social existence. "For an economic diagnosis traced to ownership of the means of production, even of the means of reproduction, does not explain everything. There is a level of reality that does not stem directly from economics," namely, the sex division that she sees as fundamental to all others (1970: 5). In this way, she reads Marxism in precisely the generative manner in which Marcuse reads Freud.

4   The End of Work

For Firestone and Marcuse, repression in the family functions to ensure the reproduction of the repressions of work. One of Freud's most seminal insights is that repression is reproduced through the Oedipus situation in the nuclear family (in a modified repetition of the domination-rebellion-restoration story of the primal father and murderous band of brothers). In Marcuse's reading of Freud, this process culminates in the transformation of a "polymorphous-perverse," timeless pleasure seeker into an instrument of clocked labor whose life is segmented between the now central imposition of work and the now marginalized "leisure":

> The conflict between sexuality and civilization unfolds with this develop-
> ment of domination. Under the rule of the performance principle, body
> and mind are made into instruments of alienated labor; they can func-
> tion as such instruments only if they renounce the freedom of the libid-
> inal subject-object which the human organism primarily is and desires
> ... the organization of sexuality reflects the basic features of the perfor-
> mance principle and its organization of society.
>
>   1955: 47

Marcuse argues that the centralizing process of sexual identity formation that Freud locates in the family "achieves the socially necessary desexualization of the body: the libido becomes concentrated in one part of the body, leaving most of the rest free for use as the instrument of labor. The temporal reduction of the libido [to 'leisure' time] is thus supplemented by its spatial reduction ... In a repressive order, which enforces the equation between normal, socially useful, and good, the manifestations of pleasure for its own sake must appear as *fleurs du mal* ... the irreconcilable conflict is not between work (reality prin-ciple) and Eros (pleasure principle), but between *alienated* labor (performance principle) and Eros" (1955: 47–50).

The capitalist segmentation of the human body and the moments of life will end with a non-repressive civilization that he sees as imminent because, among other things, the patriarchal authoritarian father has been losing his grip in the context of mass society's "depersonalization" of the superego in which the paternal object of aggression and hate is replaced by smiling teach-ers and helpful social workers. The cycle of domination-repression-restored domination is loosed from its moorings in the family. This is part of what Marcuse calls "the dialectic of civilization" that is moving toward the possibil-ity of revolution, after which the working day would be reduced to an absolute minimum, largely through the automation of production,[6] necessary labor would be re-eroticized, and the Oedipus complex, and the family that reproduces it, would "pass away."

Firestone goes even further; revolution would mean the end of the sex distinction itself ("genital differences would no longer matter culturally"). Her analysis too ends in a post-work society: because in her analysis, the sex distinction is the root of the division of labor, this too would fall away, as would labor itself – "by the elimination of labor altogether (cybernation)." In this process, then, "the tyranny of the biological family would be broken" (1970: 11). In her words:

> Marx was onto something more profound than he knew when he observed that the family contained within itself in embryo all the antagonisms that later develop on a wide scale within the society and the state. For unless revolution uproots the basic social organization, the biological family – the vinculum through which the psychology of power can always be smuggled – the tapeworm of exploitation will never be annihilated. We shall need a sexual revolution much larger than – inclusive of – a socialist one to truly eradicate all class systems.
>
> 1970: 12

Marcuse's invocation of a future "exchangeability of functions" can be read in a similar way: Progress "beyond the performance principle" would result in "satisfaction without toil" – that is, without the rule of alienated labor. Under the 'ideal' conditions of mature industrial civilization, alienation would be completed by general automatization of labor, reduction of labor time to a minimum, and exchangeability of functions. Painless gratification of needs, without toil and the repressions that allow toil to dominate our waking lives, would result in a liberation of erotic, libidinal energy "to an unprecedented degree" (1955: 153–4).

---

6   "Since the length of the working day is itself one of the principal repressive factors imposed upon the pleasure principle by the reality principle, the reduction of the working day to a point where the mere quantum of labor time no longer arrests human development is the first prerequisite for freedom" (1955: 152).

This erotic energy would, according to Marcuse, not only be strong enough to bind back the mutual primary aggressiveness that is also part of our instinctual make-up (a less repressed society would unleash less aggressiveness, and the death instinct, reinterpreted as the Nirvana Principle, would be satisfied in a less repressive, more peaceful, more connected social order); this erotic energy would also tend to self-sublimate. That is, the pleasures of sublimated bonds of affection and love, of artistic and creative work, of connection and caring, etc., would still be pursued by free people. What would end is the surplus repression of the performance principle and the repressive structures necessary, not for human survival or flourishing, but for the continuation of capitalism's endless, mindless, wasteful, and destructive exploitation and "growth."

5   The Culture of Narcissism and the Reunification of Eros

On the other hand, claims to pleasure and autonomy have been coded, by cultural conservatives on the left and the right, as insufficiently self-sacrificing and unbecoming of serious leftists ("women are starving on welfare and you are worried about orgasms? As though we couldn't worry about orgasms and poverty at the same time" (1992: xix)). In a word, narcissistic. Christopher Lasch's *The Culture of Narcissism* was only the most well-known of the moralistic harangues against sixties types who insisted, against the work ethic and family values, that pleasure and freedom in everyday life mattered. The anti-narcissists attempted to shame women's libbers with the insult. In Marcuse's analysis, though, narcissism is central to the non-repressive reunification of the two trends of Eros that he envisions: the reconciliation of the *unifying* and *gratifying* aspects of love is accomplished precisely through the release of the narcissism that proponents of women's liberation have always been criticized for.

The backlash against the sexual revolution and feminist radicalism was couched in the critique of "hedonism" as well as "narcissism" and eventually, in Willis' words, "a mood of guilt and self-doubt began to erode the sixties generation's sense of entitlement to freedom and fulfillment" (2014: 481). This was due to a culture in which there existed "a widespread unconscious conflation of self-determination with selfishness, the pursuit of personal and sexual happiness with moral corruption." According to Willis, this kind of guilt is profoundly politically dangerous because "under this unconscious burden, people fear and mistrust their desires as invitations to catastrophe." Thus, "when in the struggle for freedom and happiness, contradictions, mistakes, defeats, and the opposition of enemies inevitably come up, people doubt what they are doing. They see defeats as 'the wages of sin,' as punishments for transgressions," while also, "frustrated desire generates rage and resentment" which is then easily channeled to subaltern others as well as to "the permissive 'cultural elite'" (2014: 485).

Thus, for Willis, "Any movement that accepts this traditional moralistic take, this sense that the desire for freedom is selfish and narcissistic and frivolous, will never deal with the contradictions of the cultural unconscious that the sexual revolution unleashes. We will keep on fighting the same battles, but the reactionaries will get stronger and stronger." If we are to fight for liberation on the terrain of this kind of ambivalence, we must, in Willis' words, "unambiguously defend desire" for "it is the longing for happiness that is potentially radical, while the morality of sacrifice is an age old weapon of rulers" (1992: xx). Besides, the extension of freedom and pleasure results not in a war of all against all, nor in continued injustice, but instead in the kind of non-repressive, organic social order in which the individual and the social are no longer at odds.

In *Eros and Civilization*, Marcuse points to the figures of Orpheus and Narcissus as images of an uncompromising and generative (but totally unproductive, except of a new and non-repressive order) logic that has always been devalued by modern rationality and specifically by the performance principle – he calls them "the archetypes of another existential relation to reality." In Marcuse's reading, as Bernard Stiegler points out, narcissism is *not* solipsism; it is instead an expansive oneness with the world that grounds the free erotic sublimation that makes possible a non-repressive society: "Marcuse grounds his thought of a new form of sublimation on the notion ... of an undifferentiated, unified libido prior to the division of ego and external objects ... Primary narcissism ... engulfs the environment, integrating the narcissistic ego with the objective world" (2014: 73).

That is, Marcuse returns to Freud's first chapter in *Civilization and its Discontents* to remind us that the "primitive pleasure-ego" described there in the discussion of the oceanic feeling of the infant at the breast, does not originally distinguish between itself and the outside world: all is one in an erotic unity of connection and gratification. "Originally, the ego includes everything, later it detaches from itself the external world. The ego-feeling we are aware of now is thus only a shrunken residue of a much more extensive feeling – a feeling which embraced the universe and expressed an inseparable connection of the ego with the external world" (1962: 8).

In Marcuse's argument that Narcissus is a figure of libidinal freedom, he asserts that "narcissism may contain the germ of a different reality principle: the libidinal cathexis of the ego (one's own body) may become the source and reservoir for a new libidinal cathexis of the objective world – transforming this world into a new mode of being. This interpretation is corroborated by the decisive role which narcissistic libido plays, according to Freud, in sublimation … The hypothesis all but revolutionizes the idea of sublimation" (1955: 168–70).

Thus, for Marcuse, "narcissism, usually understood as egoistic withdrawal from reality, here is connected with oneness with the universe … [under its sway] all sublimation would begin with the reactivation of narcissistic libido, which somehow overflows and extends to objects [and constitutes] a non-repressive mode of sublimation which results from an extension rather than a constraining deflection of the libido" (1955: 153–154, quoted in Stiegler 2014: 73).

In Freud, scarcity and pain provide the impetus for the traumatic separation of the individual from the whole, but this primitive, expansive, narcissistic ego feeling remains even after the painful separation, and thus awaits (and prefigures) the post-scarcity society that Marcuse claims technological development under capitalism makes possible. In sum, Marcuse's reading of narcissistic libido grounds at a basic level his claim that an unrepressed and self-sublimating Eros is a realistic possibility. This would be an Eros in which the division between its twin imperatives of sexual pleasure and the building of society is no more.

What would a libidinal drive no longer divided against itself in this way look like? Consider Willis' essay "The Family: Love it or Leave it," in which she asserts that Wilhelm Reich's "most revolutionary assertion was … that natural sexuality is the physical manifestation of love" and that the modern bifurcation of sex and love, of sensuality and tenderness, is an effect of a sexually repressive ascetic moralism.

Democracy itself depends on the overcoming of this split between pleasure and society: "though all democratic thought is based on the premise that freedom is compatible with civilization, that under the right conditions people are capable of self-regulation, even dedicated democrats hesitate to apply this principle to family life" (1992: 106). It is possible, Willis claims, to imagine a love that is both free and responsible. In fact, it is necessary: to refuse this possibility is to "reject the possibility of love itself." She invites us to imagine a communal life that allows *both* the spontaneity of passion and the responsibility of care:

> I suspect that in a truly free society sexual love would be at once more satisfying and less terrifying, that lovers would be more spontaneously monogamous but less jealous, more willing to commit themselves deeply yet less devastated if a relationship had to end … Groups of people who agreed to take responsibility for each other, pool their economic resources, and share housework and child care would have a basis for

stability independent of any one couple's sexual bond; children would
have the added security of close ties to adults other than their biological
parents ... communal child rearing, shared by both sexes, would remove
the element of martyrdom from parenthood.

> 1992: 157–158

Here Willis illustrates precisely what Marcuse theorizes when he imagines a
non-repressive social order, a "libidinal morality" in which the split in Eros
between the drive for pleasure and the drive for social connection which Freud
claims are inexplicably in opposition to one another, is healed. In Marcuse's
words: "Against Freud's notion of the inevitable biological conflict between
pleasure principle and reality principle, between sexuality and civilization,
militates the idea of the unifying and gratifying power of Eros, chained and
worn out in a sick civilization. This idea would imply that the free Eros does
not preclude lasting civilized societal relationships – that it repels only the
supra-repressive organization of societal relationships under a principle that
is the negation of the pleasure principle" (1955: 43).

In Marcuse, the figure of Narcissus heralds this new way of being. With
Orpheus (another image of nonproductive love) Narcissus is counterposed
to Prometheus, the bringer of fire, the "culture hero of toil, productivity, and
progress through repression ... Orpheus and Narcissus (like Dionysus) stand
for a very different reality" (1955: 146). These countercultural figures animate
the Western imagination and live on in the realms of the psyche not subject to
the ego's rational reality testing – phantasy and art.

6   Mass Culture and Politics

In her analysis of capitalism and culture, Willis "mounts a polemic against
standard leftist notions about advanced capitalism – that the consumer economy makes us slaves to commodities, that the function of the mass media is to
manipulate our fantasies so we will equate fulfillment with buying the system's
products." She insists that this analysis misses the other side of culture in a
consumer society: the subversiveness whereby advertising and mass art also
undermine the system:

> By continually pushing the message that we have the right to gratifica-
> tion now, consumerism at its most expansive encouraged a demand for
> fulfillment that could not so easily be contained by products; it had a way
> of spilling over into rebellion against the constricting conditions of our

lives. The history of the sixties strongly suggests that the impulse to buy a new car and tool down the freeway with the radio blasting rock-and-roll is not unconnected to the impulse to fuck outside marriage, get high, stand up to men or white people or bosses, join dissident movements. In fact the mass media helped to spread rebellion, and the system obligingly marketed products that encouraged it, for the simple reason that there was money to be made from rebels who were also consumers. On one level the sixties revolt was an impressive illustration of Lenin's remark that the capitalist will sell you the rope to hang him with.

1992: xvi

Still, Willis consistently views the world from a working-class perspective and in some ways her quarrel with Marcuse comes from this perspective. Upon Marcuse's death, Willis wrote of *Eros and Civilization* and *One-Dimensional Man* that they "excited me because they were about problems I was struggling with – the relation of psychology to politics, the idea of a cultural revolution, the prospects for radical change in a society where most people had enough to eat" (1992: 141). Still, she sees his "apocalyptic utopianism" as closer to "nihilist pessimism" than any kind of hopeful sense of working-class agency or subjectivity. "His version of the perennial aristocratic nightmare, 'mass man,' was the passive manipulated consumer who had no autonomous desires, only socially imposed 'false needs' for the system's products and spectacles" (1992: 142). Her feminism informed this difference with the Frankfurt School disdain for pop as well: consumer goods and "frivolous" cultural forms, of course, have also always been associated by elites with not just the working class but also women and children.

Willis was critical of what she saw as Marcuse's typically aristocratic disdain for popular culture (shared, in her view, with the rest of the Frankfurt School and the New Left), the fact that "classes who take money for granted are always horrified at the naïve delight of the vulgar nouveau riche in getting and spending"; this draws a clear line between what she characterizes as a critique in which "the only revolutionary act was to stand outside the system and say *no!*," a critique for which, according to her, liberalism was at least in part a way for the ruling class to pass off its oppressions as freedoms. Against this, Willis insists that people were agents and not simply objects of the dynamics of power. She sees liberal freedoms as a concession granted by the ruling class in the face of working-class struggle for liberation – evidenced by, among other things, the fact that these liberal reforms are yanked back by capital the second it becomes possible for them to do so: "If American workers have not hated their lives enough to make a revolution, it is in part because liberalism meets some genuine human needs. But it is also because however pissed off they may be (and Americans usually are) most people, understandably, don't want to risk what they have unless they see a practical alternative and feel they have a real chance at it. In the meantime, there is struggle in small, daily ways and the opportunity to sneak out to a movie now and then" (1992: 144). Willis claims that leftists fail to see the radical potential in mass art:

> Assuming that because mass art is a product of capitalism, it is by defi-
> nition worthless – not real art at all, but merely a commodity intended
> to enrich its producers while indoctrinating and pacifying consumers.
> And again this assumption betrays a hidden conservatism. Why, after all,
> regard commercial art as intrinsically more compromised than art pro-
> duced under the auspices of the medieval church, or aristocratic patrons?
> Art has always been in some sense propaganda for the ruling classes and
> at the same time a form of struggle against them.
>
> 1992: xvi

Mass art in the sixties had a rebellious, hedonistic aesthetic. Still, rebellion, Willis admits, is not revolution. "It's not only that capitalists are experts at palming off fake rope ... neither mass art nor any kind of art is a substitute for politics" (1992: xvi). Politically, Willis was an optimist, although the reaction to the cultural radicalism, the rock and roll countercultural feminism that shaped her, came fast and furious. Nevertheless, as she famously wrote: "My deepest impulses are optimistic, an attitude that seems to me as spiritually necessary and proper as it is intellectually suspect" (1992: 81).

But Willis' optimism was never a one-sided or "mindless yea-saying" as she so devastatingly said of what she called Tom Wolfe's "failed optimism." Without complexity and a clear-eyed critical stance, midcentury pop sensibility *could* flatten into a one-dimensional cheerfulness and disavowal that was essentially anti-utopian. In her words: "The pop stance was honest up to a point. But its commitment to making the most of the existing reality excluded painful or dangerous questions about systemic change" (1992: 81). The working-class fem-inism that kept her from aristocratic disdain for the pleasures of pop also kept her from an uncritical immersion: "Of course, rebellion is not the same thing as revolution ... subversion begins to be radical only when we ask what we really want or think we should have, who or what is obstructing us, and what to do about it" (1992: xviii).

At least in *Eros,* Marcuse also saw this political potential as informed but not exhausted by the hedonism of art. In his focus on the truth value and lib-eratory potential of imagination and fantasy – the parts of the psyche "free from the control of the reality principle," because it's the part that is "born and at the same time left behind by the organization of the pleasure ego into the reality ego ... Imagination envisions the reconciliation of the individual with the whole, of desire with realization, of happiness with reason" (1955: 142–143). For him, this imagination is the content of art: "Art expressed the return of the repressed image of liberation; art was opposition ... The image of a different form of reality has appeared as the truth of one of the basic mental processes; this image contains the lost unity between the universal and the particular and the integral gratification of the life instincts by the reconciliation between the pleasure and reality principles" (1955: 145–146).

Thus, the imagination's truth is revolutionary:

> The truth value of imagination relates not only to the past but also to the future: the forms of freedom and happiness which it invokes claim to deliver the historical reality. In its refusal to accept as final the limitations imposed upon freedom and happiness by the reality principle, in its refusal to forget what can be, lies the critical function of phantasy ... that the propositions of the artistic imagination are untrue in terms of the actual organization of the facts belongs to the essence of their truth ... The relegation of real possibilities to the no-man's land of utopia is itself an essential element of the ideology of the performance principle.
>
> 1955: 149–150

7   No Surrender

In the culture wars, half measures, then, are political suicide. The backlash against sixties radicalism proved just that. As Reich's analysis shows, a little liberation without full liberation sends people running for cover in authoritarianism. Willis makes the same case in reference to the rise of Islamic fundamentalism around the globe and the strength of the religious right in the U.S.

It remains shocking that Willis is the only thinker who does not disavow the obvious fact that 9/11 was a spectacular act of sadomasochistic aggression against a massive phallic symbol. Of course she knows that other, economic and political, factors are in play. But for Willis, the left ignores the culture war between patriarchal fundamentalism and what it perceives as the West's "loose morals" at its peril. Why, she asks, would we not listen to what the attackers say themselves about their own motives? "As modernizing, liberalizing forces erode the repression that keeps rage unconscious and the social controls that keep violence contained, it becomes ever easier for a match of political grievance to ignite the gas of psychosexual tension, touching off a conflagration. Eventually, the fire is put out, for the time being. The gas remains" (2003: 99). Her Reichian analysis likens this dynamic to the rise of the Nazis in Germany. An only partial moral loosening gave rise to a fearful flight into authoritarianism.

In response to the conundrum that German rebellion took the form not of communism but of fascism:

> Reich and other psychoanalytically minded radicals, including the Marxist social theorists of the Frankfurt school, challenged the conventional economistic wisdom of the European left to argue that unconscious psychosexual conflict had played a central role in the triumph of Nazism. In the view of this Freudian left, the liberalism of Weimar had stirred up repressed longings for freedom – and rage at its suppression – that people whose characters had been formed by patriarchalism could not admit. While their anger was encouraged and legitimized by real political complaints, their underlying fear of freedom prevented them from contemplating real revolution. For the mass of Germans, then, Hitler offered a solution to this impasse: he represented the authoritarian father who commanded submission – only in this case submission entailed the license, indeed the obligation, to vent rebellious rage by supporting and participating in persecution and mass murder ... [and] indeed, the most disturbing implication of the Freudian left analysis is that Nazism was not a phenomenon peculiar to post WWI Germany but rather had fulfilled a potential inherent in patriarchal culture, even in "advanced" societies – a potential that might be activated anywhere by destabilizing political events.
>
> 2003: 100

Thus, "to examine Islamic fundamentalism through the lens of the last century's history is to discern a familiar pattern: psychopathology brought to the surface by the promise and threat of modernity and aggravated by political oppression. As with fascism, the rise of Islamic totalitarianism has partly to do with its populist appeal to class resentments and to feelings of political subordination and humiliation, but is at bottom a violent defensive reaction against the temptations of freedom. Islamic militants demonize the U.S. not simply because of its foreign policy – as so many leftists would like to believe, despite the pronouncements of the Islamists themselves – but because it exports and symbolizes cultural revolution" (2003: 101). This revolution is characterized by sexual freedom, which necessarily implies the liberation of women; the violent explosion of rebellion against it is infused with both fascination and fear. This is true of all reactionaries; Islamic fundamentalists *and* the Americans whose reaction against the sexual revolution takes the form of a Christian obsession with the "life" of the fetus, destroyed by the woman whose extra-familial sexual autonomy is now coded as "murder." In this, feminism and the rootless, cosmopolitan figure of the Jew are aligned in the patriarchal, fundamentalist, fascist imagination: both are a clear threat to totalitarian authority, a seduction, and an occasion for rage and retribution.

In considering American cultural politics since the 1960s, Willis says of the "aggressive, radical right-wing insurgency that has achieved an influence far out of proportion to its numbers" that its "potent secret weapon has been the guilt and anxiety about desire that inform the character of Americans regardless of ideology; appealing to those largely unconscious emotions, the right has disarmed, intimidated, paralyzed its opposition." When the broad left softened their stance on cultural issues, especially feminism, it reflected their own ambivalence about a politics of freedom, equality, and pleasure. The effect was, from the perspective of the Freudian analysis laid out here, predictable: "the strategy of the pandering to the right was an abject failure: Reagan was elected; the ERA lost" (and it is worth remembering that Reagan's campaign was the first to use the slogan "Make America Great Again"). "If an ambivalent public hears only one side of a question, the conservative side, passionately argued ... the passionate arguers will carry the day. Why would anyone support a movement that won't stand behind its own program?" (2006: 14).

Willis invites us to imagine a counter history. "If despite this abdication, the cultural right has met considerable popular resistance – if most people today, including many who profess to be conservatives, are reluctant to give up certain social freedoms or deny them to others – suppose the left had consistently stood up for the principle of a feminist, democratic culture? Can anyone doubt that the political landscape would be different?" (2006: 14).

A proto-fascist traditionalist authoritarianism gains strength today, even as pandemic era America has seen both the largest anti-police civil rights rebellion in a generation and what the media calls "the great resignation" – a massive work refusal and slowdown on the part of the American working class. As we continue to be engaged in the political battles around working class cultural and economic emancipation that both the early Frankfurt School and women's liberation feminists analyzed, and as the left continues to eat itself alive in battles over the universal vs. the particular, class vs. identity, mainstream vs. radical, we would do well to take their counsel to heart.

The retreat from the politics of freedom is profoundly dangerous, as the Freudian leftists discussed in this paper all make clear. And we still have a world to win. In Ellen Willis' words: "The issue, finally, is whether we have the right to hope for a freer, more humane way of connecting with each other. Defenders of the family seem to think that we have already gone too far, that the problem of this painful and confusing time is too much freedom. I think there's no such thing as too much freedom – only too little nerve" (1992: 127).

References

Firestone, Shulamith. 1970. *The Dialectic of Sex: the Case for Feminist Revolution.* New York: Bantam Books.

Freud, Sigmund. 1962 [1930]. *Civilization and its Discontents.* New York: W. W. Norton and Company.

Marcuse, Herbert. 1955. *Eros and Civilization: a Philosophical Inquiry into Freud.* Boston, MA: Beacon Press.

Stiegler, Bernard. 2014. *The Lost Spirit of Capitalism.* Cambridge: Polity Press.

Willis, Ellen. 2014. "Tom Wolfe's Failed Optimism." In *The Essential Ellen Willis,* edited by Nona Willis Aronowitz, 115–120. Minneapolis, MN: University of Minnesota Press.

Willis, Ellen. 2006. "Escape from Freedom: What's the Matter with Tom Frank (and the Liberals who Love Him?)" *Situations: Project of the Radical Imagination* 1(2): 5–20.

Willis, Ellen. 2003. "The Mass Psychology of Terrorism." In *Implicating Empire: Globalization and Resistance in the 21st Century World Order,* edited by Stanley Aronowitz and Heather Gautney, 95–108. New York, NY: Basic Books.

Willis, Ellen. 1992. *Beginning to See the Light: Sex, Hope, and Rock and Roll.* Hanover: Wesleyan University Press.

Willis, Ellen. 1992(a). "Radical Feminism and Feminist Radicalism." In *No More Nice Girls: Countercultural Essays,* 117–150. Hanover: Wesleyan University Press.

CHAPTER 2

Fascism and the Patriarchal Family

The Studies of Authoritarianism at the Institute for Social Research

Ryan Moore

1 Introduction

In his 1931 inaugural lecture as director of the Institute of Social Research, Max Horkheimer outlined a program for scholarship that would combine interdisciplinary empirical research with radical social philosophy. Five years later, the *Studien über Autorität und Familie* (Studies on Authority and the Family) was the first fruit of this program, a 2-volume work of nearly one thousand pages, published with the Institute exiled in New York City. Featuring essays by Horkheimer, Herbert Marcuse, and Erich Fromm, the *Studien* analyzed how the exercise of authority within patriarchal families generated the types of character structure that made certain individuals susceptible to fascist beliefs and actions. These initial interrogations of the connections between familial socialization and fascist politics, embodied in a sado-masochistic character structure, established the theoretical and methodological groundwork for investigations of authoritarianism in the years ahead (Jay 1996: 124–25; Kellner 1989: 40–41; Wiggershaus 2007: 38–40, 149–51).

The social-psychological analyses of fascism that followed the *Studien* veered in several directions during and after the second World War. After parting ways with the Institute, Fromm's 1941 work *Escape from Freedom* jettisoned Freud's theory of the instincts but continued to utilize the concept of "social character" in diagnosing the psychological appeal of Nazism (Fromm 1994: chaps. 5,6). His postwar works continued to examine different forms of social character (e.g., Fromm 1990a: chap. 3; 1990b: chap. 5), and he maintained a lifelong concern with the various forms of authoritarianism and destructiveness initially encountered in Germany (e.g., Fromm 1992). Meanwhile, the Institute for Social Research conducted a series of empirical works sponsored by the American Jewish Committee beginning in 1944, titled *Studies in Prejudice* (Jay 1996: chap. 7; Kellner 1989: 114–120; Wiggershaus 2007: 408–430). Each of these studies examined different aspects of anti-Semitism and authoritarian demagoguery, the best known being *The Authoritarian Personality*, conducted by T.W. Adorno with a team of social psychologists from the University

© RYAN MOORE, 2024 | DOI:10.1163/9789004686830_003

of California. The central methodological tools of *The Authoritarian Personality* were a series of questionnaires distributed to more than 2,000 respondents, which provided scales to measure anti-Semitism (A-S Scale), ethnocentrism (E Scale), political-economic conservatism (PEC Scale), and potential fascism (F-Scale) (Adorno et al. 2019).

The investigations initiated by the *Studien* in 1936 and culminating with *The Authoritarian Personality* in 1950 have had an enduring impact, influencing further studies that followed the upsurge of right-wing politics in the late 20th Century. The research of Canadian psychologist Bob Altemeyer (1981, 1996, 2006) revised and expanded the original F-Scale into a survey for measuring what he calls Right-Wing Authoritarianism. Most recently, Altemeyer has collaborated with John Dean—former White House counsel and Watergate star witness—in analyzing the authoritarian followers of George W. Bush and Donald Trump (Dean 2006; Dean and Altemeyer 2020). Indeed, *The Authoritarian Personality* along with other analyses from the *Studies in Prejudice* series acquired renewed relevance in the wake of Trump's ascendance in the Republican Party and the 2016 election (Ross 2016; Gordon 2017; Mattson 2018; Clavey 2020). Yale University hosted a conference on *The Authoritarian Personality* in February 2020, and the study has also recently been the subject of special issues of the *South Atlantic Quarterly* (Marasco 2018), *Comparative Literature and Culture* (Tomba 2021), and *Polity* (Marasco, Gerhardt, and Wetters 2022).

Recent events have demonstrated the value of data science and digital media for measuring an individual's predilection for right-wing politics, but not with the anti-fascist intentions of the Frankfurt School. The Facebook-Cambridge Analytica scandal revealed how personal data collected through social media could be used to predict a person's potential support for a variety of right-wing political campaigns, extremist groups, and conspiracy theories. Reflecting on *The Authoritarian Personality*, Moira Weigel (2022: 147) writes: "The flourishing of quantitative propaganda and personality research that the study both built on and extended not only did not cure prejudice in the United States—they ultimately proved expedient for cultivating it." Weigel proposes a new typology, an Authoritarian Personality 2.0, which maintains continuity with the vintage forms of fascism in an updated version for our present social and technological settings—a personality less likely to be characterized by conformity or conventionalism, for instance. A key new feature of the 2.0 version is its redesign for a networked society of digital media and niche markets, in contrast to the mass media and mass consumption that drew the ire of the Frankfurt School during the mid-20th Century.

The theoretical and empirical studies of authoritarianism undertaken by the Institute for Social Research have thus demonstrated their enduring influence and relevance, but they were responses to the intellectual and political currents of their own time. By the 1930s it was widely recognized that fascism had become an international movement, and some intellectuals were beginning to sense that it could not be analyzed completely in terms of economics and politics, that fascism was also a matter of social psychology. It was in this context that Wilhelm Reich first published *The Mass Psychology of Fascism* in 1933, a work that built on his prior attempts to synthesize Marx and Freud into a revolutionary politics of social and sexual liberation. Reich's diagnosis of fascism was deterministic and undialectical, but it established a critical paradigm for the Institute's subsequent investigations of the relationship between the family structure and authoritarianism. This chapter therefore begins with Reich's analysis of fascism before considering the Institute's 1936 *Studien* in closer detail. While I maintain that Horkheimer, Fromm, and Marcuse presented a more complicated picture of the intermediate social forces linking family, authority, and fascism, they did so at the expense of engaging with the issues of sexual repression and racism originally raised by Reich.

The issues taken up by Reich and the early Frankfurt School are of continuing significance for feminist theory, particularly with respect to their critique of the patriarchal family. Horkheimer's essay for the *Studien* is especially noteworthy for its historical interrogation of the family, an institution that later scholarship from the Frankfurt School would have much less to say about. Horkheimer examined the patriarchal family as a political institution whose investigation through empirical research was of paramount importance, for it is here that individuals experience their initial immersion into social relations of domination. As Robyn Marasco argues, Horkheimer's analysis illuminates how "the family matters not only for reproducing the social order, as Marxist feminists have long argued, but for orienting human beings to authority and adapting them to authoritarianism" (2018a: 798). The critical investigation of the patriarchal family as a pivotal institution for the construction of subjectivity, especially in matters of gender and sexuality, thus forms a lasting point of connection between the early Frankfurt School and contemporary feminist theory. In Marasco's words, "The family is the institution that prepares its members to assume their place in a social hierarchy, adhere to the principle of inequality, and accept the rule of authority, rational or not. The family is where we first become political subjects" (2018: 799). Fascism, in short, is often spawned in the home.

2   The Social Psychology of Nazism

Writing at the dawn of the Nazis' seizure of state power, Reich began by acknowledging the lamentable fact that fascism was not only "an international reality," but also "in many countries had visibly and undeniably outstripped the socialist revolutionary movement" (2003: 3). The triumph of fascism exposed a fatal weakness in the socialist movement and what Reich called "vulgar Marxism." In his analysis, the German Left espoused an economic determinism with the confidence that the truth of their theory would be self-evident to a growing industrial proletariat, leading to revolution whenever the objective conditions finally became sufficiently ripe. Nazism was assumed to be a regressive symptom of irrational mysticism, whose appeal would inevitably vanish when confronted with Marxist science. Mystical forms of political and religious thought had been key elements of Italian fascism, and the Nazis also invoked occultist traditions in their Aryan-esoteric theory of Ariosophy (Goodrick-Clarke 1992). In 1933, tragically, "it was the mysticism of the National Socialists that triumphed over the economic theory of socialism, and at a time when the economic crisis and misery were at their worst" (2003: 5). For Reich, this defeat exposed not just a deficient theory of politics, but a more fundamental miscalculation and oversimplification of the psycho-social forces that shape human behavior and consciousness. In his words, "the Marxists *had failed to take into account the character structure of the masses and the social effect of mysticism*" (2003: 5, original emphases).

The political rise of fascism in the face of economic crisis called on Marxists to consider the "subjective factor"—specifically the concept of ideology— to explain why things had gone so unexpectedly wrong. Yet vulgar Marxism utilized a crude base-superstructure model which posited that ideology was merely a passive reflection determined by economic forces in a unidirectional manner. This sort of reductionist thinking had resulted in psychoanalytic concepts like drives and needs being dismissed as "idealistic." Reich, on the contrary, argued that ideology must be understood as a "material force" that can have an active, reciprocal role in shaping the mode of production and state power. The victory of Nazism and the "Hitler psychosis" was presented as proof that it was "possible for an ideologic factor to produce a materialistic result" (2003: 17).

However, the Marxist concept of ideology offered only a partial explanation for Nazism's mass appeal. Reich's most original contribution was to connect ideology with his psychoanalytic notion of character structure shaped by sexual repression. He echoed Engels (1942 [1884]) in linking the origins of the patriarchal family with the development of class society, adding that the channeling of sexuality into reproduction via patriarchy was essential for maintaining and reinforcing social systems of class exploitation, male domination, and state power. Reich specifically took aim at the patriarchal family, which he derided as "the authoritarian state in miniature" (2003: 30). In his view, the family's role in repressing children's sexuality ensured the reproduction of passive subjects, children who were "afraid, shy, fearful of authority, obedient, 'good,' and 'docile' in the authoritarian sense of the words" (2003: 30). Reich distinguished between the deprivation of "primitive material needs" and the suppression of sexual needs: whereas people are often incited to rebellion when denied their material needs, sexual repression had the opposite effect in making people compliant and inhibited. "The result," he wrote, "is conservatism, fear of freedom, in a word, reactionary thinking" (2003: 31). Reich was keen to understand why people chose to conform and not rebel in the midst of deprivation and injustice, and he believed sexual repression naturally extinguished the human spirit that enabled people to resist, constituting them as docile subjects.

Though Reich was investigating Nazism in its earliest stages, his analysis was a culmination of the theory of sexuality and character structure he had been developing since the mid-1920s. Reich's concept of character initially developed by theorizing the clinical issue of resistance and different forms of blockage among patients in psychoanalysis. He described character structure as a form of "armor," a psychic shell that might momentarily defend people from existential difficulties but also limited their capacity for experience; it functioned as a "narcissistic protection mechanism" composed of "attitudes and avoidance" (Reich 1990: 157, 185; Ollman 1979: 183). This concept extended Reich's earlier theory of the orgasm in describing character structure as an obstacle to the uninhibited release of sexual energy, and thus a source for all sorts of neuroses. The armoring of character sublimates repressed sexuality and becomes manifest in what Reich described as a kind of rigidity or stiltedness in the body. Years before the Nazis actually took power, he recognized that these docile, deadened bodies could be fodder for fascism.

Reich turned his focus to the patriarchal family but analyzed how this familial structure varied among different class fractions. He maintained that Germany's lower middle classes, especially its small farmers, were the backbone of Nazism's popular support. The social conditions of the lower middle class spawned a particular sort of character structure, and this class fraction congealed into a bulwark of support for Hitler insofar as he expressed their shared anxieties and resentments. The defining feature of this character structure was a deeply ambivalent attitude toward authority, mixing reverence with rebellion, submission with sedition. This ambivalence was rooted in the intermediate social position of the lower middle class and its precarious circumstances under capitalism: threatened by the specter of proletarianization, but lacking solidarity with the actual proletariat. Hitler tapped into this ambivalence and anxiety by promising to take up the fight simultaneously against both communism and big business. Meanwhile, Reich lamented, the German Left failed to adequately address these unique circumstances of the middle classes until it was too late.

Economic production and familial relations were typically intertwined among the lower middle classes, in the form of small businesses or farms. In this environment, patriarchal control and sexual repression were nearly impossible to escape. Reich described the authoritarian family as "a factory where reactionary ideology and reactionary structures are produced," but also saw how the family was ideologically glorified as the subject of Nazi propaganda: the "'safeguarding of the family' ... is the first cultural precept of every reactionary policy" (2003: 60). Ideological discourses about the family merged with German nationalism in personifying the nation as a patriarchal family (the "Fatherland") and romanticizing the peasantry's roots in the countryside ("blood and soil"). Reich maintained that this ideological confluence of family and nation resonated most with the lower middle class, making it a stronghold of nationalism and imperialism in opposition to proletarian internationalism.

The ideological discourses of patriarchy and nationalism also converged in what Reich called the "race theory" of Nazism. Again, Nazi race theory amounted to more than an ideology insofar as it tapped into a "deeper layer" of character structure that linked authoritarianism and identification with the führer to "the belief in a 'master race'" (2003: 80). Its principal feature is the taboo against miscegenation, fueled by the idea that an elite must defend its power and alleged purity by only reproducing within its ranks, rather than contaminating their offspring with the blood and genes of inferior masses. The concern with poisoning the master race and the national body demanded a repressive creed of sexual purity and self-control: for Reich, "the core of the fascist race theory is a mortal fear of natural sexuality and of its orgasm function" (2003: 84). Sexuality is circumscribed to a reproductive function within the family, subservient to its role in propagating eugenics. Ruling class anxieties about sexuality are then projected onto the oppressed as an "alien race," whose supposedly lascivious ways are evoked to rationalize their oppression. When the lower classes begin to organize to fight for themselves, the first line of defense for the ruling class is an appeal to morality and the sanctity of the family that is meant to resonate with the intermediate classes. These middle classes stand in a precarious position that is nonetheless crucial for maintaining a patriarchal class society.

It is clear Reich presented a viable hypothesis about the relationship between patriarchy, social class, and the psychology of Nazism that anticipated the studies undertaken by the Institute for Social Research. He highlighted the "subjective factor" in the rise of fascism by utilizing the Marxist concept of ideology, but also by delving beyond ideology into the analysis of character structure. The originality of Reich's notion of character was that it advanced beyond the realm of ideas and consciousness to take up matters of sexuality and the body heretofore neglected by Marxists. This tool of character analysis was necessary to comprehend the authoritarian submission and fear of rebellion that made fascism possible: "what has to be explained is not the fact that the man who is hungry steals or the fact that the man who is exploited strikes, but why the majority of those who are hungry *don't* steal and why the majority of those who are exploited *don't* strike" (2003: 19, original emphases). In *The Mass Psychology of Fascism*, Reich grounded his previous studies of character and sexual repression in a class analysis that identified the lower middle class a crucial bulwark of nationalism, patriarchy, and racism. He was able to show how the irrationality and mysticism of Nazism grew out of this repressive environment, and in turn why it appealed to people situated in an intermediate yet insecure position within the social order.

If Reich's unique contributions are readily apparent, so too are the flaws in his undialectical conception of the relationship between nature and society, which informs his understanding of sexuality. In short, Reich views sex as a purely natural act which has simply been repressed throughout the history of patriarchal class societies. He similarly naturalizes the consequences of sexual repression in arguing that it has an innately conservative impact which limits people's capacity for rebellion. His vision of a revolutionary society of liberated individuals is one where the economic and political forces that demanded chastity and self-discipline have become superfluous, allowing people to just do what comes naturally. Reich did not perceive sexuality as a human need in Marx's sense of the term, as an historical product of the ways people engage with nature in forms of practice that, in turn, continually reshape their own needs and "human nature" (Geras 1983; Heller 2018). Marx did not draw an absolute opposition between nature and society, but rather conceptualized them in a dialectical relationship of differentiated unity that changes over time (Schmidt 2014). Marx's perspective suggests that social formations do not simply constrain but also constitute and enable expressions of human sexuality in significant ways. Reich's assumptions about the naturalness of human sexuality, and his categorical opposition between nature and society, led him to espouse a version of what Foucault (1990 [1976]) later derided as the "repressive hypothesis."

3   The Studies of Family and Authority

Reich's analysis of fascism pointed toward the pivotal importance of the patriarchal family in mediating between a material base and an ideological superstructure in order to reproduce an authoritarian character structure across
generations. The Institute for Social Research's initial studies of family and
authority investigated these same social relationships in ways that sought to
integrate theoretical critique and empirical data. Their research design, primarily based on survey questionnaires and interviews, was influenced by
Robert and Helen Lynd's landmark study of American culture in the 1920s,
Middletown. Data was collected from several international settings, including
surveys of unemployed workers and young people in Switzerland, Austria,
France, and Newark, New Jersey. The final research report would be divided
into three parts: the first contained the three theoretical essays by Horkheimer,
Fromm, and Marcuse, while the empirical data from questionnaires and studies of youth, socialization, and unemployed families comprised the study's
second and third parts. The lack of integration between these theoretical and
empirical sections, however, "dramatically illustrated the limited extent to
which a 'fusion of constructive and empirical procedures' could be spoken of"
(Wiggershaus 2007: 151). Data collection was surely inhibited by the circumstances of exile, but it seems the Frankfurt School could never fully harmonize
critical theory with social scientific research, perhaps for the same reasons
elaborated in their enduring critique of empiricism.

   The *Studien's* three theoretical essays represented a range of perspectives
that exemplified the Institute's interdisciplinary and theoretically eclectic
approach. Horkheimer discussed the family and the making of bourgeois society from an historical viewpoint, Fromm analyzed the social-psychological
dimensions of authoritarianism using Freudian categories, and Marcuse
traced the roots of fascism into the history of bourgeois thought and philosophy. Yet all three essays shared common ideas and themes that have come
to be regarded as essential features of the Frankfurt School's critical theory.
There was a generally accepted idea that the patriarchal family was a pivotal
institution in the reproduction of an authoritarian social character, but also
some hope, especially with Horkheimer and Fromm, that under different conditions family might play a more anti-authoritarian and loving role in a healthy
society. A distinction between rational and irrational forms of authority was
also a mutually shared and fundamental precept of all three essays, informing their analyses of the increasing irrationality of bourgeois social order, but
also their critiques of anarchist rejections of all forms of authority. Despite
the dire circumstances of the 1930s, they all expressed at least some degree of

confidence in the capacity to reshape society in accordance with democratic, rational forms of authority.

3.1   *Horkheimer on the Family*

Horkheimer's essay began with an overview of historical and philosophical issues that are crucial for theorizing the relationship between culture and social-economic transformation. He argued against idealist perspectives which view societies as harmonious entities progressing in accord with the development of reason, consciousness, religious and moral ideas, or "the spirit of an age." Horkheimer insisted that the wide range of practices and institutions he called culture could only be understood in relation to material forces, but at the same time he eschewed the kind of crude materialism that would simply reduce culture to economics. He allowed for the possibility that culture can be relatively autonomous, not merely a passive effect of social change. As such, "cultural spheres"—he included everyday customs and morality alongside the fields of art, religion, and philosophy—are "dynamic influences on the maintenance or breakdown of a particular form of society," and thus can actively function as "conservative or disruptive factors in the dynamism of society" (1972: 54). Thus, like Wilhelm Reich, Horkheimer recognized an urgent need to theorize the "subjective factor" in social change. Culture and ideology were not just determined but also determining, wielding a reciprocal influence in relation to the material foundations of society.

Horkheimer advanced beyond Reich, however, in identifying a "cultural lag" that made ideas and values slower to change and thus relatively independent from the mode of production. He discussed Chinese ancestor worship and the Indian caste system as examples of how ancient beliefs and patterns of authority can endure long after their material basis in society has changed. A "cultural lag" is thus characterized by the notion that "change occurs more quickly in areas immediately related to the economy than in other cultural spheres" (1972: 65). Insofar as people are passionately invested in traditional beliefs and values, culture becomes an impediment to capitalist modernization and social transformation. Horkheimer thought a kind of cultural lag was also at work, during his time, in capitalist societies transitioning from an earlier liberal form to something more monopolistic, statist, and totalitarian.

In the remainder of his essay, Horkheimer examines authority and family in terms of how their relationship to social-economic change is characterized by cultural lag. He strives to show how bourgeois thought, in lockstep with the development of capitalism, proclaimed complete freedom from traditional authority, only to surrender to "the reified authority of the economy" (1972: 83). In bourgeois philosophy, individuals are imagined to be free-thinking, self-directed actors who remain independent from nature and society. Yet even capitalists have no choice but to adapt to market forces and competitive pressures which the most powerful can never fully control. Bourgeois thought glorifies individual freedom from authority but submits to a substantively irrational economic system. Capitalism and its consequences are then perceived as an objective and inevitable form of "second nature."

Finally, Horkheimer considers the family as an institution of socialization whose major function is to reproduce authoritarian submission. The child's respect for the moral authority of the father constitutes a "first training for the bourgeois authority relationship." But here again Horkheimer distinguished between the family's pivotal role in the age of bourgeois liberalism and its diminishing power under totalitarian state capitalism. Reprising Max Weber's Protestant ethic thesis, he maintains that the patriarchal family instilled values of individual self-control and work-discipline which were "an indispensable condition of progress" in the early bourgeois era (1972: 101). But Horkheimer argues that in later stages of capitalism, the basis for a father's power and the family's role in social reproduction have eroded and become irrational remnants of an outmoded society.

The decline of a material foundation for patriarchal power opened divergent possibilities for the social relationships of family and authority. Horkheimer recognized that the family continued to function as a crucial institution for reproducing authoritarian submission. Children were socialized within the family to accept the facts of bourgeois society as inevitable and to blame the victims of capitalism for their own victimization. Patriarchy thus mediates a young person's immersion into bourgeois ideology:

> For the formation of the authority-oriented character it is especially decisive that the children should learn, under pressure from the father, not to trace every failure back to its social causes but remain at the level of the individual and to hypostatize the failure in religious terms as sin or in naturalistic terms as deficient natural endowment. The bad conscience that is developed in the family absorbs more energies than can be counted, which might otherwise be directed against the social circumstances that play a role in the individual's failure.
>
> 1972: 109

But Horkheimer also upheld the possibility that the family could serve in a critical capacity as a point of ethical resistance against bourgeois society. This was possible insofar as families were insulated from the calculating, cutthroat dealings of capitalism, and thus functioned according to an alternative logic where "relationships were not mediated by the market and the individual members were not competing with each other" (1972: 114). Horkheimer then turned to Hegel, who posited an opposition between the family, which Hegel regarded as a crucial institution for upholding ethics, and bourgeois society at large. Horkheimer criticized Hegel for absolutizing this relationship between family and society, which would blind him to Marx's later insight that the family could be colonized by egoistic forces of capitalism, thus corrupting its ethical dimension. And yet Horkheimer continued to follow Hegel in identifying a "principle of love for the whole person" embodied in the "marital community," which he associated with "womanliness" in contrast to the "manliness" of "civic subordination" (1972: 117).

To understand how these matriarchal ideals of mother-right and "womanliness" had been overthrown in creating a class society based on private property and the state, Horkheimer looked to Engels and the anthropological studies of Morgan and Bachofen. Nevertheless, he suggested that at least some residue of matriarchy and mother-right had managed to endure: "Because it still fosters human relations which are determined by the woman, the present-day family is a source of strength to resist the total dehumanization of the world and contains an element of antiauthoritarianism" (1972: 118). Horkheimer was quick to add that women's situation within the family had changed dramatically, rendering her dependent and a conservative instrument for reproducing authority. But even while recognizing that its critical potential had eroded under the weight of patriarchy, Horkheimer clearly sought to preserve more hopeful possibilities connected to the cultural lag of matriarchy. In short, "The family in the bourgeois era is no more a single and uniform reality than is, for example, man or the state" (1972: 127).

3.2   *Fromm on the Sociopsychological Dimensions of Family and Authority*

Erich Fromm's essay also presented conceptual tools for theorizing the family's role in facilitating authoritarian submission. For this task, Fromm drew from Freud's theory of the instincts and his key categories of ego, id, and superego, while also expanding Reich's analysis of character structure. Having introduced the problem of people's enthusiastic obedience to authority and emotional identification with authority figures, Fromm declared: "The only psychologist relevant in this regard is Freud, and not only because his psychological categories, as a consequence of their dynamic character, are the only usable ones, but also because he dealt directly with the problem of authority and offered important and fruitful perspectives" (2020 [1936]: 12). In 1936,

Fromm's relationship with orthodox Freudian psychoanalysis was in flux and coming to an end, as was his relationship with the Institute for Social Research. In *Escape from Freedom*, Fromm continued his analysis of sadomasochistic character formation, but he disconnected it from Freud's theories of libido, instincts, and sexuality, emphasizing the modern individual's alienated relationship with society instead. The 1936 essay for the *Studien* remained unpublished in English for many decades, because his shifting perspective meant that Fromm would have felt compelled to make substantial revisions throughout the text. But for other readers, the application of Freudian theory to these issues of family and authority is precisely what makes it uniquely compelling: for example, Wiggershaus maintains that "Fromm's essay is the best he ever wrote" (2007: 151).

Fromm focused on the concept of the superego for theorizing the internalization of authority and reconstructing Freud's inchoate sketch of social dynamics. Although Freud himself never directly confronted such issues, Fromm maintains that his concept of the superego explains how society's ruling powers can maintain their rule through measures besides violence and coercion. The costliness of a coercive apparatus, combined with the instability and unrest provoked by violence, necessitates more efficient means of social control accomplished through the superego's internalization of authority. This process of internalization is mediated through the patriarchal family, where an emotional investment in authority develops and is then projected onto all sorts of ruling powers in society. Fromm described the dialectical relationship between the superego and authority in society:

> External social force confronts the growing child in the form of its parents, and in the immediate patriarchal family especially in the form of its father. In identifying with the father and internalizing his commands and prohibitions, the super-ego as an entity is invested with the attributes of morality and power. Once this entity has been established, however, the process of identification is simultaneously reversed. The super-ego is repeatedly projected onto the ruling authority in society, in other words, the individual invests the actual authorities with the qualities of his own super-ego. Because of the super-ego's act of projection onto authority figures, the figures themselves largely evade rational critique. Credence is given to their morality, wisdom, and strength, to a great extent independently of reality. In the process, however, these authorities are in return now able to become re-internalized and support the super-ego.
>
> 2020: 15–16

Fromm criticized Freud for his unidirectional, undialectical understanding of the association between the patriarchal father and authority in society writ large. Whereas Freud correctly perceived that society's authority figures are invested with emotions that initially develop within the family, he neglected "to include the opposite notion that the father aligns himself with the dominant authority in society," thus failing to perceive how "the authority of the father himself is ultimately grounded in the authority structure of society as a whole" (2020: 18–19). The father may be the child's initial conduit into social authority, but Freud fails to see how the father himself imitates other forms of authority in society. Likewise, Fromm also criticized how Freud presented the Oedipus complex as a universal and transhistorical phenomenon rooted in nature, rather than the product of a particular form of society. Fromm would later reference these sorts of ahistorical assumptions that naturalized the patriarchal family as a major reason for his eventual rejection of Freud's libido theory and the Oedipus complex (Jay 1996: 94–98). In this essay, however, he treats the Oedipus complex as an accurate description of the conflicts and hostility embedded in patriarchy: "the structure of the patriarchal family, which fosters the incestuous desires of the son, results in the son's conflict with the father, thereby producing a revolt against him and a tendency to break apart the family" (2020: 19). Freud's categories are not rejected outright, but instead treated as historical constructs rather than psycho-biological facts.

Fromm considers the family not in the abstract but in relation to social class. Within small peasant families, all individuals embody potential sources of labor. The father-son relationship is thus "scarcely characterized by love, but rather essentially by hostility and by a tendency toward exploitation." Fromm finds a similar situation within proletarian families during the Industrial Revolution: "children were basically an object of economic utility, and no one resisted laws limiting child labor more than those parents who were economically exploiting their children" (2020: 20). In these circumstances, the conflicts of the Oedipus complex have a material basis within a particular social formation; they are not natural or transhistorical. Under different conditions where children are not valued in terms of economic necessity, there are greater possibilities for child-rearing based on "loving support and kindness." However, in considering the modern, urban families of the petit bourgeoisie—in which "the father is something like a minor post office official"—Fromm argues that the father's professional and social circumstances may lead him to exercise power over his wife and children in ways that substitute for his lack of authority in the workplace and social life outside the home. He might also live through his children in the sense of pushing them to achieve socially sanctioned goals and secure prestige that "compensates the father for his social powerlessness" (2020: 21). Thus, while the reins of immediate economic necessity have loosened, there are enduring sources of exploitation and conflict entrenched in the petit bourgeois urban family.

Fromm turns to Freud's category of the ego, which he again critiques for being vaguely and inconsistently defined. He argued that this lack of clarity was the result of an unresolved tension embedded throughout Freud's work, between a progressive belief in humanity's increasing mastery over the external world and our internal drives, and a more despairing view of our "inherent wickedness" which necessitates external suppression and means that "all attempts to achieve a society based on human happiness must inevitably fail" (2020: 24). Fromm clearly favored the former, more optimistic perspective. For him, the growth of society's forces of production created new possibilities for the human ego to strengthen. Whereas the superego represses the id's drives through a deeply irrational fear of authority, a strong ego can control and respond to those drives through rational, conscious activity that is not simply motivated by fear. Here again, Fromm treats these Freudian categories as historical rather than natural, in the way that some social conditions are more conducive to a strong ego, while conversely powerlessness in relation to the external world activates a greater sense of fear.

Utilizing the concept of character, Fromm expanded it beyond Freud's original formulation, giving it a sociological dimension as Reich had also done. He described the sadomasochistic character as a type of person who takes pleasure in submitting to more powerful authorities, but also seeks to subjugate and humiliate less powerful dependents. While "masochistic strivings almost aim to lose themselves in power," the dynamic changes in other social contexts, such that "sadistic strivings have the opposite aim of making another person into a dependent and defenseless instrument of one's own will" (2020: 41). Fromm insisted that these same tendencies could be embodied in a single individual preoccupied with authority and hierarchy. The ubiquity of sadomasochistic character structures is connected to the sense of powerlessness experienced under capitalism. Fromm maintained that seemingly objective forces of social domination create a "hopeless dependency to which the individual adapts by developing a sadomasochistic character structure" (2020: 43). The reified forms of power engendered by the capitalist system appear to be immutable and overwhelming in their capacity to determine an individual's fate.

Unfortunately, Fromm's prescriptions are painfully anachronistic given their heteronormative and homophobic assumptions. He associated the sadomasochistic character with "a relative weakness of heterosexual genitality" and "the presence of homosexual strivings" (2020: 49). Conversely, the

strong ego that Fromm viewed as an antidote to authoritarianism was characterized by the satisfaction of genital heterosexuality—not unrestrained sexual gratification, but a mastery over one's drives through conscious activity.
Upon closer reading, however, it seems that Fromm invokes "homosexuality"
more as a shorthand for the fear and hatred of women and all things feminine,
which is better described as misogyny. Those who embody a sadomasochistic
character structure have a fundamental fear of anything foreign or unfamiliar, and thus "women arouse fear in him, as they in many respects represent
a foreign and alien world on the basis of their biological and psychological
difference." Fromm writes that an authoritarian figure reacts to these fears
"by debasing women and creating a superior position for himself from the
start," and yet he maintains that this fear of women "always remains a factor
that presses in the direction of homosexuality" (2020: 49). He concludes that
"the love life of this character type demonstrates a peculiar sort of split": in
terms of sexual gratification and reproducing a family, "the average authoritarian man is heterosexual," but in psychic terms the same authoritarian type
is "homosexual" in the sense that he is "inclined to treat women with hostility
and cruelty" (2020: 50). Fromm assumes that the sadomasochistic authoritarian is a male figure, but his assumption is belied by the role of women
in New Right movements to defend patriarchy (Dworkin 1983; Klatch 1987)
and more recent currents of "female antifeminism" in contemporary fascism
(Marasco 2021).

Fromm further revealed the presumptions behind his ideal notion of character structure in distinguishing between different forms of antiauthoritarian
defiance. He drew a sharp distinction between rebellion and revolution as
forms of defiance that express "fundamentally different psychological phenomena." He described rebellion in negative terms as a form of antiauthoritarianism that is simply the inverse of submission and devotion, a juvenile
kind of reaction that retains an authoritarian character structure instead of
actually confronting and changing it. Fromm insists it is essential to distinguish between rational and irrational forms of authority, and the problem with
the "anarchist types" who inhabit a rebellious character structure is that they
simply reject all authorities, be they "reasonable or unreasonable, appropriate
or inappropriate, useful or damaging" (2020: 54). Fromm is less explicit when
it comes to explaining what he envisions as a revolutionary character structure. Yet from the overall thrust of this essay, one can surmise he associated it
with a strong individual ego that does not obtain pleasure from social relations
of domination or subordination and can use critical thought to distinguish
between rational and irrational forms of authority.

3.3   *Marcuse on Philosophies of Freedom and Authority*

Herbert Marcuse would eventually engage in an acrimonious debate with Fromm during the 1950s in *Dissent* magazine, where Fromm accused Marcuse of "instinctual 'radicalism,'" leading Marcuse to deride Fromm and others who discarded the theory of instincts as "neo-Freudian revisionists" (Rickert 1986; Robinson 1969: 195–216; McLaughlin 2017). In his 1936 essay for the *Studien*, however, Marcuse had not yet begun to fully engage with Freudian theory, and so unlike Fromm he did not utilize psychoanalytic categories to theorize the issues of family and authority. He had certainly been influenced by debates about Freud within the Institute during the 1930s, and Freudian themes and questions would soon be raised in his early essays, such as "On Hedonism" (Marcuse 1968; Jay 1996: 107–108; Kellner 1984: 155). Still, Marcuse did not engage with Freud in a serious and sustained way until the 1950s, with *Eros and Civilization* representing the crowning achievement of his efforts to synthesize Marx and Freud (Marcuse 2015; also see Marcuse 2007).

Prior to his *Studien* essay, Marcuse had written three years earlier about the issues of authority and family in German sociology. Like other members of the Institute, he had argued that the family was a key institution for socializing individuals to obey authority and conform to the social order. In times of crisis and challenges to the status quo, the family "stands in service of the defence of the bourgeoisie against the growing threat from its own ranks and from the socialist tendencies" (in Kellner 1984: 108). Marcuse criticized sociological theories which sought to identify a natural justification for the patriarchal family that made it seem eternal and immutable. Comparing various theories of the family, he concluded that they provide a "familiar apology for the existing order of power through theological, philosophical and economic constructions of all types" (in Kellner 1984: 109). However, these concerns with patriarchy did not continue in his 1936 work.

Leaving the issue of family behind, Marcuse's essay for the *Studien* critically examined the history of Western theology and philosophy on questions of authority. Contrary to bourgeois philosophy, he began by emphasizing that freedom and authority are inextricably "yoked in the same concept and united in the single person of he who is subject" (2008: 7). Bourgeois concepts of freedom, especially as formulated by Kant, had imagined that the individual could be divided into an inner realm of personal autonomy and an external realm of submission to authority. Like Horkheimer, Marcuse sought to demonstrate how bourgeois notions of individual freedom presupposed the surrender to an irrational system of social domination. As a result, "the bourgeoisie fought its greatest battles under the banner of 'Reason' but it is precisely bourgeois society which totally deprives reason of its realization" (2008: 11).

Marcuse then undertook an extensive survey of intellectual history beginning with the teachings of Luther and Calvin, before proceeding to consider
Kant as the supreme exponent of the bourgeois ideal of negative freedom.
From there, he discussed a series of criticisms and challenges to this bourgeois
notion of freedom articulated by an assortment of thinkers, from the dialectics of Hegel to the French counter-revolutionary conservatives Burke, Bonald,
and de Maistre. Finally, Marcuse arrived at a discussion of Marx, who saw that
the bourgeois split between internal autonomy and external domination was
untenable, for humanity could enter the "realm of freedom" only by overcoming the "realm of necessity": "Here for the first time freedom is understood
as a mode of real human praxis, as a task of conscious social organization"
(2008: 86). Bourgeois freedom, after all, entailed a process of dispossession
from land, the commons, and other means of production that confined "free"
wage laborers to seemingly objective forms of subordination under capitalism. Marcuse also argued that the concept of authority, no less than "freedom,"
must be treated with a dialectical sense of its "double-edged duality" in the
way Marx had. He criticized knee-jerk antiauthoritarianism in the same spirit
as Fromm, invoking Engels' essay directed against the anarchist followers of
Bakunin, "On the Principle of Authority." In Marcuse's words, "it is an 'absur-
dity' to present the principle of authority as absolutely bad and the principle
of autonomy as absolutely good" (2008: 91).

Witnessing the rise of fascism and the plunge toward a second world
war, Marcuse noted the cruel irony in which bourgeois societies supposedly
based on principles of freedom were devolving into authoritarian states. At
this stage of history, he observed, bourgeois theory had bankrupted all its
positive content in becoming nothing more than a collection of negative
counter-concepts: "it rests exclusively on the united front against liberalism
and Marxism" (2008: 101). For the final section of his essay, Marcuse looked to
Sorel and Pareto as intellectual forerunners whose theories of elitism anticipated different dynamics of authoritarianism. With his anarcho-syndicalist
mythologization of the general strike, Sorel's work was seen as "a typical
example of the transformation of an abstract anti-authoritarian attitude into
reinforced authoritarianism" (2008: 104). Marcuse made a direct connection
between Sorel's irrationalist ideas about social elites and the political triumph
of Leninist vanguardism on one side and Fascist elitism on the other. Pareto,
on the other hand, was invoked as "the first to grasp and deal with the *psychological* problem of class domination in the monopolistic phase of capitalism" (2008: 108, original emphases). For these purposes Marcuse focused on
Pareto's notions of "residues" and "derivations" that were essential for stabilizing any system of social domination—again, it was the family that played

a most significant role in "the preparation, maintenance, and transmission of authority" (2008: 110).

The overriding objective of Marcuse's essay was to show how the historical development of bourgeois thought regarding freedom and authority ironically foreshadowed the emergence of unfree, authoritarian societies. The intellectual foundations of totalitarianism, he argued, were to be found in an irrational formalism that superseded substantive rationality. While Marcuse's ideas were forged in the heat of battle against Nazism and Stalinism, they clearly continued to shape his famous critique of "one-dimensional thought" in the post-war world (1985: 2002).

4   Conclusion

The *Studien* was a formative work whose flowering of intellectual critique and methodological technique came to full fruition at the Institute for Social Research during the postwar years. If their initial attempts to integrate theory and research were not entirely successful, Horkheimer and his collaborators still blazed a trail for the innovative mixed methodology of *The Authoritarian Personality*. Although the *Studien* is perhaps best described as "a fragment of a collective 'work in progress'" (Wiggershaus 2007: 149), it does capture a remarkable, ultimately fleeting moment in the Institute's history that made it possible for the likes of Fromm and Marcuse to coexist in the pages of its first research report.

In comparison with Reich's *Mass Psychology of Fascism*, the authors associated with the Frankfurt School offered a more mediated model of the relationships connecting family, authority, and fascism. Marcuse later recalled that the Institute's members generally thought Reich proceeded too quickly and directly from material social forces to subjective factors of ideology and character. They also felt Reich had overstated the significance of sexual repression in the making of fascist social character, and likewise that his faith in the revolutionary impact of sexual liberation was delusional (Kellner 1984: 110). Yet in the process of developing a more complex and nuanced explanation of fascism, it seems the Frankfurt School scholars sacrificed the sharpness and immediacy that distinguished Reich's analysis. Persistent and urgent questions that Reich raised about the "race theory" of Nazism, for example, were not addressed by Horkheimer, Fromm, or Marcuse. If Reich can indeed be condemned as reductionist and deterministic, it also seems he was more explicit in considering class differences among families and implicating the lower middle class as a bulwark of fascism.

The theoretical analyses and empirical studies from the early years of Nazism have much to offer for contemporary critics of fascism. However, their categories and methods cannot simply be replicated in our present context, especially in light of the changing social relationships of gender, sexuality, and family. Horkheimer, Fromm, and Marcuse all observed that the classic ideal of the bourgeois family was deteriorating under the conditions of postliberal monopoly capitalism. The pressing challenge for anti-fascist scholars today is to understand how the changing landscapes of gender, sexuality, and family continue to create authoritarian personalities in an age of digital media and commodified data science. For example, Marasco (2021) asks how we are to make sense of Ashli Babbitt, the woman shot and killed by Capitol police during the January 6 insurrection and subsequently exalted as a right-wing martyr, an Air Force veteran who self-presented as "one of the guys" and was reportedly involved in an unconventional relationship ("throuple") with her second husband and his girlfriend? Just as we need a typology of the Authoritarian Personality 2.0 upgraded for our new media and niche markets that have made theories of mass society obsolete (Weigel 2022), current mutations of patriarchy and misogyny demand updated models for understanding how fascism continues to spawn in this diversifying, increasingly "unconventional" landscape of gender, sexuality, and family.

References

Adorno, Theodor, et al. 2019 [1950]. *The Authoritarian Personality*. New York: Verso Books.

Altemeyer, Bob. 1981. *Right-Wing Authoritarianism*. Winnipeg: University of Manitoba Press.

Altemeyer, Bob. 2006. *The Authoritarians*. Winnipeg: University of Manitoba Press.

Altemeyer, Bob. 1996. *The Authoritarian Specter*. Cambridge: Harvard University Press.

Clavey, Charles E. 2020. "Donald Trump, Our Prophet of Deceit." *The Boston Review*, Oct. 20. http://bostonreview.net/politics-philosophy-religion/charles-h-clavey-donald-trump-our-prophet-deceit.

Dean, John W. and Bob Altemeyer. 2020. *Authoritarian Nightmare: Trump and His Followers*. Brooklyn: Melville House.

Dean, John. 2006. *Conservatives without Conscience*. New York: Viking.

Dworkin, Andrea. 1983. *Right-Wing Women*. New York: Perigee Books.

Engels, Friedrich. 1942 [1884]. *The Origin of the Family, Private Property, and the State*. New York: International Publishers.

Foucault, Michel. 1990 [1976]. *The History of Sexuality: Volume 1, an Introduction*. New York: Vintage.

Fromm, Erich. 2020 [1936]. "Studies on Authority and the Family: Sociopsychological Dimensions." https://www.fromm-gesellschaft.eu/images/pdf-Dateien/1936a-eng .pdf.

Fromm, Erich. 1992 [1973]. *The Anatomy of Human Destructiveness*. New York: H. Holt.

Fromm, Erich. 1994 [1941]. *Escape from Freedom*. New York: H.Holt.

Fromm, Erich. 1990a [1947]. *Man for Himself*. New York: H.Holt.

Fromm, Erich. 1990b [1955]. *The Sane Society*. New York: H.Holt.

Geras, Norman. 2018 [1983]. *Marx and Human Nature: Refutation of a Legend*. New York: Verso.

Goodrick-Clarke. 1992. *The Occult Roots of Nazism: Secret Aryan Cults and their Influence on Nazi Ideology*. New York: New York University Press.

Gordon, Peter E. 2017. "The Authoritarian Personality Revisited: Reading Adorno in the Age of Trump." *Boundary2* 44(2) (May): 31–56. https://doi.org/10.1215/01903 659-3826618.

Heller, Agnes. 2018 [1976]. *The Theory of Need in Marx*. New York: Verso.

Horkheimer, Max. 1972 [1936]. "Authority and the Family." In *Critical Theory: Selected Essays*, 47–128. New York: The Seabury Press.

Jay, Martin. 1996 [1973]. *The Dialectical Imagination: a History of the Frankfurt School and the Institute of Social Research*. Berkeley: University of California Press.

Kellner, Douglas. 1989. *Critical Theory, Marxism, and Modernity*. Baltimore: Johns Hopkins University Press.

Kellner, Douglas. 1984. *Herbert Marcuse and the Crisis of Marxism*. Berkeley and Los Angeles: University of California Press.

Klatch, Rebecca E. 1987. *Women of the New Right*. Philadelphia: Temple University Press.

Marasco, Robyn. 2021. "Reconsidering the Sexual Politics of Fascism." *Historical Materialism* https://www.historicalmaterialism.org/blog/reconsidering-sexual -politics-fascism.

Marasco, Robyn, ed. 2018. "The Authoritarian Personality." *South Atlantic Quarterly* 117(4) (October): 715–19 https://doi.org/10.1215/00382876-7165818.

Marasco, Robyn. 2018a. "There's a Fascist in the Family." *South Atlantic Quarterly* 117(4) (October): 791–813.

Marasco, Robyn, Christina Gerhardt, and Kirk Wetters. 2022. "The Authoritarian Personality." *Polity* 54 (1) (January).

Marcuse, Herbert. 2015 [1955]. *Eros and Civilization: a Philosophical Inquiry into Freud*. Boston: Beacon Press.

Marcuse, Herbert. 2008 [1936]. *A Study on Authority*. New York: Verso.

Marcuse, Herbert. 2007 [1956]. "Freedom and Freud's Theory of Instincts." In *The Essential Marcuse*, edited by Andrew Feenberg and William Leiss, 159–183. Boston: Beacon Press.

Marcuse, Herbert. 2002 [1964]. *One-Dimensional Man*. New York: Routledge.

Marcuse, Herbert. 1985 [1958]. *Soviet Marxism: a Critical Analysis*. New York: Columbia University Press.

Marcuse, Herbert. 1968 [1938]. "On Hedonism." In *Negations: Essays in Critical Theory*, 159–200. Boston: Beacon Press.

Mattson, Kevin. 2018. "The Trumpian Personality." *Dissent* 65(1) (Winter): 116–22. Project MUSE.

McLaughlin, Neil. 2017. "The Fromm-Marcuse Debate and the Future of Critical Theory." In *The Palgrave Handbook of Critical Theory*, edited by Michael J. Thompson. New York: Palgrave Macmillan. https://doi.org/10.1057/978-1-137-55801-5.

Ollman, Bertell. 1979. "The Marxism of Wilhelm Reich: the Social Function of Sexual Repression." In *Social and Sexual Revolution: Essays on Marx and Reich*, 176–203. Boston: South End Press.

Reich, Wilhelm. 2003 [1933]. *The Mass Psychology of Fascism*. New York: Farrar, Straus & Giroux.

Reich, Wilhelm. 1990 [1933]. *Character Analysis*. New York: Farrar, Straus & Giroux.

Rickert, John. 1986. "The Fromm-Marcuse Debate Revisited." *Theory and Society* 15(3) (May): 351–400.

Robinson, Paul A. 1969. *The Freudian Left: Wilhelm Reich, Geza Roheim, Herbert Marcuse*. New York: Harper & Row.

Ross, Alex. 2016. "The Frankfurt School Knew Trump Was Coming." *New Yorker*, December 5 https://www.newyorker.com/culture/cultural-comment/the-frankfurt-school-knew-trump-was-coming.

Schmidt, Alfred. 2014 [1962]. *The Concept of Nature in Marx*. New York: Verso.

Tomba, Massimiliano. 2021. "Special Issue: New Faces of Authoritarianism." *Comparative Literature and Culture* 23(1): https://doi.org/10.7771/1481-4374.4010.

Weigel, Moira. 2022. "The Authoritarian Personality 2.0." *Polity* 54(1) (January): 146–80.

Wiggershaus, Rolf. 2007 [1995]. *The Frankfurt School: Its History, Theories, and Political Significance*. Cambridge: Polity.

CHAPTER 3

Family and Authoritarianism

Caio Vasconcellos and Rafaela N. Pannain

1   Introduction

Through a dialogue against the grain between Max Horkheimer and Melinda Cooper, this paper aims to shed light on the role played by the mononuclear family in two different sociohistorical periods of sharp authoritarian upsurge. While the Frankfurt scholar faced this issue *vis-à-vis* the dissolution of the liberal era after the Great Crash of 1929 and the rise of authoritarian capitalism in the 1930s and 1940s, Cooper focuses on the defense of traditional family values that aligned neoconservatives and neoliberals from U.S. Presidents Nixon and Reagan to Clinton and Obama.

On the one hand, Horkheimer drew attention to the intertwining between both the father figure and patriarchal power and the structure of authoritarianism as it existed outside the family. As if ordered by God or grounded in nature, the father – even those of a modest social and economic position – is loved and feared only due to his physical strength and the money he earns, accustoming the children and mother to respect and be afraid of the power that rebukes them.

On the other hand, Cooper points out the swift collapse in the 1970s of the consensuses around the Fordist family wage that, a few years earlier, had unified groups and individuals across a vast political spectrum. If the neoliberal economic elites discovered in the language of family values a way to obtain social support for the disinvestment of the welfare state, the neoconservatives found in the replacement of state transfers by intra-family care an opportunity to reinforce traditional moral values.

The contrast between sociohistorical periods reveals the persistence of the authoritarian and patriarchal basis in modern capitalism. While Horkheimer highlighted the pivotal role played by the traditional model of the family in giving rise to an authoritarian personality that naturalized class and gender hierarchies on the eve of Nazi fascism, Cooper, in turn, illuminates the alliance between neoconservatives and neoliberals founded on family values, strengthened in the United States from the 1970s onwards. In both democracies and dictatorships, the reproduction of the capitalist social order restores patterns of gender domination to preserve economic exploitation between classes – and vice versa. In addition to its theoretical interest, the dialogue between Horkheimer and Cooper can shed light on misogyny as a crucial element for understanding the current rise of far-right leaders and movements – as well as the antagonism and conflicts that characterize periods of democratic normality in capitalism.

2   Max Horkheimer – Crises and Family in Late Capitalism

Between the late 1970s and the early 1990s, Horkheimer's introductory essay to *Studies on Authority and the Family* evoked important critical readings from feminist intellectuals (Benjamin 1978; Jagentowicz Mills 1987; Becker-Schmidt 1991; Rumpf 1989, 1993; for another view on Horkheimer's essay, see Umrath 2018). Although it was remarkable for demonstrating his interest in reflecting on the family in sociological terms, inscribing him in a fruitful tradition of Marxist analysis on the subject, his interpretation on the historical tendencies related to the father's authority and the role/function of women within the family in late capitalism was quite contestable.

In a very influential reading, Benjamin (1978) draws attention to Horkheimer's epochal diagnosis that pronounces a tendency toward a *fatherless society* in late capitalism, i.e., a new social order structured through the replacement of paternal authority mainly by instrumental reason and bureaucratic institutions. As a kind of patriarchy without the father, this epoch stood out as a radical change in the internalization of authority – actually, as its replacement by conformity to external standards (Benjamin 1978: 35). Legitimated daily by the cultural industry, the new form of domination appeared as an objective, reified, and depersonalized set of activities and relationships. Inasmuch as the role of *pater familias* was understood by the Frankfurt scholar as definitely superseded by instrumental reason, the historical conditions of male domination, antagonism between the sexes, and the forms of resistance and fighting are also obscured.

According to Benjamin, the most questionable of Horkheimer's thoughts was the link between identification with the father and the development of *independent conscience*, i.e., the ability to maintain self-control and discipline, and to use one's own understanding without the guidance of another. Inasmuch as he circumscribed his focus to men's experience within the family, the mother seems to have no place in supporting the autonomy and independence of the children. If his concept of instrumental domination is missing the intersubjective process in general, the daughter's capacity to act is further denied by Horkheimer. While sons first internalize the father's authority, then confront it because their progenitor is unable to live up to his moral principles and taboos, daughters are completely silenced in the Frankfurt scholar's conceptual framework.

In addition to a superficial and gender-biased representation of women's experience, Horkheimer is also unable to figure out what their emancipation would mean. According to the Frankfurt scholar, even though marital union was both economically conditioned and the result of fearful coercion, romantic love could lead individuals to rebel against the family order and society (Horkheimer 2002 [1936]: 58). Despite the fact that women were becoming sexual objects and domestic servants through marriage, they sustained the place where injured individuals could find retreat. Increasingly mediated by the market, the social order became more hostile. Insofar as women suffer and fight against male domination, their structural role within the family would preserve both a principle of love and an anti-authoritarian movement.

If, nowadays, Federici (2012) calls it unpaid labor, a kind of *maternal protective love* was presented by Horkheimer as a pre-condition for the lasting spirit of rebellion of children and for the cultivation of the dream of a better condition for humanity. *Vis-à-vis* the transition from "absolute" to "relative surplus" value extraction as the most relevant mode of the exploitation of labor, and due to reproductive work becoming essential to maintaining a healthy and well-disciplined workforce, women's exploitation emerges as the Frankfurt scholar's pathway to a supposedly emancipated society:

> In the yearning of many adults for the paradise of their childhood, in the way a mother can speak of her son even though he has come into conflict with the world, in the protective love of a wife for her husband, there are ideas and forces at work which admittedly are not dependent on the existence of the family in its present form and, in fact, are even in danger of shrivelling up in such a milieu, but which, nevertheless, in the bourgeois system of life rarely have any place but the family where they can survive at all.
>
> HORKHEIMER 2002 [1936]: 114

Despite its gender bias and limits, Horkheimer's essay on Authority and Family – as well as *Authoritarianism and the Family Today*, published in 1949 – can also be scrutinized from another standpoint, highlighting the interweaving of capitalism and patriarchy. In his troubling but perhaps not descriptively inaccurate understanding on the role of women, the Frankfurt scholar draws attention to the family as a locus where male domination manifests with enthusiasm, and how the body and soul of the children are formed in line with the authoritarianism of the bourgeois world in two distinct sociohistorical contexts. If, during the 1930s, the father's power showed an intrinsic affinity to the rise of Nazi fascism, the shadow of the traditional family model would give rise to similar phenomena in the post-war period. Rather than diagnosing the full dissolution of the father's authority, Horkheimer shed light on an ideological figure depicted as someone socially and economically vulnerable, but physically strong within the family.

According to the Frankfurt scholar, the father's authority within the bourgeois family rests on two essential aspects. The obedience to men is not due to the fact that they are rational and worthy of respect or admiration, but solely because they earn or possess money and are physically stronger – and, therefore, actually or potentially violent. Like the Calvinist view of God, the father's power is absolute and unquestionable. His wishes do not need to be justified, and the children must learn with their fathers to love and fear wealth and strength from their tenderest years. Surpassing all understanding, power asymmetry and economic inequality are legitimated by moral and family values.

The inner circle of the family reproduces the social force in its totality. As if it was in accordance with God's or the father's will, society marked by the subordination of classes emerges as second nature. The immaturity of the first years of a child is perpetuated well beyond its infancy. The lesson learned within the family anticipates the authority structure of the outside world. If, as Freud (2003) puts it, what seems familiar and intimate can also mean something uncanny and unfamiliar, the real function of the modern patriarchal family is to act to convince individuals that something arbitrary and unnatural – the differences and asymmetries between social classes and individuals – must be carried in the heart.

> Because the father is *de facto* stronger, he is also *de jure* stronger. The child is not only to take the father's superiority into account; he is also to have esteem for it. In this kind of familial situation, with its determinative influence on the child's education, we find anticipated in large measure the structure of authority as it existed outside the family. According to the latter, the prevailing differences in conditions of life, which the individual finds in the world, are simply to be accepted; he must make his way within that framework and not rebel against it. To recognize facts means to accept them. Distinctions established by nature are willed by God, and, in bourgeois society, wealth and poverty seem naturally determined. When the child respects in his father's strength a moral relationship and thus learns to love what his reason recognizes to be a fact, he is experiencing his first training for the bourgeois authority relationship.
>
> HORKHEIMER 2002 [1936]: 100–101

In late capitalism, the political arena also takes advantage of those patriarchal assumptions.

A reified form of authority that perpetuates irrational hierarchies was transposed to the depths of personal life, psychological sensitivity, and the thoughts of individuals. Made widespread through commodity exchanges, the opacity of the social process reduces any human and social experience to a sequence of operations that must be followed almost automatically. The rationality that recognizes as natural the current social division of sex and labor, the distinction between capitalists and workers, and the private appropriation of material wealth conforms individuals to the authoritarian domination of social life.

As a Janus face, family values and the capitalist economy are sinking into barbarism. As hunger and the fear of wretchedness have always acted together with cultural forces and ideological beliefs to force subjects to work, so violence and the echoes of the witch-hunting in early modern Europe – "the most frightful terrorism ever exercised against a sexual group," according to Horkheimer – have also helped the family to adapt the individual to blind obedience, uncritical admiration, heteronomy, and a sense of inferiority and helplessness. In the face of the struggles of monopolies that marked the end of the liberal period, the modern order requires a new kind of individual character. While at the dawn of modernity bourgeois philosophy expressed the struggles and expectations of those who fought traditional authority and the old regime, the obscurity of the production process in a bourgeois world gives rise to the objective conditions and subjective assumptions of conformity to the social order, as well as its authoritarian submission.

If the ideology of autonomy and qualities of leadership of the independent entrepreneur in a free-trade economy was restricted by the class structure of bourgeois societies, in late capitalism this *enthusiasm for a genius* of the liberal period has been replaced by the ode to the *ruthless steadfastness* required to rule the modem masses by political and economic oligarchy (Horkheimer 2002 [1936]: 81). *Pari passu* the centralization and concentration of capital of those years, domination and violence spread through the totality of social and subjective life – the authoritarian state does not necessarily maintain the social order only by direct coercion and violence, but it rules through the appeal for direct and violent coercion spread over various spheres of society. In order to be habituated both to command and to obey, subjects must develop a lack of consideration for themselves and others. Due to the fact that even a poor man can raise hell in domestic life, the father may become an idol in a world of growing authoritarianism.

It is precisely this reified concept of authority that is applied to the supreme political leader in the modern theory of the authoritarian state. The fact that in Protestantism such authority belongs only to a transcendent being is of decisive importance religiously. This does not, however, affect the truth that the concept, whether as religious or as political, springs from the same social experience and that the opportunity for it to become in either form a basic category for understanding the world was inevitably created by the situation in the limited family of the patriarchal type.

HORKHEIMER 2002 [1936]: 104–105

Besides predisposing individuals to blind submission in an overtly authoritarian social order, the modern family – or better, its shadow – would also take care of its further developments. In *Authoritarianism and the Family Today*, the Frankfurt scholar comes back to that constellation of phenomena in the face of the so-called Golden Age of Capitalism. If, according to Horkheimer, Hitler's dictatorship tried to dispense with the family as a superfluous intermediary between the individual and the state (Horkheimer 1949: 362), the more subtle integration process in the postwar period did not persist in the same mistake.

Vis-à-vis the emergence of middle-class society, the bourgeois *pater familias* loses its economic ground and its emotional basis – as everybody is an employee, the son's and the daughter's fates depend more on their skills and work outside the house than their inheritance. Rather than just disappearing, the family and its values have turned into an abstracted form of existence updated to fulfill its former and persistent function – not to cultivate rational and autonomous individuals, but proto-fascist ones.

As an empty ideology, the family emphasizes its conventional forms. As neither the father nor the mother corresponds to their traditional roles and depictions, the private order depends on the compulsive affirmation of its appearance. Given his money and physical strength, the image of the father remains unchanged, and he is essentially identified as someone morally rigorous, rational, and a generous disciplinarian. The image projected onto women cannot elide its ambiguity. On the one hand, motherhood is linked with attributes such as practical skill, good looks, cleanliness, and health (Horkheimer 1949: 369). On the other, there is a conscious rejection of love for the mother among boys – in order to identify with the aggressor, it is necessary to persecute his victims.

The purpose of ideologies like "momism" is not to condemn women to the domestic sphere and family life. According to Horkheimer, due to her supposed weakness and dependence, the woman is perceived as a threat to the family. At the opposite pole and the main victim of the patriarchal order, she must be denied in favor of a stronger identification with power and domination. Established through an early repressed rebellion against the father, the authoritarian personality tends to develop aggressive behavior against the mother. The glorification of the father's authority is realized at the woman's expense – misogyny is the anteroom of fascism.

> Anti-femininity based on rejection of the mother sets the pattern for the subsequent rejection of everything that is deemed "different." Out-groups rejected by fascists, particularly the Jew, are often fancied as showing traits of femininity, such as weakness, emotionalism, lack of self-discipline, and sensuality. Contempt for the traits of the opposite sex in one's own sex seems to be regularly connected with a highly generalized intolerance of what is different.
>
> HORKHEIMER 1949: 369–370

3   Melinda Cooper – Crises and Family between Neoconservatism and Neoliberalism

If, according to Benjamin (1978), a pathway toward a *fatherless society* is a problematic unfolding of Horkheimer's conceptual framework, Melinda Cooper draws attention to a current tendency to identify a *general epidemic of fatherlessness* as a core problem of American families. While, during the 1960s, it was a kind of disease that especially affected impoverished women – particularly African American and Latina ones – white middle-class families would suffer from the same illness more recently, as they manifested a *career-minded narcissism*. Although it is almost common sense nowadays to people of a wide ideological spectrum, the perception of the father's absence as a crisis trigger is a symptom of a profound economic, political, and cultural change that began in the 1970s in the United States.

In *Family Values* (2017), Cooper shows how a widespread consensus around an ideal family model and gender roles has endured through the twentieth and early twenty-first centuries among policy agents in the United States. The presence of a father and an official marriage contract seem to be the two most distinctive traits of the ideal family fostered by various political decisions throughout this time.

During the New Deal welfare state era, the stable Fordist family represented that ideal. In addition to being a mechanism for the normalization of gender and sexual relationships, the Fordist family wage also structured the organization of labor, race, and class. For white families, the male breadwinner's wage guaranteed the presence of white women at home and their economic dependence on men. On the other hand, the Fordist family wage was inaccessible for black men, and African American women were relegated to agricultural and domestic labor. The New Deal welfare system thus sorted citizens according to their employment status, favoring established white male industrial workers and enforcing heterosexual normativity.

In response to the critiques of this Fordist family model, an alliance between neoliberalism and new social conservatism was forged. The latter had been formed by conservative movements from the 1960s on as a reaction to the flourishing countercultural and antinormative left. Surprisingly supportive of the inclusion of African American men within the Fordist family wage, neoliberals and neoconservatives interpreted as a threat the questioning of the sexual normativity that underpinned the authority of the family and of welfare capitalism.

If, until the 1960s, there was a consensus among Democrats and Republicans on the redistributive policies of the family wage, a major change happened when neoliberals and neoconservatives found in the idea of private family responsibility a solution to what they perceived as the crisis of the family. This passage marked the consolidation of both neoliberalism and neoconservatism as mature political philosophies, Cooper highlights.

Drawing on an American nineteenth-century tradition – which had been inspired by the much older sixteenth-century Elizabethan Poor Laws – their alternative to the New Deal welfare state aimed at reinforcing family responsibility for the care of its members. Poor laws "played a particularly significant role in the shaping of modern industrial capitalism and its signature political philosophies, first in England in the 1830s and subsequently in post-Civil War America" (Cooper 2017: 75). Indeed, in different historical periods, specific family and work duties were imposed on the lower classes by reinvented poor laws. In the post-Civil War period, the poor laws were an instrument to control enfranchised African Americans. By promoting marriage and a specific family model where men were the breadwinners and women were economically dependent, authorities intended to delegate to the family the responsibility for economically supporting former slaves, especially women and children. In spite of the unusually punitive character of the state-enforced family obligations for African American men, such laws granted patriarchal authority, reproducing in black families a socially conservative ethos. Later that century, migrants and the American white working class were also targeted by poor laws. The social conservatism reflected in such laws and their conceptions of family and gender roles was then a necessary counterpart of the laissez-faire individualism of the Gilded Age. Inasmuch as it shifted a large amount of care work onto the shoulders of women, the state's disinvestment in the process of social reproduction reinforced traditional figures of authority and domination within the family – that was the source neoliberals and neoconservatives would draw from.

In the first half of the twentieth century, the social insurance programs of the New Deal welfare state were restricted to standard male workers and their dependents, while the private family was still expected to provide economic assistance to the poor. "Although the maintenance of these [family responsibility] laws was typically justified on fiscal grounds, most commentators agree that their effect was above all punitive and disciplinary" (Cooper 2017: 92). By the 1960s, however, the process of social and cultural changes observed in sexuality and families were influencing important changes in family law and, after some legal struggle, in welfare law as well.

> By placing welfare benefits on a more secure footing and ridding them of punitive behavioral rules, the federal court decisions of this era had the effect of liberating women from the confines of private family dependence. The overall message conveyed by these rulings was that the welfare of poor women was a public responsibility on a par with that of standard male workers. Whatever their marital status, sexual history, or race, impoverished women were just as deserving of a social wage as any other citizen. At a time when middle-class women were entering the work force in growing numbers and achieving some degree of economic independence from men, unmarried women on welfare also appeared to be in reach of a social wage that was no longer mediated through a "substitute husband."
>
> COOPER 2017: 96

Neoliberals and neoconservatives considered women's economic independence from men unacceptable and, when almost all the workers were covered by social security – including women and African Americans – they portrayed the welfare state as detrimental to the family.

Neoliberals' attention focused on the increase in social spending as a consequence of the Fordist family crisis. Their prescription: to tear down the welfare state to restore the family's role in economically supporting its unwaged members. In the neoconservative rhetoric, women beneficiaries of social programs represented "an unproductive rentier class of welfare queens" financed by the blue-collar working class, which was until then the ideal Fordist family. One welfare program in particular called Aid to Families with Dependent Children (AFDC), although quite marginal, was perceived as especially contributing to the breakdown of the traditional family. A growing number of single mothers had joined the program during the postwar era, but as African American women became the majority of the beneficiaries of Aid to Dependent Children, the program became a target.

This reactionary populist discourse – as Cooper qualifies it – put the crisis of the family and traditional values and the expansion of the welfare state at the heart of the explanation of the 1970s stagflation crisis. Yet, unlike neoliberals, most neoconservatives supported the welfare state and understood that family values should be protected by the state.

> Although they rarely acknowledge or theorize this imperative, neoliberals must ultimately delegate power to social conservatives in order to realize their vision of a naturally equilibrating free-market order and a spontaneously self-sufficient family. Neoliberalism and social conservatism are thus tethered together by a working relationship that is at once necessary and disavowed: as an ideology of power that only ever acknowledges its reliance on market mechanisms and their homologues, neoliberalism can only realize its objectives by proxy, that is by outsourcing the imposition of noncontractual obligations to social conservatives. In extremis, neoliberals must turn to the overt, neoconservative methodology of state-imposed, transcendent virtue to realize their dream of an immanent virtue ethics of the market.
>
> COOPER 2017: 63

By that time, echoing the conservative populist rhetoric, the white middle class associated the stagflation crisis with the redistributive welfare programs, and the latter with the family dysfunction of the poor – a "highly racialized rhetoric," as Cooper highlights. During that period, the question of family wealth became central to political struggles. Inflation mostly depreciated the value of financial assets, having a negative impact especially for the wealth-holding classes. Even if the middle-income homeowners saw an increase in the value of their houses, this benefit was perceived as precarious. Given the stagflation scenario, the political decision not to finance "dysfunctional families" was understood as a solution to the crisis. Nevertheless, besides breaking the working and welfare classes' consensus around their economic interests, neoliberalism and its alliance with neoconservatives also fostered a significant ideological rupture. In order to protect great fortunes, the Reagan administration had to lead a moral revolution in the United States. Meritocracy and entrepreneurship became the mottos for those who understood the family as the fundamental element of society, and white middle-class homeowners switched their allegiances to the upper classes.

The 1996 Welfare Reform Act (known as the Personal Responsibility and Work Opportunity Reconciliation Act – PRWORA), enacted by the Clinton administration, expressed the victory of the alliance between neoliberalism and neoconservatism in the design of American social policy. It achieved the change in the welfare state the Reagan administration had aspired to in the early 1980s; by that time, though, these reforms were far from consensual among Republicans and Democrats. The moral justification of the law was not hidden, as it would become clear in its preamble, where marriage was characterized as "the foundation of a successful society." The welfare state was then renewed as an instrument for fostering the same conceptions of family and work as the old poor-law traditions.

As during the nineteenth century when poor laws were reinforced in the United States, promoting private family responsibility even today means the imposition of the father's authority on poor families, independently of the mother's wishes: "by detouring the payment of welfare benefits via legally designated fathers, the state reminds women that they cannot hope to find economic security without entering a relationship of personal dependence on a man" (Cooper 2017: 105). Once again, despite the punitive effects of the reform on fathers considered to be delinquent – that is, those who fail to provide for their family – the law enforced men's authority within the family. Moreover, marriage promotion and the reduction of "illegitimate births" became welfare policies expanded under the following Bush and Obama administrations.

> Much like the legal reforms that were mobilized to manage newly enfranchised slaves, PRWORA seeks to limit the potential social costs of sexual freedom among the post–Civil Rights poor by adapting and reinventing the family responsibility provisions of the poor law. And like the Freedmen's Bureau, it envisages welfare reform as a kind of demonstration project in family formation that targets African Americans in particular but aspires in the long run to extend its lessons to the wider population.
>
> COOPER 2017: 103

Poor single mothers, especially African American and other minority women, were particularly affected by Clinton's welfare reform. Punished by a heterosexual male-centered conception of the family, they were also forced, by the new legislation, to engage in work programs.

After a brief period of two decades during which the relative wages and working conditions of African American women appeared to be improving, the effect of workfare has been to brutally reinstate the historically racialized obligations of domestic servitude, in a form that responds to the imperatives of the post-Fordist service economy. African American and other minority women may well have escaped the relations of personal dependence that characterized domestic labor in white homes well into the late Fordist era. Welfare reform, however, has subjected them to new forms of unfree domestic labor outside the home and in the process places the labor of all other low-wage service workers under the shadow of workfare.

COOPER 2017: 102

In addition to a perpetual crisis, the history of the American family seems to regress to the past. Besides the restoration of moral values and traditional gender roles, and the strengthening of the father's power, the supposedly holy alliance of neoliberals and neoconservatives to reform the welfare state and the United States also intended to rescue a former economic function of the family in Western society. If, as Horkheimer puts it, the menace of disinheritance was no longer a powerful motive by which the father accomplished the obedience of his children (Horkheimer 1949: 361), Cooper shows that one of the focuses of neoliberal monetary policy in the last decades has been to reassert the private family as a vector of wealth transmission (Cooper 2017: 199). Of course, it is not an unintentional effect of the enrichment of lower and middle classes, but the result of a not so unconscious instrument to reproduce social order in capitalism, increasing its stratification of class, sex, and race.

4   Final Remarks

In her political reading of the neoliberal restructuring of the world economy, Federici (2012) highlights a permanent reproduction crisis fostered by capitalism (Federici 2012: 104). While automation has significantly reduced the labor socially necessary for the production of commodities, housework has immensely increased in the last years. Besides the fact that care work is to a great extent irreducible to mechanization, its exponential growth is a consequence of the dismantling of the welfare state. Globally widespread, the structural adjustment programs can be understood as a renewed process of primitive accumulation. Against this background, Federici points out that women have become a kind of *shock absorber* of globalization.

In her analysis of the rise of antidemocratic politics, Brown (2019) sheds light on Nietzsche's concept of resentment. In order to understand the current support for authoritarian leadership, a special kind of victimization must be taken into account. Unlike Nietzsche, Brown argues that resentment is not born from weakness, but from dethronement (Brown 2019: 177). According to Brown, the rage vocalized by Trump emerges from historically dominant groups and individuals as they feel the decline of their power. *Vis-à-vis* the displacements and losses of neoliberalism, white middle-class men have perceived their privileges to be under attack. Insofar as they are unable to fight the neoliberalization of everyday life, it drives them to hate anyone that can unseat and disdain them due to their masculinity or whiteness. In order to maintain the antagonisms of an authoritarian social order, the aggressor presents himself as a victim, while subalterns – and women in particular – are depicted as tireless and cruel predators.

In *Politics of Fear*, Ruth Wodak (2015) highlights the relevance of the "archetypical family" to the current right-wing populist parties and movements in Europe and the United States. Although it has been largely neglected by scholars, the preservation of the traditional patriarchal order of the sexes is a core element for the rhetoric of right-wing leaders and their followers. Facing changing gender relations, the ideal white middle-class Christian family is an attempt to govern and regulate women's bodies and minds (Wodak 2015: 181). However, if that conservative ideology represents the anxieties and fears of many of their voters, Wodak draws attention to a kind of gender gap in the right-wing electorate. Even when, like in the Tea Party and the National Front, women play a role in leadership, the current rise of right-wing movements is mostly supported by men (Wodak 2015: 184).

Despite the distinct sociohistorical context and the focus of their analyses, Horkheimer and Cooper contribute to the understanding of the current state of affairs. Instead of a fatherless society, the Frankfurt scholar scrutinized a family situation in which the father figure is characterized by a fundamental duality – he has the power of command within the family, whereas, outside, he must submit to the social hierarchies – the father who seems better suited to identifying with a leader like a great little man, as in Adorno's (1982 [1951]) description of fascist leadership. In this regard, the boy's identification with his father does not guarantee an autonomous and independent personality; on the contrary, it shapes an authoritarian personality. Displaced from this relationship, the mother is perceived not only as different but also as inferior. The boy's identification with the principle of authority *per se* is greater as he moves away from his mother, and begins to hate her – misogyny is the anteroom of fascism.

Besides reconstructing the economic, political, and cultural foundations of the alliance between neoliberals and neoconservatives in the United States, Cooper shows how family values were mobilized in order to break the former ideological consensus which sustained the welfare state in the previous decades, and to create a post-Keynesian capitalist order. Underlying the role of race in legitimate social and economic hierarchies, Cooper draws attention to the increasing support of both Republicans and Democrats for neoliberal and neoconservative policies. Their agreement is grounded not only in economic reasons, but also in moral values. From Nixon to Clinton or, inversely, from Obama to Reagan, changing the order of factors does not change the product. To solve the alleged crisis of the family, family responsibility and the authority of the father are the reformers' guiding principles.

If, as Horkheimer puts it, the family has contributed to forming the social cement which keeps capitalism reproducing its antagonisms, fostering an authoritarian personality that naturalizes social inequalities and idolizes domination as such, Cooper teaches us how this patriarchal family model has been enforced by the state and its social policies in recent decades in the United States. In both works, capitalism and patriarchy walk hand in hand, and manifest politically through authoritarianism and neoconservative groups, shedding light on fundamental aspects of the rise of authoritarian movements in recent American history. Moreover, Cooper teaches us that the alliance with neoconservatives has also supported the so-called progressive neoliberalism, and that Trump's simple electoral defeat, although important, does not end the problem.

References

Adorno, Theodor. 1982 [1951]. "Freudian Theory and the Pattern of Fascist Propaganda." In *The Essential Frankfurt School Reader,* edited by Andrew Arato and Eike Gebhardt, 118–137. New York: The Continuum Publishing Company.

Becker-Schmidt, Regina. 1991. "Identitätslogik und Gewalt. Zum Verhältnis von Kritischer Theorie und Feminismus." In *Fragmente Kritischer Theorie*, edited by Joachim Müller-Warden and Harald Welzer, 59–78. Tübingen: Ed. diskord.

Benjamin, Jessica. 1978. "Authority and the Family Revisited: Or, a World without Fathers?" *New German Critique*, no. 13, Special Feminist Issue (Winter): 35–57.

Brown, Wendy. 2019. *In the Ruins of Neoliberalism: the Rise of Antidemocratic Politics in the West.* New York: Columbia University Press.

Cooper, Melinda. 2017. *Family Values: Between Neoliberalism and the New Social Conservatism.* New York: Zone Books.

Federici, Silvia. 2012. *Revolution at Point Zero: Housework, Reproduction, and Feminist Struggle*. Oakland: PM Press.

Freud, Sigmund. 2003. *The Uncanny*. New York: Penguin Books.

Horkheimer, Max. 2002 [1936]. "Authority and the Family." In *Critical Theory: Selected Essays*. Translated by Matthew J. O'Connell. New York: Continuum.

Horkheimer, Max. 1949. "Authoritarianism and the Family Today." In *The Family: Its Functions and Destiny*, edited by Ruth Nanda Anshen, 359 74. New York: Harper.

Mills, Patricia Jagentowicz. 1987. *Woman, Nature, Psyche*. New Haven, London: Yale University Press.

Rumpf, Mechthild. 1993. "Mystical Aura: Imagination and the Reality of the Maternal in Horkheimer's Writings." In *On Max Horkheimer: New Perspectives*, edited by Seyla Benhabib, Wolfgang Bonss, and John McCole, 309–34. Cambridge: MIT Press.

Rumpf, Mechthild. 1989. *Spuren des Mütterlichen—Die widersprüchliche Bedeutung der Mutterrolle für die männliche Identitätsbildung in Kritischer Theorie und feministischer Wissenschaft*. Frankfurt am Main: Materialis Verlag.

Umrath, Barbara. 2018. "A Feminist Reading of the Frankfurt School's Studies on Authoritarianism and Its Relevance for Understanding AuthoritarianTendencies in Germany Today." *The South Atlantic Quarterly* 117, no. 4 (October): 861–78. https://doi.org/10.1215/00382876-7165927.

Wodak, Ruth. 2015. *The Politics of Fear: What Right-wing Populist Discourses Bean*. London: Sage.

CHAPTER 4

Rethinking "Toxic" Sovereignty?

On Horkheimer and Adorno's "Second Nature" between Nietzsche's "Bad Conscience" and Freud's "Death Drive"

Karyn Ball

The circulation of the term *toxic masculinity* has noticeably intensified between the 2014 Gamergate controversy;[1] Elliot Rodger's May 2014 killing spree in Isla Vista, California and the so-called "Incel Rebellion" enthralled by it;[2] Donald J. Trump's victory in the November 2016 election after the *Washington Post's* October 2016 release of the 2005 Access Hollywood tapes in which the candidate bragged about kissing and groping women without their consent;[3] the revelations about Harvey Weinstein's decades-long aggressive sexual exploitation of women, and the attendant rise of the #MeToo movement in 2017; the ascent and fall of billionaire sex trafficker, Jeffrey Epstein, and his legal coddling by Florida District Attorney, Eric Acosta; the ready convergence between anti-vax and anti-mask survival-of-the-fittest libertarians and white nationalist "Stop the Steal" insurrectionists; and the recent "Freedom Convoy" that snarled Canadian borders just before Vladimir's Putin's unprovoked invasion of Ukraine. Among the many beliefs, qualities, and behaviors typically attributed to "toxic masculinity" are the need to embody physical and emotional impenetrability, a harsh standard which lends itself to a hatred of vulnerability in oneself and others as well as a self-serving rejection of an ethics of compassion and the typically under- or unpaid tasks that comprise (women's) care work; a social-Darwinist winner-take-all mentality that idolizes the victorious and scorns the weak; a *droit du seigneur* sense of entitlement that quickly curdles into a petulant sense of grievance and rage when thwarted; and an embrace of violence as a means of upholding male domination.

Yet the increasing ubiquity of "toxic" attributions should give cultural critics and intellectual historians pause. As Elizabeth Pearson reminds us,

---

1 Aja Romano, "What We Still Haven't Learned from Gamergate," *Vox* (updated January 7, 2021) https://www.vox.com/culture/2020/1/20/20808875/gamergate-lessons-cultural-impact-changes-harassment-laws.

2 https://www.bbc.com/news/world-us-canada-43892189.

3 https://www.youtube.com/watch?v=PwWux5BAczk.

"[m]asculinities are relational, constructed in opposition to femininities, and enacted according to a hierarchy, in which certain masculinities are preferable to others" (1257). By extension, "[t]here can be no 'crisis' of masculinity without a norm from which the crisis deviates" (1258). Pearson rightly views the toxic stereotype as "a rhetorical device to explain broad structural issues."[4] Taking Pearson's lead, I feel called upon to reflect on the increasingly frequent recourses to this device in the mainstream press that link the masculinist performance of emotional hardness with authoritarianism while eliding the intellectual history that solidifies the persuasiveness of this connection.

The provenance of the "authoritarian personality" in Theodor W. Adorno's studies during his exile in the United States and published in 1950 is well known.[5] In Adorno's collaboration with Max Horkheimer in *The Dialectic of Enlightenment*,[6] the fascism-susceptible subject assumes its contours in their translation of Friedrich Nietzsche's critique of sovereignty building on his opposition between "first" and "second nature" in *The Genealogy of Morals*. It is in the "Second Essay" that Nietzsche seeks to denaturalize the predominant figurative logic of Western civilization's perversely punitive debtor economy through which an inadvertent failure to fulfil a promise is misrecognized as a criminal lapse of self-mastery that incurs a "debt" to society to be "paid off" with tortured flesh. The influences of Marxism, the German sociological tradition, and Freudian psychoanalysis among others spur Horkheimer and Adorno to rethink Nietzsche's schema by attending to the alienating demands of capitalist modernity depicted as an omnivalent and insatiable creditor. In the *Dialectic*, Nietzsche's conception of second nature clearly shapes Horkheimer and Adorno's emplotment of reification (mediated by Lukács) as a deformative adaptation to the capitalist injunction to perform stoic self-sovereignty by suppressing affect. Less explicitly, however, this construct might be read as vindicating Sigmund Freud's discovery of the death drive in 1920, which

---

4 Pearson has observed that "British politicians and analysts have repeatedly linked a 'crisis of masculinity' and toxicity to 'extremist' violence" (2019: 1256) whereas prior deployments of the term in the context of the "war on terror" targeted Muslim men and Islamophobes alike. To counter ahistorical and reductive equations, she recommends study of men's interior lives while taking into account intersectional cross-currents such as "class, race, or identities beyond the global North" (2019: 1259 and 1258).

5 See Theodor W. Adorno, Else Frenkel-Brunswik, Daniel J. Levinson, and R. Nevitt Sanford, *The Authoritarian Personality* (2019). This volume was part of "Studies in Prejudice" series edited by Max Horkheimer and Samuel H. Flowerman.

6 I will rely on Edmund Jephcott's translation published by Stanford University Press in 2002 unless otherwise noted.

spurs him to posit sadomasochism in 1930 as one of civilization's most infernal "discontents."

I have previously written about Nietzsche's conception of bad conscience in light of the inflections the death drive gathers between Freud's *Beyond the Pleasure Principle* from 1920 (Freud 2001), "The Economic Problem of Masochism" from 1924 (Freud 2001b), and *Civilization and Its Discontents* from 1930 (Freud 2001a).[7] Very briefly, in "The Economic Problem of Masochism," Freud elaborates on the "internalization" of a destructive death drive as "masochism" in its "erotogenic," "feminine," and "moral" forms along with its "externalization" as "sadism." As Freud states, an erotogenic "pleasure in pain" is the most fundamental of the three forms because it underlies the other two. He initially naturalizes feminine masochism "as an expression of the feminine nature" and, as such, "one that is most accessible to our observation and least problematical," though he subsequently identifies it with a perverse desire, presumably in cis-gendered men, to be copulated with and to give birth, "which are characteristic of femaleness" (SE XIX: 161 and 165).

As the most important form for Freud's purposes since it stems from "a sense of guilt which is mostly unconscious," he associates moral masochism with "a temptation to perform 'sinful' actions, which must then be expiated by the reproaches of the sadistic conscience" (SE XIX: 161 and 169). Sadism according to Freud derives from the libido's convergence with the death drive, an intersection which tasks the former with the latter's neutralization. The libido manages this task, as Freud contends, "by diverting that [drive] to a greater extent outwards,"[8] thus becoming a destructive drive [*Destruktionstrieb*] that he aligns (without citing Nietzsche) with the urge toward "mastery [*Bemächtigungstrieb*], or the will to power [*Wille zur Macht*]." Conversely, what he calls the "original erotogenic masochism" refers to the "portion" [*Anteil*] of the death drive that remains internal and "becomes libidinally bound there" (SE XIX: 163; GS XIII: 376).[9] Freud's allusion to the "will to power" in "The Economic Problem of Masochism" is striking insofar as he notoriously disclaimed Nietzsche's influence as indicated in the minutes of the Vienna Psychoanalytic Society from 1908, despite having purchased the latter's works "at some expense" in

---

7   See Ball 2006, "A Democracy Is Being Beaten".

8   As is well known, in the *Standard Edition*, the German *Trieb* is somewhat misleadingly translated as *instinct*, which elides a potentially significant distinction between instinct and drive for Freud, though they are apparently on a continuum. For the sake of precision, I have altered Strachey's translation by substituting *drive* here and elsewhere in those instances where Freud employs *Trieb*. See Freud 2001 and 1999.

9   Citing Freud 2001b and Freud 1999a.

1900 (Gay 45). It is thus left up to Freud's readers to extrapolate a relationship between Nietzsche's bad conscience and Freud's death drive.[10]

In *Civilization and Its Discontents*, Freud's 1924 derivation of masochism and sadism from the death drive undergirds his pronouncement that socialization exacerbates the very aggression it would subdue. The death drive subsequently reemerges as the motor of a sadomasochistic libidinal economy that constitutes one of the principal *Unbehagen* of Freud's *Kultur*. This dire lesson from *Civilization and Its Discontents* carries over to the Frankfurt School's revision of Nietzsche's distinction between an instinctual "first" and a deformed "second" nature.

Following a review of the "second nature" critique between Nietzsche and the Frankfurt School, I will amplify Freud's potential contribution to the motif of "internal hardness" as a poetic bridge between yesterday's authoritarian personality and today's toxic masculinity. Taking critical distance from an automatic gendering of emotional impenetrability, which, for Adorno at least, extends to the "bourgeois coldness" that permitted Auschwitz[11] will facilitate an assessment of the explanatory value of understanding toxic masculinity as a gendered death drive.

1   Toxic Sovereignties

Just because toxic masculinity is becoming a cliché does not mean it is not out to get us.[12] In a period populated by the likes of Donald Trump, Vladimir Putin,

---

10   See Richard Waugaman (1973) and my "A Democracy Is Being Beaten" (Ball 2006) for discussions and further references pertaining to this ambivalently signaled intellectual debt.

11   The full quotation from Adorno's *Negative Dialectics* reads: "Perennial suffering has as much right to expression as a tortured man has to scream; hence it may have been wrong to say that after Auschwitz you could no longer write poems. But it is not wrong to raise the less cultural question whether after Auschwitz you can go on living – especially whether one who escaped by accident, one who by rights should have been killed, may go on living. His mere survival calls for the coldness, the basic principle of bourgeois subjectivity, without which there could have been no Auschwitz; this is the drastic guilt of him who was spared" (1973a: 362–363).

12   Alex McElroy facetiously quips, "[t]oxic masculinity is so 2017," except, of course, if we are being serious: since the #MeToo moment, the men who were "trying to drop the stoicism and anger that have long warped masculinity," have seemingly lost the struggle to become a genuinely transformative force. Instead, as McElroy observes, "male vulnerability [has curdled] into something toxic" that he calls "petulant vulnerability." One symptom of the petulant mode, as McElroy diagnoses it, is the employment of "the language of vulnerability as a cudgel. If true vulnerability means accepting change, personal fallibility and the human condition of reliance on others, petulant vulnerability feigns emotional fragility

Jair Bolsonaro, Victor Orbán, Recep Tayyip Erdogan, and Rodrigo Duterte among too many others, toxic masculinity continues for the time being to accrue force as a pseudo-diagnostic shorthand for solipsistic and domineering sociopaths who resist the perceived encroachments of a liberal-democratic consensus respecting the need to promote equality and a more equitable distribution of resources as a common good. Indeed, with so many fulsome models of this veritable cliché ready-at-hand, critical endeavors to delineate the limits of its explanatory value will likely fall on deaf ears beyond academic circles. Yet it is nevertheless desirable to bear in mind the historicity of this descriptor while sidestepping the pitfalls that Pearson highlights[13] by reframing a contemporary preoccupation with toxic masculinity as a social-psychological vicissitude in the long-running critique of sovereignty.

During the years leading up to 9–11 and the first decade or so thereafter, the critique of sovereignty was conspicuously in vogue (again) as Giorgio Agamben revisited Hannah Arendt's delineation of totalitarianism in conversation with

---

as a means of retaining power." [Alex McElroy, "This Isn't Your Old Toxic Masculinity. It Has Taken an Insidious New Form." *New York Times* (January 13, 2022). https://www.nytimes.com/2022/01/13/opinion/toxic-masculinity.html].

13   Pearson is not alone in her suspicions about toxic masculinity shedding its critical leverage as it gains ubiquity. Other feminist commentators have sought to take some distance from this stereotype's intuitive appeal, which tends to naturalize its seemingly transhistorical [if this word is hyphenated, please insert the hyphen after "trans" and not as it appears in the proofs with the hyphen after the 'h']and transcultural character. Though she is not focused on toxic masculinity in particular, feminist commentator Jessica Bennett (2022) rehearses a familiar criticism from trauma studies when she decries the "seepage" of trauma rhetoric into discussions of personal pain. Her take away is that the desire to be heard in a hyper-mediatized era of the personal-is-the political multiplies recourses to the medicalizing language of pathology that serves to shore up a speaker's authority as well as their cultural capital in a crowded confessional arena.

Bennett's somewhat cynical criticism of "trauma culture" extends to terms such as *gaslighting* to describe a domination tactic commonly attributed to domestic abusers who seek to control their partners by undermining the other's confidence in their own perceptions. To the extent that *gaslighting* has, in recent years, been used to describe not just Trump's lies, but the Republican party's tactics as a whole, it is not surprising to see some pundits argue that the American people are in an "abusive relation" with the former president and his MAGA minions in the House and Senate whose favorite tactic in recent years is to project their own malfeasance onto their accusers. It might be time to formulate an approach that reconstructs American politics through the lens of the "bad" or "abusive" relationship. On Trump and the GOP as abusers, see Nadine DeNinno 2020; Chauncy Devega (2020), Abigail R. Esman, and Dahlia Lithwick (2020); Ibram X. Kendi (2019); Tanya Lewis (2021); Bandy X. Lee, Harper West, and Kevin Washington (2020); Amil Niazi (2020); Anna North (2021); Stephanie Sarkis (2018); Tanya Selvaratnam (2021); and Andrew Tasker (2021). On gaslighting in general, see Amanda Kippart (2021).

Auschwitz survivor Primo Levi and one-time Nazi juror Carl Schmitt in order to rethink Michel Foucault's conception of biopolitics.[14] This nexus of mediations zigzagged ambivalently with Jacques Derrida's career-long contributions to the critique of sovereignty (sometimes in response to Emmanuel Lévinas), beginning with his successive deconstructions of the metaphysics of presence and his linguistically-turned recourses to the psychoanalytic unconscious to chart fatally-performative symptoms of self-derailed authority in Western thought. While both philosophical projects attracted significant scholarly attention in the context of the "war on terror" and the attendant passage of the United States "Patriot Act,"[15] they missed the opportunity to engage with poststructuralist, feminist, and queer discussions about gender performativity as originally conceptualized by Judith Butler. In their own dialogues with Agamben's conception of "bare life" from 2004 and 2010, Butler refined his contribution to the critique of sovereignty by setting forth a more intersectionally nuanced ethics of precarity that attended to the relative vulnerability of various groups in an increasingly global scene.[16]

Though academic feminists are mostly familiar with recent critiques of sovereignty as well as Butler's performativity thesis, in interventions published in popular venues, they understandably shy away from detailing complex intellectual histories and theoretical debates. The broad strokes favored in short commentaries about toxic masculinity nevertheless benefit from a sedimentation of connections that bolster their familiarity over time.

In a discussion of the circumstances surrounding Trump's first impeachment in 2019, Bonnie Mann (2019) elaborates on the "aspiration to sovereign masculinity [that] expresses itself most exuberantly in hyperbolic displays of power."[17] Summarizing the historian Gail

---

14   At the risk of repeating a commonplace, Agamben endeavors to redeem sovereignty from the potentially exaggerated tactical divergences of a post-Marxist Foucault who was proposing a behavioral-discursive diffusion of superstructural power and knowledge that would qualify if not displace a foregoing over-emphasis on consciousness and the state. See Giorgio Agamben, *Homo Sacer: Sovereign Power and Bare Life* (1998), *Remnants of Auschwitz: The Witness and the Archive* (1999), and *State of Exception* (2005). Though the publication (in Italian and English) of the first two volumes of Agamben's *Homo Sacer* series preceded 9–11, the attacks and subsequent U.S. "war on terrorism" made his renewed interrogation of sovereignty seem prescient.

15   https://www.fincen.gov/resources/statutes-regulations/usa-patriot-act.

16   See Judith Butler's *Precarious Life: The Powers of Mourning and Violence* (2004) and *Frames of War: When Is Life Grievable?* (2010).

17   Bonnie Mann, "Marie Yovanovich's Courage." *The New York Times* (10/19/2019) https://www.nytimes.com/2019/10/19/opinion/marie-yovanovitchs-moral-courage.html.

Bederman,[18] Mann cites "America's obsession with this kind of masculinity," which dates back to the Progressive Era "when white men feared 'civilization' was making them weak, invented Tarzan, and reinvented white masculinity as a copy of their own fantasy of dangerous, primitive, black and indigenous manhood." Thereafter, "sovereign masculinity is not associated with rationality or the life of the mind, but," as Mann recounts it, "with a fantasy of instinct-driven, primitive potency. It scorns deliberation, negotiation, alliances with others, and the intellectual life." To amplify her point, Mann quotes a revanchist post-9-11 treatise by conservative Harvard political philosopher, Harvey Mansfield, whose ideal form of manliness "would be the one where the man is the source of all meaning, where nothing else has meaning unless the man supplies it." Yet if sovereign man likens himself to a god whose "word instantiates truth," then, as Mann suggests, it follows that he is also "not subject to the law because he is a source of law for others."

The stakes of this fantasy could not be higher according to Mann who worries that the "cultural purchase" of MAGA toxicity brings the United States perilously close to authoritarianism. Ruth Ben-Ghiat echoes Mann in a recent commentary on Paul Gosar's anime-style video featuring an avatar of the Arizona Congressional representative "[saving] the nation, attacking President Biden with swords and killing Representative Alexandria Ocasio-Cortez."[19] In an age of "lawless masculinity," as Ben-Ghiat refers to it, Gosar's fantasy "takes a page[...] straight out of the authoritarian playbook," which not only polices behavior, but, as Ben-Ghiat emphasizes, also features "the *removal* of checks on actions deemed unethical in democratic contexts (lying, thievery, even rape and murder)." In this respect, Ben-Ghiat contends, lawless masculinity has operated as "a lubricant of corruption, normalizing behaviors and redefining illegal or immoral acts as acceptable, from election fraud to sexual assault." It should therefore surprise no one that Trump, in a "classic authoritarian fashion," has "attracted collaborators by making it easier for men to act on their desires without fear of punishment."

According to Ben-Ghiat, the lawless masculinity stereotype assumes that a "real man takes what he wants, when he wants it, whether in the bedroom, the workplace, or politics, and pays no penalty." As the contemporary GOP continues to idolize Trump not despite of but because of his crimes, it has, as Ben-Ghiat suggests, openly subscribed to a lawless-masculine ethos with

---

18   See Gail Bederman, *Manliness and Civilization: A Cultural History of Gender and Race in the United States, 1880–1917* (1996).

19   https://twitter.com/tedlieu/status/1457865685464276997. Cited by Ben-Ghiat in "Welcome to the Age of Lawless Masculinity".

its attendant authoritarian politics. For this reason, she warns, that as "the Republican quest to destroy democracy intensifies, so will abusive, predatory, and criminal behavior be further enabled and justified."[20]

It is worth pointing out that the intuitive appeal of Mann's "sovereign" and Ben-Ghiat's "lawless masculinity" depends on unacknowledged slippages between the traditional ideal of the stoic hero who silently sacrifices his own emotional needs to rescue or provide for others and the macho thug who perpetrates violence against those who threaten his psychological boundaries. These commentaries do not mention Klaus Theweleit's two-volume *Male Fantasies* appearing in English in 1987 and 1989 respectively, where he tracks motifs in the proto-fascist *Freikorps'* novels, letters, and autobiographies depicting "feminine" and "racial" threats to German male self-sovereignty. In a move that seems to reflect enthusiasm for Gilles Deleuze and Félix Guattari's post-humanist and post-psychoanalytic metaphors, Theweleit, oddly, distances himself from his Frankfurt School forbears when he dismisses their "attempt to thrust Freud and Marx (or vice versa) onto a single pedestal" in order finally to "create the homunculus, the omniscient one, from a retort" (Theweleit 1987: 416). Yet even if Theweleit might be justified in rebuking his predecessors for ignoring "the things that happen in, and to, human bodies (psychic matter)," in the *Dialectic*, Horkheimer and Adorno conspicuously endeavor to explain how people in capitalist societies come to desire their own subjection; it is therefore an exaggeration to claim, with Theweleit channeling

---

20   Ruth Ben-Ghiat, "Welcome to the Age of Lawless Masculinity," *The Atlantic* (November 19, 2021) https://www.theatlantic.com/ideas/archive/2021/11/lawless-masculinity-gop /620732/. This was, after all, the "macho" administration that, in 2019, restricted the legal definition of domestic abuse to physical acts of harm, thereby legalizing sexual, psychological, and economic injury. While defending "men accused of sexual harassment and sexual assault, including Supreme Court Justice Brett Kavanaugh," Trump also bestowed "high-profile government positions" on the white nationalist Steve Bannon among others "who were accused of sexual harassment, domestic abuse, or inappropriate workplace behavior." See Maya Oppenheim, "Trump Administration 'rolling back women's rights by 50 years' by changing definitions of domestic violence and sexual assault." *Independent* (January 24, 2019). https://www.independent.co.uk/news/world/americas/trump-domes tic-abuse-sexual-assault-definition-womens-rights-justice-department-a8744546.html. (cited by Ben-Ghiat in "Welcome to the Age of Lawless Masculinity"). In the meantime, Fox News and Republican Senator Josh Hawley of Missouri have called for a defense of "'traditional masculine virtues,'" or what Hawley identifies as "'courage and independence and assertiveness'" over and against "a left trying to 'feminize' men." "Senator Hawley Delivers National Conservatism Keynote on the Left's Attack on Men in America" (November 1, 2021). https://www.hawley.senate.gov/senator-hawley-delivers-national -conservatism-keynote-lefts-attack-men-america [cited by Ben-Ghiat in "Welcome to the Age of Lawless Masculinity"].

a post-psychoanalytic *Anti-Oedipus*, that "[t]hey have no category for the desiring-production of the unconscious, from which all reality, 'psychic' as well as 'social,' derives" (Theweleit 1987: 416).[21] To counter Theweleit's biting-the-hand-that-feeds-him dismissal of their "*Ideologiekritik*," I will extend Horkheimer and Adorno's Marxist renovation of Nietzsche's second nature figure and "bad conscience" as such with a reading of how Freud's death-driven trauma theory might be read as a latent figurative logic for their concept of reification.

2   Second Nature and/as Nietzsche's "Bad Conscience"

In *The Origin of Negative Dialectics*, Susan Buck-Morss attaches the idea of "second nature" to Adorno's endeavor to "[expose] the historical dimension in that which appeared to be natural"; hence, while "'[f]irst nature' referred to the sensual world, including the human body" as the site of "the concrete, particular nature to which the course of history did violence," "second nature" was, as Buck-Morss parses it, "a negating, critical concept which referred to the false, mythical appearance of given reality as ahistorical and absolute" (1979: 55). The problem that the second nature concept would help to address, in her words, was that "either social conditions were affirmed as 'natural' without regard for their historical becoming, or the actual historical process was affirmed as 'essential'" at the expense of a genuine recognition of the "irrational historical suffering of which history was composed. In both cases," Buck-Morss adds, "the result was the ideological justification of the social order" (1979: 54). To counteract this elision, Adorno's dialectical analysis of the opposition between "nature" and "history" purported to redeem the "critical negativity" of these concepts from their reification as theoretical pregivens by emphasizing their mutually determining double character: the appearance of the natural would be demystified as second nature and, conversely, the appearance of the historical would be revealed as the domain of first nature (1979: 54).

---

21   Here is Theweleit's comment in full: "All of the lines of scientific research based purely on ideological criticism, or *ideologiekritik* (headed by the Frankfurt School), and all of the theoretical approaches that practice historical-materialist-philosophical-metapsychological manipulations in an attempt to thrust Freud and Marx (or vice versa) onto a single pedestal – and *finally* create the homunculus, the omniscient one, from a retort – ignore the same basic area: the things that happen in, and to, human bodies (psychic matter). They have no category for the desiring-production of the unconscious, from which all reality, 'psychic' as well as 'social,' derives" (Theweleit 1987: 416).

Drawing from the philosophical and sociological continuum connecting G.W.F. Hegel to Karl Marx to Max Weber to György Lukács,[22] Adorno includes "second nature" in a "constellation of critical concepts together with 'fetish,' 'reification,' 'enchantment,' 'fate,' 'myth,' and 'phantasmagoria' which were used to see through the mysterious 'natural' appearance of objects in their 'given' form to the historical dimension of their production." The intent, as Buck-Morss characterizes it, was to slough off "the mythical aura of their legitimacy" (1979: 55). In the *Dialectic of Enlightenment*, Horkheimer and Adorno show how the intensifying "rationalization and 'disenchantment' of society did not lead progressively to a rational social order," as Buck-Morss paraphrases it, "but instead to new structures of domination in the forms of monopoly capitalism and political totalitarianism" (1979: 61). Among the most prominent refrains in the *Dialectic* is that reason is "the tool for the domination of nature"; however, in its close conjunction "with self-renunciation and bourgeois asceticism" and the program of stoic restraint as such, Horkheimer and Adorno contend that reason "had turned 'against the thinking subject himself'" (1979: 61 citing Horkheimer and Adorno, 1972: 26). The result of this inversion, as they recount it, is that "[r]ational control of inner and outer nature was reflected in the very form of Enlightenment thought: logical abstraction led not only to the reification of cognition," as Buck-Morss summarizes, "but also to the domination of the content of thought by the concepts," thereby legitimating violence to "first nature" (Buck-Morss 61). In effect, then, Buck-Morss reads the book as enacting "a *critical negation* of that rationalist, idealist, progressive view of history which in bourgeois society had itself become 'second nature,'" a critique they pursue "*for the sake of* the Enlightenment and the rationality which it promised" (1979: 61).

In this connection, Buck-Morss additionally draws attention to the influence on the *Dialectic* of Walter Benjamin's "On the Concept of History" from 1940, as Horkheimer and Adorno advance his agenda to "dismantle the myth of the history of progress" (1979: 60). In the frequently cited "Angel of History"

---

22   Susan Buck-Morss notes that the heritage of *second nature* includes Hegel's invocation of it "to expose the externality of forms as mere appearance," but Adorno's revision of this term in "The Idea of Natural History" is more overtly indebted to Lukács' "*Die Theorie des Romans* [*The Theory of the Novel*], in which 'second nature' was used to describe the alienated world, emptied of meaning, 'created by man yet composed of things which have become lost to him, ... the world of convention'" (Buck-Morss 1979: 55 citing Adorno, "Die Idee der Naturgeschichte" 1973: 355). Less germane for Adorno, according to Buck-Morss, is Lukács' employment of this figure in *History and Class Consciousness* as a synonym for "Marx's concept of 'fetish' in his analysis of bourgeois conventions in terms of the commodity structure" (1979: 55).

image from thesis IX, the critique of the bourgeois-historical narrative of progress that transpires in homogeneous and empty time paves over a pile-up of catastrophic suffering sedimented with failed revolutionary possibilities that a messianically-inclined Benjamin would seek to reanimate. Benjamin viewed the transitoriness of nature "as a source of suffering, but at the same time, because its essence was change, it was the source of hope" (1979: 57). Horkheimer and Adorno's second nature critique is infused with the spirit of Benjamin's mandate to extricate Marxist historiography from the bourgeois myth of progress, which not only reifies history by neutralizing its transitory dynamic but also overlooks the abiding inherence of class struggle.

Buck-Morss' commentary on second nature stresses the Frankfurt School's repudiation of Enlightenment progress narratives which accords with a broader Marxist insistence on historicizing phenomena as the dialectical crux of political-economic developments and sociocultural conditions. At the same time, second nature conceived critically as reification is poetically evinced as the "hardening," or solidification of natural and historical flux through the rationalizing forces of abstraction that homogenize work time and occult the socially coercive relations goading production. Though Buck-Morss is aware that Nietzsche's affirmation of becoming versus stasis clearly influences the Frankfurt School insistence on respecting transitoriness in both nature and history (1979: 48), she does not dwell on the role that Nietzsche's figurative logic plays in the *Dialectic*. As I will demonstrate below, this influence becomes still more conspicuous in Horkheimer and Adorno's predication of second nature as the inter- and intrasubjective precipitate of a culture that instrumentalizes self-mastery at the expense of instinctual first nature.

As a term that sometimes references the expropriation of history, *reification* calls for its own historicization. Buck-Morss correctly identifies the term's critical valence with Marx's and then Lukács' depiction of the commodity fetishism through which the promise of happiness that auraticizes goods occults the coercive and exploitative social forces structuring the labor that produced them. Yet to the extent that commodity fetishism encodes a broader social-psychological logic, it references not only the impact of transactional thinking that "thingifies" humans in reducing them either to their use- and/or their exchange-value but also the calcification of abstract ideas or values, such as love, intimacy, and justice that evacuates their historical contingencies. This might mean "ontologizing" them – attributing stasis and/or actuality to an historically sedimented and shifting idea or, in the language of ideology critique, it might involve naturalizing a sociocultural construction, thereby eliding the fluctuating political-economic conditions and social forces shaping its emergence as an historical phenomenon.

The early sociological tradition after Marx advances an increasingly robust concept of reification to designate the alienating impacts of industrialized labor organization. Within this trajectory, Ferdinand Tönnies' atomizing *Gesellschaft* (society) displaces organic, tradition-imbedded *Gemeinschaft* (community).[23] Rationalization hereafter designates the forces that intellectualize, abstract, classify, compartmentalize, and thus bureaucratize social relations in keeping with Taylorist standards that dissect the space and time of discrete tasks to promote efficiency and productivity in the workplace. One of the contextually motivated questions pursued in the *Dialectic* is how the Enlightenment inherited fetishism of science that raises it to the status of a hegemonic myth intersects with the rationalization of labor divisions to generate the kind of subject formations that eventuate in Auschwitz. What Horkheimer and Adorno add to the sociological account of rationalization is an enunciation of the logic of internalization whereby people harden themselves against the harshness of the domination they experience between the workplace and institutions. In my reading, this logic infuses Nietzsche's emplotment of an inverted second nature from *On the Genealogy of Morals* with Marxist concerns about how profitability is instrumentally effectuated through multifariously overlaid modes of disinterested intellectualization.

Of course, concerns about how the embrace of abstraction deforms consciousness are not unique to Marx and the German sociological tradition. According to the "genealogy" offered in Nietzsche's "Second Essay" on "'Guilt,' 'Bad Conscience' and the Like,"[24] memory is a technology that demarcates self-forgetting animals from humans who must be threatened with pain to perform sovereignty by keeping their promises and paying their debts above all. The proximity between *guilt* and *debt* through the German word *Schuld* suggests a figurative debtor economy to Nietzsche in which any kind of personal, social, or professional lapse can be perceived as incurring a "debt." Among Nietzsche's ostensible aims in the "Second Essay" is to defamiliarize the naturalized slippage between an unfulfilled promise and an unpaid debt. Toward this aim, he invokes the medieval creditor's putative right to carve out a morsel of flesh from a prodigal debtor. This gory morsel henceforward operates as a metonym associating guilt and debt with pain and punishment. Of course, since a piece of someone's flesh is not worth much, its main value, as Nietzsche emphasizes, stems from the enjoyment-in-cruelty it begets; he hereby intimates how

---

23 See Ferdinand Tönnies' *Community and Society* (2002) originally published in German under the title *Gemeinschaft und Gesellschaft* in 1887.

24 See Nietzsche 1969.

sadistic pleasure becomes the blood-limned currency of a barbaric culture that converts inadvertent lapses of self-mastery into punishable crimes.

Nietzsche decries the injunction to perform self-sovereignty that propels humans to seek to become consistent, reliable, and "calculable." "To ordain the future in advance" as the fulfillment of a "long chain of will," Nietzsche writes, "man must first have learned to distinguish necessary events from chance ones, to think causally, to see and anticipate distant eventualities as if they belonged to the present, to decide with certainty what is the goal and the means to it, and in general be able to calculate and compute." In short, "[m]an himself must first of all have become *calculable, regular, necessary*, even in his own image of himself, if he is to be able to stand security for *his own future*, which is what one who promises does!" (§1:58). Toward this end, humans rein in, not only their "will to power" as Nietzsche's term for first-natural instincts to overcome, aggress, create, become, and transcend, but also their attendant affects, a vital fundament of passion and unpredictability.

Particularly remarkable in §16 of the "Second Essay" is Nietzsche's deployment of visceral imagery to evoke the self-destructive repercussions of man's *internalization* as "all those instincts of wild, free prowling man [are] turned backward *against man himself*." Bestowed with a soul, this inwardly-turned man is hereby "forcibly confined to the oppressive narrowness and punctiliousness of custom, impatiently lacerated, persecuted, gnawed at, assaulted, and mal-treated himself"; he is, as Nietzsche dramatizes it, "this animal that rubbed itself raw against the bars of its cage as one tried to 'tame' it" (§16: 85). Declaring "war against the old instincts upon which his strength, joy and terribleness had rested hitherto," man *inverts* them – an act of violence perpetrated by a guilt-hardened "second nature" against the instinctual "first" (§16: 85).

As Western civilization embraces guilt, bad conscience translates into a toxic *self-hatred*, according to Nietzsche, since it impels subjects to despise instinctual nature, to favor calculation and restraint over spontaneity and the animal's self-forgetful enjoyment. It is in this respect, too, that bad conscience is not only "morally masochistic" in Freud's sense, but also sadistic, since those who internalize ascetic ideals that demand restraint scorn those who do not or cannot perform self-sovereignty by fulfilling promises, paying debts, or consistently quelling their emotions.[25]

---

25   In "The Economic Problem of Masochism," Freud takes pains to distinguish a sadistic superego from a masochistic ego. He describes individuals who give the "impression of being morally inhibited to an excessive degree, of being under the domination of an especially sensitive conscience, although they are not conscious of any of this ultramo-rality. On closer inspection, we can see the difference there is between an unconscious

It is in the context of his critique of sovereignty that Nietzsche denounces the "mastery of affects" precipitated by the instinct-deforming "internalization of man" (§3: 62). Internalization constitutes the crux of bad conscience as the name Nietzsche gives to a figurative logic whereby the domination exerted from without modifies inner life, which then recalibrates social existence as the "civilized" act out their guilt by policing themselves and others. *Ressentiment* exacerbates this paranoid and sadomasochistic debtor's economy insofar as second-natured subjects hate not only themselves; they simultaneously resent and envy those who unrepentantly exercise a vigorously first-natural will to power.

Horkheimer and Adorno restage Nietzsche's preoccupation with the "denial of nature in human beings" into an episode in the technological domination of nature. Rationalization might therefore be said to commence in "the moment when human beings cut themselves off from the consciousness of themselves as nature," and thus expropriate "all the purposes for which they keep themselves alive" (*Dialectic* 42–43). Second nature is, in the *Dialectic*, a deformation that results when modern subjects turn the Enlightenment *ratio* that would regulate nature inward *against* humans themselves. Echoing Nietzsche, Horkheimer and Adorno contend that "pleasure has learned to hate itself, in its totalitarian emancipation it remains mean and mutilated through self-contempt." Moreover, such self-hating pleasure "is still in the grip of the self-preservation inculcated in it by the reason which has now been deposed" (*Dialectic* 24). Yet whereas "Second Essay" Nietzsche embraces the will to power as "first nature," Horkheimer and Adorno are inclined to treat the concept of nature dialectically to avoid mythologizing it; they consequently invert the Enlightenment's embrace of the myth of a "mature" intellect that belittles ignorance, superstition, and fear along with the terrors of an external nature it would rule. This dialectical inversion locates fear in first nature while discerning rigidity as a prehistorical defense against that fear in second nature.

---

extension of morality of this kind and moral masochism. In the former, the accent falls on the heightened sadism of the super-ego to which the ego submits; in the latter, it falls on the ego's own masochism which seeks punishment, whether from the super-ego or from parental powers outside. We may be forgiven for having confused the two to begin with; for in both cases, it is a question of a relationship between the ego and the super-ego (or powers that are equivalent to it), and in both cases what is involved is a need which is satisfied by punishment and suffering. It can hardly be an insignificant detail, then, that the sadism of the super-ego becomes for the most part glaringly conscious, whereas the masochistic trend of the ego remains as a rule concealed from the subject and has to be inferred from his behaviour" (SE XIX: 168–169).

From Nietzsche, Horkheimer and Adorno borrow the figurative logic of an inward-turning, self-punishing subject whose instincts have been deformed through socialization and, most particularly, the need to perform "calculability." Lukács' revision of Weber's account of rationalization sediments this theorization of a second-natural subject who becomes at once *calculable and calculating* in myriad socioeconomic arenas. The workplace injunction to "compartmentalize" intimacy by confining it to familial relationships in the domestic sphere reflects the bureaucratic and Taylorist infrastructure of a functionally differentiated economy. As the petrified inside comes to mirror the domination exerted from without, the enlightened purportedly lose their spontaneity and responsiveness, or what might be viewed as the sensory and affective conditions for forming (revolutionary) solidarities. The *Dialectic*'s Marxist critique of this inter- and intrasubjective seepage thus extends Nietzsche's debt- and guilt-driven figuration of bad conscience as a self-destructive subjugation of instinctual nature into a theory about emotional hardening as modern mimicry, an anthropologically archaic adaptation to rationalization.

In configuring "toxic masculinity" as a performative stylization of affective fossilization, I am, in effect, reformulating this identity cliché as a second-natural reaction formation against the shamefully "childish" and "feminine" residues of fear and vulnerability that belong to a sloughed off first nature as well as its alternately uncanny and traumatic eruptions. Yet while this stylization manifestly incorporates toxic masculinity's characteristic sadism toward those who capitulate to civilizing constraints, its less acknowledged masochistic valence warrants critical and theoretical attention. In pursuing this line of inquiry in the next section, I will amplify the figurative logic at stake in Freud's hints in the second chapter of *Beyond the Pleasure Principle* about the "mysterious masochistic trends" that foreshadow the emergence of the "death drive" in the fifth chapter, before I reassess the prospect of viewing toxic masculinity as a gendered death drive.

3   Second Nature and/as Freud's "Death Drive"

In *The Human Motor: Energy, Fatigue, and the Origins of Modernity* (1992), Anson Rabinbach historicizes the scientific-materialist notion of a "unity of matter and motion in energy [that] succeeded in erasing the distinction between [work and energy]" (1992: 5). As Rabinbach notes, this central doctrine spurred the efforts of physiologists, social hygienists, engineers, psychologists, and social reformers "for whom fatigue represented the threshold of human limitation" but one that society "should strive to bring under the control of medicine, technology and politics" (1992: 44). The trope of a "human motor" geared toward conserving energy and forestalling entropy hereafter conjoins an emerging positivist orientation in the still incipient social sciences of the late nineteenth-century with the middle-class fantasy of "a body without fatigue" (1992: 44).[26]

Rabinbach's intellectual history of the human motor trope valuably contextualizes a figurative logic that shapes shifting understandings of science across multiple disciplines still in their early stages in the late 19th and early 20th centuries when Freud was formulating his most fundamental concepts. Indeed, as Jean Laplanche (1989) has shown, Freud's conspicuous endeavors to constitute psychoanalysis as a science borrow from multiple sources – whatever facilitates his thinking. In effect, then scientific ideas that might have been briefly current or already outmoded at the time surface along with citations of philosophy and literature as metapsychological figures or bridges between concepts. Because figurative logics cannot be assessed epistemologically as either "true" or "false," when turning to Freud, a conventional focus on the plausibility of the evidence he provides for causal claims breaks down. The question his interdisciplinary bricolage poses to contemporary readers is therefore similar to literature's: does his assemblage of figures resonate with our experience and expand our understanding of symptomatic behavior, or not?

Freud makes prominent recourse to the human motor trope in *Beyond the Pleasure Principle*, where the titular concept indebted to G.T. Fechner regulates a psychophysical apparatus that produces "pleasure" by neutralizing "unpleasure" defined as excess tension. In accordance with Freud's insistence on the "economic" valence of his trauma theory, his extenuation of the pleasure principle implies that if the management of this excess overwhelms the system, then its capacity for other kinds of work is strained and entropy results.

After introducing the repetition compulsion in war veterans' nightmares as disconcerting evidence against his repressed wish thesis from the *Traumdeutung*, Freud hints at the death drive in the second chapter of *Beyond the Pleasure Principle* when he alludes to the "mysteriously masochistic trends of the ego" (SE XVIII: 14). While this insinuation is not unpacked before the fifth chapter, Freud's "mysteriously masochistic trends" emerge from his analysis of what he refers to as his grandson Ernst's *"fort-da* game," which the

---

26   Rabinbach (1992) provides me with a means of bridging the Frankfurt School configuration of "second nature" with Freud's language for the death drive when he contends that Horkheimer and Adorno align positivism with "the attributes of inorganic nature" at the same time as it models "its method and goals on the social project of conquering and dominating nature" (16).

psychoanalyst mainly interprets as an active symbolization of the infant's passively-incurred anxiety when his mother leaves the room. At this juncture, the "mysterious trends" reference presages the seemingly self-destructive edge of compulsive repetition that otherwise appears to carry out the pleasure principle's conventional thermodynamic goal by gradually emptying out an event's traumatic charge, thereby creating the economic conditions for a sense of psychological mastery on a preconscious or conscious level. Yet this explanation does not appear to satisfy Freud, who feels impelled to look deeper still into the very origins of life and death as *evolutions* that he must first invent in order to discover.

Commenting on the "conservative" disposition of the drives for which the death drive seemingly serves as both an origin and a model, Freud argues that the "goal of life" cannot be a new, never yet realized state but rather an "*old state of things, an initial state from which the living entity has at one time or other departed and to which it is striving to return by the circuitous paths along which its development leads.*" Freud hereby arrives at the following pronouncement: "If we are to take it as a truth that knows no exception that everything living dies for *internal* reasons – becomes inorganic once again – then we shall be compelled to say that *'the aim of all life is death'* and, looking backwards, that *'inanimate things existed before living ones'*" (XVIII: 38).

The psychoanalyst cobbles an awkwardly mixed image here. Though it is inert, a corpse is not genuinely "inorganic," since only organic life can die; nevertheless, Freud metonymically associates death with the tension-free "inanimacy" of the inorganic (SE XVIII: 38). He hereafter postulates an evolution whereby "the qualities of life were at some time evoked [*die Eigenschaften des Lebenden erweckt*] in inanimate matter by the action of a force of whose nature we can form no conception [*ganz unvorstellbare Krafteinwirkung*]." It is, then, the tension created by this mysterious introduction of force into "what had hitherto been an inanimate substance," which, according to Freud, "endeavoured to cancel itself out [*sich abzugleichen*]" (SE XVIII: 38; GS XIII: 40). Freud thus stages the "phylogenesis" of an urge to revert to lifelessness as the *first* drive ["*es war der erste Trieb gegeben, der, zum Leblosen zurückzukehren*"] (SE XVIII: 38; GS XIII: 40).[27]

Goaded by "ever more complicated *détours*," Freud speculates that his paradigmatic organism is diverted from immediately reaching its aim to revert to an inorganic thing-like numbness by purging *all* systemic tension (SE XVIII: 39).

---

27   Freud emphasizes the "*conservative* nature of living substance" (SE XVIII: 36) before visualizing the paradox elaborated above whereby life's awakening triggers an organism's counteractive urge to revert to pre-organic inertia.

It is this paradoxical figuration of *life* as the 'circuitous paths' through which a being "ward[s] off any possible ways of returning to inorganic existence other than those which are immanent in the organism itself" that resolves Freud's titular mystery about what lies beyond the pleasure principle: the death drive is, at once, an economic reaction against the trauma of life and a *primal fate* inscribed preternaturally in the very *substance* of living matter (SE XVIII: 39). And it is here, then, that we also come to an inescapable paradox: a systemic compulsion to conserve energy by reverting to inorganic calm might be the ultimate defense against stress-induced entropy, but it would be a Pyrrhic victory for death on life's behalf.

The metonymy Freud orchestrates between death, calcification, the inanimate, and the inorganic illuminates the potentially psychoanalytic presentiment of the Frankfurt School's conception of reification as a product of a death-driven second nature. To flesh out this connection, it is worth recalling Freud's earlier evocation of the inorganic from the fourth chapter of *Beyond*. This previous recourse is crucial to Freud's parable about a "little fragment of living substance suspended in the middle of an external world charged with the most powerful energies" (SE XVIII: 27). He tells us that this organism would be killed "if it were not provided with a protective shield [*Reizschutz*] against stimuli" (SE XVIII: 27; GS XIII: 26). By virtue of its contact with the stimuli barrage, Freud contends, the "outermost surface ceases to have the structure proper to living matter, becomes to some degree inorganic and thenceforward functions as a special envelope or membrane resistant to stimuli." Freud celebrates this "death" as a noble sacrifice that safeguards "all of the deeper [layers] from a similar fate," unless the external forces are sufficiently intense to breach the shield, which transpires in instances of trauma. In addition, the protective skin "must above all endeavor to preserve the special modes of transformation of energy operating in it against the effects threatened by the enormous energies at work in the external world." In suggesting that such preservation encourages "a leveling out [*gleichmachenden*] of [these external energies] and hence toward destruction" (SE XVIII: 27; GS XIII: 27), Freud's fable about the genesis of the simplest life form's "'baked through'" crust (SE XVIII: 26) also foreshadows the death drive's numbing work.

Reading further, we find this fable operating as an analogy: it prefigures Freud's "first topography" in which the selective and protective perceptual-conscious system [Pcpt.-Cs.][28] corresponds to the vesicle's quasi-inorganic

---

28   As J.B. Pontalis and Jean Laplanche state, Freud's *topographical* standpoint "implies a differentiation of the psychical apparatus into a number of subsystems" with "distinct characteristics or functions and a specific position vis-à-vis the others, so that they may

outer skin whereas permanent traces are confined to the depths. How Freud visualizes the development of the vesicle's coarsened membrane implies that the perceptual-conscious system is not merely *deadened* by a stimuli barrage, but that it becomes, itself, *deadening* in its function to protect the inner layers from an onslaught of stimuli; in this respect, its fate harbingers Freud's inauguration of the death drive in the fifth chapter, where he once again associates inorganic matter with death.

Even though there is no reference to Freud's "little vesicle" in the *Dialectic*, as Adorno's correspondence with Benjamin attests, the former would have been familiar with the latter's treatment of it from "On Some Motifs in Baudelaire." In this context, Benjamin does not seem to be interested in the Freudian death drive's masochistic valence, which, indeed, he never mentions. In the third section of "On Some Motifs," Freud's *Bläschen* from the fourth chapter of *Beyond* serves instead to illustrate the value of Marcel Proust's distinction between voluntary and involuntary memory from *In Search of Lost Time* as the literary reproof to an "ahistorical" Henri Bergson.[29] In this context, Freud's vesicle of living substance herewith becomes emblematic of the destructive impacts of modernity upon perception, experience, and memory that displace *Erfahrung* (long-term collective experience imbricated in tradition) with *Erlebnisse* (fleeting experiences). Adopting Freud's "assumption that 'emerging consciousness takes the place of a memory trace,'" leads Benjamin citing Freud to a "basic formula" to the effect that "'becoming conscious and leaving behind a memory

---

be treated, metaphorically speaking, as points in a psychical space which is susceptible of figurative representation." Laplanche and Pontalis identify two topographies in Freud's configuration of the psyche. In the first, which I am referencing above, Freud distinguishes between the *Unconscious, Preconscious* and *Conscious*, "each of which has its own function, type of process, cathectic energy and specific ideational contents" (1973: 449 and 450–451). The second comprises the three agencies of *id*, or the "instinctual pole of the personality"; the *ego* "which puts itself forward as representative of the whole person, and which, as such, is cathected by narcissistic libido"; and the *super-ego*, "or agency of judgment and criticism, constituted by the internalisation of parental demands and prohibitions" (1973: 452). Freud functionally delineates the first topography in *Beyond the Pleasure Principle* when he contends that "excitatory processes that occur in *other* systems leave permanent traces behind in them which form the foundation of memory." At the same time, he rejects the prospect that stimuli leave such traces in the perceptual-conscious system which, as he infers, must retain a capacity "for receiving fresh excitations." In effect, then, apart from unexpected and overwhelming events that Freud classifies as traumatic, "excitatory processes do not leave behind any permanent change in [the conscious-system's] elements but expire, as it were, in the phenomenon of becoming conscious" (SE XVIII: 24–25).

29   See Ball 2015, "In Search of Lost Community: The Literary Image between 'Proust' and 'Baudelaire' in Walter Benjamin's Modernization Lament".

trace are incompatible processes within one and the same system'" (Benjamin V4: 317).

Additionally crucial to Benjamin's argument is Freud's characterization of the perceptual-conscious system for which *"protection against* stimuli is almost more important than the *reception* of stimuli" (Freud XVIII: 27). This insistence on the thermodynamic limits of the system for sorting external stimuli bolsters Benjamin's expansion of Freud's trauma theory to enunciate the "threat of shocks" proliferated by modernity. In this vein, Benjamin reads between the second chapter of *Beyond the Pleasure Principle* where Freud identifies the shock that results from a lack of preparedness as a crucial element of trauma and the fourth chapter where he demarcates a functionally-differentiated first topography. Hence Benjamin's extrapolation that "[t]he more readily consciousness registers these shocks, the less likely they are to have a traumatic effect" (Benjamin 4: 317). In short, shocks intensify the habit-hardened selectivity that distinguishes modern defenses against a potentially damaging stimuli siege whereas an aptitude for integrating them preempts it.

As is well known, Benjamin honors Baudelaire's poetry for "parrying" these shocks, thereby dramatizing the historicity of a shift in the reception of lyric poetry, which loses its audience as capitalist modernity's increasingly defensive perceptual apparatus favors (fleeting) *Erlebnisse* at the expense of (collective) *Erfahrung*. For Benjamin, the selective-and-protective function that Freud ascribes to the perceptual-conscious system inclines moderns toward fleeting experiences because it buffers the force of the stimuli that enter it. This operation privileges the kind of stimuli that pass through without being absorbed. Reading between Baudelaire, Proust, and Freud, Benjamin infers that perceptual "hardening" diminishes responsiveness and flexibility; henceforth, a *regression* of our defenses is required to permit the prospect of unexpected emergences such as the irruption of "involuntary memory," Proust's literary (and deconstructive) correlate to Bergson's "pure memory."[30]

Although Horkheimer and Adorno do not cite Freud's vesicle story, in the "Elements of Anti-Semitism" chapter in the *Dialectic*, they seem to echo Benjamin's mediation of this image as support for his claim about a deadened perceptual-conscious system that proliferates *Erlebnisse* over and against *Erfahrung*. As "consciousness itself succumbed to a process of reification [*Verdinglichung*]," Horkheimer and Adorno observe, "[c]ulture was entirely

---

30   As I argue in "In Search of Lost Community" (2015), the conspicuousness of the artifice entailed by Proust's magisterial depiction of "involuntary memory" in *In Search of Lost Time* belies the alleged spontaneity of its tea-soaked madeleine triggered resurgence, thereby deconstructing the opposition between involuntary and voluntary memory.

commoditized, disseminated as information which did not permeate those who acquired it." As a result, "[t]hought becomes short-winded, confines itself to apprehending isolated facts" while "[i]ntellectual connections are rejected as an inconvenient and useless exertion." Once the "developmental moment in thought, its whole genetic and intensive dimension, is forgotten and leveled down [*nivelliert*] to what is immediately present, to the extensive," the conditions for critical reflection that counteracts paranoia have already been preempted (2002: 163/2000: 207).[31]

While neither Benjamin nor Horkheimer and Adorno mention the death drive, there is a striking overlap in the poetics of their thinking about the modern decay of perceptual flexibility that recalls Benjamin's Freud recourse from his "Motifs." The figurative connection I am accentuating here is the identity between reification and internal hardening, and sensory and affective calcification as such. Benjamin takes up this motif explicitly in his attention to Freud's phylogenetic figuration of a deadened and quasi-inorganic "cortical layer" from his primal *bläschen* parable recounting the evolution of functional differentiation between the perceptual-conscious system (*Pcpt.-Cs.*) and the psyche's "deeper layers," including what the psychoanalyst refers to as the unconscious-system. As presented in the *Dialectic*, the concept of reification as second nature presumes that such "deadening" does, indeed, leak into interior domains. This figurative logic is manifest in poetic language that resonates with Freud's imagery but with at least one crucial difference: in keeping with Nietzsche's and Benjamin's emplotments of Western consciousness, Horkheimer and Adorno reconstitute death-driven numbness as an *adaptation* to the demand for conformity under capitalism rather than as a phylogenetic antecedent.

Second nature and the death drive might be read as coinciding again as Horkheimer and Adorno excoriate identitarian thinking and thus transfigure Freud's theory of primary and secondary narcissism into *ratio*. In this connection, it is helpful to remember that, for Freud, primary narcissism involves the immediacy of self-love represented by the *ideal-ich* (ideal ego) before the impact of socialization while secondary narcissism oriented by the *ich-ideal* (ego ideal) amalgamates and interiorizes familial and institutional demands as a regulative fiction. Pivotal here is Freud's proposition from the 1914 "Introduction on Narcissism" essay (2001d) that secondary narcissism

---

31   Critical reflection is doomed when "[t]he present order of life allows the self no scope to draw intellectual or spiritual conclusions" (Horkheimer and Adorno 2002: 163). On the motif of paranoia in the *Dialectic of Enlightenment* see Ball 2005, "Paranoia in the Age of the World Picture: the Global 'Limits of Enlightenment.'"

spurs the need to bolster self-love and avoid ostracism by meeting expectations; it depends, in Lacanian terms, on internalizing the Other's gaze.

Freud's "secondary narcissism" definition structurally resonates with
Nietzsche's bad conscience, since an inculcated need to perform sovereignty
impels promise-making subjects to identify with calculability as a behavioral
standard. Echoing Nietzsche, the Frankfurt School links the need to perform
sovereignty with an investment in self-sameness, yet such unity is impossible
(as the psychoanalytic theory of the drives presumes), and its appearance must
be continually resignified. Sadomasochism attends this anxiety-limned performance to the extent that subjects punish themselves along with everyone else
whose simulation of coherent self-mastery remains unpersuasive.

Critically alluding to Kant, Horkheimer and Adorno treat the longing for
unified consciousness as a modern symptom. This longing defines a subject
that learns "how to impart a synthetic unity not only to the outward impres-
sions but to the inward ones which gradually separate themselves from them,"
and, in so doing, "retroactively constitute the self. The identical ego is," thus,
"the most recent constant product of projection" (2002: 155).

In the third chapter of *Beyond*, Freud offers a potential explanation for this
identitarian projection in noting that the conscious and unconscious ego's
resistance to change "operates under the sway of the pleasure principle: it
seeks to avoid the unpleasure which would be produced by the liberation of
the repressed" (SE XVIII: 20). If the goal of treatment, in contrast, is to encourage "the toleration of that unpleasure through an appeal to the reality principle" (20), then it is forestalled by the provenance of the compulsion to repeat
in "the unconscious repressed" (20). From a phylogenetic standpoint, the
implication is that economic functions are unconscious: the systemic need to
defuse excess tension nonvoluntarily spurs repetition that will wear it down;
on an ontogenetic level, unconsciously mobilized repetition seems to indicate
an urge to (return to and) stay the same at all costs: to remain numbly inert
(like death) rather than work through one's pain.

To the extent that compulsive repetition signals the blunting work of the
death drive as a radicalized pleasure principle, it evokes the identitarian circu-
larity that Horkheimer and Adorno following Nietzsche decry.[32] Further material for this connection emerges in a dense footnote at the end of the sixth
chapter of *Beyond*, where Freud charts the shifts in his *Trieblehre* between the
"Introduction: On Narcissism" from 1914, "Instincts and their Vicissitudes" from

---

32   See in particular Nietzsche's "On Truth and Lie in an Extra-Moral Sense" (Nietzsche
      1976ryt).

1915, and his conjuring of the life and death drives in 1920. A close reading of this note reveals a slippage between the ego drives and the death drive (SE XVIII: 60–61). Very briefly, after recalling his opposition between the narcissistic ego and the sexual object drives, Freud posits a new dualism between Eros and Thanatos, or the life and death drives respectively. While it makes sense to unite the survival instinct with the urge to reproduce the species under the life drive, there is an unexplained potential alignment between the former ego drives and the new death drive, which I interpret as follows. What if the Freudian death drive is mobilized on behalf of the unconscious ego's investment in self-sameness – in performing sovereignty as reliability and calculability over and against the changes that fracture the primary narcissistic fiction of coherent unity? Extrapolating to the Frankfurt School theory of reification as second nature, we might now see how the capitalist demand for calculable productivity entails consistent emotional suppression that is facilitated by internal hardening. As the "professional" masters affects by deadening them, they preserve energy for more work while smoothing the paths of others pursuing the same or related ends. To the extent that heteropatriarchal capitalism not only performs this figurative logic but upholds it as a norm, it *ontologizes the death drive*.[33] "What we are left with," in Freud's words, "is the fact that the organism wishes to die only in its own fashion" (SE XVIII: 39).

In "The Elements of Anti-Semitism" chapter of the *Dialectic of Enlightenment*, Horkheimer and Adorno echo Nietzsche in contending that "self-preservation as a natural drive like other impulses, has a bad conscience." As they emphasize, "only bustling efficiency and the institutions created to serve it – mediation, apparatus, organization, systematization as ends in themselves – enjoy the esteem, in practice as in theory, of being deemed reasonable" (2002: 72). In this instrumental context, the stoic ideal of silent mastery exacerbates a rational ego image that "has been forged by hardening itself against" the anxious self-preservative behaviors associated with "first nature" (2002: 148). From the standpoint of this ideal, then, "any emotion is finally embarrassing" because it betrays the incompleteness of internalized domination (149).

Along with Nietzsche, Freud's emplotment for "uncanny" returns of the repressed seemingly infuses Horkheimer and Adorno's revision in the "Elements of Antisemitism" chapter of Benjamin's and Roger Caillois'

---

33 Rethinking toxic masculinity as an expression of a second-natural death drive might benefit from a reassessment of Herbert Marcuse's concept of *surplus repression* from *Eros and Civilization* (1974) where he defines it as an over-adaptation to capitalist modernity.

respective variations on an anthropological mimesis motif.[34] "What repels [the blinded] as alien is all too familiar," according to Horkheimer and Adorno, insofar as it comprises signs of a repudiated and punished first nature. The paranoid self-hatred that results from such repression goads those "blinded by civilization" to lose contact with their own first-natural fear except "through certain gestures and forms of behavior they encounter in others, as isolated, shameful residues in their rationalized environment" (2002: 149). Freud's primal death drive thus appears to resurface here in Horkheimer and Adorno's second-natural compulsion to annihilate any symptoms of "regression" to a first-natural survival anxiety: "These numb human reactions are archaic patterns of self-preservation: the tribute life pays for its continued existence is adaptation to death" (2002:148).

But what could it possibly mean to "adapt" to death? Horkheimer and Adorno declare that "[p]rotection as petrified terror is a form of camouflage. Where the human seeks to resemble nature, at the same time it hardens itself against it" (2002: 148). By recoding such "hardening" as a mode of reification, Horkheimer and Adorno recast Nietzsche's "mastery of affects" as camouflage in a technological society, a mimetic defense against socioeconomic survival threats that parallels Freud's paradoxical origin story for the death drive's emergence as a defensive reaction against the traumatic introduction of life itself. In Horkheimer and Adorno's Marxist version of this story, the fetishism of science as "observed regularity" is a form of compulsive repetition that manifests itself in stereotypes and everyday life. The internalization of this compulsion is, thus, "an adaptation to lifelessness in the service of self-preservation" that automates "mental processes," thereby converting them "into blind sequences." As human expressions become "both controllable and compulsive," we see how

---

34   In the opening paragraph of "On the Mimetic Faculty," Benjamin proclaims the human "gift for seeing similarity [as] nothing but a rudiment of the once powerful compulsion to become similar and to behave mimetically. There is perhaps not a single one of [man's] higher functions in which his mimetic faculty does not play a decisive role" (1999: 720). Michael Taussig notes that Roger Caillois' "memorable essay on mimesis," "Mimicry and Legendary Psychasthenia," originally appeared in "the noted Surrealist journal, *Minotaure*, in 1935 (two years after Benjamin wrote his piece on mimesis [entitled "On the Mimetic Faculty"], in Paris too)." Taussig thumbnails the essay as follows: "In a dizzying journey through insect biology, aesthetics of excess, theories of sympathetic magic, and the miming body as a self-sculpting camera, Caillois suggests that mimesis is a matter of 'being tempted by space,' a drama in which the self is but a self-diminishing point amid others, losing its boundedness" (1993: 33–34). Unfortunately, despite its importance, I will need to defer a longer exploration of this complex motif to a future essay. See Roger Caillois, "Mimicry and Legendary Psychasthenia" (1984) and Michael Taussig, *Mimesis and Alterity: A Particular History of the Senses* (1993).

"the blind mastery of nature, which is identical to farsighted instrumentality" reveals itself, in Horkheimer and Adorno's figuration, to be death-driven: "all that remains of the adaptation to nature is the hardening against it" (149).

4   Toxic Implantation(s)

It bears mentioning again that Freud's first topography as evinced in his "little vesicle" parable analogizes a functionally differentiated economy that must set aside energy to support the perceptual-conscious system's selective protection against external stimuli to save the deeper layers. It is in this respect that Freud's evolutionary account of the stimuli barrage-hardened membrane's economic function overlaps with the Marxist motif of internal compartmentalization as an impact of ubiquitous rationalization.[35] To the extent that Horkheimer and Adorno anthropologize the bourgeois stoic's emotional coldness as a second-natural regression to mimicry in a technological society, they also recognize how the little vesicle's deadened cortical layer has moved *inside*.

The question remains as to what lessons, if any, the Frankfurt School's treatment of the internal hardness motif might offer to an understanding of the masculinist disposition associated with the term *toxic masculinity*. In the interests of taking critical distance from this gender cliché, I have positioned Horkheimer and Adorno's recourse to Nietzsche's second nature concept as a revision of the Marxist-sociological theory of reification. I have also sought to illustrate how Freud's death drive imagery sheds light on the figurative logic of Nietzsche's "mastery of affects" insight at the crux of his definition of bad conscience as well as Horkheimer and Adorno's view of stoicism, and bourgeois coldness as such. The poetics of this configuration delineate interior hardening as the byproduct of a second-natural adaptation to the forces of

---

35   Horkheimer and Adorno specifically comment on Freud's second topography of the ego, id, and superego as a refraction of a functionally differentiated economy: "The psychological small business – the individual – is meeting the same fate [as the old-style specialist shop expropriated by the department store]. It came into being as the power cell of economic activity. Emancipated from the tutelage of earlier economic stages, individuals fended for themselves alone: as proletarians by hiring themselves out through the labor market and by constant adaptation to new technical conditions, as entrepreneurs by tirelessly realizing of the ideal type of *homo oeconomicus*. Psychoanalysis has portrayed the internal small business which thus came into being as a complex dynamic of unconscious and conscious elements, of id, ego, and superego [...]. The subjects of the drive economy are being psychologically expropriated, and the drive economy is being more rationally operated by society itself" (2002: 168).

domination: cis-gendered men's *ressentiment* against supposed incursions upon their sense of entitlement is based on a secondary-narcissistic ideal of decisiveness, unquestioned authority, stoic containment and "silent strength" as such, a repressive deformation of emotional life that spurs a hatred of vulnerability and justifies their privilege in a hierarchy of weak and emotionally "leaky" others who fail to sustain this death-driven mimicry of *ratio*. Since anyone who expresses emotional complexity or who requires compassion bears the potential to rattle those in thrall to stoic restraints, toxic-masculines are often identified by their sadistic tendency to lash out angrily – not only at their gendered, sexual, racial, religious, and national others but at other men who do not consistently perform emotional aloofness.

At the same time, if we focus too much on emotional impenetrability fetishism as a defining feature of toxic masculinity, we miss the broader perspective implied by Horkheimer and Adorno's denunciation of stoicism. In referring to it as a "bourgeois philosophy," Horkheimer and Adorno repudiate stoicism for making it "easier for the privileged to look what threatens them in the eye by dwelling on the suffering of others. It affirms the general," they write, "by elevating private existence, as protection from it, to the status of a principle. The private sphere of the bourgeois is an upper-class cultural asset which has come down in the world" (2002: 76).[36] One implication is that stoicism is, at once, a déclassé virtue and a regressive mimesis of automation in a technological society; another is that emotional coldness is a death-driven reaction formation against suffering. The more brutally this society abandons certain populations to precarity, the more paranoid and "toxic" self-loathing will become among those whom the heteropatriarchy once revered as sovereign agents of survival.

Finally, the figurative logic whereby Horkheimer and Adorno convert Nietzsche's critique of second nature into a theory of reification illuminates the toxic-masculine type's enmeshment in a narcissistic misrecognition of first-natural aggression as the content of "true" sovereignty. If the will to power is perceived as an expropriated entitlement, then its domestication generates self-loathing, paranoia, and *ressentiment*. At the same time, when Freud portrays the deadening of a primal organism's cortical layer as a "sacrifice" made on behalf of the system's capacity for work, this sacrifice loses its presumed nobility when it re-emerges as a death-driven repetition geared toward leveling out

---

36   It should be pointed out that Horkheimer and Adorno do not restrict stoicism as mimicry to antisemitic gentiles insofar as it also operates as a vehicle of assimilation for the Jewish bourgeoisie. As Horkheimer and Adorno acknowledge, "whenever they sacrificed their difference to the prevailing mode, the successfully adapted Jews took on in exchange the cold, stoical character which existing society imposes on human beings" (*Dialectic* 138).

the trauma of life itself. To the extent that Horkheimer and Adorno's critique of bourgeois stoicism lambasts internal hardening as a regression into mimicry in an increasingly automated world, a seething performance of emotional containment might strike us as outmoded, if not also as an uncanny return of the repressed. In its exaggerated campaign against vulnerability and compassion, toxic masculinity potentially attests to the rise of a third nature taking revenge on a death-driven society that no longer venerates the sovereignty of the sacrifice it requires.

References

Adorno, Theodor W. 1973. "Die Idee der Naturgeschichte." *Gesammelte Schriften* Band 1: *Philosophische Frühschritten*. Ed. Rolf Tiedemann. Frankfurt am Main: Suhrkamp Verlag. 345–365.

Adorno, Theodor W. 1973a. *Negative Dialectics*. Trans. E.B. Ashton. Seabury, New York.

Adorno, Theodor W., Else Frenkel-Brunswik, Daniel J. Levinson, and R. Nevitt Sanford 2019. *The Authoritarian Personality*. Verso.

Agamben, Giorgio. 1998. *Homo Sacer: Sovereign Power and Bare Life*. Trans. Daniel Heller-Roazen. Stanford University Press.

Agamben, Giorgio. 1999. *Remnants of Auschwitz: the Witness and the Archive*. Trans. Daniel Heller-Roazen. Zone Books.

Agamben, Giorgio. 2005. *State of Exception*. Trans. Kevin Attell. University of Chicago Press.

Ball, Karyn. 2006. "A Democracy Is Being Beaten." *English Studies in Canada* 32.1: 45–76.

Ball, Karyn. 2015. "In Search of Losat Community: the Literary Image Between 'Proust' and 'Baudelaire' in Walter Benjamin's Modernization Lament." *Humanities* 4: 149–180; doi:10.3390/h4010149.

Ball, Karyn. 2005. "Paranoia in the Age of the World Picture: the Global 'Limits of Enlightenment.'" *Cultural Critique* 61 (Fall 2005): 115–147.

Bederman, Gail. 1996. *Manliness and Civilization: a Cultural History of Gender and Race in the United States, 1880–1917*. University of Chicago Press.

Benjamin, Walter. 2003. "On Some Motifs in Baudelaire." In *Selected Writings Volume 4: 1938–1940*. Edited by Michael W. Jennings. Cambridge: Harvard University Press, 313–55.

Benjamin, Walter. 1999. "On the Mimetic Faculty." In *Selected Writings Volume 2: 1927–1934*. Edited by Michael W. Jennings, Howard Eiland, and Gary Smith. Translated by Rodney Livingstone and Others. Cambridge: Harvard University Press. 720–722.

Bennett, Jessica. 2022. "If Everything Is 'Trauma,' Is Anything?" *New York Times* (February 4, 2022). https://www.nytimes.com/2022/02/04/opinion/caleb-love -bombing-gaslighting-trauma.html.

Buck-Morss, Susan. 1979. *The Origin of Negative Dialectics: Theodor Adorno, Walter Benjamin, and the Frankfurt Institute.* Free Press.

Butler, Judith. 2004. *Precarious Life: the Powers of Mourning and Violence.* Verso.

Butler, Judith. 2010. *Frames of War: When Is Life Grievable?* Verso.

Caillois, Roger. 1984. "Mimicry and Legendary Psychasthenia." Trans. John Shepley. *October* 31 (winter 1984): 16–32.

DeNinno, Nadine. 2020. "Will.I.am Likens Trump Supporters to People in an AbusiveRelationship." *New York Post* (November 3, 2020). https://nypost.com/2020 /11/03/will-i-am-likens-trump-supporters-to-people-in-an-abusive-relationship/.

Devega, Chauncy. 2020. "Interview with Dr. Seth Norrholm: How to Survive the Physical, Financial, and Emotional Abuse of the Trump Era." *Salon* (December 21, 2020). https://www.salon.com/2020/12/21/dr-seth-norrholm-how-to-survive-the -physical-financial-and-emotional-abuse-of-the-trump-era/.

Esman, Abigail R. and Dahlia Lithwick. 2020. "America Is Attempting to Exit an Abusive Relationship: and It's When the Woman Finally Leaves that Things Tend to Get Violent." *Slate* (December 15, 2020). https://slate.com/news-and-politics/2020 /12/trump-america-abusive-relationship-exit.html.

Freud, Sigmund. 1999. *Jenseits des Lustprinzips.* In *Gesammelte Werke Volume XIII.* Frankfurt am Main: Fischer Taschenbuch Verlag. 1–66.

Freud, Sigmund. 1999a. "Das Ökonomische Problem des Masochismus." In *Gesammelte Werke Volume XIII.* Frankfurt am Main: Fischer Taschenbuch Verlag. 369–383.

Freud, Sigmund. 2001. *Beyond the Pleasure Principle.* In *The Standard Edition of the Complete Psychological Works of Sigmund Freud Volume XVIII (1920–1922).* Edited and translated by James Strachey in collaboration with Anna Freud. New York: Vintage, 1–64.

Freud, Sigmund. 2001a. *Civilization and Its Discontents.* In *The Standard Edition of the Complete Psychological Works of Sigmund Freud Volume XXI (1927–1931).* Edited and translated by James Strachey in collaboration with Anna Freud. New York: Vintage. 59–145.

Freud, Sigmund. 2001b. "The Economic Problem of Masochism." In *The Standard Edition of the Complete Psychological Works of Sigmund Freud Volume XIX (1923– 1925).* Edited and translated by James Strachey in collaboration with Anna Freud. New York: Vintage, 157–170.

Freud, Sigmund. 2001c. "Introduction: on Narcissism" and "Instincts and Their Vicissitudes." In *The Standard Edition of the Complete Psychological Works of Sigmund Freud Volume XIX (1914–1916).* Edited and translated by James Strachey in collaboration with Anna Freud. New York: Vintage, 67–102 and 105–139.

Gay, Peter. 1984. *Freud: a Life for Our Time*. New York: Norton.

Horkheimer, Max and Theodor W. Adorno. 2000. *Dialektik der Aufklärung: Philosophische Fragmente*. Fischer Taschenbuch Verlag.

Horkheimer, Max and Theodor W. Adorno. 1972. *Dialectic of Enlightenment: Philosophical Fragments*. Trans. John Cumming. New York, NY: Herder and Herder.

Horkheimer, Max and Theodore W. Adorno. 2002. *Dialectic of Enlightenment: Philosophical Fragments*. Ed. Gunzelin Schmid Noerr. Trans. Edmund Jephcott. Stanford University Press.

Kendi, Ibram X. 2019. "Trump Is in an Abusive Relationship with America." *The Atlantic* (August 1, 2019) https://www.theatlantic.com/ideas/archive/2019/08/trump-doe snt-really-love-america/595231/.

Kippart, Amanda. 2021. "A Guide to Gaslighting: a Comprehensive Look at this Confusing Tactic That Makes You Doubt Your Reality." *Domesticshelters.org* (October 20, 2021). https://www.domesticshelters.org/articles/ending-domestic-violence/a -guide-to-gaslighting?gclid=CjoKCQiAjJOQBhCkARIsAEKMtOoVpACQ-L2g_Ylc4 _UMvfniruVh3BFUVtYditfTQoH3QnNWdHIbgHAaAmQiEALw_wcB.

Laplanche, Jean. 1989. *New Foundations for Psychoanalysis*. Trans. David Macey. Blackwell.

Laplanche, Jean and J.B. Pontalis. 1973. *The Language of Psycho-Analysis*. Trans. Donald Nicholson Smith. New York: ww. Norton & Company.

Lee, Bandy X., Harper West, and Kevin Washington. 2020. "How to Escape Our Abusive Relationship with Trump." *The St. Louis American* (May 2, 2020). http://www .stlamerican.com/news/columnists/guest_columnists/how-to-escape-our-abus ive-relationship-with-trump/article_8398a8c0-8c93-11ea-a8c3-c36d17325c6a.html.

Lewis, Tanya. 2021. "The 'Shared Psychosis' of Donald Trump and His Loyalists: Forensic Psychiatrist Bandy X. Lee Explains the Outgoing President's Psychological Appeal and How to Wean People from It." *Scientific American* (January 11, 2021). https: //www.scientificamerican.com/article/the-shared-psychosis-of-donald-trump-and -his-loyalists/.

Mann, Bonnie. 2019. "Marie Yovanovich's Courage." *The New York Times* (10/19/2019) https://www.nytimes.com/2019/10/19/opinion/marie-yovanovitchs-moral-cour age.html.

Marcuse, Herbert. 1974. *Eros and Civilization: a Philosophical Inquiry into Freud*. Beacon Press.

Niazi, Amil. 2020. "Putting Trump behind Us Is Like Exiting an Abusive Relationship: It Takes Time." *The Guardian* (November 25, 2020). https://www.theguardian.com/us -news/2020/nov/25/trump-trauma-experts-abusive-relationship.

Nietzsche, Friedrich. 1976. "On Truth and Lie in an Extra-Moral Sense." In *The Portable Nietzsche*. Ed and Trans. Walter Kaufmann. New York: Viking Press. 42–47.

Nietzsche, Friedrich. 1969. "Second Essay: Guilt, Bad Conscience, and the Like." *On the Genealogy of Morals and Ecce Homo.* Translated and Edited with a commentary by Walter Kaufmann. Random House, 57–96.

North, Anna. 2021. "'People Are Not Okay': the Mental Health Impact of the Trump Era." *Vox* (January 28, 2021). https://www.vox.com/2021/1/28/22249273/trump-presidency-trauma-covid-19-2020-election.

Oppenheim, Maya. 2019. "Trump Administration 'rolling back women's rights by 50 years' by changing definitions of domestic violence and sexual assault." *Independent* (January 24, 2019). https://www.independent.co.uk/news/world/americas/trump-domestic-abuse-sexual-assault-definition-womens-rights-justice-department-a8744546.html.

Pearson, Elizabeth. 2019. "Extremism and toxic masculinity: the Man Question Reposed." *International Affairs* 95.6: 1251–1270.

Rabinbach, Anson. *The Human Motor: Energy, Fatigue, and the Origins of Modernity.* Berkeley, CA: University of California Press, 1992.

Romano, Aja. "What We Still Haven't Learned from Gamergate," *Vox* (updated January 7, 2021) https://www.vox.com/culture/2020/1/20/20808875/gamergate-lessons-cultural-impact-changes-harassment-laws.

Sarkis, Stephanie. 2018. "Donald Trump Is a Classic Gaslighter in an Abusive Relationship with America." *USA Today* (October 3, 2018) https://www.usatoday.com/story/opinion/2018/10/03/trump-classic-gaslighter-abusive-relationship-america-column/1445050002/.

Selvaratnam, Tanya. 2021. "America Has Been in an Abusive Relationship: This Is How We Get Out." (February 22, 2021) https://www.glamour.com/story/america-has-been-in-an-abusive-relationship-heres-how-we-get-out.

Tasker, Andrew. 2021. "GOP Gaslighting People about Covid, Election, Jan. 6." *Sun Journal* (August 3, 2021). https://www.sunjournal.com/2021/08/03/andrew-tasker-gop-gaslighting-people-about-covid-election-jan-6/.

Taussig, Michael. 1993. *Mimesis and Alterity: a Particular History of the Senses.* London: Routledge.

Theweleit, Klaus. 1987. *Male Fantasies Volume 1: Women, Floods, Bodies, History.* Trans. Stephen Conway in collaboration with Erica Carter and Chris Turner. Foreword by Barbara Ehrenreich. University of Minnesota Press.

Theweleit, Klaus. 1989. *Male Fantasies Volume 2 Male Bodies: Psychoanalyzing the White Terror.* Trans. Erica Carter and Chris Turner in collaboration with Stephen Conway. Foreword by Anson Rabinbach and Jessica Benjamin. University of Minnesota Press.

Tönnies, Ferdinand. 2002. *Community and Society.* Translated and edited by Charles P. Loomis. Mineola, New York: Dover Publications, Inc.

Waugaman, Richard. 1973. "The Intellectual Relationship between Nietzsche and Freud." *Psychiatry* (November 1973): 459–67.

PART 2

Power, Truth, and (Non)Identity

∵

CHAPTER 5

Marcuse's "Feminine Principle" and Non-binary Subversions

Mary Caputi

Much of the early Frankfurt School writings on the topics of gender and sexuality are infused with pessimism, arguing that the social construction of these topics in the West has been deleteriously impacted by capitalism. When the human body is read through the filter of market mechanisms, both masculinity and femininity answer to an instrumentalist mindset that pauperizes the lives of men and women. With sexuality, for instance, what might be an expression of love, desire, or simply attraction has been distorted by the intervening forces of economic exchange, reducing human values to market variables. And because capitalism's logic pervades so much of everyday life, we fail to recognize its commercializing influence even where intimacy is concerned. "Love for the prostitute is the apotheosis of empathy with the commodity," writes Walter Benjamin in his unfinished *Arcades Project* (Benjamin 1999: 511).

Both gender and sexuality's co-optation in Western culture is precisely what causes Herbert Marcuse to theorize the possibility of alternatives, that is, ways of experiencing the body that resist the logic of capitalism and its attendant repression. In *Eros and Civilization: a Philosophical Inquiry into Freud,* Marcuse introduces the concept of the "feminine principle" which offers a way out of this co-optation (Marcuse 1974 [1955]). Under changed socio-economic relations less driven by market forces and competitive, accumulative values, he argues that a new "feminine" principle contravenes the premise that the body's meaning resides in its dutiful, output-driven delivery. Less called on to perform in the workplace thanks to rearranged economic organization, the body would no longer exist solely as an instrument of labor, a means of achieving the demands of the market; rather, with capitalist values attenuated by left-leaning principles, a new experience of love and desire would rescue human subjectivity from its current state of alienation. Under such changed material conditions, the demanding "work-world" of civilization would not exert such a dominant force, Marcuse insists, such that repression and gratification, toil and pleasure, would no longer exist as starkly polarized opposites.

Throughout *Eros and Civilization,* Marcuse thus argues against the Freudian claim that repression and its attendant malaise represent the inevitable victors of the civilized world. For Freud, it is internalized taboo, law-inducing moral strictures, and deferred gratification that safeguard culture against the unlawful impulses and transgressive desires of the body. Expressions of aggression and sexual desire are especially curtailed by civilization's "reality principle," according to Freud, which thwarts the release and gratification sought by the potentially subversive "pleasure principle." In sum, civilization necessitates repression: the more civilized the society, the more repression it presupposes. Yet for Marcuse, this erroneous premise demands revisiting since he remains unconvinced that a flourishing culture rests upon such exigencies, or that taboo constitutes civilization's defining element.

Epitomized in the figures of Orpheus, the mesmerizing lute player, Narcissus, the beautiful youth in love with himself, and Pandora, the first mortal woman, the feminine principle opposes the work-world of civilization; it stands for an immediate and ample fulfilment that need not be acquired through labor and deferred gratification. Instead of the "workism" that has only become increasingly pronounced in our globalized, neoliberal economy, it invokes an "aesthetic dimension," a receptive fluidity which resonates with the "negative," a-systematic quality of Adorno's negative dialectics.[1] The aesthetic dimension stands in contrast to the formal logic of instrumental rationality that is grounded in *ratio*'s reductionist, calculated thinking of equivalences and formulae; in other words, it stands opposed to those aspects of Enlightenment rationality that Max Horkheimer and Theodor Adorno most repudiate in *Dialectic of Enlightenment* (2002 [1944]). These reductionist principles, *ratio*'s instrumental logic of equivalences, are what caused the Enlightenment's project to turn back on itself and deliver not expansiveness but domination; not a rational and comfortable world, but one characterized by violence, irrationality, and disaster; not a more humane civilization, but – amidst European fascism – a nightmare.

Conversely, the aesthetic principle that Marcuse endorses privileges a dialectical, intuitive sense that resists the logical reductionism of the analytic mind, and remains more open to difference and the incommensurate possibilities of a-systematic thought. Thus, resisting the one-to-one identifications of formal logic, Marcuse's feminine principle eschews closed, binary systems and the rigidity of structuralism in favor of "the image of joy and fulfilment; the voice which does not command but sings; the gesture of receptivity which offers and receives; the deed which is peace and ends the labor of conquest"

---

1 For a discussion of "workism," see Derek Thompson, "Workism Is Making Americans Miserable," *The Atlantic*, February 24, 2019, https://www.theatlantic.com/ideas/archive/2019/02/religion-workism-making-americans-miserable/583441/, accessed October 27, 2021.

(Marcuse 1974 [1955]:162). In the context of the twenty-first century, this principle allows for values having nothing to do with the globalized neoliberal enterprise, instead making room for connection and receptivity, reparations toward the earth and toward injured populations, and an ethos of sustainability rather than constant economic growth.[2]

Yet on balance, the optimism of Marcuse's feminine principle – both gendered and sexual – surely stands overshadowed by other early Frankfurt School texts wherein the calculating, formal logic of instrumental rationality appears to triumph over an aesthetically grounded sensibility. Reading *Eros and Civilization,* a mid-twentieth century text, in the context of today's economic system marked by dramatic inequalities of wealth, increased poverty, and a squeezed middle class, one wonders whether his optimism has any hope of revival. The neoliberal logic of the market seems to permeate all aspects of life in the West such that working harder, "smarter," and longer with ever-increasing productivity appears as an unquestioned desirable objective. With computers, smartphones, and social media as staples of everyday life, we are constantly reminded of the neoliberal ethos that seeks constant growth and a constantly refreshed capitalist expansion. At the extreme, one wonders whether our culture is even aware of the extent to which the logic of exchange has extinguished the aesthetic dimension now occluded by global capitalism's extensive reach.

Perhaps there is hope. Might the contemporary celebration of gender and sexual *fluidity,* the refusal to be caught in a binary that constrains and confines the traditional interpretation of these categories, suggest the possibility of a revived optimism? Contemporary culture has moved eminently beyond binaries and now embraces an array of identifying possibilities that confuse and confound standard readings of male and female, masculine and feminine, hetero- and homosexual. With welcome and celebrated confusion, the resultant mêlée embodied in LGBTQIA2S+ perhaps frees the human body from the regulations of formal logic, since the intellectual strictures that governed for so long are now loosened. Today's many articulations of alternative identities – trans, genderqueer, nonbinary, two spirited, a-gendered – surely operate to undermine the West's time-honored categories that bolster closed intellectual systems such as heteronormativity, and thus dissolve the body's commodification to which Benjamin refers. And if fluidity challenges if not replaces

---

2   There exists a copious literature on the topic of economic degrowth and sustainability. See especially Serge Latouche, *Farewell to Growth,* translated by David Macey, Cambridge, UK: Polity Press, 2009; Ekaterina Cherkovskya, Alexander Paulsson, and Stefania Barca, *Toward a Political Economy of Degrowth,* Lanham, MD: Rowman & Littlefield, 2019.

traditional gender and sexual binaries, the resultant a-systematic reading of things may well usher in an ideology unaligned with instrumental rationality, one closer to Marcuse's feminine principle that can operate beyond the constraints of taboo, proscription, and a life heavy with restrictions.

But does the new gender and sexual fluidity go that far? Do they *undo* binaries as they currently exist in ways invocative of Marcuse's aesthetic dimension and Adorno's negative dialectics? In this chapter, I first examine early Frankfurt School authors' pessimism regarding sexuality, pressing the issue of how sexual expression remains constrained by economic relations and the liberal ethos of market ideology. Focusing first on Horkheimer and Adorno's *Dialectic of Enlightenment*, I examine the book's second excursus on the Marquis de Sade's Juliette whose many exploits align sexual libertinism with instrumental rationality (Horkheimer and Adorno 2002 [1944]). Juliette's profane, guileful behavior seemingly confirms Horkheimer and Adorno's pessimism regarding human interaction – gendered and sexual – since the Enlightenment. The chapter then asks whether the gender-bending, non-conforming twenty-first century emancipation from the binary truly deals a blow to traditional norms. It inquires whether the freedom that accompanies LGBTQIA2S+ subversions of identity affirm the possibility of Marcusean optimism grounded in aesthetic, not instrumental, rationality. The chapter will argue that the new fluidity can at times fall short of the larger philosophical claims of aesthetic rationality given the perils of identity politics. Nevertheless, the possibility of a freer approach to the body is implied in the effort to undo masculine and feminine norms, and this approach *can* inspire a new aesthetics that at the very least anticipates aesthetic rationality.

1   De Sade's Justine/Juliette Dichotomy and the Replaying of Patriarchal Norms

Composed in 1944, Horkheimer and Adorno's Dialectic *of Enlightenment* does not readily appear to foretell the optimism of Marcuse's 1955 *Eros and Civilization*. Rather, it has been received as a text that studies the doomed unravelling of the concept of enlightenment which, over time, has ironically come to denote its opposite: not the triumph of rationality, secular wisdom, or even common sense, but myth-making, story-telling, blind faith in "science" meant to deliver progress when in fact it delivers ruin. Throughout its pages, the text builds on the premise that, during the course of Western history, the seventeenth- and eighteenth-century Enlightenment abandoned its more noble potential and engaged in a far crasser version of intellectual pursuit; it devolved to its least commendable form in ways that unfortunately gained cultural capital. Leaving behind its negative, dialectical abilities that breed the a-systematic, aesthetic dimension, the Enlightenment went from dispelling myth to creating it, from liberating humanity to enslaving it anew in a false, reconstituted chimera of "science."

In their analysis of this misbegotten mission which betrayed its own guiding principles, Horkheimer and Adorno fault the prevalence of scientism as the leading agent behind this wrong turn, for the latter relies too heavily on a systematized, reductionist approach to the world hostile to dialectical intervention. It binds the world into stringent categories rather than opening it up to investigation, and colonizes our experience in ways that shut down intellectual curiosity. "For the Enlightenment, only what can be encompassed by unity has the status as an existent or an event," they write: "its ideal is the system from which everything and anything follows" (Horkheimer and Adorno 2002 [1944]: 4). System, order, and unity all buttress instrumental rationality, giving meaning to things only as they confirm the overarching logic of human mastery and control. "Formal logic was the high school of unification," they write. "It offered Enlightenment thinkers a schema for making the world calculable ... [the] number became enlightenment's canon ... Bourgeois society is ruled by equivalence" (Horkheimer and Adorno 2002 [1944]: 4).

While science can serve humankind in progressive and ennobling ways, its oversold misinterpretation – scientism – leads to a hyperextension of its dominating form, allowing the thinking mind to believe that it can comprehend, categorize, domesticate, and ultimately control the world. Unlike myth, which maintained the inscrutable distance between what could be understood and what remained unfathomable, the seventeenth- and eighteenth-century Enlightenment instead claimed a neat correspondence between the world and what the mind can grasp, insisting that material existence and cognitive understanding stand unproblematically aligned. In sum, in its efforts to dispel myth and subsequently disenchant the world for human betterment, it actually *created* the myth that everything is reducible to unifying, domesticating thought: "[T]he myths which fell victim to the Enlightenment were themselves its product" (Horkheimer and Adorno 2002 [1944]: 4). Hence modernity's Enlightenment becomes its own myth; meanwhile, "[m]yth becomes enlightenment," a point to which we will return later (Horkheimer and Adorno 2002 [1944]: 6).

In their analysis of enlightenment's development throughout Western history – that is, the dialectic that betrays the ambitions of Enlightenment and instead devolves to its opposite – Horkheimer and Adorno include an excursus focused on sexuality. "Juliette or Enlightenment and Morality" considers a debauched, dissipating moral dimension of sexual expression as it has been co-opted in modernity and interpreted through the lens of capitalist exchange and formal, instrumental logic. Focusing on the Marquis de Sade's cruel, cal-culating heroine as found in his novel, *Juliette, or Vice Amply Rewarded* (1968 [1797–1801]), the authors thus consider a private, interpersonal dimension of Enlightenment's dialectical unravelling and the demise of an enlightened out-look. They argue that the novel demonstrates how traditional gendered and sexual expressions replay and reconfirm modernity's logic of exchange, built on the premise that even the most intimate human interactions must reflect market mechanisms. In keeping with this logic, all forms of sexual expression reduce to a quantifiable value in order for them to have purpose: the body's meaning resides in its exchange value, not in any inherent or aesthetic worth. The unrestrained libertinage of de Sade's Juliette, whose debauchery extends to murder, operates on the principle that the human body must serve a purpose aligned with capitalist principles: sexual encounters are for self-promotion and other ulterior motives. They are rife with calculation, a clear expression of instrumental rationality.

Adding to their first excursus wherein Homer's Odysseus also uses instru-mental rationality to outwit, outmaneuver, and evade his obstacles, this second excursus focuses on Juliette's weaponizing of the female body to obtain what she needs. And although the time frame and social settings differ consider-ably – ancient Greece as opposed to eighteenth-century France – the parallels between Odysseus and Juliette remain striking. Both are fighters, he a Greek warrior returning from Troy and she a woman in a man's world, orphaned early in life with no money of her own. Both use the de-aestheticized, reduction-ist logic of exchange to fight their battles and obtain what they need which, in Juliette's case, results in her defiance of every moral rule that undergirds eighteenth-century French society and that she originally learned in a convent. Yet, as de Sade suggests by making her an anti-heroine, Juliette simply imple-ments the rules established by the reigning social order, and thus exemplifies the form of rationality that proves most efficacious and thus most sensible. She is "scientific" to the degree that she calculates the odds and measures the outcomes: the humanity of others is not what matters, but only the tangible rewards that they can bring her. Her mentality is singularly strategic. "Science stands in the same relationship to nature and human beings in general as insurance theory stands to life and death in particular. Who dies is unimport-ant; what matters is the ratio of incidences of death to the liabilities of the company" (Horkheimer and Adorno 2002 [1944]: 66).

Both Homer's Odysseus and De Sade's Juliette thus succumb to the pow-ers of this mythical, unifying system ruled by ratio, or equivalence; both want and need to get ahead, to secure their position in the world. "Thinking, as understood by the Enlightenment, is the process of establishing a unified, scientific order and of deriving factual knowledge from principles" (Horkheimer and Adorno 2002 [1944]: 63). In clever and inventive ways, Odysseus deceives his opponents, performing such well-known acts as plugging up the ears of his oarsmen to prevent them from hearing the Sirens, telling the Cyclops Polyphemus that his name is "Nobody," and offering a large wooden horse as a means of entering Troy by stealth. He thus exercises a dissembling, faithless form of reasoning for the purposes of protecting himself and outsmarting his opponents. Yet one can hardly argue with his intended goal, for following victory in Troy he simply wishes to return home and resume his old life; he is simply trying to survive. For him, reason operates instrumentally to deliver a desired end; it perceives the world strategically, gauging expenditures and measuring outcomes.

To be fair, Juliette is also merely trying to survive, making use of those weapons available to her as an orphaned woman in a man's world. Not wishing to lose sight of her plight, we should not overlook the fact that her only recourse is to her mind, her body, and whatever favors she can garner from friends, lovers, and acquaintances. Yet the Machiavellian dimension of her character goes beyond the task of mere survival; she does not simply ward off danger but employs instrumental rationality in a nefariously self-promoting manner that uses others in the worst sense. Unlike Odysseus, she employs her mind and body not simply to escape imminent danger, but in order to advance her impoverished status and be allowed to get ahead socioeconomically in a world often hostile to women. A consummate libertine and lover of depravity, she will stop at nothing: she murders, deceives, betrays, blasphemes, and generally defies all moral standards in an effort to improve her life.

In ways consistent with Enlightenment myth-making and formulaic logic, then, Juliette reduces everything to simple equations whose purpose is to ascertain what she might gain; thus, something is "good" only if it breeds desired results. Her actions do not contravene Enlightenment culture, but embody its logic; she is a product of her time. "Juliette's *credo* is science," Horkheimer and Adorno write. "She abominates any veneration which cannot be shown to be rational: belief in God and his dead son, obedience to the Ten Commandments, preference of the good to the wicked, salvation to sin" (Horkheimer and Adorno 2002 [1944]: 76). By her own standard of measurement, Juliette's exploits serve her well, for she ultimately becomes a rich widow who leads a life of pleasure and dissipation. While Odysseus is never cruel or unnecessarily violent, Juliette inflicts pain and destroys life in order to ameliorate her own.

Importantly, the libertine Juliette stands pitted against her virtuous sister, Justine, whose sad life of abuse suggests the powerlessness to which women were subjected. The unfortunate protagonist of *Justine, or the Misfortunes of Virtue* (2013 [1797]) exemplifies a life of feminine martyrdom that clings dutifully to the moral law subjugating women. Try as she might to remain unblemished, Justine's moral rectitude forever plunges her into abusive situations wherein scoundrels and rogues take advantage of her. Unlike her sister, Justine never abandons the religious training she learned in the convent, yet her vulnerability in a hostile society causes her to transgress the moral law against her wishes. The degree to which the libertine Juliette disregards Christian teachings equals the degree to which the pious Justine upholds them; yet ironically the surrounding society rewards the former while punishing the latter, who suffers poverty, misfortune, and loss right up to her violent death by a lightning bolt. Clearly, the Justine/Juliette juxtaposition reconfirms the age-old Madonna/whore, angel-in-the-house/madwoman-in-the-attic dichotomy, which keeps both sisters confined to male-defined roles.

Indeed, even Juliette, who seemingly plays the system against itself with remarkable cleverness, in fact abides by *masculinist* rules: she is *upholding* a sexist dichotomy invented by patriarchy. If she appears to empower women by suggesting that they use the system against itself, a closer look reveals her complacency in Enlightenment logic, for she willingly plays out one side of the traditional, male-defined Madonna/whore binary. She is not as original as one might think; at least, this represents one plausible reading of de Sade's novel. Angela Carter's insightful reading of the text takes seriously this interpretation of things, arguing that Juliette in fact does not outsmart gendered dichotomies, but rather obeys them. Carter's *The Sadeian Woman and the Ideology of Pornography* (1978) insists that a laudatory interpretation of Juliette – the "smart" woman who turns things to her advantage – is too simple, and that to readily endow de Sade with a feminist sensibility needs further scrutiny. It is too easy, Carter maintains, to simply affirm the author's feminism given his treatment of the Justine/Juliette dichotomy, for we cannot simply align feminism with anything that promises personal advancement. Is feminism necessarily on the side of instrumental rationality, or any other form of thinking for that matter, that promises individual gain? Is it "feminist" to play by aggressive, self-interested masculinist rules rather than to rethink those rules altogether? Again, we should appreciate the limited options available to Juliette and the difficulties of navigating life as a solitary woman in eighteenth century France. Yet if we proclaim de Sade as an unequivocal champion of women thanks to the outcome delivered by Juliette's nefarious methods, perhaps we fail to consider whether Juliette's "enlightenment" hasn't "eradicated the last remnant of its own self-awareness" (Horkheimer and Adorno 2002 [1944]: 2). Justine and Juliette mirror one another: "Both are women whose identities have been defined exclusively by men" (Carter 1978: 77). Carter elaborates:

> [T]he woman who makes no bones about selling herself will soon adopt the ideology of the small shopkeeper and identify her interests with the status quo ... By accepting the contractual nature of sexual relations, even if on her own terms, she imprisons herself within them just as securely as a wife does ... If marriage is legalised prostitution, then prostitution is itself a form of group marriage.
>
>   1978: 59

Although Carter does not employ the language of critical theory, her analysis joins the Frankfurt School's juxtaposition between instrumental and aesthetic rationality. Her reading of de Sade's notorious heroine, whose malicious acts correspond neatly to the mirrored opposite of Justine's moral goodness, cele-brate the work world principles of capitalist enterprise, and fail to corroborate Marcuse's feminine principle more attuned to an aesthetic understanding of the world. And as Horkheimer and Adorno's excursus makes clear, the immoral – or perhaps amoral – behaviors that Juliette exemplifies stand commensurate with the Enlightenment ethos, since what is "good," "right," and "just" is that which gets the job done efficiently. Enlightenment morality thus has noth-ing to do with rethinking the binaries, gendered or otherwise, that undergird Western civilization; it has nothing to do, in other words, with rethinking the rules of the game. Juliette exhibits no imagination when it comes to that; she obediently plays by the rules offering "bad" for Justine's "good."

    Carter thus deploys a decidedly feminist intervention into Horkheimer and Adorno's second excursus, agreeing with them that "Enlightenment" has reverted to its opposite, since Juliette is not outside the system but stands decidedly ensconced within it. From Odysseus to Juliette, enlightenment's trajectory from antiquity to the eighteenth century has consistently erred on the side of a myth-making ethos that favors domination over nature, control over other people, and the finely honed interpersonal skills that allow one to get ahead: being "enlightened" means being on top of your game, invincible. Certainly, the neoliberal ethos of current Western civilization promotes this reading of things, for as Carter herself observes, so much of what today passes as a "smart" woman coincides precisely with Juliette's enterprising, ambi-tious spirit, minus the murder and mayhem. Elsewhere, I have argued that so much of what constitutes "power feminism" today – a.k.a. "lipstick," "sti-letto," and "babe" feminisms – in fact reproduces a muscled-up, tough-talking masculinist ideology, thus buying into the very logic that needs reconsideration (Caputi 2013).

This tendency to reconfirm rather than challenge the status quo might seem discouraging to those wishing to depose the neoliberal mindset in favor of something more humane. If feminism's oppositional imagination has been domesticated, where does that leave us? How does that help liberate Marcuse's "feminine principle" and truly introduce Adorno's "negative," a-systematic dialectics into our understanding of gender and sexuality? Fortunately, though, there are other players in the field and other responses to the logic of the market. Power feminism, for instance, does not represent the full array of feminist schools of thought, just as other groups committed to a more progressive, forward-looking understanding of gender and sexuality insist on a more maverick reading of these categories. Much work has been done in terms of rethinking these categories both in the realm of social movements and legislation as well as in the area of gender and sexuality studies. Indeed, by any standard our society's interpretation of gender and sexuality has undergone considerable change, often moving in the direction of the negative fluidity promoted by Marcuse's aesthetic, "feminine principle" and Adorno's negative dialectics. But do these inroads truly correspond to what critical theorists envisage?

2   LGBTQIA2S+, an Apt Site for Negative Dialectics?

Today's LGBTQIA2S+ movement is to be credited with having vastly widened the playing field of gendered and sexual persona and allowed many expressions of identity to flourish. The old binary of male and female, masculine and feminine, heterosexual and homosexual has been superseded by an array of possibilities that grant far more freedom and positive expression to forms of identity previously considered aberrant, thereby changing the discourse surrounding the individual's lived experience of identity. Not only is more fluidity granted to one's self-definitions, as seen in queer or "questioning" persons, but it is no longer necessary to uphold the binary at all, as with two-spirited individuals who identify with an array of definitions and practices. Politically, then, the term "LGBTQIA2S+" is slightly misleading in that it suggests an integrated social movement with a homogenized center that unites a wide spectrum of people. In fact, the various identities included in the acronym differ considerably one from another and share only the effort to oppose an ensconced heteronormativity. While they pursue different political ends, it is fair to say that they share the common aim of dismantling the stigma of homophobia and the conceit of heterosexuality's comfortable status as they seek to validate forms of gender and sexual identity that were formerly deemed deviant. Hence, despite their differences, there is solidarity in their efforts to undo gender and sexuality and discredit any effort to locate truth or fixed meaning in the body and its expressions.

By any standards, the movement's many successes in the past fifty to sixty years have brought about radical change in mainstream society's acceptance of LGBTQIA2S+ communities. In the Western world, the groups included under this umbrella have gained tremendous ground in terms of their social profile, their civil rights, and their efforts to mainstream alternative lifestyles unaligned with traditional heterosexual patterns. While resistance still exists among those who oppose these communities' right to self-expression, many significant battles have been won that at least point in the direction of a society that validates rather than occludes the many varieties of gender and sexual identities which, after all, have long been in practice. "So it is a question of developing within law, psychiatry, social, and literary theory a new legitimating lexicon for the gender complexity that we have been living for a long time," Judith Butler explains (Butler 2004: 31). In the United States, there can be no denying that the public at large has dramatically changed its attitude toward non-heterosexuals as witnessed in the openly gay and lesbian persons in public service, such as U.S. Secretary of Transportation Pete Buttigieg, as well as in their extensive inclusion in the media, the arts, and the academy.

Yet LGBTQIA2S+ represents a wide-reaching umbrella comprised of disparate parts, some of which stand in disagreement with one another. Given the variety of struggles in question, we can ask whether any of these non-binary subversions address the concerns of critical theorists such as Marcuse and Adorno. In challenging gendered, heterosexual norms, are members of the collection meaningfully invoking the feminine principle that opposes the neoliberal ethos; are they approaching the negative dimension of Adorno's negative dialectics? The answer, of course, is some but not all. For while it is possible that gender and sexuality's undoing may include the deconstruction of categories altogether, many people contained under the acronym LGBTQIA2S+ do not seek such radical change; rather, they simply seek admittance to the set of norms that mainstream heterosexuals already take for granted. Understandably and without apology, they simply wish to enjoy what those who abide by the binary have always been allowed to enjoy.

The advances made in LGBTQIA2S+ civil rights and the latter's general acceptance by society at large illustrates this clearly. At the federal level, Supreme Court rulings and legislation such as *Lawrence v. Texas* (2003), the Matthew Shepard and James Byrd Jr. Hate Crimes Prevention Act (2009), and *Obergefell v. Hodges* (2015), as well as the extensive reach of the Civil Rights Act of 1964, all testify to the inroads made by those seeking protection under the law as non-heterosexuals. Thanks to the realization of such protections and the notable shift in public opinion regarding non-binary expressions, those seeking inclusion in a traditional lifestyle can easily claim that much progress has been made. They have opened many doors that were previously closed such that younger persons today have far more flexibility in terms of lifestyle choices. A relatively open-minded sensibility now prevails, albeit unevenly; at least in politically progressive communities around the country, discrimination against those included under the umbrella has waned.

Yet not all members of the heterogenous umbrella want assimilation into mainstream society, since the strictures of that mainstream – marriage, children, shared property, "family" living – are many. The assumption that non-binary persons unaligned with any distinct gender or sexual identity desire the same things as, say, gays and lesbians wishing to marry, rings false; not everyone wants a "normal life" (Spade 2015). Moreover, it further overlooks and alienates those who do not identify with traditional roles, occluding their existence from the social landscape and thereby imposing further hardship on them. Arguing for equal protection of LGBTQIA2S+ under the law thus does not speak to all members of the group, and has the inadvertent consequence of actually hurting those uninterested in equal protection by confirming their outlier status. "An integral part of equal protection rhetoric is the argument that the individuals being discriminated against deserve to be treated equivalently to the dominant groups within society," Courtenay W. Daum explains. "This equality-based rhetoric, however, presupposes that assimilation is an important and desirable end goal of the LBGTQ movement" (Daum 2017: 358). Many non-binaries resent the assumption that heterosexuality represents the idealized model that everyone should follow, and that they themselves are simply variants on a binary-based norm. "In reality," Daum continues, "many gays and lesbians do not want access to marriage predicated on heteronormative values or monogamous legally sanctioned relationships of any kind" (Daum 2017: 360).

Implicit in Daum's argument is recognition of the fact that the LGBTQIA2S+ experience does not replay the time-honored binary that undergirds traditional articulations of gender and sexuality. The dualisms that have long prevailed in the West – male/female, transcendence/immanence, the Madonna/whore dichotomy, culture/nature – are not featured in the alternative iterations of identity to which the LGBTQIA2S+ community gives expression. Rather, the heterogeneous umbrella extends beyond and thus subverts the time-honored assumption that gender and sexuality always line up according to previously established definitions. Indeed, an important gift of the movement resides in the fact that it moves away not only from heteronormative privilege, but also from the assumption that the classic binaries that support heteronormativity must always hold. Some identities resist categorization and dualistic schematization; they move beyond the old parameters and thus dispel with the need for assimilation. For instance: "Queer theory recognizes identity as unstable, fluid, and multifaceted," Daum explains, "and argues against group-based identity politics as a means of political and legal reform" (Daum 2017: 361).

This gesture of arguing against group-based identity politics, of insisting on the "unstable, fluid, and multifaceted" nature of human experience, frees gender and sexuality from appropriating categories and allows for the singular uniqueness of each individual's lived experience. Defying appropriation, it invokes Adorno's negativity; resisting formal logic, it makes possible Marcuse's feminine principle. As an example, two-spiritedness resists the mandate that a person identify one way or another and be linked inexorably to preordained definitions that staunch variety. Learning from Indigenous peoples, it opens the possibility that one person claim both feminine and masculine persona as well as a trans identity. Similarly, those identifying as "ace" enjoy platonic relationships with no expression of physical attraction, thereby avoiding the entire question of where they fall on the spectrum of possibilities. They avoid appropriating language altogether and thus allow the immediacy of their experience to prevail over definitions and categories: language is demoted as a transmitter of meaning given that its homogenizing, distorting power pauperizes lived experience. Yet thinking beyond gendered and sexual categories by letting go of identity's powerful hold is something that relatively few of us have ever done. Because we typically understand these categories as integral to human experience, most of us cannot imagine dispelling of their central place in our lives.

Heath Fogg Davis illustrates this point by demonstrating the vital importance we attach to our sexual and gendered identities and the difficulty that we have in thinking beyond them (Davis 2017). Keenly aware of the crucial role that we assign to these, he explores the many ways in which we are indoctrinated into thinking that a sexual, gendered identity constitutes a *sine qua non* of who we are, that it indeed reveals a truth about our being and thus constitutes a touchstone of our existence. In *Beyond Trans: Does Gender Matter?*, Davis comments on the manner in which this category accompanies us throughout our lives and thus gains currency as an essential part of living. "Checking or clicking on a sex-identity box is so routinized that many of us have never questioned it," he writes. "These boxes continue to appear on the papers and screens in front of us throughout our lifetimes. And sex markers stay with us until the time of our death when our death certificates describe us as having been male or female" (Davis 2017: 14). Implicit in Davis' observation lies the possibility of diminishing the importance of a sexual or gendered identity and releasing the categories from any supposed moorings. It might be possible, in other words, to undo sex and gender such that neither is credited with revealing a "truth" about us or establishing a core without which our lives would be meaningless. Sex and gender would then be revealed as markers always open to interpretation and thus performative in nature, neither pre-existing nor culturally stable, but always contingent and fluid.

Such fluidity is consistent with the "feminine principle" identified by Marcuse, a principle whose "image of joy and fulfilment" (Marcuse 1974 [1955]: 162) moves beyond the binaries that have long defined gender and sexuality in the West. Dispelling of these binaries allows for the interpretive openness of Adorno's negative dialectics and differs markedly from the closure that can potentially characterize identity politics. It is this *interpretive openness*, this *cognitive suppleness* that I wish to emphasize since it strikes me as most essential to the feminine principle that Marcuse endorses. True, fluidity cast as an open-ended *identity* may not always be the same thing as fluidity in human *perception*, in how we grasp the world and think about it. For indeed even an unconventional, non-conforming identity can become rigid and dogmatic in its performative iteration; even an iconoclast can become dictatorial. As with any form of identity politics – in fact, any politics – positions can harden and assume a stance inconsistent with their own earlier iterations.

However, if we consider those aspects of the LGBTQIA2S+ umbrella that address not how identities express themselves in society, but how we grasp them intellectually, then we are closer to what is "negative" in Marcuse's feminine principle, "the voice which does not command but sings; the gesture of receptivity which offers and receives" (Marcuse 1974 [1955]: 162). The fluidity implicit in this description indicates an intellectual resilience, a cognitive dynamism that surely resonates with Adorno's negative dialectics wherein subject and object stand mutually interpenetrated. It reveals a willingness to forever negotiate our cognitive categories and remain open to interpretations as yet unimagined. To illustrate my point, I return to *Dialectic of Enlightenment*, this time emphasizing the first excursus on Odysseus in his encounter with the Sirens.

3   "Archaic Supremacy": the Sirens' Song and the Power of Aesthetic
       Receptivity

In their first excursus on Odysseus, Horkheimer and Adorno emphasize the Greek hero's use of instrumental rationality, that form of logical reasoning that repeatedly comes to his aid. Without the ability to think strategically and in linear fashion, Odysseus would never have been able to surmount the many trials that he encountered on his epic journey. He therefore serves as the perfect model of that form of Enlightenment rationality that the authors are keen to criticize, that form of "enlightenment" so reliant on *ratio* that only understands unity, conformity, and system. It thus seeks to dominate anything that threatens to escape its grasp, hoping for predictability where novelty or uncertainty exist. This form of "enlightened" thinking cannot tolerate the unknown and cannot grasp the fact that some things are unknowable: "Nothing is to remain outside," Horkheimer and Adorno write, "since the mere idea of 'outside' is the real source of fear" (Horkheimer and Adorno 2002 [1944]: 11). This passion for unity, conformity, and system is but the overt expression of an underlying violence that must control things and that cannot abide those subversive forces that counter the reach of instrumental rationality.

In order to retain control, this epistemic system made manifest through Odysseus' valiant acts categorically refuses to allow the natural world to disturb the disenchanted, disenchanting progress of Western culture; it will not allow nature's unappropriated elements to threaten the achievements of science or the scientific mind so revered in Western culture. Nature is to be dominated, brought under the control of a scientific regimen. "What human beings seek to learn from nature is how to use it to dominate wholly both it and human beings. Nothing else counts" (Horkheimer and Adorno 2002 [1944]: 2). That which threatens or subverts this control over nature must ultimately be appropriated; otherwise, it is not acknowledged. "For the Enlightenment, only what can be encompassed by unity has the status of an existent or an event" (Horkheimer and Adorno 2002 [1944]: 4). True, Odysseus is able to survive life-threatening situations and continue on his journey home thanks only to his use of formal, instrumental logic. In this way, he "turns out to be the prototype of the bourgeois individual" marked by "unwavering self-assertion;" he prefigures bourgeois values (Horkheimer and Adorno 2002 [1944]: 35). His memorable encounters with strange creatures and cunning plots might thus all be grouped together under the heading of "ways to outsmart one's opponent" or "ways to subdue the power of nature." For indeed, it is Odysseus' stalwart thinking and undying resourcefulness that make him a hero of the Homeric legend as he unfailingly overcomes adversity.

Nevertheless, it is possible to approach one adventure, his encounter with the Sirens, from a slightly different angle and thus perceive a mitigated interpretation of his cunning. A subtle shift in our reading of this famous Homeric episode can deliver a version of the story that errs more on the side of the aesthetic sensibility, something closer to Marcuse's feminine principle. Odysseus' voyage back to Ithaca occasions his encounter with the Sirens, the seductive half-women, half-bird creatures whose enchanting song is reputedly impossible to resist. Their mellifluent singing is as beautiful as it is dangerous, for many sailors have been lured to their island, unable to resist the captivating sound of their voices, and there met their demise. A pile of bones on the shores where the temptresses sing testify to the fact that their charming allure will surely lead to one's death; in art, they are frequently depicted tantalizing Odysseus by trying to approach him and his oarsmen.[3] Aware of this danger alloyed to pleasure, Odysseus employs his strategic thinking and devises a way to both hear the Sirens' enchanting song and avoid their danger: he will plug up the ears of his oarsmen so that they cannot hear the singing, and simultaneously have himself tied to the mast. In this way, with his own ears unplugged, he will be able to hear the creatures' beautiful music without gesturing to his oarsmen to go to their shore; he will be able to enjoy the power of nature without being subject to its treacherous impulses.

In their excursus, Horkheimer and Adorno emphasize the thematic consistency of the Homeric tradition as it is repeated in the Sirens' episode. Once again, Odysseus outsmarts his opponents, employing his cunning and strategic logic to ensure his own survival in the face of danger. He remains the prototypical bourgeois individual and proceeds according to the nature-dominating principles of the Enlightenment. While he recognizes the power of nature over any mental faculty, his formal logic allows him to prevail, beguiled by the Sirens' enchanting music and yet not falling prey to their death-dealing influence. It is thus the hero's savvy, his formal logic, that Horkheimer and Adorno stress:

> Odysseus does not try to steer a different course to the one past the Sirens'
> island ... he realizes that however he may consciously distance himself
> from nature, as a listener [*Hörender*] he remains under its spell ... But he
> has found a loophole in the agreement, through which he eludes it while
> fulfilling its terms ... Technically enlightened, Odysseus acknowledges
> the archaic supremacy of the song by having himself bound ... But he has
> taken the precaution not to succumb to them even when he succumbs.
>
>   2002 [1944]: 46

---

3 For example, Alexander Bruckmann's 1829 painting, "Odysseus and the Sirens," clearly depicts a pile of bones that testify to the Sirens' fatal influence.

Hence even as he admits to nature's "archaic supremacy," the Homeric hero succeeds in outsmarting its superiority and asserting the instrumental rationality of bourgeois individualism. Whatever subversive elements threaten to controvert formal logic, the myth teaches us, can be overcome through forethought and creative ingenuity.

Yet not everyone is so convinced that the encounter with the Sirens proves reducible to a mind-over-matter analysis, or that the episode has such a pat finish to it. Morton Schoolman prefers to shift the emphasis slightly, focusing more on Odysseus' desire to hear the temptresses in the first place. In his excellent *Reason and Horror: Critical Theory, Democracy, and Aesthetic Individuality*, Schoolman argues that the Greek's cunning strategy nevertheless reveals the remnant of nature's power, the desire to be overwhelmed by nature and to encounter what we cannot control (Schoolman 2001). In other words, it reveals the double mediation between mind and matter, subject and object which, in keeping with negative dialectics, never allows either pole of the dialectic to take complete precedence. Neither concrete material reality nor cognitive apprehension claim the upper hand, but remain interpenetrated. On some level, then, Odysseus is reminded – perhaps *longs to be reminded* – of his participation in a world not dominated by the logic of unity (that is, of alignment between subject and object, of identity politics) but overwhelmed by that which escapes categorization. Perhaps he longs to be overpowered by nature with its chaotic, a-systematic forces. Schoolman explains that, having discovered the "loophole in the agreement," Odysseus can experience the aesthetic reasoning that informs Marcuse's feminine principle:

> Odysseus is [not] without opportunities to ... design some sort of praxis, whereby he typically resorts to cunning to cheat the deities while coincidentally ensuring an aesthetic receptivity to the difference in the world the deities represent ... [yet he is] aesthetically receptive to a world of difference ... we must acknowledge that Odysseus' actions reflect a degree of enlightened self-possession or aesthetic individuality.
>
> 2001: 57–58

Read in this light, the Homeric tale of a valiant warrior and king of Ithaca displays the principle, not of enlightenment as myth, but of myth as enlightenment. For in his eagerness to hear the Sirens' tantalizing music that will surely overpower his rational capacity, Odysseus points to the power of nature as it resists human cognitive categories, the "archaic supremacy" of our embodied, natural existence whose dynamics we cannot fully domesticate. The myth proves enlightening in its aesthetic receptivity, instructing us about the limits of human cognition and the dangers of identitarian thought. We learn of our intellectual feebleness and recognize the mind as forever enmeshed in a relationship of double mediation with concrete, material reality and historical specificity, as Odysseus' desire to be seduced by musical incantation – to lose himself to nature – so clearly shows.

4   Conclusion: the Feminine Principle as Political Praxis

In this chapter, I have asked whether the many non-binary expressions of sexual and gendered identity that typically comprise the LGBTQIA2S+ collective correspond to Marcuse's "feminine principle," a principle that endows sex and gender with subversive rather than conformist potential. The hopeful attributes that Marcuse confers on this principle allow it to meaningfully contravene the neoliberal logic of unchecked economic gain and for-profit politics that so often go unchallenged. For as we have seen, this worldview is even confirmed and perpetuated by schools of thought that should otherwise prove contrapuntal: de Sade's Juliette in many ways resonates with today's "smart" woman who applauds the neoliberal logic of "workism" and perpetuates masculinist values. Superficially feminist, she in fact reconfirms the social order that she is trying to outsmart. But do non-binary individuals, those who on principle avoid the strictures that organize how we think about sex and gender, fare differently and truly encapsulate the "negative" thinking of Marcuse's principle, the open-ended negativity contained in Adorno's dialectics?

I think, at times, they can. We have seen the cautioning position of Daum as she perceives a possible conformism and troublingly staid quality in certain advancements made on behalf of the LGBTQIA2S+ community. She correctly points out that advancements such as same-sex marriage indeed address the interests of *some* LGBTQIA2S+ members and ensure the protection of their equal rights and civil liberties. These landmark events can be deemed a "victory" as they normalize homosexuality and mainstream what was long deemed deviant. Yet identification with the mainstream may well be both the strongpoint and the simultaneous weakness of this "victory," Daum argues, since many non-binary, non-heterosexual persons have no interest in conforming to social norms. Because triumphant Supreme Court cases and Acts of Congress seemingly speak for the entire LGBTQIA2S+ community, or at least are billed as doing so, those non-conformists uninterested in heterosexual norms are further ostracized and rendered invisible. What is deemed "progress" in fact contains a regressive impulse and a missed opportunity; it fails to acknowledge the lived reality of those not on the mainstream's radar. Daum explains that for many under the LGBTQIA2S+ umbrella, "fighting for access to hetero-normative institutions such as marriage is counterproductive and threatens to undermine the radical transformative potential of the LGBTQ rights move-ment" (Daum 2017: 361).

Daum is correct: it is counterproductive because it prolongs the identitarian logic contained in identity politics. It curtails the progressive element located in Marcuse's "feminine principle" and fails to liberate gender and sexuality from the shackles of formal logic. Without denying the gains from which many gays and lesbians rightfully benefit, the "progressive" element of, say, *Obergefell v. Hodges* conforms to a mainstream neoliberal lifestyle and upholds the sta-tus quo built around capitalism, consumerism, the time-honored division between public and private, and the traditional family. Such advancements extend a heterosexual lifestyle to those formerly denied access, but do not inquire into the oppression that this lifestyle implies. It welcomes in those previously excluded, but never queries the harm that the mainstream embod-ies. Jeremiah J. Garretson laments the fact that so many fail to perceive this loss, which only proves how invisible and disempowered the truly progressive elements of the movement remain. If "progress" has been made that tethers the LGBTQIA2S+ community to the mainstream, "does this mean that a post-identity queer liberationist politics is less likely to succeed at a mass level, ver-sus a politics based around a shared identity like "gay" or "lesbian?"" (Garretson 2017: 265). Garretson hopes for the former, "a post-gender, liberationist politics, one in which the distinctive social categories ... then evaporate and recede" (Garretson 2017: 266).

In its eschewal of formal, identitarian logic, such a "post-identity" politics surely resonates with Marcuse's feminine principle and its embodied opti-mism. It surely foreshadows the undoing of gender in ways that open up cat-egories of human identity in ways that allow for the joy and generosity that Marcuse envisages. For if something as integral to the human experience as gender and sexuality demand not the use of instrumental rationality, but of its aesthetic counterpart, then a liberationist politics undergoes assimilation into our everyday lives where it can truly have an effect.

References

Benjamin, Walter. 1999. *The Arcades Project,* trans. Howard Eiland and Kevin McLaughlin. Cambridge, MA: Belknap Press.

Bruckmann, Alexander. 1829. *Odysseus and the Sirens.* Oil on canvas. Staatsgalerie Stuttgart, Stuttgart.

Butler, Judith. 2004. *Undoing Gender*, New York: Routledge.

Caputi, Mary. 2013. *Feminism and Power: the Need for Critical Theory*. Lanham, MD: Lexington Books.

Carter, Angela. 1978. *The Sadeian Woman and the Ideology of Pornography*. New York: Pantheon Books.

Cherkovskya, Ekaternia, Alexander Paulsson, Stefania Barca. 2019. *Toward a Political Economy of Degrowth*. Lanham, MD: Rowman & Littlefield Publishers.

Daum, Courtenay W. 2017. "Marriage Equality: Assimilationist Victory or Pluralist Defeat?" In *LGBTQ Politics: a Critical Reader*, ed. Marla Brettschneider, Susan Burgess, and Christine Keating, 353–373. New York University Press.

De Sade, Marquis. 1968 [1797–1801]. *Juliette*, trans. Austryn Wainhouse. New York: Grove Press.

De Sade, Marquis. 2013 [1797]. *Justine, or the Misfortunes of Virtue,* trans. John Phillips. Oxford, UK: Oxford University Press.

Fogg Davis, Heath. 2017. *Beyond Trans: Does Gender Matter?* New York: New York University Press.

Garretson, Jeremiah J. 2017. "The How, Why, and Who of LGBTQ 'Victory:' A Critical Examination of Change in Public Attitudes Involving LGBTQ People." In *LGBTQ Politics: a Critical Reader*, ed. Marla Brettschneider, Susan Burgess, and Christine Keating, 252–269. New York: New York University Press.

Horkheimer, Max and Theodor Adorno. 2002 [1944]. *Dialectic of Enlightenment*, trans. Edmund Jephcott. Stanford, CA: Stanford University Press.

Latouche, Serge. 2009. *Farewell to Growth*, trans. David Macey. Cambridge, UK: Polity Press.

Marcuse, Herbert. 1974 [1955]. *Eros and Civilization: a Philosophical Inquiry Into Freud*. New York: Beacon Press.

Schoolman, Morton. 2001. *Reason and Horror: Critical Theory, Democracy, and Aesthetic Individuality*. New York: Routledge.

Spade, Dean. 2015. *Normal Life: Administrative Violence, Critical Trans Politics and the Limits of Law*. Durham, NC: Duke University Press.

Thompson, Derek. 2019. "Workism Is Making Americans Miserable." In *The Atlantic*: February 24. https://www.theatlantic.com/ideas/archive/2019/02/religion-workism -making-americans-miserable/583441/.

CHAPTER 6

Towards a Critical Identity Politics

Butler, Adorno, and the Force of Non-identity

Tivadar Vervoort

> If you find your body refusing [...] "normal" modes of life, don't
> despair – realize your gift!
>
> HARDT AND NEGRI 2000: 216

∵

1   Introduction

From the sixties onwards, a myriad of new social movements demanded the
Left to diversify its emphasis on socio-economic struggles. Feminist, decolonial, anti-racist, and queer politics had obviously started to emerge many
decades earlier, but as the Marxist model of social revolution increasingly lost
its self-evidence during the twentieth century, Leftist politics could no longer
justify its sole emphasis on class conflict. As a result, radical Leftist movements
broadened their scope beyond economic redistribution to include the emancipation of particular social groups oppressed along axes distinct from (but
intersecting with) socio-economic exploitation. However, as contemporary
discussions about "wokeness" and cancel culture signal, the "New" Left came
to be criticized for overemphasizing the demands for recognition of subordinated social identities. According to these allegations, "identity politics" would
only reproduce the "otherness" of oppressed groups, and replace the struggle
for social transformation with mere moralizing, or even policing. Supposedly,
then, the emphasis on identity politics is said to blind the Left from questioning more fundamental forms of social domination.

In its original formulation, however, The Combahee River Collective
understood identity politics as a universalist emancipatory demand "to be
recognized as human, levelly human" (The Combahee River Collective 2014
[1977]: 247). In that sense, identity politics might be nothing more than a
"strategic essentialism", as Gayatri Chakravorty Spivak has put it (1990). The

question remains, how strategic such essentialism can be. As Judith Butler reminds us, "[t]he mobilization of identity categories for the purposes of politicization always remains threatened by the prospect of identity becoming an instrument of the power one opposes" (1999 [1990]: xxvi; cf. Haider 2018, 2020). As a consequence, identity claims entail a problematic paradox: subordinated social groups must affirm the identity upon which their subordination is based to challenge their oppression. Or again, "[t]he internal paradox of this foundationalism [of identity politics] is that it presumes, fixes, and constrains the very 'subjects' that it hopes to represent and liberate" (1999: 189).

To come to terms with this paradox, this paper argues for a "critical identity politics" that presupposes a critically reflexive stance towards the identity categories that it mobilizes. To develop such a critical identity politics, I return to the reflexive stance typical of Frankfurt School critical social theory in general, and Theodor W. Adorno's work on identity thinking in particular.[1] My claim is that Judith Butler's comments on the paradoxes of identity politics resonate with the reflexive attitude that Adorno's critical social theory proposes towards identity claims. More precisely, I aim to show that Butler's emphasis on the exclusionary effects of the gender dichotomy vis-à-vis a plurality of experiences of the self, echoes Adorno's reflections on the subsumption of difference under universally applicable concepts. Indeed, in *Giving an Account of Oneself*, Butler comments that Adorno "refers to a situation in which 'the universal' fails to agree with or include the individual" (2005: 7). If identities are both given as well as made, emancipatory struggles should turn categories of identity against themselves to transgress the forms of oppression and subordination that their given form constitutes. To foreclose the reification of social identities, then, a critical identity politics requires the reflexive stance typical of the critical social theorist. Or, as Butler has put it with explicit reference to Adorno: "when the 'I' seeks to give an account of itself, an account that must include the conditions of its own emergence, it must, as a matter of necessity, become a social theorist" (Butler 2005: 8).

In the following, I will first revisit Butler's theory of the performativity of gender and its repercussions for the possibility of an identity politics. Secondly, I will shortly discuss Adorno's critique of identity thinking and stress

---

1   I have connected "the epistemological problem of critical theory" with questions around identity politics before in Vervoort 2020.

his emphasis on a critical engagement with reason's own categories of identi-fication. Thirdly, I will claim that Butler's theory of performativity is commensurable with Adorno's dialectical account of identity. Finally, I will argue for a critical identity politics by drawing connections between Butler's emphasis on alterity as a resource for contestation and the preponderance of the non-identical in Adorno's negative dialectics.

2   Performativity and the Paradox of Identity

Judith Butler's work on the performativity of gender (Butler 1999 [1990], 2004b, 2011 [1993], 2013 [1997]) is oftentimes regarded as the theoretical inaugura-tion of third wave feminism (see e.g. Grady 2018; Hekman 2000). Rather than addressing the oppression of women as evolving from a structural, asymmet-rical power-relation between two fundamentally opposed sexes – as in the case of second-wave feminism – Butler suggests that "the presumed univer-sality and unity of the subject of feminism is effectively undermined by the constraints of the representational discourse in which it functions" (1999: 7). Accordingly, Butler's work aims to create room for the struggles of those indi-viduals who do not feel represented by feminist discourses characterizing sex as an essential feature of the subject. As they put it recently:

> My argument was that it should be possible for all sorts of people to enter into the feminist movement without identifying with a restrictive category of gender [...] I sought to expand the vocabularies, the ways of understanding gender and its complexity, so that feminism did not require a premature and costly conformity to restrictive identity catego-ries to make its claims.
>
> BUTLER 2021: 35[2]

Butler's pathbreaking redefinition of feminist politics beyond the founda-tional dichotomy of the sexes aims to circumvent the "reification" (1999: 8; 34) of sex and gender by approaching the categories of "woman" and "man" as constituted by the sedimentation and repetition of interlocking discursive

---

2   Or again, Butler writes: "In *Gender Trouble*, I was concerned to show, among other things, that the available terms for establishing self-recognition as a woman were constraining for many who lived outside the heteronormative matrix (called "compulsory heterosexuality" at the time), and I called for more complex and inclusive terms so that those people who could not easily identify with the category of women still had a social place in language" (2021: 36).

utterances and performative gestures. As Butler puts it in *Undoing Gender,* "the binary of man and woman as the exclusive way to understand the gender field performs a regulatory operation of power that naturalizes the hegemonic instance and forecloses the thinkability of its disruption" (Butler 2004b: 43). Accordingly, Butler understands the performative repetition of gendered gestures to *produce* sex, instead of presupposing the givenness of the biological dichotomy of the sexes.

In the introduction to the second edition of *Gender Trouble,* Butler explains they derived the notion of performativity from Derrida's reflections on Kafka's story "Before the Law." They argue that in Derrida's comments, "the one who waits for the law [...] attributes a certain force to the law for which one waits" just like gender functions as "an expectation that ends up producing the very phenomenon that it anticipates" (Butler 1999: xiv). Hence, the performativity of gender does not simply point to gender as an "act" in the sense of a voluntarist choice, nor is gender performative in the sense of a theatrical staging. Rather, the performativity of gender signifies how gender identities participate in a "historically contingent epistemic regime" consisting of a "sustained set of acts, posited through the gendered stylization of the body" (1999: xv, see also 178) that produces and reproduces sex and gender. As such, the performative gestures of gender identities are both the products of the given gender discourse and its reproduction. Or, as Butler puts it succinctly: "There is no gender identity behind the expressions of gender; that identity is performatively constituted by the very 'expressions' that are said to be its results" (Butler 1999: 33).

In sum, then, the dichotomy between male and female gender identities is part of a discursive horizon that (1) is constantly reiterated and reified by gender performances, and (2) constrains the available categories for the understanding of the self to that discursive horizon. As there is no essential kernel or foundation that justifies given social identities – like those of gender – beyond their performative reiteration,

> acts, gestures, enactments, generally construed, are performative in the sense that the essence or identity that they otherwise purport to express are fabrications manufactured and sustained through corporeal signs and other discursive means. That the gendered body is performative suggests that it has no ontological status apart from the various acts which constitute its reality.
>
> BUTLER 1999: 173

By understanding gender as a discursive framework that installs a naturalized dichotomy between men and women, Butler can articulate a critical toolkit to delve into the forms of power and domination such discourse implies.

Moreover, as far as Foucault is right to claim that there is power where there is resistance (Foucault 1998), Butler's theory of performativity also implies the possibility to subvert gendered identities by reappropriating the way gendered utterances and acts are repeated and distributed. The performativity of gender identities thus also implies the possibility to resist the dominant discursive regime, and to alter social identities. Indeed, Butler explicitly stresses that their emphasis on performativity "was to establish the play of freedom within forms of social construction" to "[insist] that freedom can be found within the scene of social constraints" (Butler 2021: 37–38). As such, the notion of performativity counteracts the essentialist categories of classical feminist theories. As Butler points out in an interview in *Artforum*, "[a] number of people feel caught between categories or outside of them in some ways. [...] [S]uch people are an enormous political resource that has been lost through the insistence on coherent identity" (Butler and Kotz 1992). Consequently, Butler's reflections on the performativity of gender imply a politics that recasts the role of identity: rather than grounding an "identity politics" in the essential dichotomy of two sexes, Butler's politics of performativity questions how identities are constituted by norms and discourses from the outset, to subsequently question, mock, redefine, reappropriate, and subvert them from the standpoint of who do not fit in.

Indeed, Butler explicitly tries to find "political possibilities" in "a radical critique of the categories of identity" that is no longer constrained by "identity as a common ground" (1999: xxix). They argue for a critical approach towards identity that builds upon "a coalition of sexual minorities that will transcend the simple categories of identity [...] and dissipate the violence imposed by restrictive bodily norms" (1999: xxvi). Such a politics must move beyond reference to "essential difference" as the latter "forecloses in advance the emergence of new identity concepts in and through politically engaged actions" (1999: 21). Rather, Butler wants to disentangle the paradox of identity politics by affirming that

> Paradoxically, the reconceptualization of identity as an effect, that is, as produced or generated, opens up possibilities of 'agency' that are insidiously foreclosed by positions that take identity categories as foundational and fixed. For an identity to be an effect means that it is neither fatally determined nor fully artificial and arbitrary.
>
> 1999: 187

In sum, Butler's theory of performativity implies that a critical attitude towards the epistemic regime of gender should center around the political potential of resignifying identity categories. In such a *critical* identity politics, the reference to identity is not omitted altogether. Rather, Butler redirects identity politics to those instances where "[g]ender norms are 'resignified' by bodies that are not supposed to embody them" (Butler 2021: 40–41). Still, they emphasize that discursive utterances and performative gestures – even if they initially emerge from the margins – risk becoming reified into a matrix of power. Insofar as all reification is a forgetting, as Adorno has it, the tendency from resignification towards reification demands any form of emancipatory identity politics to place its categories under constant critical scrutiny. As such, one could argue that Butler reverses the paradox of identity politics in an "enthusiastically dialectical" (Stoetzler 2005: 347) way: their understanding of identity as a performative effect does not foreclose the possibility of a politics of identity, but rather encourages a *critical* identity politics that demands a constant reflection on the discourses which mediate the constitution of identity. As such, Butler's politics of performativity continues to carry along a dialectical approach to social reality that they, as a philosopher, have always been well-acquainted with. This dialectical figuration hints, as we will see, towards the shared concerns with identity between Butler's work and the critical theory of Adorno.

3   Adorno's Philosophy: from Failure to Critique

Adorno too is an outspoken critic of identity thinking. As early as in "The Actuality of Philosophy" (Adorno 1977 [1931]), he argues that the presupposed identity between thought and reality obscures the fundamentally differentiated and heterogeneous character of existence. Adorno expresses his critique of identity thinking even more explicitly in his magnum opus *Negative Dialectics,* which could be considered as the philosophical-methodological justification of his critical social theory at large (Honneth 2006: 12). In its "Introduction," Adorno reflects on the possibility of philosophical critique in an era after the failure of the social transformations promised by idealist philosophies of history. Adorno, of course, has the Marxist appropriation of the Hegelian philosophy of history in mind, according to which the contradiction between forces and relations of production would eventually run into crisis, culminating into a social revolution. Even if this Marxist teleology of history did not materialize, Adorno contends, this Hegelian strand of thought proved to be right in understanding concepts of thought as historically and socially sedimented categories.

The problem that Adorno signals is that the tensions and contradictions within these sedimentations lost their emancipatory promise. Together with Max Horkheimer, Adorno already discussed in *Dialectics of Enlightenment* that the use of reason to escape from the barbarity of nature has itself become a dominating force, with the instrumental rationalities of capitalism and fascism as prime examples. More precisely, reason's instrumentalization in modern capitalism has effectively created a social order that excludes rather than liberates thoughts, practices, and experiences differing from the functional logic of the capitalist form of life. Borrowing from Georg Lukács' *History and Class Consciousness*, Adorno recognizes the force of identity thinking in the capitalist "commodity form" that subsumes any thought or practice under the generally applicable form of capitalist life (cf. Vervoort 2021). Hence, the need for a reflexive approach to reason not only follows from the failure of reason's emancipatory dedication, but also from its reversal: the suffering caused by fascism and capitalism. Adorno's project to formulate a negative dialectics should therefore be considered as an effort to formulate a way of doing philosophy that regards the force of reason, and especially its tendency to presuppose an identity between thought and reality, with suspicion, while at the same time preserving an historical-dialectical understanding of the meaning and significance of concepts of thought. To do so, Adorno limits the role of philosophy to a reflexive posture towards its own categories. Philosophy, in the first place, is "obliged to ruthlessly criticize itself" (Adorno 2004: 3).[3]

The stringency of such a philosophy of self-critique is exemplified by Adorno's critical theory of society. Strikingly, he notes that, in late capitalism, "[w]hat proved idle in theory was ironically confirmed in practice" (2004: 23). Whereas the theoretical unity between concept and reality, subject and object, or philosophy of history and revolutionary praxis remained but a projection of idealist philosophies, particular, social practices within the capitalist form of life are in fact totally subsumed under the general categories of capitalist reason. Like Lukács, then, Adorno emphasizes that every praxis is eminently theoretical (1966: 147, cf. 2003b: 798, 2008: 58): capitalist social practices are formed by the instrumentalization of the same spirit of theoretical reason that should have brought forth a transformative revolutionary praxis. Following this observation, Adorno cannot judge practices and rationalities of capitalist social life as false according to a transcendent, rational view of the good life. Rather, as he famously claims in *Minima Moralia,* it is impossible to foster the good life – theoretically or practically – within the falseness of the wrong life.

---

3   Here and elsewhere, I have slightly amended the translation.

As an alternative, Adorno formulates a negative dialectics that takes issue with reason's very claim or capacity to have the last word about social reality. Adorno traces the identification of thought with its object back to Kant's transcendental philosophy, but locates its "mobilization" in Hegel's dialectical idealism which, according to him, "represents the attempt to incorporate into philosophy whatever is heterogeneous, philosophy's other" (2008: 57). Even though Adorno compliments Hegel for giving philosophy the capacity "to think substantively" (2004: 7), he emphasizes that the identity that Hegel sought between concepts and their objects was imprisoned in its own "circle of identification", unable to grasp anything outside of its own framework of thought. As he puts it in his lectures on negative dialectics, Hegel attempted "to comprehend the non-identical, albeit to comprehend it by identifying it" (2008: 59). Consequently, rational thought came to identify only itself. By questioning the possibility to rationally conceptualize, schematize, and penetrate the multitude of experiences that make up social life, Adorno aims to call attention to moments that are non-identical with the form of reason governing society. It is with reference to these moments of non-identity between experience and reason that Adorno hopes to shed light on the contradictory character of the capitalist form of life. Hence, Adorno regards the tendency to presuppose an identity between thought and reality with suspicion: if the possibility of emancipation follows from those moments that do not fit the mode of thinking under which things are subsumed, the philosopher ought to use its concepts with care.

To counteract the self-referentiality of thought and call attention to moments that are non-identical to the reification of social life, Adorno underscores the primacy, *Vorrang* or preponderance, of the *object*. He argues that "philosophy should seek its contents in the unlimited diversity of its objects. It should become fully receptive to them without looking to any system of coordinates or its so-called postulates for backing" (2008: 81). Without pleading for the autonomy of objectivity or a crude materialism or empiricism,[4] which he considers just as socially construed as the categories of thought (1966: 184, cf. 186, 193),[5] Adorno directs philosophical critique towards "nonconceptuality, individuality, and particularity" (*Begriffslosen, Einzelnen und Besonderen*) (1966: 21, 2004: 8). The utopic counterimage to idealist dialectics that Adorno sketches, aspires "to use concepts to unseal the nonconceptual with concepts,

---

4   "Tatsächlich kann keine [...] die facta bruta an den Haaren herbeischleppen und [...] die Einzeldinge in die Texte kleben." (Adorno 1966: 23).
5   "Trotz des Vorrangs des Objekts ist die Dinghaftigkeit der Welt auch Schein." (1966: 190).

without making it their equal" (2004: 10). As such, Adorno's problematization of the identity between concepts and their objects prefigures Butler's emphasis on the incompleteness of foundationalist categories of identity. In *Negative Dialectics*, he indeed argues that

> If a stroke of undeserved luck has kept the mental composition of some individuals not quite adjusted to the prevailing norms – a stroke of luck they have often enough to pay for in their relations with their environment – it is up to these individuals to make the moral and, as it were, representative effort to say what most of those for whom they say it cannot see or, to do justice to reality, will not allow themselves to see.
>
> ADORNO 2004: 41

Although Adorno discusses alleged alternatives to idealist philosophy such as the works of Husserl, Heidegger, Sartre, Bergson, Scheler, Simmel, and Merleau-Ponty – some of whom influenced Butler's thought directly or indirectly – he concludes that these merely represent a "false concreteness" according to which an authentic account of reality would be possible without the mediation of reason. The denial of such mediation, for Adorno, only reproduces identity thinking: thought is supposed to be capable of identifying things in the world as if it were able to capture things directly in their singularity. The goal of Adorno's negative dialectics is to show that such an approach to reality precisely excludes the heterogeneity – and thus the fundamental irrepresentability – of those parts of the world that are lost when things are subsumed under the categories of thought. Instead, the self-reflexive form of philosophy that Adorno proposes aims to deconstruct the unifying force of concepts of reason. Indeed, Adorno contends that the social world is in fact far more heterogeneous than its conceptualization makes us believe (2003a: 89). As Deborah Cook summarizes, then, the problem Adorno's negative dialectics revolves around is that "no concept can fully grasp non-conceptual material things because concepts are subjective constructs rather than objective entities" (Cook 2013: 966). Hence, everything heterogeneous must compromise its heterogeneity when encountering the categories of identification.

Although Adorno stresses that it is impossible to conceive of anything without concepts, he leaves open the possibility to transgress the Hegelian logic of "identity between identity and non-identity" by means of a critique of conceptual thinking *through* concepts. Such critique of society from the standpoint of philosophy presupposes a reflexive stance towards thought itself, to make room for what it excludes: the non-identical. Hence, the aim of Adorno's philosophical project is to formulate an immanent critique of the coercive force of identity thinking to make room for what is heterogeneous to it. As such, his version of dialectics is only negatively "achievable": as a negativist critique (cf. Jaeggi 2005), it does not refer to a normative framework, utopian prospect, first nature, or true objectivity to justify its conclusions. Rather, negative dialectics aims to undermine the reification of the world by questioning existing categories of identity under reference to the glimpses of non-identity that in themselves remain inaccessible. Or, as Adorno puts it, "[i]t is concerned with what is heterogeneous to itself without reducing it to prefabricated categories" (2008: 66). Again, Adorno does not renounce conceptual thinking altogether, but contends that we cannot do without concepts, so that thought should self-reflexively question *how* it uses its concepts. Critical social theory should reach "by way of the concept, to transcend the concept" (2004: 15) – that is, enable the disenchantment of philosophical concepts and encourage the possibility to sink into what is heterogeneous to it – without identifying the latter with its ready-made universals. Negative dialectics takes issue with reason's tendency to think in identity categories, and mobilizes reason itself to question its own tendency towards identity thinking. As such, it opposes the Kantian effort to create a synthesis out of the chaotic diversity (*Mannigfaltigkeit*) of experience. In its anti-systematicity, it aims to be receptive to philosophy's "open and unshielded part" (2004: 20), acknowledging rather than denying the aporic nature of knowledge and thinking. In a nutshell, this is how a critical identity politics could respond to its paradoxical conjuncture: as there is no way around a strategic recourse to identity in emancipatory politics, a reflective attitude towards the categories it mobilizes forms the necessary precondition implied by its emancipatory efforts.

4   The Persistence of Dialectics in Butler's Work

It might seem as if Butler's Foucauldian work on the discursive power of gender is miles away from Adorno's dialectical considerations on identity thinking. Still, in the 1999 introduction of Butler's "juvenal" (Butler [1987] 1999: xiv) monograph *Subjects of Desire*, they state that "all of [their] work remains within the orbit of a certain set of Hegelian questions: What is the relation between desire and recognition, and how is it that the constitution of the subject entails a radical and constitutive relation to alterity?" (1999: xx). Moreover, Butler stresses that during their doctoral research, they "worked in the traditions of phenomenology, hermeneutics, and the Frankfurt School while seeking to acquire a background in German Idealism" (Butler 1999: xiii; cf. Butler

2021). Hence, Butler's philosophical background, if anything, comes remarkably close to Adorno: like him, they worked specifically within the tradition of the Frankfurt School and dealt extensively with Hegelian dialectics. It could therefore be said that Butler's work on gender identity has always been informed by the same philosophical questions as Adorno's negative dialectics. In the following, I will consider how Butler's discussion of identity politics is indeed commensurable with Adorno's negative dialectics as far as both problematize how the constitution of regimes of thought excludes heterogeneous experiences and demand a reflexivity towards the use of categories of identity.

Carrie Hull, Marcel Stoetzler and, more recently, Alexandra Colligs have already traced the resonances between Adorno's negative dialectics and Butler's theory of gender (Colligs 2021, 2022; Hull 1997; Stoetzler 2005). Stoetzler, for one, contends that Butler's critique of dialectics "leaves out what is *outside* the *Hegelian concept* of dialectics," namely the possibility of an Adornian "*negative dialectics*" – even though such negative dialectics shares Butler's "rejection of 'identitarian thinking'" (2005, 358). Moreover, Stoetzler claims that Adorno's negative dialectics refers to "a perspective where the societal compulsion to 'have' or 'be' an identity could vanish," whereas Butler would not. As such, Stoetzler reverses the negativistic approach of Adorno's critique of identity thinking. From an Adornian perspective, the outside of a dialectics of identification can only be referred to negatively, by way of criticizing positive and reifying forms of identification. Any direct reference to "objectivity" or the vanishing of social compulsion lies beyond the capacities of thought.

Hull, on the other hand, reads Butler's *Bodies that Matter* to contend that Butler, like Adorno, conceives of "no access to matter prior to its conceptualization in thought and language" (Hull 1997: 23). Indeed, the "matter" of sex, for Butler, is just as discursively produced as its gendered conceptualization. Like Adorno, Butler explicitly considers materiality as the "imposition of a form" (cf. the Introduction of Butler 2011; 1997: 23) rather than as an autonomous point of reference. Still, Hull adds that, for Butler, "relative outsides or margins […] are also constitutive of reality" as far as "the 'other' to any thought category, while lying outside of that category, is intimately connected to it" (1997: 24) whereas, according to Hull, Adorno would argue that "the abject outside maintains a distinctness owing directly to its objectivity" (1997: 25, cf. 31).

Hull is right to emphasize the distinctness of Adorno's non-identical. Her use of the term "objectivity" rather than "non-identity" to describe the distinctness of the outside of reason, however, confuses Adorno's argument. Adorno would be wary to understand the non-identical as constitutive for thought because of its distinctness. The negativity of Adorno's dialectics implies that the distinctness of its outside can only come to the fore in conceptualized constellations. Reason itself is fundamentally incapable to grasp the distinctness of its outside. Still, Colligs too argues that Adorno is committed to the primacy of a material reality. As we have seen, however, Adorno's negative dialectics explicitly argues against a crude empiricism that claims access to an authentic materiality. It is only through the identification of the non-identical that the outside of reason, as a (de)formed objectivity, becomes accessible to reason. As such, the materiality of the non-identical can only be known as an objectivity mediated by identity thinking. Like Butler's reference to alterity, the non-identical can only be thought through hegemonic concepts, norms, or discourse. The outside as an outside, on the other hand, fundamentally preserves its alterity.

As such, Butler's treatment of materiality remains close to Adorno's treatment of the non-identical: both Butler and Adorno recognize the preponderance of an alterity that escapes hegemonic and reified social forms, a non-identical instance that only becomes schematized into an objective form once it encounters conceptual and discursive frameworks. The outside of thought is co-constitutive of conceptuality, but loses its distinctness in its interaction with the forms that make it discursively and rationally accessible.

In *Gender Trouble*, however, Butler allegedly already replaced – or even "rejected" (cf. Butler, Osborne, and Segal 1994: 35; Stoetzler 2005: 344) – the dialectics between inside and outside for a Foucauldian genealogical approach towards discourse. Indeed, they write that "[t]he Hegelian model of self-recognition [...] presupposes a potential adequation between the 'I' that confronts its world [...] and the 'I' that finds itself as an object in that world. But the subject/object dichotomy [...] conditions the very problematic of identity that it seeks to solve" (1999: 183). From an Adornian perspective, however, the outside of a dialectics of identification can only be found negatively, by way of criticizing the dialectics of identification. His orientation towards the non-identical implies an effort to find glimpses of hope in a reified world that has no outside. Hence, as far as we understand Butler's emphasis on the "outside" as a negativist critique of its incomplete and violent identification and objectification, their position is closer to Adorno's than Hull, Stoetzler, and Colligs suggest.

When we take a closer look at Butler's explicit engagements with Adorno's work, this point proves its plausibility. In the essay "What is Critique," inspired by both Foucault's 1978 lectures on the same topic (Butler 2003; Foucault 2015, see also Foucault 2020), Butler already describes Adorno's conception of critique "as part of a praxis [...] to apprehend the ways in which categories are themselves instituted, how the field of knowledge is ordered, and how what it suppresses returns, as it were, as its own constitutive occlusion" (2003b: 305).

Butler explicitly endorses Adorno's negativist approach to critique, explaining critique as "always a critique *of* some instituted practice, discourse, episteme, institution" (2003b: 304). Countering the alleged break between their Hegelian and Foucauldian works, they suggest that Foucault's notion of critique, in an analogous way to Adorno, aims to "question the limits of our most sure ways of knowing" (2003b: 307). As such, Butler contends that critique surfaces because "one has already run up against a crisis within the epistemological field in which one lives" (2003b: 307). For Butler, critique emerges when "[t]he categories by which social life are ordered produce a certain incoherence or entire realms of unspeakability" creating a "tear in the fabric of our epistemological web" (2003b: 307). Hence, Butler argues that the outside of discourse emerges as a non-identical moment producing a crisis within the discourse of identity thinking that it, in its alterity, does not fit. Like Adorno's "preponderance of the object," then, Butler's emphasis on alterity can only manifest itself as a moment of distinctness that shows itself to be crisis-prone or even incomprehensible within the hegemonic discourse.

In *Giving an Account of Oneself* (2005), that grew out of Butler's Adorno-lectures in Frankfurt, they indeed describe Adorno's model of critique as "implicated in a social temporality that exceeds its own capacities for narration" while "the perspective of 'I' has no story of its own that is not also the story of a relation – or set of relations – to a set of norms" (2005: 8). Butler comes to emphasize subjectivity as always already situated in intersubjective relationships. They suggest that Adorno's immanent mode of critique allows for the development of an understanding of subjectivity that moves away from an understanding of the subject as a mere product of discourse (cf. 2005: 15), as the latter cannot account for "the desire to recognize another or be recognized by one" (2005: 22). In other words, Butler now understands subjective identities as relational, granting that social norms are the instances that provide "the terms that make self-recognition possible" (2005: 22). Hence, they argue that "what I can 'be'" is always already conditioned by "a regime of truth that decides what will and will not be a recognizable form of being" (2005: 22).

In short, Butler now claims that hegemonic discursive identities provide social norms as "a framework for the scene of recognition" (2005: 22). Accordingly, Butler stresses the "social dimension" of subjectivity to emphasize that alternative social ontologies can only arise through an engagement with given norms and categories of identity. It is in this sense that they refer to Adorno's negative dialectics as a model of critique that problematizes "claims of collectivity [that] turn out not to be collective, when claims of abstract universality turn out not to be universal" (Butler 2005: 8). Motivated by Adorno's emphasis on the social embeddedness of the subject, Butler comes to conceive of subjectivity as formed "in relation to a set of codes, prescriptions, or norms" (Butler 2005: 16). They argue that self-formation is always bound to norms that "precede and exceed the subject" (2005: 16). Consequently, forms of subjectivity that are non-identical to hegemonic discourses of the self – such as those of the gender dichotomy – can only emerge if their practices critically engage with "the limits of the historical scheme of things" (2005: 19). According to Butler, then, these norms are encountered "through proximate and living exchanges, in the modes by which we are addressed and asked to take up the question of who we are and what our relation to the other ought to be" (2005: 31). In the years after, Butler increasingly delves into such "ungrievable" subjectivities that are "outside" the scope of recognition, and insofar as these subjectivities manifest themselves politically, are positioned to push the limits of institutionalized discourses (Butler 2004a, 2005, 2009, 2013; Chambers 2008). Accordingly, Butler comes to contend that the contestation of norms presupposes that subjects risk their "intelligibility and recognizability" (2005: 133). Indeed, when subjectivities deviate from prevalent norms in society, they risk their self-identity. Hence, answering the question "Who are you?" (2005: 134) can be the first step towards reflexive modes of subjectivity that could contest the reification of social discourses.

5   The Negative Dialectics of Identity and Difference

My contention is that a reflection on the relation between Adorno's philosophy of non-identity and Butler's reflections on subjectivity can provide the building blocks for a critical identity politics. In fact, Nancy Fraser already described Butler's emphasis on the dynamics between identification and deconstruction as "close to Theodor Adorno's attempt to articulate a non-identitarian mode of thinking" (Fraser in Benhabib 1995: 74). The transformative potential of a critical identity politics would not only lie in the representation of subordinated identities per se, but rather in the critical stance towards the very identities it mobilizes. As we have seen, Butler explicitly claims that "[i]dentity categories are never merely descriptive, but always normative, and as such, exclusionary" (Butler 1994: 14). Their reflections on the entanglements of social norms and the exclusionary effects of identity thinking highlight that a political mobilization of identity categories should be "necessarily subject to continual deconstruction" within a "dialectic" that is itself "a political resource" (Butler in Benhabib 1995: 69). As Carolyn Culbertson points out, for Butler, "it is necessary both to occupy socially-situated subject positions and, meanwhile, to interrogate the conditions of these positions, opening up their foundations to contestation" (Culbertson 2013: 451).

Adorno also directs emancipatory practices towards the dialectical tension between identity categories and their residues. Although he contends that critique does not easily "liquidate" the system (2004: 24), his critique of identity thinking as well provides an elementary building block for a critical identity politics. Even if Adorno suggests that the totality of society is subsumed under the commodity form, this subsumption of society under identity categories always remains aporic, and thus not *entirely* total. Experience continues to be full of contradictions, precisely because the generality of identity categories is incapable of encompassing all the particularities they purport to identify. Hence, what transgresses identity thinking, the non-identical, should not be considered as an original, authentic, or objective moment of reality. Rather, the possibility of critique lies in the aporia where "the object of a mental experience is an antagonistic system in itself – antagonistic in reality, not just in its conveyance to the knowing subject that rediscovers itself therein" (Adorno 2004: 10).

By considering both subjective universals and external objectivity as socially constructed, negative dialectics wants to point towards the differentiated heterogeneity lying outside of the rationality of philosophical thought. Adorno proposes to express these non-identical relations between concepts and individuals by means of "models" or "constellations" that lay bare the aporia in a system of identities by leaving the non-identity between particulars and universals intact. As there is no way around concepts in thought, their incompleteness vis-à-vis the particular necessitates one to "cite" other concepts (*herbeizitieren*) from which said constellations emerge. In this way, Adorno invokes a genealogical dimension into the critique of identity thinking: the shifting meaning of constellations of concepts shows that their universality is not atemporal but *becomes* and changes under certain conditions. Consequently, Adorno's strategy to unleash the heterogeneity of the non-identical limits itself to the examination of conceptual constellations beyond which the non-identical lies: the non-identity between universals and their referents demands a multiplicity of concepts to approach any particular. The critique of concepts *is* conceptual; it is through the constellation of concepts that their genealogy, their social construction, their historicity, contingency, and their incompleteness can be shown.

Ultimately, Adorno's critique of dialectics shows that the *Schein* of reconciliation excludes the possibility of emancipation. His critical theory revolves around the de- and reconstruction of constellations within which objectivity is immersed. What is implied is that social critique only becomes possible when the concepts that organize the social order are historicized. When the non-identical is left irreconciled, that is, not submerged under a universal concept, it can be experienced as non-identical to it, thus encouraging experiences that contest the timelessness of universal thought schemata. Moreover, through a constellational critique, the critical social theorist is positioned to "compose" new conceptual categories that account for their incompleteness (1966: 57). Constellations relate themselves to the heterogeneity of the non-identical, by acknowledging that the non-identical will remain outside their scope. Philosophy that self-reflexively takes the non-identical into consideration without aiming to subsume it under its categories, thus tasks itself with perpetually questioning the identification of conceptual mediations with their objects.

What is provided by the non-identical, then, is not objectivity as such; nor is negative dialectics an effort to establish the truth of the non-identical. The non-identical establishes the limit (*Grenzwert*) which philosophy cannot cross when observing and criticizing its object. Still, critique is aimed at this limit and, in addition, at questioning how, why, where and by whom it is drawn. In Adorno's philosophy, therefore, emancipation is only possible by taking issue with the rationality of identity thinking. As he puts it: "Only if things might have gone differently; if the totality is recognized as a socially necessary semblance, as the hypostasis of the universal pressed out of individual human beings; if its claim to be absolute is broken – only then will a critical social consciousness retain its freedom to think that things might be different someday" (2004: 323).

I have shown that, for Adorno, thought itself plays a crucial role in the exclusion of the heterogeneous and non-identical. What is at stake, for Adorno, is not a mere 'metaphysical' problem. Rather, Adorno understands the acknowledgement of the non-identical as a crucial prerequisite for the possibility of emancipation. As Deborah Cook points out, "those who refuse, or are unable, to identify themselves with society and its norms – or with what Adorno often called the 'universal' – suffer" (2013: 673). It is this primordial suffering, which is indeed an important theme in Adorno's social critique, that is reminiscent of Butler's emphasis on subjectivities caught between categories or outside of them. The refusal of the norms of society, however, cannot be separated from the activity of critical thought. Rather, for Adorno, thought preserves the potential to resist what is imposed upon it. When categories of identity are experienced as repressive or subordinating, the possibility of resistance is implied, since the experience of oppression creates the very aporia that unmasks the subsumption of society under its totalizing concepts as false.

As far as Cook is right that "[Adorno's] critique of identity thinking extends to the stereotyping and compartmentalization of individuals and groups"

(2018: 102), this observation also extends to Butler's problematization of the exclusionary effects of gender categories. Indeed, Butler understands "the field of differential relations from which all particular identities emerge" as "limit-less," and the "incompleteness" of identities as "a direct result of its differential emergence" since "no particular identity can emerge without presuming and enacting the exclusion of others" (2000: 31). Hence, their theory of performa-tivity is directed to "emphasize the way in which the social world is made – and new social possibilities emerge – at various levels of social action through a col-laborative relation with power" (2000: 14).

What follows is that the emancipation of the socio-economically exploited, people of color, queer people, women, and any other subordinated group should aim at a liberation *from* the fundamentally *incomplete* concepts that cannot account for the heterogeneity of their members. Indeed, Adorno pro-poses to criticize concepts through concepts, just as identities can be ques-tioned through identities, to show that identities can never grasp the non-identical. Such dissolutions clear the way for an orientation towards the future in which new forms of subjectivity, beyond given identities, can flourish. Indeed, in "Progress," Adorno alludes to an idea of emancipation as the setting free of the radical *difference* between individuals, writing that "[h]umanity can be thought only through this extreme form of differentiation, individuation" (Adorno 2005, 151). As such, Adorno's reflections on the fundamental incom-pleteness of identity categories prefigure Butler's reference to the political potential of the marginal perspective of alterity that does not fit into hege-monic identity categories. His negative dialectics shows that thought has the tendency to level out all differences residing within the heterogeneous social world. Again, for Adorno, this is not a mere philosophical observation, but a social critique. The subsumption of non-identical particulars under universal identities produces a social world that does not allow for deviations from uni-versals. Hence, the task of critical theory is to point out how thought itself is invested in this mode of thinking.

Both Butler and Adorno, then, argue that general concepts of identity play a decisive role in establishing the limit between reified social categories and their outside. They both aim to lay bare how *abstracta* shape our reality, and they both criticize their universal validity to facilitate the possibility to resist the order they constitute. Moreover, Butler's proposal to solve the paradox of identity politics by a strategy of "subversive repetition" of identity is prefigured by Adorno's distrust towards reason's tendency to identity thinking – even if we cannot do without it. When Butler points to the fact that "theories of feminist identity that elaborate predicates of color, sexuality, ethnicity, class, and able-bodiedness invariably close with an embarrassed 'etc.' at the end of the list," they maintain that such a "Hegelian" mode of identification "conditions the very problematic that it seeks to solve" (1999: 196). With Adorno, we can explain this painful "etc." as referring to the non-identical: it points to the fact that identity thinking always remains incomplete. By accounting for this incompleteness, identity politics can remain true to its emancipatory moment without lapsing into a representational politics. Both Adorno and Butler allude to these non-identical possibilities that become feasible when given truths, norms, identities, and power relations are criticized. They argue for a form of resistance that does not aim at improving the representation of a subordinated identity, but at the emancipation of *all* individuals in their singularity. The complicity of identity thinking with given norms in society requires a constant critical approach towards identities themselves. Questioning and criticizing relations of power and the identity categories they build upon, is fundamental for political resistance that wants to move beyond the social and epistemic orders we find ourselves in.

References

Adorno, Theodor W. 1966. *Negative Dialektik*. Frankfurt am Main: Suhrkamp.

Adorno, Theodor W. [1931] 1977. "The Actuality of Philosophy." *Telos* 1977(31): 120–33.

Adorno, Theodor W. 2003a. "Postscriptum." In *Soziologische Schriften. Gesammelte Schriften Band 8*, 86–92. Frankfurt am Main: Suhrkamp.

Adorno, Theodor W. 2003b. "Resignation." In *Kulturkritik und Gesellschaft II. Gesammelte Schriften Band 10.2*, 794–99. Frankfurt am Main: Suhrkamp.

Adorno, Theodor W. 2004. *Negative Dialectics*. London: Taylor & Francis.

Adorno, Theodor W. 2005. *Critical Models: Interventions and Catchwords*. New York: Columbia University Press.

Adorno, Theodor W. 2008. *Lectures on Negative Dialectics: Fragments of a Lecture Course 1965/1966*. Cambridge: Polity.

Benhabib, Seyla, ed. 1995. *Feminist Contentions: a Philosophical Exchange*. New York: Routledge.

Butler, Judith. [1990] 1994. "Contingent Foundations: Feminism and the Question of 'Postmodernism.'" In *The Postmodern Turn*, edited by S. Seidman, 153–70. Cambridge University Press.

Butler, Judith. 1997. *The Psychic Life of Power: Theories in Subjection*. Stanford, CA: Stanford University Press.

Butler, Judith. [1990] 1999. *Gender Trouble: Feminism and the Subversion of Identity*. New York: Routledge.

Butler, Judith. [1987] 1999. *Subjects of Desire: Hegelian Reflections in Twentieth Century France*. New York: Columbia University Press.

Butler, Judith. 2003. "What Is Critique?" In *The Judith Butler Reader*, edited by S. Salih, 302–22. Malden, MA: Blackwell Pub.

Butler, Judith. 2004a. *Precarious Life: the Powers of Mourning and Violence*. London/New York: Verso.

Butler, Judith. 2004b. *Undoing Gender*. New York/London: Routledge.

Butler, Judith. 2005. *Giving an Account of Oneself*. New York: Fordham University Press.

Butler, Judith. 2009. *Frames of War: When Is Life Grievable?* London/New York: Verso.

Butler, Judith. [1993] 2011. *Bodies That Matter: On the Discursive Limits of "Sex."* Abingdon/New York: Routledge.

Butler, Judith. [1997] 2013. *Excitable Speech: a Politics of the Performative*. 1st ed. Routledge.

Butler, Judith. 2021. "Recognition and the Social Bond: a Response to Axel Honneth." In Ikäheimo, Heikki, Kristina Lepold, and Titus Stahl, eds., *Recognition and Ambivalence*, 31–54. New York: Columbia University Press.

Butler, Judith, and Liz Kotz. 1992. "The Body You Want: an Interview with Judith Butler." *Artforum* 82–89.

Butler, Judith, Ernesto Laclau, and Slavoj Žižek. 2000. *Contingency, Hegemony, Universality: Contemporary Dialogues on the Left*. London: Verso.

Butler, Judith, Peter Osborne, and Lynne Segal. 1994. "Gender as Performance." *Radical Philosophy* (67): 32–39.

Chambers, Samuel. 2008. *Judith Butler and Political Theory: Troubling Politics*. 1st ed. Routledge.

Colligs, Alexandra. 2021. *Identität und Befreiung: Subjektkritik nach Butler und Adorno*. Frankfurt: Campus Verlag.

Colligs, Alexandra. 2022. "Zwei Formen der Kritik an Identität. Zum Verhältnis von Kritischer Theorie und Queerfeminismus." In *Kritische Theorie und Feminismus*, edited by K. Stögner and A. Colligs, 225–46. Berlin: Suhrkamp.

Combahee River Collective. 2014. "A Black Feminist Statement." *Women's Studies Quarterly* 42(3/4): 271–80.

Cook, Deborah. 2013. "Adorno, Foucault and Critique." *Philosophy and Social Criticism* 39(10): 965 81.

Cook, Deborah. 2018. *Adorno, Foucault and the Critique of the West*. London/New York: Verso.

Culbertson, Carolyn. 2013. "The Ethics of Relationality: Judith Butler and Social Critique." *Continental Philosophy Review* 46(3): 449–63.

Foucault, Michel. 1998. *The Will to Knowledge*. Harmondsworth: Penguin Books.

Foucault, Michel. 2015. "Qu'est-ce que la critique?" In *Qu'est-ce que la critique? Suivi de La culture de soi*, edited by H.-P. Fruchaud and D. Lorenzini, 33–80. Paris: Vrin.

Foucault, Michel. 2020. "What Is Enlightenment?" In *Foucault Reader: an Introduction to Foucault's Thought*, edited by P. Rabinow, 32–50. London: Penguin Books.

Grady, Constance. 2018. "The Waves of Feminism, and Why People Keep Fighting over Them, Explained." *Vox*, March 20.

Haider, Asad. 2018. *Mistaken Identity: Race and Class in the Age of Trump*. London/New York: Verso.

Haider, Asad. 2020. "Identity." *History of the Present* 10(2): 237–55.

Hardt, Michael, and Antonio Negri. 2000. *Empire*. Cambridge, MA: Harvard University Press.

Hekman, Susan. 2000. "Beyond Identity: Feminism, Identity and Identity Politics." *Feminist Theory* 1(3): 289–308.

Honneth, Axel. 2006. "Einleitung. Zum Begriff der Philosophie." In *Theodor W. Adorno: Negative Dialektik*, edited by A. Honneth and C. Menke, 11–28. Berlin: Akademie Verlag.

Hull, Carrie L. 1997. "Materiality in Theodor W. Adorno and Judith Butler." *Radical Philosophy* (84): 22–35.

Jaeggi, Rahel. 2005. "'No Individual Can Resist': Minima Moralia as Critique of Forms of Life." *Constellations* 12(1): 65–82.

Spivak, Gayatri Chakravorthy. 1990. "Criticism, Feminism, and the Institution." In *The Post-colonial Critic: Interviews, Strategies, Dialogues*, edited by S. Harasym, 1 16. New York: Routledge.

Stoetzler, Marcel. 2005. "Subject Trouble: Judith Butler and Dialectics." *Philosophy and Social Criticism* 31(3): 343–68.

Vervoort, Tivadar. 2020. "Krisis, identiteit en kritiek." *Krisis | Journal for Contemporary Philosophy* 40(1): 60–67. https://doi.org/10.21827/krisis.40.1.37055.

Vervoort, Tivadar. 2021. "Towards a Critique of Reification as a Critique of Forms of Life." *Metodo* 9(2): 291–326. https://doi.org/10.19079/metodo.9.2.291.

CHAPTER 7

Adorno, Foucault, and Feminist Theory
The Politics of Truth

Lambert Zuidervaart

So far as we know, Theodor Adorno (1903–1969) and Michel Foucault (1926–1984) never met. Nor, for the most part, did they read each other's work. Yet their critiques of Western society are strikingly similar—so similar, in fact, that they have drawn comparable criticisms from Jürgen Habermas and Axel Honneth. They have also received analogous defenses from feminist Critical Theorists, such as Amy Allen and Deborah Cook, who challenge Habermas and Honneth's criticisms.

Central to these disputes lie issues concerning rationality, normativity, and the prospects for social transformation. Habermas takes Adorno and Foucault to task for so totalizing their critiques of modern rationality that no normative basis remains for their critiques (Habermas 1987: 106–30, 266–93; Bernstein 1991: 142–71). Likewise, Honneth criticizes both of them for neglecting the normative implications of social practices and social struggle (Honneth 1991). By contrast, Amy Allen, addressing the concerns of post- and decolonial theory, turns to Foucault and Adorno for worthy alternatives to the Eurocentric progressivism of Habermas and Honneth. According to Allen, Foucault and Adorno call "those who have inherited the project of Enlightenment to live up more fully to its normative ideals of freedom, inclusion, and respect for the other" (Allen 2016a: 165).[1] So too, in response to Habermas's criticisms, Deborah Cook argues that both Adorno and Foucault have sufficient normative grounding for their social critiques—Adorno, in the process of determinate negation; Foucault, in the history of resistance; and both of them, in a commitment to autonomy. According to Cook, such grounding makes them more astute critics than Habermas is of a society where economic exchange and political power

---

1 I should note that, whereas here Allen focuses on Foucault's early writings, especially his 1961 *History of Madness*, the criticisms I have cited from Habermas and Honneth pertain primarily to Foucault's middle writings, especially his 1975 *Discipline and Punish*.

predominate, and it lets them hold open the possibility of radical social transformation (Cook 2018: 142–51).[2]

Complex issues are at stake in these responses to Foucault and Adorno. There is no way to sort all of them out in one article. Nor do I intend to review the extensive literature on debates between Habermasians and Foucaultians concerning rationality, normativity, and social transformation.[3] Instead, let me focus on two concepts at the heart of these debates, ones that contemporary feminists need to revisit, namely, the ideas of power and truth. The concept of power has played a central role in feminist theories; the concept of truth, not so much.[4] Yet I shall argue that both concepts should be central to feminist critical theory.

I am especially concerned about the *relation* between power and truth, for here, it seems to me, lie both crucial insights and disturbing blind spots in Foucault and Adorno's critiques. Moreover, even when this relation is not explicitly thematized, it engenders many of the disputes about Foucault and Adorno in feminism and Critical Theory. My aim is not to resolve such disputes. Yet I do want to find a better way to think about power, truth, and their relation—better both conceptually and with respect to a contemporary political environment where powerful authoritarian populists not only try to undo the accomplishments of the feminist movement but also dismiss the importance of truth.

My discussion has three stages. First, I compare Adorno and Foucault's conceptions of power, with an emphasis on the connection between interactional and macrostructural forms of power. Next, I compare their conceptions of truth, with a focus on the interrelation between truth and power. Then, aiming to retrieve insights relevant for contemporary feminism, I offer critical reflections on their conceptions of truth and power and argue that feminist critical theory needs to develop both a new conception of truth and a sufficiently normative critique of power.

---

2   Cook briefly mentions Honneth's criticisms of Adorno and Foucault but does not address them.

3   In addition to the works already cited, see, for example, McCarthy 1991: 43–75; Kelly 1994; Hoy and McCarthy 1994; Ingram 2005; and Petherbridge 2013.

4   This is not to deny the crucial work done in feminist epistemology and feminist science and technology studies on the topics of knowledge and truth, however. Among the many books one could mention are Harding 1986, Haraway 1989, Longino 1990, Collins 1991, Code 1991, Alcoff 1996, and Hartsock 1998. For a survey of such contributions, see Anderson 2020.

1   **Power Dynamics**

1.1   *Feminism and Forms of Power*
Power is a protean concept, and it is the topic of countless contentions among
feminist theorists. Amy Allen (2016b) maps many of these feminist disputes
in an illuminating article titled "Feminist Perspectives on Power." In the first
place, she says, disagreements arise over whether power is best regarded as
influence ("power-over") or agency ("power-to").[5] These disagreements spill
over into disputes about whether, in my own vocabulary, power is primarily
interactional (i.e., occurring in the interrelations, practices, and institutions
that configure human agency and influence) or primarily macrostructural (i.e.,
occurring in or via the large-scale structures that organize social life—today,
arguably, civil society and economic and political systems). Whereas liberal
feminists and care theorists tend to emphasize agency and interactional power,
feminists who are critical theorists in the broad sense tend to emphasize influence and macrostructural power.[6] Moreover, what Allen calls "phenomenological feminist approaches" (e.g., Iris Young) and "analytic feminist approaches"
(e.g., Ann Cudd) often emphasize both interactional and macrostructural
power, as indicated, for example, by Sally Haslanger's calling attention to both
"agent oppression" and "structural oppression" (Haslanger 2012: 311–38).
      Even if one acknowledges both interactional and macrostructural forms of
power, however, questions remain about how these two forms interconnect—
whether, for example, one form has precedence over the other, and whether
their interconnection undergoes sociohistorical shifts. For, like race and class,
issues of gender transect what I have distinguished as macrostructural and
interactional forms of power. That is why Nancy Fraser rightly argues that the
injustices suffered by women and people of color in the contemporary West
can only be adequately addressed by a politics that properly combines striving
for socioeconomic equality with struggles for cultural recognition. Gender and
race are what she calls "paradigmatic bivalent collectivities." They encompass
both "political-economic dimensions and cultural-valuational dimensions."

---

5   In an earlier and more extensive discussion, Allen also distinguishes solidarity ("power-
    with") from influence and agency, arguing that a feminist conception of power must include
    all three senses of power in order to understand "masculine domination, feminine empower-
    ment and resistance, and feminist solidarity and coalition-building" (Allen 1999: 123).
6   Under *critical theory* in the broad sense, I include what Allen distinguishes as radical,
    socialist, intersectional, and poststructuralist feminists. When referring specifically to the
    Frankfurt School tradition, I capitalize *Critical Theory*. Feminists in the tradition of Critical
    Theory usually align with critical theory in the broad sense rather than with, say, liberal fem-
    inism or care theory.

For such bivalent collectivities, "both socioeconomic maldistribution and cultural misrecognition ... are primary and co-original" (Fraser 1997: 19). In other words, the injustices the members of these collectivities suffer arise from power dynamics in both the macrostructures of society (especially the proprietary economy and the administrative state) and the patterns of social interaction (i.e., in interrelations, practices, and institutions) and, as Fraser argues, they require a suitably "bivalent" response.

Because both Adorno and Foucault, each in his own way, thematize the interconnection between interactional and macrostructural power, their social critiques remain relevant for feminist theory and politics. By highlighting questions about how these forms of power interconnect and making them central to a critique of Western society, Adorno and Foucault make indispensable contributions to feminist critical theory, as well as to other modes of critical theory such as queer theory, postcolonial theory, and critical race theory. Yet they have different conceptions of both interactional and macrostructural power. In these differences one can discern conceptual problems that, I argue, feminists should not perpetuate. These problems become especially pressing when one considers how power and truth interrelate.

1.2 *Foucault: Disciplinary Power and Biopolitics*

The most prominent concepts of power in Foucault's work, and certainly the ones that have attracted the most discussion and debate, occur in genealogical writings from the mid-1970s. These include *Surveiller et punir* (1975; in English, Foucault 1977) and *La Volenté de savoir* (1976, the first volume in *The History of Sexuality*) as well as essays, interviews, and lectures from the same time. Deborah Cook and Amy Allen rightly point out that these writings deploy two closely related concepts of power, namely, disciplinary power and state biopower (Cook 2018: 31–60; Allen 2008: 48–60). Foucault claims that these are distinctly modern forms of power. They have developed since the end of the eighteenth century, and they have gradually supplanted earlier forms of power.

That is why common social-critical concepts of power such as repression and domination, which Foucault himself had used in earlier writings, fail to capture how power operates in contemporary society. Hence, for example, he rejects what he calls "the repressive hypothesis" with respect to modern sexuality—the hypothesis "that modern industrial societies ushered in an age of increased sexual repression" (Foucault 1978: 49). He also insists that a "juridical" or "sovereign" theory of power, one which posits a sovereign ruler wielding control over social subjects by enforcing the rule of law, is inappropriate for understanding modern society (Foucault 1980b: 121–5), where power primarily flows through disciplinary practices and institutions and via state-sanctioned biopolitics.

Foucault regards modern power as a relation rather than either a substance or a nonrelational property. More specifically, as Allen suggests, it is a strategic relation in which opposing forces struggle to get the other to do what each wants (Allen 2008: 49–50). It is also productive, rather than repressive, aiming for results, rather than mere control: modern power "traverses and produces things, it induces pleasure, forms knowledge, produces discourse" (Foucault 1980b: 119). In contrast to the juridical or sovereign theory of power, then, what Allen calls Foucault's "strategic model" sees modern power as dispersed across society rather than concentrated in one institutional complex or macrostructure, as generated in myriad interrelations, practices, and institutions, and as aimed at results over which individual subjects might have little or no control.

Indeed, rather than think of individual subjects as "having" power, we should regard them as effects and conduits of power, Foucault says: "[O]ne of the first effects of power is that it allows bodies, gestures, discourses, and desires to be identified and constituted as something individual. The individual is not ... power's opposite number; the individual is one of power's first effects. The individual is in fact a power-effect, and ... to the extent that he is a power-effect, the individual is a relay: power passes through the individuals it has constituted" (Foucault 2003: 29–30).[7] Hence, one general effect of power in modern society is the subjection (*assujettisement*) of individuals, in a double sense: they are subject to relations of power, and they are constituted as subjects by the effects of power.

Although this does not mean that individuals are no more than the effects of power, it does mean that resistance to modern power must take the form of a struggle against subjection, a process Foucault calls "desubjection" (*désassujettisement*). This struggle involves both critical reflection on how power constitutes the subject and deliberate refashioning of the subject, using what Foucault calls technologies of the self. The freedom of individuals, then, lies not in an escape from power but in "strategically reworking the power relations to which we are subjected" (Allen 2008: 68).[8] In the first instance, these are relations of disciplinary power.

---

7   For an earlier translation of the first two lectures (i.e., January 7 and 14, 1976), see Foucault 1980c.

8   Foucault's account of subjection raises difficult questions about whether and how individual subjects can have the autonomy seemingly required to undertake both critical reflection upon, and deliberate transformation of, contemporary technologies of the self. Amy Allen argues in detail that Foucault does indeed give an account of such autonomy, although she thinks it needs to be supplemented by a more Habermasian approach, one that provides an

1.2.1   Disciplinary Power

Foucault explains the disciplinary model of power in *"Society Must Be Defended,"* lectures he gave in 1976, around the time of the "Truth and Power" interview I have already cited. Contrary to liberal and Marxist misconceptions, he says, disciplinary power is not a contractually negotiable private possession, nor is it simply political power aimed at economic ends. Instead, it is "exercised ... in action" and is "primarily ... a relationship of force" (Foucault 2003: 14–15). But how is power exercised? Not as oppression (which would presuppose a contractual model of legitimacy), nor as repression or top-down domination. Rather, disciplinary power operates by producing multiple "discourses of truth" that have "powerful effects." And such operation is not peripheral or optional: our society needs power-produced truth "in order to function" (Foucault 2003: 24).

Moreover, that is precisely how contemporary power flows—not from a central authority or a predominant macrostructure (e.g., State or economy) but via a wide diversity of practices and institutions to which individuals are subject. This implies, in turn, that, far from *possessing* power, individuals always simultaneously *submit to* and *exercise* power, and such power flows from the tiniest mechanisms into "increasingly general mechanisms" and even into "forms of overall domination" (Foucault 2003: 29–30).[9]

Indeed, the circulation of disciplinary power does not so much rely on ideological constructs as on instruments for creating and accumulating knowledge: "the observational methods, the recording techniques, the investigative research procedures, the verification mechanisms" (Foucault 2003: 33). This sort of power makes possible the extraction of time and labor from human bodies; it is "exercised through constant surveillance" (in what Foucault describes as a *surveillance society*) (Foucault 2003: 35–6); and it operates via the discourses of the human sciences—especially those tied to clinical knowledge (e.g., psychology, sociology, and the medical sciences). These disciplinary discourses do not seek to sort out what is legally or morally legitimate or right.

"intersubjective account of subjectivity and autonomy" grounded in "communicative interaction" (Allen 2008: 69). Although I think such questions about autonomy are crucial, I do not address them here.

9   In a short 1977 interview, Foucault hypothesizes that power, which is "co-extensive with the social body," occurs in relations of power that take multiple forms (not simply prohibition or punishment) and are "interwoven with other kinds of relations (production, kinship, family, sexuality) for which they play at once a conditioning and a conditioned role." Moreover, the interconnections among diverse relations of power "delineate general conditions of domination," and domination is organized into "global strategies" that make use of these power relations—albeit not without resistance, since "there are no relations of power without resistances" that can also be "integrated in global strategies" (Foucault 1980a: 142).

Instead, they aim to establish and enforce what is normal, thereby leading to what Foucault calls a *normalizing society* (Foucault 2003: 38–9).

For Foucault, the only viable and worthwhile alternative to such normalizing disciplinary power would not be an absence of power, and it certainly would not be reversion to the outdated sort of sovereign power from which the normative concepts of legitimacy and right stem. Instead, it would be a "nondisciplinary"—but also nonsovereign—form of power, tied to a new "antidisciplinary"—but also nonsovereign—form of right (Foucault 2003: 39–40).[10]

1.2.2   State Biopower

Although Foucault emphasizes the interactional form of power, which he calls disciplinary, he does not deny that power also takes a macrostructural form in the modern West. This is what he labels *biopower*, and he locates it primarily in how the administrative state intersects a capitalist economy. Foucault insists, however, that state biopower relies heavily on the operations of disciplinary power. Whereas disciplinary power targets individuals—as students, workers, prisoners, patients, and the like—biopower aims at entire populations and sometimes even at the human species as a whole.

Together, these two interlinked forms of power—disciplinary power and state biopower—make up a characteristically modern mode of power that, as Allen puts it, is "simultaneously individualizing and totalizing" (Allen 2008: 56). The first volume to *The History of Sexuality* describes this modern mode as a "power over life" having two interlinked "poles of development." The first pole centers on disciplining the individual body, optimizing its capability, making it more useful and docile, and integrating it into systems of control. Foucault calls such disciplinary power over life, exercised in schools, armies, prisons, and other institutions, an *"anatomo-politics of the human body."* The second pole of development focuses on what Foucault labels "the species body" as the basis for human survival and biological reproduction. It involves state supervision of entire populations, of births and deaths, public health, and the like. Foucault calls such state biopower over life a *"bio-politics of the population"* (Foucault 1978: 139).

According to Foucault, the development of sexuality was one of the most important ways in which these two forms of power over life conjoined in the

---

10   Although he does not deny that, along with disciplinary mechanisms, sovereignty remains one of the two essential components within modern society's general mechanism of power, Foucault refuses to give sovereignty either explanatory or normative preference. It persists, he suggests, primarily as a way to conceal how disciplinary power operates even in the democratic procurement of individual rights (Foucault 2003: 37).

nineteenth century. Also important, however, was how capitalism developed. On the one hand, the techniques of disciplinary power across diverse institutions such as the family, schooling, and medicine prepared a ready work force. On the other hand, techniques of state biopower made it possible to connect population growth with "the expansion of productive forces and the differential allocation of profit" (Foucault 1978: 141). Similar observations can be made about the domains of law and politics.

The main point, however, is that we cannot properly resist contemporary forms of subjection if we do not understand how both interactional (disciplinary) and macrostructural (state supervised) forms of power have developed and have become tightly intermeshed. That is why, on its own, neither a Freud-inspired diagnosis of sexual "repression" nor a roughly Marx-inspired diagnosis of economic "exploitation" or "oppression" will suffice for the purposes of Foucaultian social critique. That is also why feminist critical theorists, who tend to emphasize both influence and macrostructural power, find Foucault's work so important. Their challenge, as it was for Foucault, is to envision normative pathways along which the subjection of women can be not only resisted but also transformed, a topic I return to below.

1.3   *Adorno: Three Modes of Domination*
When Jacques Derrida accepted the City of Frankfurt's Theodor W. Adorno Prize in September 2001, he called himself an "heir to the Frankfurt School" for whom Adorno was an "adoptive father." Derrida thereby presented himself as a sibling rival to Jürgen Habermas. If Derrida could thus pose as Adorno's "other son," then both the similarities between Foucaultian and Adornian critiques of modernity and the striving between Foucault and Habermas over the legacy of the Enlightenment suggest, as Allen indicates, that we should regard Foucault as Adorno's "other 'other son.'"[11] This is especially so with regard to what Honneth has labeled "the critique of power" (Honneth 1991).

Yet there are also significant differences, as I hope to show, and they point to underlying issues that neither Foucault nor Adorno could adequately address. These differences are suggested by the title of the book by Adorno and Max Horkheimer to which Foucault shows the greatest affinities[12] and

---

11   Allen 2016a: 164, 250n1. In a more general way, David Couzens Hoy had already argued in 1994 that French poststructuralism—especially Foucault—is "an alternative way of continuing the tradition of [Frankfurt School] critical theory"—i.e., an alternative to Habermas (Hoy and McCarthy 1994: 144).

12   In 1978, asked about how his thought related to the early Frankfurt School, Foucault said Adorno and his colleagues "had tried, earlier than I, to say things I had also been trying to say for years," especially with regard to "the effects of power in their relation to [modern]

that Habermas most vigorously criticizes:[13] *Dialectic of Enlightenment*. For although, like Adorno and Horkheimer, Foucault conducts a genealogy of the imbrication of power and rationality, unlike them, he does not construe this as a universal-historical dialectic. Nor does Foucault hold out the hope, however dim, that such imbrication could be loosened or overcome. Unlike Foucault, as Peter Dews puts it, "Horkheimer and Adorno envisage a genuine dialectic of Enlightenment" (Dews 1987: 210). These differences are reflected in the term Adorno prefers when he talks about power, namely, domination (*Herrschaft*). Adornian social critique unfolds as a critical reflection of the dialectic of domination, within the utopian horizon of possible liberation. What makes late capitalist society in its entirety false, Adorno says, is how it lets domination occur through the process of economic exchange, a process that leaves no gender, class, or race unscathed.

A frequently cited passage from *Negative Dialectics* in "World Spirit and Natural History" captures the gist of Adorno's social critique. In this passage Adorno responds to the Hegelian concept of universal history as a continuous, dialectical, and progressive unfolding of spirit (*Geist*). Let me quote it at length and then comment.

> Universal history must be [both] constructed and denied. After [recent] catastrophes and in view of future ones, it would be cynical to assert a self-manifesting and all-encompassing world plan for the better. This, however, is no reason to deny the unity that welds together the discontinuous, chaotically splintered moments and phases of history—the unity of control over nature [*Naturbeherrschung*], progressing into domination [*Herrschaft*] over human beings and finally over inner nature. No universal history leads from savagery to humanity, but one does indeed lead from the slingshot to the megaton bomb. It culminates in the total threat of organized humankind against organized human beings, in the epitome of discontinuity. Hegel is thereby horribly verified and stood on his head ... History is the unity of continuity and discontinuity. Society preserves itself not despite its antagonism but by means of it: objectively, the profit motive [*Profitinteresse*] and hence the class relation are the motor

---

rationality ... Couldn't it be concluded that the Enlightenment's promise of attaining freedom through the exercise of reason has been turned upside down, resulting in a domination by reason itself, which increasingly usurps the place of freedom?" (Foucault 2000a: 273).

13   See especially the chapter titled "The Critique of Instrumental Reason" in Habermas 1984, 1987, vol. 1: 339–99.

of the process of production on which everyone's life depends and whose primacy portends the death of all. And this implies what is reconciling in the irreconcilable: because it alone lets people live, a changed life would not even be possible without it. What historically created that possibility can just as well destroy it.

ND: 314/320[14]

In other words, human history is a dialectical process of ever more expansive domination that simultaneously creates both the real threat of Earth's complete destruction and the conditions for a possibly post-dominative future.

When compared with Foucault's accounts of disciplinary power and state biopower, three features stand out in this passage. First, if, as Foucault claims, there is a distinctly modern mode of power, then Adorno would want to emphasize how this develops *from* earlier modes of power. Whereas Foucault locates historical discontinuity in irreversible shifts from one "regime of truth" to the next (e.g., in his terms, from the classical to the modern), Adorno locates historical discontinuity in the antagonism that drives historical development *across* different "moments and phases," an antagonism that now threatens to destroy everyone and thereby bring history to an end, in "the epitome of discontinuity."

Second, whereas Foucault disavows or downplays continuity across different regimes of truth and historical modes of power, Adorno emphatically asserts such continuity. It occurs, he says, in the unfolding of domination within three mutually intertwined modes, which we can distinguish as subjugation (of nature), exploitation (of some human beings by others), and repression (of nature within human existence). These three modes of domination take different shapes in different historical settings. Yet their mutual entwinement is, if you will, a historical constant. And at its core that constant is one of antagonism, antagonism between humans and nature, among humans, and within human existence. In this sense history is, as Adorno says, "the unity of continuity and discontinuity."

Third, whereas Foucault stresses the dispersion of modern power across interrelations, practices, and institutions, such that not even state biopower can properly be called "domination," Adorno forthrightly continues a Marxian emphasis on the capitalist economic system, with its class conflicts and private

---

14   Citations of Adorno's books use abbreviations and give pagination first in the German original and then in the English translation. I cite existing English translations where possible and silently emend them when necessary. Dates immediately after titles indicate when the German originals were first presented or published.

ownership of the means of production, as the key to modern modes of domination. As Deborah Cook shows, this emphasis on the economic macrostructure does not combine easily with a Foucaultian emphasis on diverse power relations and the subjection of individuals to them. Whereas Adorno would want to say the forms of modern power that Foucault diagnoses are anchored in the late capitalist economy, to which the administrative state is also subordinate, Foucault repeatedly stresses that capitalism itself relies heavily on the modern development of disciplinary power and state biopower (Cook 2018: 39–55).

Given Adorno's emphasis on the antagonistic unity of domination as anchored in the capitalist economic system, two other differences from Foucault emerge, in sentences I omitted from the passage cited. First, the primary motivation for Adorno's critique of domination does not lie in a desire for individual freedom but rather in the need to remove suffering. This motivation lies at the heart of Adorno's critique of Hegel who, Adorno says, transfigured "historical suffering" into a conduit for the world spirit's progress rather than recognizing how suffering has persisted, albeit "with breathing spells," throughout human history until now (ND: 314/320). A really transformed society would be one where suffering is mitigated or removed. Although Cook occasionally suggests that Foucault shares Adorno's concerns in this regard, I do not find suffering to be a primary motivation for Foucault's critique of power. Rather, individual desubjection is.[15]

So too, whereas Foucault is wary about specifying a general pattern or principle that governs all the diverse power relations in modern society, Adorno has no such qualms. The principle that governs all three modes of domination as well as everyone and everything subject to them is what Adorno calls the "all-subjugating principle of identity" (alles unterjochenden Identitätsprinzip). This principle turns the nonidentical—i.e., whatever resists imposed identity and instrumental rationality—into something to be feared (ND: 314–15/320). To the extent that the historical process of enlightenment follows the principle of identity and serves blind domination, it is, in Horkheimer and Adorno's memorable phrase, "mythical fear radicalized" (DA: 32/11).

This suggests, however, that the principle of identity is not in fact "all-subjugating," and the process of domination is not all-powerful. There is more to people and things than the identity they acquire under late-capitalist conditions, and there are forms of resistance not even blind domination can wipe

---

15   At the same time, however, unlike Martin Shuster, I also do not regard Adorno's philosophy of history, with its inherent critique of domination, as primarily motivated by a quasi-Benjaminian concern for the sacredness of "every unique human life" and "the irreducible singularity of every moment and every life" (Shuster 2018: 59).

out. Hence an Adornian social critique would point to this "more," without subsuming it under the principle of identity, and it would enact such resistance, without reinforcing patterns of domination. Although some of this will involve the sorts of individual change that Foucault calls desubjection, the context for such self-transformation lies in the historically evolved structure of a society where a capitalist economy dominates other macrostructures, social interrelations, and individual lives. Moreover, as we shall see, both a social critique of domination and resistance to it require a different idea of truth.

2   Truth Matters

2.1   *Feminist Contentions*

In a debate with Judith Butler during the early 1990s over the implications of postmodernism for feminist theory and politics, Seyla Benhabib worried that postmodernism had produced a "retreat from utopia within feminist theory." Recalling the phrase Max Horkheimer used in a telling interview one year after Adorno died (Horkheimer 1970), Benhabib describes utopian thinking as "the longing for the 'wholly other' (*das ganz Andere*), for that which is not yet," without which, she says, "not only morality but also radical transformation is unthinkable." Absent this "regulative principle of hope," she suggests, postmodernism will seduce feminists into contentedly and self-destructively "singing the swan song of normative thinking in general" (Benhabib in Benhabib et al. 1995: 30).[16] Although Benhabib mentions Lyotard in this context, Butler's appropriation of Foucault's critique of power lies at the center of her worry.

Butler, for their part, prefers to speak of poststructuralism rather than postmodernism, and they say the "fine point" poststructuralism makes is that "power pervades the very conceptual apparatus" that tries to sort out how power works, "including the subject position of the critic." Moreover, "this implication of the terms of criticism in the field of power is *not* the advent of a nihilistic relativism incapable of furnishing norms, but, rather, the very precondition of a politically engaged critique. To establish a set of norms that

---

16   A longer version of this essay appears as chapter 7 ("Feminism and the Question of Postmodernism") in Benhabib 1992: 203–41. The original exchange among Benhabib, Butler, and Fraser occurred at a symposium on feminism and postmodernism sponsored by the Greater Philadelphia Philosophy Consortium. It was published first in the journal *Praxis International* (July 1991) and then, expanded by a contribution from Drucilla Cornell, in a German volume titled *Der Streit um Differenz* (Frankfurt am Main: Fischer Verlag, 1993).

are beyond power or force is itself a powerful and forceful conceptual practice that sublimates, disguises, and extends its own power play through recourse to tropes of normative universality" (Butler in Benhabib et al. 1995: 39). With that move Butler turns the debate into one about the entanglement of power and validity as well as both the possibility and the desirability of a normative social critique[17]—and not about utopian thinking.

Indeed, Benhabib's worry about a retreat from utopia gets lost in her exchange with Butler—her own response to Butler says, "issues of subjectivity, selfhood, and agency" (implicitly, not utopia) lie at the core of their disagreement (Benhabib in Benhabib et al. 1995: 108). When the theme of utopian thinking does return, in Drucilla Cornell's contributions, it receives mostly dismissive responses: Benhabib objects to Cornell's wishing to reinscribe "a utopian female sexuality" (Benhabib in Benhabib et al. 1995: 116),[18] Butler questions how to understand "the deconstructive notion of 'the constitutive outside'" (Butler in Benhabib et al. 1995: 142), and Nancy Fraser worries that Cornell's "quasi-Lacanian/Derridean framework" does not adequately "permit us to ... infuse all of our work with a normative critique of domination and injustice" (Fraser in Benhabib et al. 1995: 159, 164). The actual role of utopian hope in feminist theory and politics—which Cornell's response to Benhabib emphasizes, appealing to Adorno and Benjamin (Cornell in Benhabib et al. 1995: 148–9)—is left unaddressed.

This lack is doubly unfortunate. First, it weakens feminist critiques of power. Second, it keeps feminist critical theorists from reimagining the idea of truth that their critiques silently presuppose—silently, because questions about truth only come up sideways in *Feminist Contentions* (1995) and do not receive direct attention. In the social critiques that Foucault and Adorno offer, by contrast, questions concerning truth and its interrelation with power are front and center. At the same time, as we shall see, the differences in how they understand these matters raise central issues for feminists to address, not least of which is the role of hope in feminist theory and politics.[19]

---

17   For succinct summaries of the debate along these lines, with an emphasis on "the problem of the subject" and its relation to power, see Allen 2008: 4–10, and Allen 2018: 529–32.

18   But see "Feminism and Postmodernism," where Benhabib acknowledges Cornell as a feminist who "seeks to retain this utopian element even while affirming postmodernist philosophy" (Benhabib in Benhabib et al. 1995: 34n29).

19   On the political importance of cultivating utopian hope, see the Ernst Bloch-inspired reflections in Weeks 2011: 175–225.

2.2   *Foucault: Regimes of Truth*

Foucault explains how power and truth interrelate in the wide-ranging and well-known 1976 interview titled "Truth and Power," first published in 1977. The interview proposes that scholars and professionals should understand their political role in post-war France as being "specific intellectuals" who take up struggles over disciplinary power in the interactional sectors where they live or work, such as "housing, the hospital, the asylum, the laboratory, the university, family and sexual relations" (Foucault 1980b: 126). These are sites of power. They are simultaneously sites of truth. And, to sustain sector-specific political struggles, scholars and professionals must understand the interrelation between truth and power. For, Foucault says, "truth isn't outside power, or lacking in power ... Truth is a thing of this world: it is produced only by virtue of multiple forms of constraint. And it induces regular effects of power" (Foucault 1980b: 131). Hence truth is not an alternative to power, nor is it a sacred space from which to critique and resist power. Rather, truth—specifically, social-scientific truth—is how power—specifically, disciplinary power—operates.

To capture such interlinkage, Foucault introduces the notion of a *regime of truth*. The term *regime* implies that a nexus of truth *and* power emerges historically and can undergo "a global modification" (Foucault 1980b: 113). A regime of truth is the dynamic, historically conditioned pattern that governs which sorts of statements and claims are acceptable and authorized, along with the discursive means and methods valorized and "the status of those who are charged with saying what counts as true" (Foucault 1980b: 131). Because authority, sanctions, and valorization are built in, a regime of truth regulates how power is exercised in a society. It constrains social conduct, and it helps produce the practices and institutions that organize social life.

According to Foucault, the modern regime of truth places scientific discourse and organizations at the center, in conjunction with ongoing economic and political demands for scientifically established truth. That means institutions of education and information, where truth claims attract wide-spread contestation, have an especially prominent role in the modern circulation of truth, and these are themselves under the control of major political and economic "apparatuses" (e.g., universities and media). Because of the modern emphasis on scientific discourse and the role of scientific discourse in political and economic systems, intellectuals need not only to engage in sector-specific struggles over truth but also take on the entire modern regime of truth, in "a battle about the status of truth and the economic and political role it plays." For Foucault, the aim of what he calls "a new politics of truth" would not be to free truth from power as such. Rather, the aim would be to detach "the power of truth from the forms of hegemony ... within which it operates at the present time" (Foucault 1980b: 132).

Foucault leaves little doubt that truth is a central concern within his critique of the modern West. As he says in another interview from around the same time, he regards the "problem of truth" as "the most general of political problems" (Foucault 1987: 111).[20] Less apparent, however, is exactly what he thinks truth and its interlinkage with power involve. This is exacerbated by Foucault's strong tendency to use general concepts such as power and truth as no more than historically specific categories. Rather than discuss the nature of power in general, for example, he prefers to discuss historically distinct forms of power. Nevertheless, in order to draw a distinction between premodern "juridical" power, on the one hand, and modern "disciplinary" power, on the other, Foucault must presuppose that they belong to the same conceptual field—i.e., that both categories are in fact concepts of power and hence have something significant in common.

What they have in common, in the first instance, is that they are about relations and processes, and not about either substances or nonrelational properties. As we have seen, power, for Foucault—and not only disciplinary power—is a relational concept. It primarily pertains to the social relations whereby certain social forces influence human identities, lives, and conduct. Secondarily, it also pertains to the social relations within which human agents respond to such influences. Depending on the historical era and societal structure, such relations can be top down, bottom up, or side-to-side, and that is a matter for genealogical investigation. But in any case, power is a relational concept.

So is Foucault's mostly implicit general concept of truth. Reconstructed from other publications both earlier and later than the 1976 "Truth and Power" interview, his concept regards truth as a complex, conceptually articulated, and methodically secured relation between epistemic subjects and the objects of their search for knowledge (which objects, in the social sciences, include epistemic subjects).[21] Although he does not restrict truth to what the sciences,

---

20   The interview stems from 1978. It first appeared in 1980, followed by an English translation in 1981.

21   See especially Foucault 1972. Although written before the genealogical studies of truth and power that I have cited, this book establishes key claims about objects of discourse and levels of knowledge that Foucault neither abandoned nor revoked. See also the dictionary entry on "Foucault," which describes Foucault's project as a "critical history of thought" that analyzes "the conditions under which certain relations of subject to object are formed and modified, insofar as those relations constitute a possible knowledge [savoir]" (Florence 1998: 459). The editor explains that this entry from the early 1980s for the Dictionnaire des philosophes was written mostly by Foucault and signed

especially the social sciences, aim to achieve, Foucault's concept of truth is a version of what some would delimit as scientific truth, as distinct, for example, from artistic truth or religious truth.

When Foucault speaks of a regime of truth, then, he claims that, to understand how power works in modern society, we must understand the relation between two relational concepts. Further, the relation between power and truth is such that we cannot have one without the other. In that sense, power and truth are *inter*relational concepts. On the one hand, as a specific sort of relation between the subjects and objects of knowledge (objects that can include subjects), truth is a necessary condition for the exercise of power in modern society. If, as Foucault says in a later interview, relations of power are ways of influencing the actions of "acting subjects" (Foucault 2000b: 340), then such influence usually requires the influencing agency to strive for truth-claiming knowledge about the acting subject and its actions. That's what is implied, in part, by calling a dominant form of modern power "disciplinary": it depends upon the deployment of knowledge achieved in scientific or scientifically informed disciplines.

On the other hand, as a relation of social influence and response, power is a necessary condition for pursuing and achieving truth as a specific epistemic subject/object relation. For this relation is not one that occurs in the abstract. In the modern West (roughly from the late eighteenth century onward), Foucault points out, we have increasingly relied on scientific and professional discourses to establish what is true, have employed scientific procedures and instrumentation to distinguish between true and false statements, and have authorized scientists and professionals to say what counts as true. Despite the dismissal of science and the celebration of "alternative facts" among contemporary authoritarian populists, a Foucaultian might say they have not provided any genuine alternative to the truth-producing discourses, truth-sorting mechanisms, and truth-claiming authorities within the modern regime of truth. And these discourses, mechanisms, and authorities are themselves ways in which power is exercised, ways in which how people live, act, and understand themselves are influenced, for good or ill.

Yet this last phrase—"for good or ill"—introduces an issue that Foucault never resolves—indeed, barely addresses. For he fails to think through the normative implications of power and truth as *relational* concepts. To posit truth as a specific sort of epistemic subject/object relation is to broach the question

---

pseudonymously "Maurice Florence." I discuss Foucault's general conception of truth at greater length in Zuidervaart 2023.

whether there are better and worse forms of this relation. So too, to regard power as a relation between social forces and human agents is to suggest that there might be better and worse forms of this relation for society and human life. Moreover, if these concepts are *interrelational*, if they are mutually necessary (but not sufficient) conditions for each other, then the question arises whether certain forms of the epistemic relation are more or less conducive to better forms of power and whether, conversely, certain forms of the social influence/response relation are more likely to support the sorts of knowledge needed or desired. These are questions for which, so far as I can tell, Foucault has no response.[22]

2.3   *Adorno: Truth as Constellation*

Similar questions arise in Adorno's dialectical critique of domination. Unlike Foucault, however, Adorno does not ignore or avoid them. Rather, he makes them central to what, countering Hegel, he calls negative dialectics. Indeed, they are the underlying topic in "Self-Reflection of Dialectics" (*ND*: 397–400/ 405–8), the last of the "Meditations on Metaphysics" that conclude *Negative Dialectics*. There Adorno asks whether metaphysics, understood as knowledge of the absolute (*Wissen vom Absoluten*), can avoid the horns of a dilemma bequeathed by Hegel's dialectic: either dialectical thought claims to conceptually grasp the absolute, and thereby poses as itself being absolute, or it declares the absolute to be something wholly other, beyond the grasp of dialectical thought, and thereby subscribes to a double-truth theory reminiscent of outmoded medieval philosophy. Although Adorno's negative dialectics rejects any attempt to absolutize thought and its results,[23] it also regards positing two kinds of truth as "incompatible with the idea of the true" (*ND*: 397/406). How can negative dialectics escape this dilemma without entirely giving up on

---

22   Although this is not the same issue as the alleged "cryptonormativism" in Foucault's genealogical critique of power, it is closely related. "Cryptonormativism" refers to Foucault's supposedly invoking norms that he cannot justify because to justify them would require an appeal to universals like "justice" whose validity transcends the current regime of truth. See Habermas 1987: 282–6, which favorably cites the 1981 version of the essay by Nancy Fraser, "Foucault on Modern Power: Empirical Insights and Normative Confusions," now in Fraser 1989: 17–34.

23   See in this connection Adorno's lectures on metaphysics, where he says the idea that "thought and its constitutive forms are *in fact* the absolute" is "really the thesis of the whole metaphysical tradition" (and not, for example, simply of Hegel's absolute idealism). Adorno refers in this connection to his own critique (in *Metakritik der Erkenntnistheorie*) of Husserl's "logical absolutism" for treating the pure forms of thought as absolute rather than historically contingent (*MCP*: 99).

metaphysics and thereby also surrendering the idea of truth which, as Adorno had said a few pages earlier, is "the highest" (*die oberste*) among metaphysical ideas (*ND*: 394/401)?

Such talk of metaphysics, double-truth theory, and knowing the absolute might seem remote from both Adorno's social critique and feminist critical theory. Nevertheless, what motivates Adorno's concern here is not simply how to respond to the Western metaphysical tradition and Hegel's absolute idealism. Rather, it emerges from his own understanding of the dialectic of domination. For the "all-subjugating principle of identity" (*ND*: 314/320) that governs all three modes of domination also governs the theoretical critique of domination. Yet resistance to blind domination requires the critical theorist to appeal to an emphatic idea of truth that points beyond identitarian domination. How is that possible?

Adorno's response involves several moves. First, he recognizes the double character of dialectical thought with respect to the universal history of domination. Dialectics is, he says, both the imprint (*Abdruck*) and the critique of this "universal context of delusion" (*Verblendungszusammenhang*). Second, he insists that, as such a critique, dialectical thought must challenge its own participation in domination. In "one last move," dialectics must "turn against itself" (*ND*: 397/406). It must engage in self-critique. Third, in turning against itself, dialectical thought must also point beyond the dialectic of domination that until now has held sway, also within thought. Specifically, dialectical thought must point beyond the principle of identity and the economic exchange principle it mirrors and reinforces. For the capitalist economic principle that nothing has value except insofar as it can be exchanged for something else (and thereby generate private profit) is precisely what scientific and technological efforts to impose conceptual identity on things both echo and sustain. And pointing beyond the exchange and identity principles is precisely what Adorno does, throughout the entire book, to be sure, but especially in these concluding pages.

But what does pointing beyond the dialectic of domination come to? As Adorno immediately indicates, it involves logically grasping and resisting the coercive character (*Zwangscharakter*) of logic itself—the tendency in modern philosophy, science, and society, for example, to think that scientific truth is the only truth. In thereby relativizing the principle of identity, while still following it, negative dialectics can envision what truth would be like if the dialectic of domination were in fact superseded in both thought and society: truth would be to do justice to "the nonidentical that would emerge only after the identity-compulsion [*Identitätszwang*] dissolved" (*ND*: 398/406). In the meantime, to pursue such truth requires, together with a self-critique of dialectical thought, "micrological" investigations of life and society. These would bring matters into a "legible constellation" from which we can begin to discern what things would be like if they were no longer ruled by the all-subjugating principle of identity—i.e., what they would be like in their nonidentity. Because such micrological thinking is devoted to "the absolute"—because, in pursuing truth, it tries to do justice to the nonidentical that would emerge after the identity-compulsion has dissolved—it shows solidarity with metaphysics—which traditionally absolutized thought itself—"in the moment of its collapse" (*ND*: 400/408).

This combination of dialectics and micrology—of Hegel and Walter Benjamin, if you will—yields a distinctive conception of truth in Adorno's philosophy. Truth, he often says, is a constellation, and it cannot be restricted to scientific truth. Thus, for example, as an alternative to Husserl's alleged "logical absolutism"—his idealizing the laws of logic and removing them from anything empirical—Adorno portrays truth as a "constellation" of both subjective and objective moments and as a "force field" that cannot be pinned down as "an entity" (*ME*: 79/72). In other words, truth is relational and processual, and it is not a substance or nonrelational property, despite what most Western philosophers since Aristotle have thought.[24]

To that extent, then, Adorno's conception of truth resembles Foucault's: both of them regard truth as relational and processual. As a constellation, however, the idea of truth is more complex than the relation between epistemic subject and object that, with his concerns about scientific knowledge and disciplinary power, Foucault emphasizes. At various places Adorno calls attention to other intersecting polarities within the constellation of truth: along with the subject/object dialectic there are polarities between universal and particular, between concept and thing, and between identity and nonidentity. Truth consists in the ongoing mediation of such polarities. Unlike Foucault, however, Adorno thinks of these polarities as unfolding within a universal dialectic of domination, such that there is an important continuity across historical epochs.

For this reason, as I have argued elsewhere, the dialectic between history and transcendence is the most decisive polarity in Adorno's conception of truth (Zuidervaart 2018), and it has no parallel in Foucault's thought. Briefly, the dialectic between history and transcendence lies in a tension between the historical rootedness of the idea of truth and the possibility that the course

---

24   A few pages earlier, Adorno says Husserl's attempt to bracket out empirical existence is based on "that residual concept of truth which is common to all bourgeois philosophy, with the exception of Hegel and Nietzsche," a concept that treats truth as the residue left after the labor of actual thinking has been erased (*ME*: 76–7/70).

of history could dramatically change. On the one hand, we would not have the idea of truth if it had not emerged from a dialectic of enlightenment in which, as Adorno says at one point, the subject "wrestles free from illusion [*Schein*]" (*ND*: 368/375). On the other hand, even though until now such critique of untruth has repeatedly contributed to the domination of nature, self, and others, the idea of truth must also point to the possibility that untruth will not have the final word, that the history of domination from which this idea emerges could indeed give way to freedom. This possibility emerges both from the capacity thought retains to think otherwise and from the refusal of the dominated to submit entirely to an imposed identity (i.e., from the nonidentical).

Accordingly, Adorno says the "surplus beyond the subject" and "the truth-moment in what is thing-like ... touch in the idea of truth" (*ND*: 368/375). And what sustains such touching is the possibility that the course of history is not inevitable, that a fundamentally different society is possible, a society in which blind domination and needless suffering have ended. Adorno calls this possibility "the humanly promised other of history" (*ND*: 396/404). The pursuit of truth, then, requires both an unsparing critique of domination and a persistent hope for complete social transformation.

Because such hope is required, the pursuit of truth cannot do without what Benhabib called utopian thinking. She was right to worry that Foucaultian social critique undermines this element in feminist theory. At the same time, however, Foucault's detailed exposés of how the pursuit of scientific truth both supports and receives support from disciplinary power makes one wonder whether and how a complete social transformation would in fact be possible. At what point does utopian thinking tip over into nothing more than socially necessary illusion?

Hence Foucault and Adorno leave feminist critical theorists with two inter-related challenges. One is to think through normative implications of the interrelation between truth and power. The other is to try to envision prospects for social transformation that neither ignore nor totalize the dialectic of domination. Let me provide preliminary responses to each challenge in turn.

3   Power, Truth, and Social Critique

3.1   *Social Domains of Truth*

Earlier I suggested that Foucault fails to consider whether certain forms of power and truth are better or worse, both intrinsically and in relationship to each other. Behind this suggestion lies the intuition, partially shared by Adorno, that in modern society there is more than one social domain of knowledge and hence more than one sort of truth. For example, one can regard artistic truth as a distinct sort of truth that cannot be either reduced to scientific truth or replaced by it. If that is so, then one can also ask how the sort of truth that art offers differs from scientific truth and provides something science lacks.

One can also consider both whether either art or science is more conducive to desirable forms of power and whether the more desirable forms of power are more likely to support either artistic or scientific truth. Even if it is so that disciplinary power is the predominant form of interactional power in contemporary society and that scientific truth is the primary way in which disciplinary power is produced and ratified, this would not preclude there being alternative forms of power and truth within the historically emergent architecture of society. Such alternative forms could allow resistance to take shape and help inspire a normative critique of dominant power relations. This could provide a more nuanced understanding of feminist struggles against subjugation. It could also provide a way out of the conceptual binds within Foucaultian feminist accounts of (de)subjection with respect to (individual) freedom and (societal) determinism.[25]

To recognize more than one social domain of truth need not commit one to a version of the double-truth theory, however. Adorno is right that the idea of truth rules out such dividing and conquering. But he also says this idea is a constellation, and that suggests there can be more than one "star"—i.e., social domain of truth—and yet all the stars make up one constellation. To posit one constellation and so avoid a double-truth theory, however, would require a holistic conception of truth that neither restricts it primarily to scientific truth, à la Foucault, nor renders it mostly counterfactual, à la Adorno (*"das Absolute wäre"*). Moreover, to avoid simply counterfactualizing or subjunctivizing truth as a whole, one would need a more nuanced account of the interrelation between truth and power than Adorno and Foucault provide.

3.2   *Normative Critique of Power*
This is especially so with regard to the universal dialectic of domination in Adorno's philosophy of history. As we have seen, Adorno construes this dialectic as an emergent and antagonistic continuity among three modes of domination that both threatens complete destruction and makes possible a post-dominative future. For that future to arrive, the principle of identity could

---

25   See in this connection the illuminating discussion of Judith Butler's work in chapter 4 ("Dependency, Subordination, and Recognition: Butler on Subjection") in Allen 2008: 72–95.

no longer be imposed on nature, human relations, and individual lives. This understanding of domination as a universal-historical process raises two sorts of questions for which Adorno lacks adequate answers.

One question concerns normative alternatives to identitarian domination. If the imposition of identity governs destructive modes of domination, ones that in their violence create persistent suffering, human and otherwise, then what would be a better way to connect the pursuit of identity with the exercise of power? Although Adorno points to micrology as an alternative, it is hard to see how this theoretical model of nonidentitarian thought would either generate or support better ways to connect identity and power in either science or politics.

A second question concerns qualitative distinctions among the three modes of domination. Might Adorno's insistence on continuity in domination and a single all-subjugating principle occlude the sorts of nonidentities that not even the most pervasive dialectic can eliminate? Specifically, aren't there qualitative differences among the subjugation of nature, the exploitation of humans, and self-repression, such that, even within the continuity of domination, each points to its own sort of alternative and calls for its own sort of normative critique? The exercise of human power with respect to so-called nature has different normative implications than it does with respect to either other humans or one's self. As I have argued elsewhere,[26] attempts to control nonhuman life and existence become problematic when they fail to promote interconnected flourishing among all creatures; they become destructive when they try to promote human wellbeing at the expense of other creatures. Patterns of thought that identify "nature" as no more than a realm of objects for human mastery are, as Adorno recognizes, inherently violent, and they feed into destructive control, into the subjugation of "nature."

Yet violence toward "nature" cannot be equated with violence toward other human beings. The exploitation of one class or gender or race by another, for example, involves a one-sided *social* distribution of power; it is not simply the exercise of human power with respect to nonhuman creatures, even when the exploiters treat the exploited as mere things. This one-sided distribution persistently promotes the apparent flourishing of one group at the ongoing expense of another, whose members suffer as a result. Such social violence is not only destructive—directly so for the exploited and indirectly for the exploiters—but also normatively problematic: it rejects fundamental

---

26   See the chapter "Globalizing Dialectic of Enlightenment" in Zuidervaart 2007: 107–131.

expectations of solidarity and justice without which, as members of society, human beings cannot flourish.

So too, the domination of what Adorno calls inner nature— in the words of *Dialectic of Enlightenment,* the "denial of nature in the human being for the sake of mastery [*Herrschaft*] over extrahuman nature and over other human beings" (*DA*: 78/42)—is qualitatively different from either the subjugation of "nature" or the exploitation of other humans. How an individual relates to one's own corporeal needs and sensuous happiness is different from how humanity relates to "nature" and how groups engage in social struggle. Moreover, not all self-denial is destructive or illegitimate, as Adorno himself recognizes; without some degree of self-denial individuals could hardly have agency or exercise power. So, we need to distinguish between self-denial that is indeed problematic and that which is not. I mark this distinction with the words *repression* and *sublimation.* Whereas repressing one's own needs and desires is problematic, sublimating them into a larger life-project, into pathways of personal flourishing, is not.

Reformulated, then, Adorno's thesis of historical continuity in domination claims that subjugation of nature, social exploitation, and self-repression unavoidably feed into and off one another both historically and in late capitalist society. To break the grip of domination would require undoing all three modes of domination. Hence the urgency of challenging the "all-subjugating principle of identity." If, however, these are not the only ways in which power has been and currently is exercised—if, in fact, nonviolent control, nonexploitative social struggle, and nonrepressive self-relations have occurred in the past and are currently available—then the critique of domination can become more nuanced, and the hope for social transformation can become less desperate.

3.3   *Collaboration and Social Hope*

Here the shape of interactional and macrostructural forms of power and their interrelation, which both Adorno and Foucault thematize, become decisive. For if the only forms of interactional power historically available are power-over (influence) and power-to (agency), as Foucault's diagnosis of disciplinary power suggests; if macrostructural forms of political and economic power hold sway in contemporary society, as Adorno claims; and if these forms of interactional and macrostructural power not only interlink but reinforce each other, as both Foucault and Adorno seem to indicate, then critique and resistance would seem futile and social transformation impossible. Then the utopian hope that Benhabib rightly says feminists need would become merely utopian in a pejorative sense. I call this the dilemma of historically ill-founded utopian hope.[27]

I can envision two ways to respond to this dilemma. One would be to acknowledge a third and intrinsically intersubjective form of power in human history and contemporary society, a form Amy Allen calls "power-with." Derived from Hannah Arendt's definition of power as the human ability to act in concert, power-with is a capacity people enact together to accomplish a shared end. We can call it *collaboration*. In describing it, however, I have modified Allen's definition. Allen defines power-with as "the ability of a collectivity to act together for the attainment of an agreed-upon end or series of ends" (Allen 1999: 127). I have modified her definition because not all power-with involves collectivity (e.g., in a friendship or intimate partnership), and I do not think prior agreement is always required in order to exercise power-with. Indeed, it is important to break completely with a contractualist notion of power if one wants to understand the distinctive qualities and potentials of collaborative power.

As Allen points out, feminism and other collective movements of resistance and critique depend heavily on collaboration. So do many of the interrelations and practices that make up the fabric of daily social life. Unless one regards all such collaboration as merely a conduit or target of disciplinary power and domination—a position I regard as both cynical and empirically incorrect—one can look to such social movements and modes of interaction for ways to empower social transformation.

A second way to respond to the dilemma of ill-founded hope would be point to historically emergent and shared, albeit contested, expectations concerning social life. I call these expectations societal principles, and I argue that they hold for the entire array of interrelations, practices, institutions, and macrostructures that organize life in contemporary society. Together with the pursuit of interconnected flourishing, fidelity to such expectations is the hallmark of truth. For truth is a dynamic correlation between human fidelity to societal principles and a life-giving disclosure of society. And truth is not an otherworldly idea. Rather, the process from which shared expectations and possibilities for flourishing emerge is the same history where disciplinary power and a dialectic of domination occur.

These expectations and possibilities are, if you will, the penumbra of problematic power. They emerge not in the absence of power but in the very exercise of power both interactional and macrostructural. For people cannot be

---

27   See in this connection the related discussion of what I call Adorno's "objectification of hope" in Zuidervaart 2007: 66–76.

faithful to societal principles such as solidarity and justice without collaborating, exerting influence, and exercising agency. Nor can they pursue interconnected flourishing in a power vacuum. Accordingly, every social domain of truth, whether science, art, or religion, for example, is simultaneously a domain of power, and a normative critique of power must ask which sorts of power are most conducive to truth in each domain.

Politics, I have argued elsewhere, is one such domain.[28] It is the domain where people struggle for power to achieve justice and where they struggle over justice from positions of relative power. Such empowered struggles for justice typically aim to liberate people and other creatures from oppression. Accordingly, the exercise of political power is subject to normative constraints: it must either promise or actually accomplish justice and freedom, and it must be suitable in this regard. Moreover, the justifiability and suitability of power are intrinsic to politics as a social domain of truth. Without them, in the long run, neither justice nor freedom would be achieved.

If justice and freedom have in fact been achieved in the past, and if justifiable and suitable forms of political power are available in the present, then there are genuinely political reasons to hope for social transformation. Such hope need not be merely utopian, even though there is more to the social transformation needed than politics alone can achieve. For contemporary society as a whole needs what I call a "differential transformation,"[29] and that will not occur in the absence of fundamental economic change.

Like Foucault and Adorno, feminist critical theorists have offered sophisticated critiques of power. But we have run stuck, it seems to me, because we have not developed a sufficiently nuanced account of the normative interrelation between truth and power. To do that, I have suggested, feminist critical theorists need to reexamine Foucault's genealogy and Adorno's negative dialectics to ask what forms of power these have ignored or overlooked. And, given the prominence of truth for both Foucault and Adorno, that will also require a new conception of truth, one that neither restricts truth to science nor treats it as a counterfactual idea, but locates it instead in the historically emergent and malleable social domains of truth.[30]

---

28   See the chapter "Truth and Politics" in Zuidervaart 2023.

29   See the chapter titled "Macrostructures and Societal Principles: An Architectonic Critique," in Zuidervaart 2016: 252–76.

30   An early draft of the Foucault materials in this chapter received illuminating comments from Joshua Harris, Dean Dettloff, and the late Deborah Cook. I wish to thank them here. I also thank Joshua Harris, Christine Payne, and Jeremiah Morelock for their perceptive and constructive remarks on the first draft of this chapter. I dedicate it to the memory of my fellow Adorno scholar Deborah Ellen Cook.

References

Adorno, Theodor W. 1970. *Zur Metakritik der Erkenntnistheorie: Studien über Husserl und die phänomenologischen Antinomien*, in *Gesammelte Schriften* 5 (Frankfurt am Main: Suhrkamp, 1970), 7–245. *Against Epistemology: a Metacritique; Studies in Husserl and the Phenomenological Antinomies* (1956), trans. Willis Domingo (Cambridge, MA: MIT Press, 1982). [Abbreviated *ME* in this chapter.]

Adorno, Theodor W. 1973. Negative Dialektik, in *Gesammelte Schriften* 6 (Frankfurt am Main: Suhrkamp, 1973), 7–412. *Negative Dialectics* (1966, 1967), trans. E. B. Ashton (New York: Seabury Press, 1973). [Abbreviated *ND* in this chapter.]

Adorno, Theodor W. 2000. *Metaphysics: Concept and Problems* (1965), ed. Rolf Tiedemann, trans. Edmund Jephcott. Stanford, CA: Stanford University Press, 2000. [Abbreviated *MCP* in this chapter.]

Alcoff, Linda Martín. 1996. *Real Knowing: New Versions of the Coherence Theory*. Ithaca: Cornell University Press.

Allen, Amy. 1999. *The Power of Feminist Theory: Domination, Resistance, Solidarity*. Boulder, CO: Westview Press.

Allen, Amy. 2008. *The Politics of Our Selves: Power, Autonomy, and Gender in Contemporary Critical Theory*. New York: Columbia University Press.

Allen, Amy. 2016a. *The End of Progress: Decolonizing the Normative Foundations of Critical Theory*. New York: Columbia University Press.

Allen, Amy. 2016b. "Feminist Perspectives on Power." *The Stanford Encyclopedia of Philosophy* (Fall 2016 Edition), ed. Edward N. Zalta. URL = <https://plato.stanford.edu/archives/fall2016/entries/feminist-power/>.

Allen, Amy. 2018. "Critical Theory and Feminism." In *The Routledge Companion to the Frankfurt School*, eds. Peter Gordon, Espen Hammer, and Axel Honneth, 528–41. New York: Routledge.

Anderson, Elisabeth. 2020. "Feminist Epistemology and Philosophy of Science." *The Stanford Encyclopedia of Philosophy* (Spring 2020 Edition), ed. Edward N. Zalta. URL = <https://plato.stanford.edu/archives/spr2020/entries/feminism-epistemology/>.

Benhabib, Seyla. 1992. *Situating the Self: Gender, Community and Postmodernism in Contemporary Ethics*. New York: Routledge.

Benhabib, Seyla, Judith Butler, Drucilla Cornell, and Nancy Fraser. 1995. *Feminist Contentions: a Philosophical Exchange*. New York: Routledge.

Bernstein, Richard J. 1991. "Foucault: Critique as a Philosophic *Ēthos*." In *The New Constellation: the Ethical-Political Horizons of Modernity/Postmodernity*, 142–71. Cambridge, MA: MIT Press.

Code, Lorraine. 1991. *What Can She Know? Feminist Theory and the Construction of Knowledge*. Ithaca: Cornell University Press.

Collins, Patricia Hill. 1991. *Black Feminist Thought: Knowledge, Consciousness, and the Politics of Empowerment.* New York: Routledge.

Cook, Deborah. 2018. *Adorno, Foucault and the Critique of the West.* London: Verso.

Dews, Peter. 1987. *Logics of Disintegration: Post-Structuralist Thought and the Claims of Critical Theory.* London: Verso.

Florence, Maurice. 1998. "Foucault." In Michel Foucault, *Aesthetics, Method, and Epistemology: Essential Works of Foucault, 1954–1984, Vol. 2,* ed. James D. Faubion, trans. Robert Hurley et al., 459–63. New York: The New Press.

Foucault, Michel. 1972. *The Archaeology of Knowledge and the Discourse on Language* (1969 and 1971), trans. A. M. Sheridan Smith. New York: Vintage Books.

Foucault, Michel. 1977. *Discipline and Punish: the Birth of the Prison* (1975), trans. Alan Sheridan. New York: Pantheon Books.

Foucault, Michel. 1978. *The History of Sexuality*, Vol. 1: *an Introduction* (1976) trans. Robert Hurley. New York: Random House, Vintage Books.

Foucault, Michel. 1980a. "Powers and Strategies" (1977). In *Power/Knowledge: Selected Interviews and Other Writings 1972–1977*, ed. Colin Gordon, 134–45. New York: Pantheon Books.

Foucault, Michel. 1980b. "Truth and Power" (1977). In *Power/Knowledge: Selected Interviews and Other Writings 1972–1977*, ed. Colin Gordon, 109–33. New York: Pantheon Books.

Foucault, Michel. 1980c. "Two Lectures" (1976). In *Power/Knowledge: Selected Interviews and Other Writings 1972–1977*, ed. Colin Gordon, 78–108. New York: Pantheon Books.

Foucault, Michel. 1987. "Questions of Method: an Interview with Michel Foucault" (1980). In *After Philosophy: End or Transformation?*, eds. Kenneth Baynes, James Bohman, and Thomas McCarthy, 100–17. Cambridge, MA: MIT Press.

Foucault, Michel. 2000a. "Interview with Michel Foucault" (1980). In *Power: Essential Works of Foucault, 1954–1984, Vol. 3*, ed. James D. Faubion, trans. Robert Hurley et al., 239–97. New York: The New Press.

Foucault, Michel. 2000b. "The Subject and Power" (1982). In *Power: Essential Works of Foucault, 1954–1984, Vol. 3*, ed. James D. Faubion, trans. Robert Hurley et al., 326–48. New York: The New Press.

Foucault, Michel. 2003. *"Society Must Be Defended": Lectures at the Collège de France, 1975–76*, ed. Mauro Bertani and Alessandro Fontana, trans. David Macey. New York: Picador.

Fraser, Nancy. 1989. *Unruly Practices: Power, Discourse, and Gender in Contemporary Social Theory.* Minneapolis: University of Minnesota Press.

Fraser, Nancy. 1997. *Justice Interruptus: Critical Reflections on the "Postsocialist Condition."* New York: Routledge.

Habermas, Jürgen. 1984, 1987. *The Theory of Communicative Action*, trans. Thomas McCarthy. 2 vols. Boston: Beacon Press.

Habermas, Jürgen. 1987. *The Philosophical Discourse of Modernity: Twelve Lectures* (1985), trans. Frederick G. Lawrence. Cambridge, MA: MIT Press.

Haraway, Donna J. 1989. *Primate Visions: Gender, Race, and Nature in the World of Modern Science*. New York: Routledge.

Harding, Sandra. 1986. *The Science Question in Feminism*. Ithaca, NY: Cornell University Press.

Hartsock, Nancy C. M. 1998. *The Feminist Standpoint Revisited and Other Essays*. Boulder, CO: Westview Press.

Haslanger, Sally. 2012. *Resisting Reality: Social Construction and Social Critique*. New York: Oxford University Press.

Honneth, Axel. 1991. *The Critique of Power: Reflective Stages in a Critical Social Theory*, trans. Kenneth Baynes. Cambridge, MA: MIT Press.

Horkheimer, Max. 1970. *Die Sehnsucht nach dem ganz Anderen: Ein Interview mit Kommentar von Helmut Gumnior*. Hamburg: Furche-Verlag.

Horkheimer, Max, and Theodor W. Adorno. 1987. *Dialektik der Aufklärung*, in Max Horkheimer, *Gesammelte Schriften, Band 5: 'Dialektik der Aufklärung' und Schriften 1940–1950*, ed. Gunzelin Schmid Noerr (Frankfurt am Main: Fischer Taschenbuch, 1987). *Dialectic of Enlightenment: Philosophical Fragments* (1947), ed. Gunzelin Schmid Noerr, trans. Edmund Jephcott (Stanford, CA: Stanford University Press, 2002). [Abbreviated *DA* in this chapter.]

Hoy, David Couzens, and Thomas McCarthy. 1994. *Critical Theory*. Oxford: Blackwell.

Ingram, David. 2005. "Foucault and Habermas." In *The Cambridge Companion to Foucault*, ed. Gary Gutting, 2nd ed., 240–83. Cambridge: Cambridge University Press.

Kelly, Michael, ed. 1994. *Critique and Power: Recasting the Foucault/Habermas Debate*. Cambridge, MA: MIT Press.

Longino, Helen. 1990. *Science as Social Knowledge: Values and Objectivity in Scientific Inquiry*. Princeton, NJ: Princeton University Press.

McCarthy, Thomas. 1991. "The Critique of Impure Reason: Foucault and the Frankfurt School." In *Ideals and Illusions: On Reconstruction and Deconstruction in Contemporary Critical Theory*, 43–75. Cambridge, MA: MIT Press.

Petherbridge, Danielle. 2013. *The Critical Theory of Axel Honneth*. Lanham: Lexington Books.

Shuster, Martin. 2018. "The Philosophy of History." In *The Routledge Companion to the Frankfurt School*, eds. Peter Gordon, Espen Hammer, and Axel Honneth, 48–64. New York: Routledge.

Weeks, Kathi. 2011. *The Problem with Work: Feminism, Marxism, Antiwork Politics, and Postwork Imaginaries*. Durham, NC: Duke University Press, 2011.

Zuidervaart, Lambert. 2007. *Social Philosophy after Adorno*. Cambridge: Cambridge University Press.

Zuidervaart, Lambert. 2016. *Religion, Truth, and Social Transformation: Essays in Reformational Philosophy*. Montreal: McGill-Queen's University Press.

Zuidervaart, Lambert. 2018. "History and Transcendence in Adorno's Idea of Truth." In *The Routledge Companion to the Frankfurt School*, eds. Peter Gordon, Espen Hammer, and Axel Honneth, 121–34. New York: Routledge.

Zuidervaart, Lambert. 2023. *Social Domains of Truth: Science, Politics, Art, and Religion*. New York: Routledge.

CHAPTER 8

The Disintegration of Autonomy
Jill Johnston's Anti-criticism

Frida Sandström

On May 21, 1969, American cultural critic Jill Johnston organizes the public panel "The Disintegration of a Critic," at Loeb Student Centre at New York University, a location used frequently by the ongoing student and new left movement, as in the case of the Angry Arts Week in 1967.[1] In her press release for the panel, which was the third in a series of panels on dance and citique, Johnston describes the program as a "final solution to a personal problem which I would hope to have some effect on all those caught in a similar trap if indeed they see it that way" (Johnston 2019 [1969]: 194). She furthermore explicates the intent to offer her name "as a sort of sacrifice [...] of a disintegration of criticism," which she views as an "outmoded form of communication." This kind of communication, Johnston makes clear, is a question of the critic's alienation of the artist, and vice versa. Furthermore, she underscores the problem with the modern concept of history, and how it is 'imposed' on people by means of domination from transcendent, critical subjects – including herself. This, Johnston argues, makes it impossible to imagine history autobiographically:

> I am now interested solely in autobiographical history, from the cradles as well as from the history of an (our) archetypal past. As anything else I see both immediate and more remote history as imposed upon people from without and the people who take it as unwilling to accept the responsibility for deciding what their own history is, dependent always upon judgment the authority of one who assumes it in the historical guise of the father of the Judaic-Christian patriarchal tradition. That this dependence will continue to exist I see as fate for the present yet equally fated to terminate in the near future, as a state of affairs family, educational and cultural and finally political. Having been a so-called critic I fall into the cultural category and even the panel May 21st is meant to illustrate,

---

1 See for example Frascina, Francis. *Art, Politics and Dissent: Aspects of the Art Left in Sixties America.* (1999: Manchester University Press).

as an art event of the "object lesson" variety, the demise of a particular
critic who both literally and figuratively (or intellectually) disintegrated.
> Ibid. 193–194

What Johnston manifests in this paragraph is that she takes the 'termination' of
the critic in her own hands, by 'terminating' her own activity, which is her "final
solution to a personal problem." This is Johnston's "disintegration of a critic,"
a procedure which, in the format of a panel, is made as public as art criticism
itself. What Johnston terminates, I suggest, is critical mediation of sensations,
abstracting these away from the subjects embodying them as experiences. An
alienation which in the long run distances history of art and society writ large
from people's diverse experiences of it. To counter this, Johnston suggests the
model of the autobiography, which inverts these logics and departs from the
sensuous experience itself, without making it an object of critique. As Johnston
makes clear, she is herself someone who upholds this 'dependence' on critical
mediation, that she calls the 'authority' of the critical subject. What Johnston
describes as her 'object lesson' can therefore be described as a self-critique
regarding the subject position that she occupies as a critic. It is an 'object lesson'
that makes her own practice as a critic *an object* of her critique. This self-critique
and objectification-as-*objection*—a refusal of the transcendental subject—is
something that Johnston developed throughout her activity as a critic of visual
art, dance, performance, and music, and which reached its culmination with her
'disintegration' panel. In this chapter I will discuss Johnston's art criticism and
social activism in relation to her 'Disintegration' panel, to understand whether
and how the critic's subject disintegrates by this objective transformation, or
self-objectification, and furthermore what alternative subjectivities emerge
instead. Theodor W. Adorno's notion of de-subjectivization, what I understand
as a social critique of objectivity, will here function as a framework for a discussion of Johnston's activity in the period of her disintegration. Simultaneously,
Johnston's disintegration will allow for an extended understanding of Adorno's
concept of art as having "a double character" (Adorno 2002 [1970]: 299).

The present chapter will show how this concept relates not only to the
form and concept of art, but also to the form and subject of art criticism. For
example, Adorno argues that "the subject's reflection upon its own formalism
is reflection upon society" (Adorno 2005 [1969]: 257). This means, I argue, that
self-reflection for Adorno always implies a level of social critique. Such critique
is manifested by Johnston's 'object lesson' as referred to in the press release
above. It can be understood to regard the societal relations embedded in the
objective form of the critic's subject. Johnston's 'lesson' also takes place in a
conjunctural specific context where the relation between theory and praxis is

debated in critical theory as well as in social movements. From the perspective of that debate, I attempt to understand Johnston's art criticism and social critique through a similar dialectics. I argue that the complicated relationship between subjectivity and subjectivization as manifested in Johnston's activity makes it essential to understand her case through the lens of Adorno's writings on the subject-object and the theory-praxis dialectics. Despite the shared conjunctural specificity, neither Adorno nor Johnston caught the other's attention. Yet through Marcuse's collegial relation to Adorno and Johnston's reading of Marcuse (most probably as introduced by Gregory Battcock) there is a historically specific link between them. Furthermore, it is clear that the conflictual relation between the subject and form of art and of social movements is as present for Adorno as it is for Johnston. Via Johnston's disintegration, we may understand the social forms of Adorno's desubjectivization as they play out in the struggle for sexual rights, otherwise ignored by him. Hence my contribution to 'feminism' in relation to the Frankfurt School is an attempt to point out the queering capacity of Adorno's aesthetics, which are essential to revitalize in the present conjuncture.

1   Johnston's Anti-criticism

One of the speakers in Johnston's disintegration panel was her friend and colleague, art critic Gregory Battcock. In a column written shortly after the panel, published in the magazine *Gay*, Battcock discusses what he calls Johnston's "anti-criticism" (Battcock 2019 [1969]: 221). With anti-criticism, Battcock extends the avant-garde notion of 'anti-art' to the figure of what he describes as the 'anti-worker.' As he argues, the anti-worker's "reconstruction of the sensibility" will end what he describes as "intellectual class stratification." I propose that we can understand such an imagined reconstruction quite like Johnston's objective transformation – in her terms a disintegration of 'authority.' In the column, Battcock argues:

> The anti-worker has to liberate himself from the prevailing terminology, classifications and categorizations. In criticism (quiticism) only Jill Johnston and Gene Swenson have, so far, been able to do it.
>   Ibid 222[2]

---

2   To this note it needs to be added that Gene Swenson had attended Johnston's earlier panel with an invasive approach, quite like Johnston, at Town Hall in April 1971. See for example

I interpret what Battcock describes regarding the reconstruction undertaken by the anti-worker as a liberation from both theoretical concepts used in art critical judgments and the concept of history as referred to by Johnston. Yet the "prevailing terminology" that Battcock mentions can also be understood in a broader sense of socially restraining epistemology, when it comes to identifications in terms of race, gender, and sexuality. These are the concepts that Battcock points toward as both aesthetic and social problems. Battcock's twofolded approach to critique can also be understood to be Johnston's aim with her disintegration, which demands subjectivity to be critiqued both aesthetically and socially. Only so can the conceptual alienation imposed by critical subjects on people and things during art critical judgments – which alienate these not only from the concept of art but also from a general historical consciousness – be refuted. Johnston's *disintegration* of critique and Battcock's *reconstruction* of sensibility are appear both as social critiques of Hegelian aesthetics and the absolute concept of history that follows with it. I believe that Battcock and Johnston are approaching the so called 'end of art' on two levels: abstract, in terms of critique, and socially, in terms of the new, immediate relations, that they suggest as alternatives to the formal, objective ones. In the two following sections I will describe how this played out in Johnston's critique and social activism. I will start by discussing what a social critique of an aesthetic judgment may imply for the subject of critique. Which, in this context, is Johnston herself. This brings me back to Adorno.

In the introduction to *Negative Dialectics*, Adorno writes that "The double character of the [philosophical] system" demands us to transpose critical thinking from the abstract to the concrete, 'individual moments' (Adorno 1973 [1966]: 24–25). He writes:

> To comprehend a thing itself, not just to fit and register it in its system of reference, is nothing but to perceive the individual moment in its immanent connection with others. Such antisubjectivism lies under the crackling shell of absolute idealism. It stirs in the tendency to unseal current issues by resorting to the way they came to be. What the conception of the system recalls, in reverse, is the coherence of the nonidentical, the very thing infringed by deductive systematics. Criticism of systems and asystematic thought are superficial as long as they cannot release the

---

Johnston, Jill. "The Unhappy Spectator," in *Marmalade Me*. Wesleyan University Press 1998, pp. 199.

cohesive force which the idealistic systems had signed over to the transcendental subject.

Ibid 25–26

What Adorno states above, which summarizes his negative dialectics, is that
the individual, i.e., the subject, must be understood in non-coherent constellation with other subjects. It therefore must be understood socially, as an *objective* constellation which enables its own subjective mediation. The "idealistic
system" that Adorno mentions refers to his critique of Heideggerian ontologies and Hegelian dialectics. Instead of understanding rational reflection as
identical and hence absolute, Adorno stresses the irrationality of such perception, and underscores the need to imagine social relations between different
'outcasts,' what he describes as 'negative identity.' In Johnston's words as cited
in the previous section, as much as according to Adorno's Benjaminian concept of history, such 'negative identities' must be understood as experiences
that are not mediated by her supposedly critical subjectivity. What Johnston
does, I suggest, is to mediate the 'outcast' of her own critical objectivity, which
I propose as being her sexual subjectivity. In this sense, Johnston critiques art
criticism *socially*. Importantly, this process must be understood to take place
both immanently and objectively with regards to her own activity, quite like
Adorno's "dialectics of the cultural critic," which he argues must both participate in culture 'and not' (33). Johnston hence makes her critical subjectivity
the *object* of her reflection. The 'antisubjectivism' that Adorno refers to in the
introduction to *Negative Dialectics* can in this context be understood as the
means to perceive relations between individual moments (of Johnston as critic
and as lesbian), via their *difference*.

According to the logics of formalist art criticism and formal social relations
of labor writ large, the concepts of art, gender and sexuality, appear as fragmented experiences that are forced into total forms and shapes. The objects of
these are muted by absolute forms of subjectivity, which Johnston in this case
embodied as critic. The objects of this formalism can be understood as historical experiences of sexual identity, which by means of Johnston's proposed
disintegration may self-reflect *despite* the compulsive concepts imposed upon
them, including the historical consciousness that formal mediation instigates.
Accordingly, the self-reflection of the objects enables an alternative historical
consciousness. This, I suggest, is what Johnston describes as an autobiograph-
ical writing of history in her press release to the Disintegration panel. It is also
this practice that Johnston undertakes after the panel, when she leaves art criticism for two decades. She then focuses solely on her own biography, and the
role of art and writing therein. To fully understand the process of disintegration,

we will read some formalist art criticism – and critique of such – written by Johnston in the mid-1960s. We will start by approaching the context in which this writing took place.

From McCarthy's racist anti-communism in the 1950s, to Richard Nixon's "Vietnamization" in 1969, the period and context of Johnston's late art critical writing was dominated by the 'sexual revolution' which emerged from a longer struggle for gay rights. While the American 'Homophile Action League' stated that 'We are living in an age of revolution', the Gay Liberation Front was formed as "a self-proclaimed revolutionary group" during the Stonewall movement in 1969 in New York. As Western European universities were occupied, the annual meeting of the American Psychiatric Association was stormed by gay liberationists in 1970 (Drucker 2015: 199). In addition to references to the concept of revolution, strikes reoccurred in many segments of civil society. 1969 saw the founding of Art Workers' Coalition (AWC) in New York, where an artworker's identity was introduced as an alternative or niche to an working class identification. (Bolt 2023: 212) A prominent spokesperson for AWC was American art critic Lucy Lippard, who raised her voice for feminist art workerism, and who herself identified as an artworker. While this identity was central to artistic debates at the time, it was both conceptualized and refused when initially coined, as in the case of Ad Reinhart's *Satirical Sketch for an Artist Strike* (1961), and Lee Lozano's durational pieces *General Strike* (1969), followed by her *Drop Out Piece* (1970 –), before and after the founding of AWC. All works are examples of explicit negations of anything such as a collective identity of the artist.[3] Furthermore, the negation of an identification as artist or worker coincided with critiques of the concept of art, from the avant-garde to critical theory and social movements during this period. Through Johnston's engagement in the movement for sexual liberation during the late 1960s and early 1970s USA, as both art critic and radical lesbian, we will look at the relation between art criticism and the social relations that emerge in the formation of social movements that *oppose* or *negate* the current order. Therefore, the 'social' in social critique gains a double meaning: late modern capitalist relations on the one hand, and the social movements against these, on the other.

The changes in modern dance during the period and context of this study are central for an understanding of Johnston's personal and professional turning points. As public manifestations against local repression and international military interventions reoccurred in the USA during the late 1950s

---

3   For a further discussion on art strikes, see Stewart Martin, "Art Strikes: An Inventory," *Mute*, 1 May =2020. https://www.metamute.org/editorial/articles/art-strikes-inventory (retreived 27 September 2023).

and early 1960s, the 'everyday' bodily movements undertaken by people active in social struggles entered the American dance theatres. According to dance theorist Sally Banes, the Cold War had an essential impact on the late modern dance scene, (Banes 1987, XX) resulting in the 1962 founding of the Judson Dance Theatre. Judson built on the 1950s American avant-garde: Merce Cunningham, (Banes 1982: 167) and John Cage – whose 'chance techniques,' tasks, and event-scores were pivotal for the founders. Central to these activities was the everyday movement of anyone, as in the case of people assembling on the streets against social injustice. Furthermore, many of the performance works and choreographies that emerged from Judson critiqued U.S. military inventions ongoing at the time (Banes 1994: 15). Judson was a communal space, influenced by the ambulant presentation forms of the Living Theatre (Banes 1982: 168). During its two first founding years, practitioners from various fields met weekly, to perform for critics such as Johnston (Ibid. 167). These meetings took the form of practice sessions, where Johnston not only attended presentations but also joined the training, along with visual artists such as Robert Morris, Robert Rauschenberg, and other non-dancers (Johnston 1971: 43) who also frequented the weekly sessions (Banes 1994: 212). Johnston thus took the position as both *performer* and *spectator*, which later came to be crucial for her negotiation with art criticism. In Johnston's very first essay on dance, published in 1955, entitled "Thoughts on the Present and Future Directions of Modern Dance," she hints that a "rebel group" will take over the Northern American dance scene (Banes 1994: 4). After the first Judson Dance Theatre concerts, she describes the activities as "a revolution of dance" (Johnston 2019 [1963]: 19). The manifold meaning of revolution in this context and period is not coincidental. A decade later, in 1965, Johnston writes: "I see a scope of action on many fronts, involving artists and spectators, beyond the present horizon" (ibid. 41).

The immanent critique of modern dance undertaken by the Judson'ers deeply influenced Johnston's way of thinking and writing, both aesthetically and socially. In her Dance Collumn in the *Village Voice,* titled "Communications," from in 1965, Johnston criticizes dance's dependence on media and communication to 'sell,' as a problem for the artform. She writes:

> Dance is not property, not in the sense that painting and sculpture are materials of exchange in a supply and demand economy including all stabilized objects.
>
> JOHNSTON 1965; MCGOVERN ET AL. 2019: 41

Writing this from the position of a critic, Johnston is deeply involved in the valorization of artworks, both in aesthetic and economic terms. She knows well the relation between an art critical judgment and the economic value of an artwork in circulation and how this decides the future economic possibilities for the laboring artist. When Johnston writes that "Dancers are not bought and sold," but rather "sell" or "lease" themselves, (ibid.) this includes Johnston too, as a critic. I argue so since I understand Johnston's critique of the 'object' of critique to be her own subjectivity. This makes Johnston's self-reflection immanent quite like in the critical practice of the conceptual artworks about which she wrote and with whom she shared most of her life during this period. Yet her critique is not only immanent to its social constellation, i.e., social – it is also objective, i.e., aesthetic. These dialectics are what make it possible to apply Adorno's theory of the artwork on Johnston's subjectivity as a critic, which I will develop further soon. If we now understand Johnston's writing on the dancer as a self-reflection which in fact implies herself as object, she is, too, "not bought and sold," but formally 'leased' to the form of presentation of a work of art, i.e., she is 'leased' to undertake the practice of art criticism. This is also the reason for Johnston's type of writing. As she puts it herself in the same column: "The problems are circular. A low economy is a cause of deficient communications and vice versa" (ibid 42). This includes Johnston's own social and economic situation.

While the circular problems that Johnston points out in "Communications" are still the case in contemporary art production and critique, the lack of 'discourse' around dance which according to Johnston's argument causes a weak historical consciousness for young practitioners has a double meaning in this historically specific context, and especially for Johnston. When dancers during this period were taught to work according to a formal, modernist concept of dance, this formalism and historical 'absolutism' can also be understood to *halt* the 'revolution in dance' that Johnston points towards, a revolution which she describes to overthrow the relation between spectator and work of art, in constant flux at Judson Dance Theatre.

2   A Blinded Consciousness

In the conjunctural specific context in which Johnston describes the revolution in dance to take place, the risk for a 'halt' of the revolutionary process that she warns of in "Communications" would not only affect the dance scene but also the social movements with which these dance practices were interwoven. I suggest that it was precisely this interweaving of dance and upheaval that caught Johnston's attention, at the time. A halt, then, could be caused by a missing self-reflection regarding the practitioner's or activist's objective relations, as sexualized, racialized, or otherwise structurally opressed. This could, for example, be the consequence of too big a trust in formalist critique. 'Revolution,' in Johnston's terms, must therefore be understood beyond the question of genre: it concerns aesthetic and social forms of social struggle, manifested in artistic activities at the time. Besides the critique of the American post-war military engagement, this includes the struggle for raising a common consciousness regarding class, sexual differences, and race. From this perspective, what Johnston refers to as 'a lack of theory' of modern dance, which in her view alienates dancers and choreographers from their history, can be understood beyond the dance theatre and rather as a struggle for social and sexual rights. In other words, it is a critique of a lack of historical consciousness of sexualized and racialized subjects. Johnston writes:

> When there's nothing to see there's nothing to talk about. When there's nothing to talk about everybody is in the dark. The people may come and go in the rooms, but they continue to talk about the pictures that are available to be seen.
>
> JOHNSTON 1965; MCGOVERN ET AL. 2019: 44

The question of 'talking' for Johnston, I interpret, is a way of being 'trapped' in a specific historical consciousness that ignores a large part of the population, including Johnston's own subjectivity as a lesbian. To 'talk' can therefore be understood as a way to imagine otherwise, which is what Johnston does herself. By disintegrating the art critical subjectivity that upholds such a singular 'picture,' alternative imaginaries are brought forth in Johnston's practice. This is what she instigates when intersecting formalist critique with reflections on the social reality that both preconditions and results from this activity in the first place. She does so throughout the 1960s. In a Dance Column from 1961 titled "Cunningham in Connecticut," Johnston writes:

> It Is not easy to see. Outside the theatre, living as we do, most of us see very little with our eyes wide open. In action the eye absorbs space forms to function; in repose the eye becomes a facial decoration as sight turns inward. And our training is such that when we do look for non-functional reasons, it is usually at something huge and spectacular, like cathedrals or sunsets. And even then it is rare to see more than a general outline. Or to see more and still enter. That is the crucial transition, from seeing to entering. Not only crucial but mysterious, so I won't say any more except to note that I think most people who go to dance concerts don't see very

well, not even dancers, sometimes dancers especially, and most often critics, who must attend special classes in becoming blind.

JOHNSTON 1961; MCGOVERN ET AL., 2019: 15

Let's stay briefly with the absorption that Johnston describes in the paragraph above. Interestingly, absorption is precisely what post-Kantian art critic and art historian Michael Fried describes in 1980 as an alternative to his forerunner's, Clement Greenberg's, concept of 'immanence in painting'. In a book on the Enlightenment art critic, Denis Diderot, Fried develops further Diderot's praising of painted subjects that are 'absorbed' by what they are doing. Fried states that the beholder must be 'neutralized' to not 'distract' this absorption (Fried 1988: 68). Therefore, the spectator must be as absorbed by their activity (art criticism) as is the subject depicted in the work of art. Fried writes:

> Put just barely figuratively, it is as though the presence of the beholder threatened to distract the dramatis personae from all involvement in ordinary states and activities, and as though the artist was therefore called upon to neutralize the beholder's presence by taking whatever measures proved necessary to absorb, or reabsorb, those personae in the world of the painting.
>
> Ibid

Like Diderot in his *Essais sur la peinture* from 1765, Fried distinguishes "a man who presents himself in society and a man who is engaged in action." To 'academicize' the social context of the subject painted, Diderot argues, would damage the activity by which they are absorbed. This would turn the 'neutral' space in which the subjects are absorbed into a theatre, and the subjects would be stiff actors. In 1967, Fried argued the same regarding the abstract object art in the context that Johnston writes about. In the infamous essay, entitled "Art and objecthood," Fried called works which extended the form of art to the whole exhibition space and all the social relations within it, theatrical. By positing these activities as 'objecthood,' and not 'art,' he explicitly described them as 'degenerated' (Fried 1998 [1967]: 164). In this respect, the 'revolution' that Johnston pointed toward above was not only a question of genre, but also of social identification, whose concepts and laws restrained non-normative subjects in this context and period (and still today). I suggest that it was the presence of these subjects that Fried ignored in his art theory.

Regarding Fried's ignorance, I suggest that critical reflections of the context in which art is represented and of the social relations that follow such representation has the capacity to extend social identification beyond established concepts, including the concept of art. When Fried stresses how 'theatrical' artistic actions are literal object formations and not objective art, he also refuses to accept these artistic appearances as subjective, enacted by people and not things. If we now return to Johnston's comment on absorption above, it may be Fried's absorptive critique (sometimes only turning inward, toward its own dominating identity) that she points out. In this sense, the 'blindness' of the social actor that Johnston refers to is the consequence of such absorption, which at the time was dominating in formal dance education as well as in art criticism, and in the modus operandi of the McCarthyist nation state writ large. To disrupt this absorptive formalism – which Fried describes as a kind of 'reabsorption' of the subjects depicted in the artwork – away from their distracting spectators, demands a social critique of the context in which the work plays out. Such social critique must include the context of the critic himself, which Fried obviously refuses. To stay with this 'specialized' blindness, in Fried's words an 'absorbed consciousness' (Fried 1988: 68) would, in Johnston's terms, halt 'the revolutionary consciousness' of the dancer/social actor. Therefore, the blindness spreads to society writ large. Let us repeat one sentence by Johnston: "Outside the theatre, living as we do, most of us see very little with our eyes wide open" (JOHNSTON 1961; MCGOVERN ET AL. 2019: 15).

Besides the relation to a recurring critique of virtuosity and skill amongst the Judson'ers who refused to uphold ballet aesthetics,[4] Johnston's aversion toward specialization also reflects her own activity as a critic, as made clear above. From the position of a formalist art critic like Fried himself, Johnston twists her objectivity by 'taking classes' *not* to be "blind." As an alternative to this blindness, she is socially involved in the works and the contexts that she attends, as we see in her texts. This includes practice sessions and surrounding social events at Judson, as much as personal relations that led up to the founding of Judson one year after the publication of Johnston's column in question. Either way, Johnston's engagement with dance 'behind the scenes' led her to the conviction that an understanding of dance needs to include a knowledge of the circumstances in which the dancers work, which in fact is closely related to the knowledge of the labor and means of production behind the artform itself. This is, again, closely related to the activity that Johnston herself also undertook as a critic. From this perspective, it is essential to discuss what kind of social relations and identifications this labor upholds, and by what means? In a 1965 column entitled "Critic's Critic," Johnston writes:

---

4 See, for example, Lambert 1999, Wikström 2021.

> Criticism wears me out – it's like riding a bike up and down the country hills in a race against a phantom judge. I'll take a plot of level territory and stake out a claim to lie down on it and criticize the constellations if that's what I happen to be looking at.
>
> JOHNSTON 2019 [1965]: 39

In this short paragraph, it seems like Johnston is not only herself judging art critically, but also acting under a "phantom judge." Be it a social stigma or the social relations of labor, the relation between the subject and object of art criticism is in movement in Johnston's case, for good and for bad. In the words of Diana Theodores, "[s]he seemed as conscious and questioning of the art of her criticism as the work she viewed" (Theodores 1979: 86). These works were occasionally transposed with herself, which led to the process of disintegration.

3   Overlapping Subjectivities

Prior to 1969, Johnston identifies as straight and understands her struggles and troubles with identity to be purely individual (Johnston 1983: 79). As she approaches 1969, her critique intertwined the 'revolution in dance': sexuality, gender, race, and class, both in terms of content and form. From this time on, she uses her thus far supposed heterosexual identity as a Trojan horse, or a 'found' object (Johnston 1998: 79). That is, she writes from the position of the formal art critic, while subverting this writer's position and subjectivity with immanent or direct references to social relations that disentangles the very subjectivity that this writing presupposes. Johnston's supposedly 'neutral' subjectivization as an art critic is hence 'troubled,' to use Judith Butler's notion, by her negation of a heterosexual identity. This brings us to the relation between non-gender and non-identity, crucial for the processes that Johnston's case highlights. Such a process allows us to understand Adorno's negative dialectics in a new light, in terms of sexual difference.

Already in 1965, Johnston writes that she 'subverts' her Dance Columns in the *Village Voice* (Johnston 1983: 76). And as the column transforms along with her social and sexual identification, it is consequently renamed "Dance Journal," to better reflect the daily life that Johnston extensively came to include in her critique (Andy Warhol 2019 [70]: 201). In 1971, it is simply titled "Jill Johnston," representing Johnston's self-representation coming from her alternate mode of subjectivization, as mentioned above. In the afterword to Johnston's collection of essays entitled *Marmalade Me* (1971), dance theorist Sally Banes argues that Johnston here acknowledged "what had in fact become the subject of her column" (Johnston 1998b: 313), namely: herself. While Johnston herself attests retrospectively that it was through Stonewall that she came out as a lesbian, (Johnston 1998a: 79) it is mostly in her writing and not on the streets that this took place. On July 2, 1970, Johnston came out as a radical lesbian in print:

> I don't recall any decision to declare my sexuality, in print, as though it should necessarily have interested anybody in any case. It happened that the column was moving at that time away from the theatre of dance and happenings toward the theatre of my life as a personal solution to among other things the Cagian philosophy – which I had until then taken seriously in the context of other people's work – of the continuity and inseparability of life and art. Gradually the life became the theatre became the column. The life being everything of course included everything. Sex was especially interesting since I was in love with a beautiful girl and we were having a very good time of it, at home and on the road. This was embarrassing. I didn't really want to make trouble for myself. Nobody ever gave me reason to believe that I would be adored and acclaimed for loving my own sex.
>
>   JOHNSTON 2019 [1970]: 72–73 AND JOHNSTON 1998b [1970]: 313

While the research on Johnston's activity as a social actor in the movement for sexual liberation is in process (Warner 2012; Manning et al. 2020), the role that this activity played for her art criticism is less discussed. As mentioned above, which I will discuss in depth below, I understand the relation between art criticism and social movement as manifested in Johnston's activity as a historically specific case for the dialectics of theory and praxis – the transcendental subject and the abstracted or commodified object – both critiqued and negated by Johnston. This does not mean that I want to reduce art criticism to theory, or social protest to praxis. Rather, I would like to explicate how the case of Johnston allows for an extended discussion of these dialectics, from the perspective of her disintegration. Importantly, this process is a question of her appearances as a public figure, in social struggle as well as in formal contexts of art and politics. For example, during a benefit ceremony for a women's strike on August 26, 1970 – a "disaster for women and a minor triumph for me," (Johnston 1973: 45) as Johnston calls it – she interrupted the ceremony by stripping to her underpants and jumping into a pool in the garden of the house in question. In a column published in the lesbian journal *The Ladder,* the situation is contextualized as radical lesbianism:

During Miss Steinem's talk, Jill Johnston took her swim. She identified herself as a writer and a Lesbian and said her swim was in protest of those in the movement for women's liberation who don't like Lesbians. While not advocating unorthodox swims, this episode does dramatically illustrate the one major weakness in the women's liberation movement. Unlike any other "minority" group, women have the power to literally take over the world tomorrow. If they will band together to do so; all they have to do is accept all women.

> The Ladder 1970: 30[5]

Johnston, who had not yet come out as a lesbian at this point, had quite a different account of the event:

A lot of people said and wrote I went into the pool to protest the discrimination against lesbians by feminists, but I wasn't nearly so organized.

> JOHNSTON 1973: 16

Johnston's approach to the domination of formalist art criticism that she herself undertook during the late 1950s and early 1960s was as disorganized as her social activism. But if we are to discuss it methodologically, we could stake out two tendencies. On the one hand, it took form in a way that made her critique immanent to the works discussed. On the other hand, Johnston made it *social*. While the first approach is exemplified in the Dance Column "Inside "Originale"," from 1964—the column entitled "Pain, Pleasure, Process," also from 1964, involves the way that Johnston weaves her social relations into her art critical reflections. In the first, Johnston describes life to always be "a new mixture of habit and improvisation," calling John Cage "an inventor in a medium that he has made his habit," (McGovern et al.: 36) while also acting out this habit *outside* of the artform. If this means that Cage includes daily life in his artistic methods, Johnston rather made critique her habit in daily life. That is, she extended art criticism to her social context. Furthermore, and in reverse, she also extended her social context to the object of her critique, occluded by formalist critics like the mentioned case of Fried.

"Inside "Originale"," is significant for Johnston since it was written from within the artwork in which she also was invited to act a role quite like herself. In this sense, Johnston both enabled the piece, partook in it, and critiqued

---

5   This recurring column, entitled "Cross Currents," is published unsigned, but can be assumed
    to be authored by the journal's editor, Barbara Grier.

it. She thus took the position of the art critic, the performer (the artist), and the social actor (the audience). This approach is like Johnston's simultaneous partaking in the weekly Judson sessions, along with many other artists whose works she also reviewed, such as Robert Morris. In the mid-1960s, in which the column in question was published, Johnston's reviews are often written from a formal perspective, as in the case of "Pain, Pleasure, Process." It concerns artist and Judson'er Robert Morris's two artworks *Card File* (1962) and *Box with the Sound of Its Own Making* (1961). In Johnston's writing, these works serve as examples for her engagement with the art object as both autonomous and social, which includes the artist's subject as much as her own subjectivity as a critic. In "Pain, Pleasure, Process," Johnston understands Morris' works quite different to Fried's argumentation regarding 'art objects.' She describes them as "[objects] illustrating the object," that is: mediations of the artform which critically reflects its formal conditions of possibility *as art* and consequently, the conditions of possibility of the subjectivity of the artist and the critic. Johnston writes: "Process becomes explicit in the product. The process is contained in the product. Process and product become the same thing" (Johnston 1971, 43). This 'process' is not only a question of the production of the art object; it is also the critical reflection *from within* the "sensuous character of value," as Stewart Martin describes the work of art (Martin 2007: 23). This reified form, which I discuss in depth below, is in Johnston's terms the 'object' which she makes her own 'lesson,' as stated in her press release to the Disintegration panel. Hence the object in question is also sexual, which is a central point to this chapter.

Discussing conceptual works of art like the ones by Morris, British philosopher Peter Osborne describes the consequence of an artistic, linguistic expression as a *withdrawal* of subjectivization "from the realization of the work *back to an idea*." In my reading this means that by making the social relations of artistic production the work's form *and* content, such social reality is sedimented in the work's aesthetic form and can consequently not only be 'read' as an autonomous semblance (of art). Rather, must it also be approached as a *social fact* (fait social, Adorno 2002 [1970]: 241), immanent to the artwork's form and sometimes to its title in conceptual artworks. This process, characterizing a tendency in modern art and dance to be dominated by the de-subjectivization of the artist in the 1960s, (Osborne 2013, 66) is significant for Johnston's own development as art critic. This is what Adorno in the *Negative Dialectics* calls antisubjectivism. I argue that Johnston de-subjectivizes as a critic by calling her writing an artform. This makes her anti-criticism an anti-subjectivism, since both artwork and critic's subject become 'objects illustrating the [other] object'. I propose that they are artworks that illustrate the condition of possibility for art, and for its presupposed subjects – including

Johnston's own aesthetic and social subjectivities, which are in stark conflict prior to 1969. I therefore suggest that there is an antisubjectivim in process when Johnston describes her 'object lesson' as a disintegration in May 1969. During this process the de-subjectivization of Johnston as a critic is withdrawn back to the *idea* of critique, immanent to the sensuous experience. Hence the 'object' in question can, when embodying a latent subjectivity, imagine this subjectivity otherwise. I believe that this is what Johnston does.

As a self-objectified critic, who merges her critique of the artwork with that of herself, Johnston merges her own presupposed art critical *subjectivity* with her *objectified* role as a worker, and with her *self-objectification* as a sexual subject. This is best documented in Johnston's autobiographic montage book *Lesbian Nation* (1973) in which her critical writings are re-edited as a biography in process. These examples are often traced outside of Johnston's publications, in her social activities. During the theatrical convention "Dialogue on Women's Liberation" at Town Hall, East Hampton, in May 1971,[6] Johnston refused to leave the stage when her speaker's time was over. Eventually, she was joined on stage by two other women. When asked, again, to wrap up her remarks, the three performed "a comic and erotic make-out session" (Manning et al. 2020: 113). Refusing to stop and thereafter interrupting the more conservative speaker Diana Thrilling's speech, Johnston made her critique of conservative feminism clear in action. In *Lesbian Nation*, she reflects over her own contribution: "town hall at least gave people something else to think about," adding that her "original intention for town hall was to launch my career as a boxer" (Johnston 1973:17). In dance scholar Claire Croft's words on the Town Hall convention, Johnston "forced an evening initially pitched as a debate of women versus men into an exploration of the *many* ways to be a woman in public" (Manning et al. 2020: 117).

In the above example, Johnston's 'overlap' of subjectivities not only questions formalist art criticism as a practice, but also the subjectivization of the critic, as autonomous and social fact. Her case therefore echoes what Osborne describes as the 'artist-critic': actors who self-reflect their artistic labor at the level of the artworks' form, which linguistically is presented as its *content* (Osborne 2013: 57). Johnston's activity can also be understood in line with what Jasper Bernes describes as "the critic of the artist-spectator or writer-reader," (Bernes 2017: 14) which in the 1960s emerged in the form of a "qualitative critique of work" (16). While the 'artist-critic' opposes formal art criticism and its

---

6   In 1979, the filmed convent was released as a documentary by Chris Hegedus and D. A. Pennebaker, entitled *Town Bloody Hall*. https://www.historicfilms.com/tapes/9658.

presupposed artforms, the "qualitative critique of work" extends a critique of artistic labor to a critique of labor in general, from the perspective of the laboring artist. Both Osborne's and Bernes' notions suggest alternative art critical positions and functions. They are indeed useful for a further understanding of the relation between praxis and theory (critique) in the context of artistic practice. They also are examples of what it would mean to critique art from within a social context. Yet as already made clear above, Johnston also critiques social contexts from within her art criticism's formal relations. This is what makes her critique social, even though she did not write from within a social struggle. Rather was the social struggle immanent to her writing. This is specific for the case of Johnston: she situated her social struggle within her own, formal relations as critic. It is with this approach that she extends her critique to life writ large – not the other way around. Today, contemporary discussions concerning the relation between critique and social relations are bound up to the notion of a "socially engaged art criticism," introduced by art historian Grant Kester with the journal *FIELD. A Journal of Socially Engaged Art Criticism* (2016). This notion suggests that art criticism is not social itself, which the case of Johnston's double character proves. Hence, when art criticism is critiqued socially, it disintegrates rather than being 'socialized'. My focus below is how this disintegration matters for the art critic as part of a social struggle for sexual rights. This can also help us to understand better how struggle relates to changing conceptions of art and of artistic practices in this period and context.

4   Johnston's Social Critique

For British philosopher Stewart Martin, 'anti-art' mediates art's supposed autonomy *critically* (Martin 2000: 203). In my reading, this means that anti-art self-reflects the semblance of autonomy that the aesthetic form upholds in the alienated form of a modern artwork, as described by Adorno in *Aesthetic Theory*. Adorno writes: "The purposefulness of artworks requires the purposeless, with the result that their own consistency is predicated on the illusory; semblance is indeed their logic" (Adorno 2002 [1970]: 101). Hence, the very 'value' of art as commodity is dependent on the mediation of its 'uselessness' as aesthetic form, autonomous from any kind of monetary objectification. Yet the commodified artwork *seemes* to be non-commodified, as aesthetic form. This is the semblance of autonomy that art upholds with its double character. If we return to Adorno's paragraph of the double character of the philosophical system and hence of critical thought, as cited above from *Negative Dialectics*, this means that art criticism cannot only rely on its individual objectivity, independent of all social relations that mediates the artwork as 'fait social'. Rather must the critic understand herself as fait social, i.e., as an object of (her own) critique. In its immanent reflection as artwork, the work of art sheds light on its own 'performance,' i.e., the labor by means of which it comes into being.[7] I propose that Johnstojn does the same thing, when reflecting socially over her own objectivity. This, I think, is what Adorno strives for when he describes anti-subjectivism as a model for perceiving relations between individual moments, via their *difference,* as discussed above.

As I will discuss in this section, Johnston undertakes her own disintegration by understanding her criticism as an artform. This allows us to understand her "anti-criticism," in Battcock's terminology, as a way for Johnston to mediate her art critical subjectivity – which also may be interpreted as semblance – *critically,* as suggested by Martin in the case of the artwork. This 'double mediation,' understood as a negation in Adorno's terms, underscores what I call the double character of the art critic. To outline how Johnston puts this aspect to practice, I have discussed the ways in which her art critical activities and their relation to her social context allows us to understand the role that her 'anti-criticism' plays for her art criticism. This has shown the following: if Johnston's 'disintegration' concerned *the subjectivity of the art critic* rather than *the object of art,* then her social critique – here interpreted as her anti-criticism – must, too, be understood in terms of how Johnston's art critical subjectivity related to the context of social struggle in which she was involved. In the next section, I will discuss the role of sexual identity at play in this relation, to show that in this historically specific context, 1965–1975, self-reflected objectivities – what I understand as the dialectics between *self-objectification* and *subjectivization* – coincide in the model of antisubjectivism which suggests new forms of subjecthood, at stake in the social struggle in which Johnston is involved. This equally means, I argue, that heteronomous relations (socially determined relations and forms of social repression) and autonomous forms (the value form, the subjects of art and of critique) are mutually confronted in Johnston's anti-criticism. They are so by means of a self-reflection over existing social conditions for critical thought. This reflection by Johnston brings us to a historically specific discussion regarding the relation between (social) *praxis* – what Marx describes as labor and what Adorno approaches as self-reflected objectivities – and (autonomous) *theory.* In other words, it is a discussion regarding possible

---

7 For further reading on the relation between the notion of performance and labor, see Josefine Wikström, *Practices of Relations in Task-Dance and the Event-Score: A Critique of Performance* (Routledge 2021).

social forms of critique, and in reverse, the possible critique enacted within social mobilization against reigning forms of oppression.

In Johnston's case, I suggest that theory and praxis coincide in the following way: if the subjectivization that transcendental critique (and hence, too, formalist art criticism) implies is a central precondition for the formalist art critic's presupposed *objectivity*, then Johnston's activity as a lesbian activist shows an example of another kind of subjectivization. This subjectivization is mediated by means of a social critique of its abstracted form, i.e., as a *self-objectification*. This is what I, in this context, describe as *praxis*. If Johnston's heteronomous experience as a lesbian activist coincides with her autonomous semblance as art critic, her critical subjectivity consequently becomes an object of her own social critique in the process of disintegration. The process of disintegration is hence a process that complicates the supposed dialectics of art criticism and modern subjectivity: of theory and praxis. But as I will show, any objection to critical subjectivity demands a differently imagined subjectivity to undertake this objection, i.e., this critique. In Johnston's case, this is how her 'double' self-criticism plays out. It is also what Adorno, as mentioned from *Negative Dialectics*, describes as "the coherence of the nonidentical" (Adorno 1973 [1966]: 24–25), which in Johnston's case is manifested by Johnston as social actor and as critical subject. Therefore, critical subjectivity is not outlasted but mediated *differently*, by means of its social relations. I even dare to argue that critical subjectivity is mediated by means of its immanent *difference* to itself. In Johnston's case, a non-heterosexual identity.

In "Marginalia on Theory and Praxis," written alongside a longer correspondence with Marcuse on the German student movement in 1969, Adorno warns of the neglect of theory as 'false praxis,' (Adorno 2005 [1969]: 265) to spread amongst his student's social actions. Such false praxis would, in Adorno's point of view, risk developing into what the action emerged against in the first place. He argues that "Immediate action [...] is incomparably closer to oppression than the thought that catches its breath" (ibid.: 274). Furthermore, Adorno warns for any individual interest to 'belong' to a collective, in this case a revolutionary movement, or to identify with slogans rather than developing arguments – what he describes as "the dialectical reversal into irrationalism" (ibid.; 276). In *Aesthetic Theory*, authored during the same period, Adorno approaches the subject quite differently. In his drafted introduction to *Aesthetic Theory*, he writes that "the ways available to experience and thought that lead into artworks are infinitely many, yet they converge in truth content. This is obvious to artistic praxis, and theory should follow it much more closely than it has" (Adorno 2002 [1970]: 354). What these two examples make clear is that artistic and revolutionary praxis are not quite the same for Adorno.

To exemplify the way in which theory and praxis should follow what is not formally represented by an artwork, Adorno describes a collaboration between musicians during the rehearsal of a string quartet, during which one is asked by the other to contribute with "whatever critique and suggestions occurred to him." This critique of the colleague's performance allows for a "transformation of aesthetic comportment" and furthermore "transformations of the comportment of the subject," as part of the "changes in the representational level" (ibid.). Consequently, the collectively altered form of the work also transforms its subjectivization. That is, it opens for the unrepresented, non-subjectified, in art. This is what Adorno misses amongst his students' attempts to cohere with a party line. The collectively – yet undertaken by individuals – altered means for subjectivization that he points out in the interaction between the musicians is not far from Johnston's activity. She, too, stays within her individual activity, but immerses this into that which this activity formally is not. As mentioned above, she describes her writing to be an 'artform' in "Critics' Critic":

> One reason I'm writing this piece about criticism is that I just read Clive Barnes on criticism in the *Times*. With all respects to Mr. Barnes and I liked his article on criticism, I don't think of myself as a "parasite," which is the term Mr. Barnes used in referring to one who practices criticism. I was about to say: – one who practices the ART of criticism, which brings me back to what I said about staking out a claim to being an artist. And speaking of artists, why is it that more dancers don't practice the art of writing about their work?
>
> JOHNSTON 2019 [1965]: 39

This 'claim' outlined by Johnston doesn't make her a 'collaborator' of any of the artists whose works she reviews. Rather, the notion of collaboration is important on a different level. Namely, on the level of social relations between artists and Johnston herself, which throughout the 1960s informs a growing part of her writing. This level of "collaboration" in terms of intimate relationships also differentiates Johnston from her contemporary art critic colleague Lucy Lippard, who in the introduction to *Six Years,* published in 1973, argues that "a critic's medium is always artists; critics are the original appropriators" (Lippard 1997: XV). As we read above, Johnston makes clear that she did not understand herself to be a "parasite," since her practice was an artform *too*. Her activity as a critic is an 'artform,' she claims, adding that dancers too 'should' write like that (JOHNSTON 2019 [1965]: 40). Hence, Johnston's above-mentioned callout to dancers to write dance criticism themselves not only reflects the indistinction between artist and critic as in the aforementioned case of musicians in Adorno's *Aesthetic Theory*. It also reflects Johnston's own practice. Different from Lippard, Johnston appropriates *her own* social relations and treats these as found (art) objects, close to the methods of the artists that she reviews (which, in turn, often are included in Johnston's social relations). This method is confirmed by Judson member Yvonne Rainer, who in 1970 describes the annoying experience of reading Johnston's thoughts about their relation in print:

> I get very mad at Jill when she repeats something I say in her column or when I find out she's mad at me through reading the *VV*. She avoids direct communication. That's her trouble that's my trouble that's everybody's trouble. End sermon. Sorry Jo.
>
> RAINER 1974 [1970]: 317

Adorno's writing on cultural critique is useful for a further discussion of Johnston's case, and the social relations that her criticism presupposed and produced. In the essay "Cultural Criticism and Society," Adorno argues that the critic cannot be purely immanent; its consciousness must transcend "the immanence of culture," into the social whole (Adorno 1983 [1955]: 29). In this sense the critic is not only autonomous, but also socially subjected, much like how Adorno describes the double character of art. This is also what Johnston shows an example of as a 'double character' of the critic, and which is made even more obvious if we are to compare her with contemporary critics in her field at the time. While most critics active in the context and during the period of study – such as Lippard (1937 –) or Douglas Crimp (1944–2019) – are known for having joined feminist groups, the early gay movement, or the founding of The Art Workers' Coalition, while simultaneously holding on to the subjectivity as an art critic and sometimes also curator, Johnston goes further.

At this stage in our discussion, it is important to underscore that Johnston not only questions formal art criticism as a practice, but also the presupposed subjectivities that follow with such a practice. What kind of subjectivization is enabled during a critical reflection of a work of art, and by whom? I suggest that Johnston's critique does not primarily concern the objectivity of the artwork as form, but rather her own subjective formation as a critic, presupposed in the encounter with the artwork. Such formation can in Johnston's context be understood as a white, cis-heterosexual European male subject. As already discussed, Johnston's reflection of critical subjectivity is in fact the object of her art criticism. This object is also herself when restrained by the norms governing the critic's subject. In this sense, the disintegration of art criticism is Johnston's praxis for a remodeling of this 'object'––as subject. A sexual subject. On a concrete level, the process plays out in the way that Johnston reviews artworks and performances from a formal art critic's perspective, while simultaneously confronting the critical subjectivity of hers, which is mediated by this objectivity. This objectivity is simultaneously confronted by the heteronomous relations, which Johnston finds within the objectivity of her critique (and not outside of this). These heteronomies are not only a question of her relation to and partial involvement in the social struggle for sexual liberation, but also of the cultural industry that Johnston's art critical engagement is an inherent part of. While Johnston's labor as art critic (what she describes as the biking "up and down the country hills" (JOHNSTON 2019 [1965]: 39)) therefore affirms capitalist social relations, I argue that her simultaneous activity as a radical lesbian activist, which also plays out in her texts, *negates* these. They do so since Johnston's 'disintegration' not only concerns the subjective relations of aesthetic forms but also those of the value form, which I, with Johnston as example, have shown to interrelate. This interrelation is also the point of the dialectics pointed out with Adorno's model of the 'double character'.

As pointed out by Osborne, the double character of the artwork as socially subjected and yet autonomous is also to be understood as the bourgeois subject, quite like Marx before him described capital to be both social and autonomous, when embodied by living labor (Gordon et al. 2020: 310). This makes it quite useful to imagine a double character of a critic, but Adorno never does so himself. Instead, he uses the notion of 'the dialectical critic of culture.' This critic, he writes, must both "participate in culture *and not* participate. Only then does he do justice to his object and to himself" (Adorno 1983: 33). In the case of Johnston, this dialectic of participation applies equally in the context of art and in that of social movements, both of which she is part of "and not," by the reason that her involvement in the first informs her involvement in the other, and vice versa. Hence Johnston's engagement as art critic and social activist allows her to mediate her social struggle in art critical texts published formally as columns. This furthermore enables her to mediate her social relations critically, while socializing this very mediation. Hence this social critique depended on an aesthetic *distance* that she upheld within the social context in which she immediately took part as a critic – a distance which simultaneously was confronted socially by Johnston, in her social actions as much as in her writing. In this case, Adorno's dialectics of cultural and transcendent critique, which may be understood as the dialectics of art critical subjectivity, extends the relation between critique and anti-criticism vis-à-vis autonomous art and anti-art. Let me explain how.

In his reading of *Aesthetic Theory*, Martin points out that Adorno mobilizes the artwork's semblance of autonomy *against* the autonomy of capital. This is the social reality of the modern artwork, which Martin describes to be "a sensuous fixation of abstraction, of the value-form, and not immediately abstract" (Martin 2000: 23). If we are to understand the case of Johnston via this model, i.e., art criticism personified by herself as seemingly autonomous, it is mobilized *against itself* as commodified labor. As autonomous and social fact; *subject and object of critique,* Johnston's anti-criticism appears to be the form in which these dialectics do not collapse but forces their respective subject forms to *disintegrate* in new forms of subjectivity. My proposal is that Johnston's anti-criticism is a social critique of her own practice and hence of her presupposed heterosexual identification as art critic. By understanding this social critique as Johnston's practice, we may understand how it caused critical subjectivity to disintegrate into *different* forms of subjectivity.

5   Johnston's Sexual Subjectivization

"Only by immersing its autonomy in society's imagerie can art surmount the heteronomous market," writes Adorno in *Aesthetic Theory* (Adorno 2002 [1970]: 21). In the case of Johnston, I suggest that this "imagerie" can be understood as the struggles undertaken in social movements, in the 1960s USA, such as the struggle for sexual liberation to which Johnston was affiliated. As in the context of modern art at the time, also here, the 'culture industry' plays a big part, for better or for worse (and often worse) (Drucker 2015: 171). Consequently, Johnston's engagement with the art market and the movement for sexual liberation coincides with their commercialization, an opportunity for Johnston that she also was critiqued for when becoming too 'famous' as a public figure. Johnston's 'immersion' of autonomy into these heteronomies is therefore not only a question of the autonomy of art being immersed in a heteronomous context of social struggle, but also of an activation of the subjective experiences (what Adorno calls truth content or negative identity) which are deselected in a formal art critical judgment, within these processes. By means of the activity of these experiences, heteronomy of the market was negated as much as the autonomy of art and capital, by means of Johnston's anti-criticism. As the above cited argument by Adorno makes clear, art's negative dialectics are a question of *surmounting by immersion*. And if "[t]he absolute artwork converges with the absolute commodity," (Adorno 2002 [1970]: 21) in the form of a critique and as a simultaneous product of capitalism, Johnston's case proves that this is also the case for criticism: the art critic encounters herself as an absolute commodity and simultaneously autonomous, both of which she confronts as a sexual subject. This is possible since Johnston's public lesbianism was not fully absorbed by the social relations of capital, which is a different case today.

The question of reification, of art and social subjects, is central to Johnston's double character. It is also central to the way in which her anti-criticism mediates her sexual subjectivity, which otherwise would be occluded by her formal art critical subjectivity and by herself as commodified laborer. As part of this anti-criticism, Johnston self-objectifies by emphasizing different social relations that are immanent to her formal critique. In other words, the relations that enable her as a critic, for example the de-selection of certain subjects and experiences from the aesthetic form of art. The self-objectification that Johnston undertakes is manifested by Johnston when she calls her writing an artform. In *The Reification of Desire,* (2009) Queer Marxist Kevin Floyd extends on Marx's concept of self-objectification as explicated in Marx's "Theses on Feuerbach" from 1845 and in the "Economic and Philosophic Manuscripts" from 1844. Against an orthodox Marxist critique of reification as outlined by György Lukács, Floyd underscores Marx's emancipatory emphasis on praxis as further developed by Marcuse at the time of Johnston's activities. This not only includes the double character of a person as both autonomous and socially subjected to sexual or racial repression––it also refers to how the identification with a sexual identity may surmount this repression. According to Floyd's suggestion, such identification surmounts in Marx's transcendent upheaval of capitalist abstractions, quite like Marcuse's writing on Eros (Marcuse 1955). For Floyd, this means that the reified subject, produced by abstraction, (Marx 1992: 387) also may subjectify *differently,* as part of this process; that is, in negation to governing forms of subjectivity, of one-dimensionality as Marcuse called it (Marcuse 1964). Hence de-subjectivization as self-objectification allows for different kinds of subjectivization.

Informed by Foucault and Marcuse, Floyd argues that the capitalist alienation of the subject not only includes people's productive, but also social and reproductive skills, such as sexual experience. Therefore, suggests Floyd, self-objectification entails the emergence of new sexual subjectivities. The self-inflicted reification of sexual desire hence surpasses the modern subject's self-valorization as laborer and allows for alternate abstractions which 'occupy' the value form and from there redefines sexual subjectivity (Floyd 2009: 69). This process is, too, quite close to how Adorno describes the subjection of historic experience (negative identity) in self-critical artforms. Quite like he describes the double character of the philosophical system, he describes the model of art as a constellation through individual *difference,* as we have discussed before. It is this difference *as praxis* that Floyd underscores, arguing that it reaches beyond the "heterosexual matrix" as Judith Butler calls it. Floyd hence suggests that the laboring body can be more than a commodity (73), even though it is part of an extended process of accumulation and exploitation. In Peter Drucker's critique of Floyd's proposal, "[t]his does not mean that the gay/straight binary is anything to cheer about, any more so than capital's exploitation of labor" (Drucker 2015: 166). Yet the historically specific double bind of emancipation and repression that Floyd describes as embedded in the self-objectified laborer is helpful for a better understanding of Johnston's 'double character,' which is far from only aesthetic.

While social struggles and capitalist relations are "imprinted in the structure of artworks," any literalness in terms of content, such as 'political opinions,' obscures their truth content, Adorno argues in *Aesthetic Theory* (Adorno 2002 [1970]: 232). Therefore, 'real partisanship' can only appear at the level of an artwork's *form*, not in the *content* of a work or in an explicit political manifestation, he concludes. If Adorno most probably would argue that the social movements in which Johnston engaged as a critic did not fulfil this – as they did indeed imply opinions – it is also possible to understand Johnston's social critique as an artform as such. Furthermore, we can understand these social movements in line with how Adorno describes the social content in art as something that "inheres in individuation, which is itself a social reality" (233). Individuation can therefore be understood in line with the objectification in which the artwork-as-commodity becomes subjectivized, just like Floyd suggests the alternative subjectivization of a sexual subject takes place. Therefore, the subjectivized artwork enters a dialectical relation to praxis. This we already have discussed as antisubjectivism and de-subjectivization. Yet if for Adorno, the artwork's self-consciousness is mediated by its commodity form as what Osborne calls a "substitute for authentic working-class reality" (Osborne 2020: 310), then Floyd's suggested sexual subjectivization by means of a reification of sexual desire, 'substitutes' a *queer reality*. I believe that Johnston's case merges both the historical consciousness of the artwork and of the sexual subject.

The social reality in which the respective subject's negative subjectivization of artwork and sexual subject takes place is indeed the capitalist relations in which the movement for sexual liberation also emerged in this period and context. In the historically specific context of this struggle, right before and soon after Stonewall, such subjectivization was not given. Neither was it for Johnston. In the act of writing – what she called an artform – resides the social reality that her art critical subjectivity excluded. When critically mediating this social reality by means of this kind of writing, Johnston' art criticism included her engagement in the movement for sexual liberation. It is a reality that otherwise would not have been mentioned in the words authored by her in the context of art criticism, but which through her double character is given a voice. It is imprinted in the structure of her writing, independent of its explicitness. In a *Village Voice* column from 1970, entitled "Of This Pure But Irregular Passion," Johnston writes:

> I had been misbehaving at the heterosexual loft artist parties for instance. Dancing with my heterosexual female friends, if they would. Things like that. Angry. I was angry. I saw nothing in the society around me to affirm a sexual choice that finally I had to make to clarify my life.
>
> JOHNSTON 2019 [1970]: 74

From the perspective of the 'negative identity' that Johnston embodies as lesbian in the subjective body of an art critic, it is possible to draw a parallel between Adorno's description of the artwork's negative dialectics and her art critical writing, which I have done throughout this chapter. I have done so in terms of what I propose as the double character of the critic. Yet it needs to be emphasized that this perspective is only possible because Johnston calls her writing an artform, which makes it both art and non-art (to use Freid's notion) – and anti-criticism (to use Battcock's concept). The resulting 'figuration,' which I suggest that Johnston's art critical writing enables, therefore "articulates the wordless and mute contradictions" in the (sexual) social reality that enables it (by being excluded from it), and in which Johnston lives and acts. Adorno describes this 'articulation' as a *praxis* that "does not act directly," which clearly reflects his restraints toward direct political action and "committed art" (Adorno 2002: 232). As for Johnston, the non-direct action undertaken from within her objectivity as art critic, reflects her indirect participation in social movements as an occasionally idolized writer. Yet when calling her indirect participation an artform, she gives form to her own subjectivization as a lesbian, which her art critical subjectivity otherwise neglected. This combines Adorno's aesthetic subjectivization with Floyd's sexual one. It also emphasizes the social and aesthetic character of praxis, which furthermore emphasizes the immanent relation of praxis and theory – in this sense: critique.

If Johnston's sexual subjectivity emerges *in negation* to her art critical subjectivity and yet within its form, she is not immersing her critical autonomy into the social heteronomy in which she lives and works. Rather does her writing also take form immanently and yet *against* a social reality that opposes the presupposed objectivity of art criticism. This social reality resides within the 'artform' of Johnston's writing. It is from the perspective of the act of giving form to this subjectifiation that Johnston also reflects the social objectivity of her art critical subjectivity, which simultaneously becomes an object for her social criticism. Yet different from Johnston's art critical judgment, this social critique and hence anti-criticism is historically specific. By negating the form of her art critical subjectivity *from within* the autonomy that it presupposes, her praxis restructures meaning of art (and sexuality) like the case of Adorno's musicians. In other words, it allows for new kinds of subjectivities to emerge in the negation of the social objectivity of Johnston-as-critic. And which during her panel in May 1969 causes this subject to disintegrate. Art's double character is therefore reflected in Johnston's double subjectivization, which is both socially figured and aesthetically formed. The form of art, British philosopher Gillian Rose wrote after Adorno, embeds not only a "crisis of meaning" (qua form) but also a "restructuring of meaning" (Rose 2014: 167). If we understand meaning as the social (sexual) content of the artwork, Johnston's case extends it to her writing "art" and hence to her social reality as lesbian. In this sense, what Rose calls a crisis of meaning can be understood as a *negative figuration* of subjectivity and hence an antisubjectivism in the form of art. This absented subjectivity is not the work's content, but something which speaks for an unspoken 'inside,' as Adorno describes Beckett's *Endgame* (Adorno 1982 [1961]). The restructuring of meaning, then, is the process of an alternatively imagined subjectivization that gives shape to these silent expressions (or, rather, silenced, in this context of sexual repression). In Johnston's case, her sexual subjectivity is expressed from within the form of formal writing, and not immediately on the streets. It causes a social disintegration of her formalist art criticism as much as of her heterosexual identity. The example of Johnston hence provides a social as much as a queer perspective of Adorno's model of the artwork, which is essential for an understanding of feminism in relation to critical theory, today.

References

Adorno, Theodor W., *Aesthetic Theory*. [1970] Trans. Tiedemann, Rolf. London: Continuum 2002.

Adorno, Theodor W., *Critical Models*. [1969] Trans. Pickford, Henry W. Colombia University Press 2005.

Adorno, Theodor W., *Negative Dialectics*. [1966] Ashton E.B., Trans. London and New York, Routledge 1973.

Adorno, Theodor W., *Prisms*. [1955] Nicholsen, Shierry Weber and Weber, Samuel, Trans. New York: MIT Press 1983.

Adorno, Theodor W., Jones, Michael T., "Trying to Understand Endgame." [1961] *New German Critique* No. 26, Critical Theory and Modernity (Spring – Summer, 1982), pp. 119–150.

Banes, Sally. *Terpsichore in Sneakers: Post-modern Dance.* Wesleyan University Press 1987.

Banes, Sally. "The Birth of the Judson Dance Theatre: "A Concert of Dance" at Judson Church, July 6, 1962." *Dance Chronicle*, Vol. 5, No. 2. London and New York: Taylor & Francis, Ltd. 1982.

Banes, Sally. *Writing Dancing in the Age of Postmodernism*, Middletown, Conn: Wesleyan University Press; Hanover: University Press of New England 1994.

Banes, Sally. "Jill Johnston, Signaling Through the Flames," in Jill Johnston, *Marmalade Me (Revised And Expanded Edition)*, Hanver: University Press of New England, (1971), 1998b

Battcock, Gregory. "THE LAST ESTATE," *New York Review of Sex*, July 1969, in Johnston, Jill, McGovern, Fiona, Sullivan, Megan Francis, Wieder, Axel, ed. Jill Johnston. *The Disintegration of a Critic.* Bergen Kunsthall, Stenberg Press 2019.

Bernes, Jasper. *The Work of Art in the Age of Deindustrialization.* Stanford, California: Stanford University Press 2017.

Bolt, Mikkel. *Dialog med de døde.* Aarhus: Antipyrine 2023.

Drucker, Peter. *Warped. Gay Normality and Queer Anti-Capitalism.* Historical Materialism, Brill 2015.

Floyd, Kevin. *The Reification of Desire. Toward a Queer Marxism.* Minneapolis and London: University of Minnesota Press 2009.

Frascina, Francis. *Art, Politics and Dissent: Aspects of the Art Left in Sixties America.* Manchester: Manchester University Press 1999.

Fried, Michael. *Absorption and Theatricality: Painting and Beholder in the Age of Diderot.* Chicago University Press 1988.

Fried, Michael. "Art and Objecthood," *Artforum*, June 1967, in Fried, Michael, *Art And Objecthood. Essays and Reviews.* Chicago and London: Chicago University Press: 1998.

Johnston, Jill. *Admission Accomplished: the "Lesbian Nation" Years (1970–75)* London: Serpents Tail, 1998a.

Johnston, Jill. "Communications," *Village Voice,* November 14, 1965, in Johnston, Jill, McGovern, Fiona, Sullivan, Megan Francis, Wieder, Axel, ed. Jill Johnston. *The Disintegration of a Critic.* Bergen Kunsthall, Stenberg Press 2019.

Johnston, Jill. "Critic's Critic," *Village Voice*, September 16, 1965, in Johnston, Jill, McGovern, Fiona, Sullivan, Megan Francis, Wieder, Axel, ed. Jill Johnston. *The Disintegration of a Critic.* Bergen Kunsthall, Stenberg Press 2019.

Johnston, Jill. "Cunningham in Connecticut," *Village Voice*, September 7, 1961, in Jill Johnston, McGovern, Fiona, Sullivan, Megan Francis, Wieder, Axel, ed. Jill Johnston. *The Disintegration of a Critic*. Bergen Kunsthall, Stenberg Press 2019.

Johnston, Jill. "Inside "Originale"," *Village Voice*, October 1, 1964, in Johnston, Jill, McGovern, Fiona, Sullivan, Megan Francis, Wieder, Axel, ed. Jill Johnston. *The Disintegration of a Critic*. Bergen Kunsthall, Stenberg Press 2019.

Johnston, Jill. "Judson Concerts #3, #4," Village Voice, February 28, 1963, in Jill Johnston, McGovern, Fiona, Sullivan, Megan Francis, Wieder, Axel, ed. Jill Johnston. *The Disintegration of a Critic*. Bergen Kunsthall, Stenberg Press 2019.

Johnston, Jill. "Lesbian/Feminism Reconsidered," *Salmagundi*, Fall 1982-Winter 1983, No. 58/59 pp. 76–88 Skidmore College.

Johnston, Jill. *Lesbian Nation*, New York: Simon & Schuster 1973.

Johnston, Jill. "Pain, Pleasure, Process," Village Voice February 27, 1964 in Johnston, Jill, *Marmalade Me (New and Expanded Edition)*, Hanver: University Press of New England, (1971), 1998b.

Johnston, Jill. "PRESS RELEASE," 1969, in Johnston, Jill, McGovern, Fiona, Sullivan, Megan Francis, Wieder, Axel, ed. Jill Johnston. *The Disintegration of a Critic*. Bergen Kunsthall, Stenberg Press 2019.

Lambert, Carrie, "Moving Still: Mediating Yvonne Rainer's "Trio A"" *October*, Vol. 89. (Summer, 1999), pp. 87–112.

Lippard, Lucy, R. *Six Years. The Dematerialization of the Art Object from 1966 to 1972* Berkeley and Los Angeles, University of California Press, 1997.

Manning, Susan, Ross, Janice, Schneider, Rebecca, ed. *Futures of Dance Studies*. University of Wisconsin Press 2020.

Marcuse, Herbert. *Eros and Civilisation*. Beacon Press 1955.

Marcuse, Herbert, *One-Dimensional Man*. Beacon Press, 1964.

Martin, Stewart, "Art Strikes: an Inventory," Mute Magazine, 1 May 2020. Source:https://www.metamute.org/editorial/articles/art-strikes-inventory(retreived 27 September 2023).

Martin, Stewart, "Autonomy and Anti-Art: Adorno's Concept of Avant-Garde Art," *Constellations* 7:2, June 2000.

Martin, Stewart. "The Absolute Artwork Meets the Absolute Commodity," *Radical Philosophy* 146. Nov/Dec 2007.

Marx, Karl. "Economic and Philosophic Manuscripts," *Early Writings*. Trans. Rodney Livingstone and Gregor Benton. London: Penguin Books, 1992.

McGovern, Fiona, Sullivan, Megan Francis, Wieder, Axel, ed. *Jill Johnston. The Disintegration of a Critic*. Bergen Kunsthall, Stenberg Press 2019.

Osborne, Peter, "Adorno and Marx," In *A Companion to Adorno*, Gordon, Peter E., Hammer, Espen, Pensky, Max, eds. Wiley-Blackwell: 2020.

Osborne, Peter. *Anywhere or Not at All*. London: Verso 2013.

Rainer, Yvonne, "Yvonne Rainer," *Cultural Hero*, "Jill Johnston: Exposed," ed. Les Levine, no 14, 1970, in Yvonne Rainer, W*orks,* The Press of the Nova Scotia College of Art and Design, Halifax. New York University Press, New York 1974.

Rose, Gillian, *The Melancholy Science. An Introduction to the Thought of Theodor W. Adorno.* London: Verso 2014.

Theodores Taplin, Diana "On Critics and Criticism of dance," Theodores Taplin Diana (ed.), *New Directions in Dance. Collected Writings from the Seventh Dance in Canada Conference Held at the University of Waterloo,* Canada, June 1979, Toronto, Pergamon Press, 1979.

The Ladder, October-November 1970, Vol. 15, No. 1 and 2. See: https://documents.alexanderstreet.com/d/1003347911.

Warhol, Andy, "Andy Warhol," *Cultural Hero*, "Jill Johnston: Exposed," ed. Levine, Les, no 4, 1970, in McGovern, Fiona, Sullivan, Megan Francis, Wieder, Axel, eds. Jill Johnston. *The Disintegration of a Critic.* Bergen Kunsthall, Stenberg Press 2019.

Warner, Sara. *Acts of Gaiety. LGBT Performance and the Politics of Pleasure.* University of Michigan Press, 2012.

Wikström, Josefine. *Practices of Relations in Task-Dance and the Event-Score. A Critique of Performance.* London: Routledge, 2021.

PART 3

Intersectional Investigations

∵

CHAPTER 9

Historical Traumas in the Critiques of Theodor Adorno and Joy James

Jana McAuliffe

Contemporary feminist politics and theory are deeply influenced by feminists of color whose work produced the rigorous tools that enable intersectional analysis. Intersectionality is not one theory or approach; this term refers, broadly, to feminist work committed to the idea that the category "woman" does not function universally, that gendered experience and gendered social justice struggles are deeply entwined with other aspects of social life, including, but not limited to, race, class, sexuality, ability, and nationality. Influential thinkers including Audre Lorde, Kimberlé Crenshaw, and Angela Davis have pushed feminist thinking and organizing to continually question who is the subject of feminism, to problematize in whose name and for whose benefit feminism works, and to interrogate any use of a social identity category that would signify monolithically (Lorde 2007; Crenshaw 1991; Davis 1983). One consequence of this is that racial justice can be understood as an ethical and political feminist commitment, and an intersectional critique of institutionalized white supremacy in the contemporary United States will critically engage the role gender plays in racist power.

   It is from this understanding of feminist theory that I put into conversation the conceptual work of the contemporary political theorist Joy James and the Frankfurt School philosopher Theodor W. Adorno. I focus on the concepts each thinker uses to confront the trauma caused by historical violence. Reflecting on the foundational violence of slavery for the United States, James developed the term *Captive Maternals* to demonstrate how racial capitalism steals and relies on the "labor and time" of Black women and other oppressed caretakers (James 2016: 259). On James' analysis, "Captive Maternals provided the reproductive and productive labor to stabilize culture and wealth" used to develop and to maintain U.S. democracy (James 2016: 256). Responding to a different foundational violence, Adorno asserted after the horrors of World War II that one cannot write poetry and, ultimately, one cannot live, and that Hitler has imposed upon humanity an imperative that Auschwitz never happen again (Adorno 2002: 110). *Auschwitz* for Adorno invokes the mechanized cruelty and horror of the concentration camps and the existential guilt that all subjects now bear because of this historical trauma. As I will explore more fully below, each thinker's work presents an effective method for making the relevance of history on the present understood and felt.

Such methods are important for critical social theory, as the determination of what history matters now, and how it matters, plays a crucial role in the constitution of political community. At the time of this writing, there is significant political strife surrounding history, as exemplified in the political contestations concerning whether The 1619 Project and other "Critical Race Theories" should be taught in schools. Such political disputes raise deep questions about the identity of the nation: what is the United States and who is the U.S. American citizen? What history formed them? If that history is violent, what does that imply about those of us who live and work and form our identities in this nation? Following through on the legacy of intersectional analysis in addressing such historical questions reveals that they will likely remain unsettled, as they do not have one final answer. This chapter operates from the point of view that the enslavement of Black people is a fundamental trauma that helped form the development of the United States and the identity of U.S. Americans. The genocidal conquest of Indigenous people is as well; I do not engage that history here, but it would be necessary to a full treatment of the historical violence significant to the development of the United States. Although it occurs much later, the Holocaust is another historically significant violence that impacted the development of the nation. Even if that could be agreed upon (which it currently is not), *how* that history continues to inform the present will be different depending upon the different social locations of citizens. Even within political solidarity groups, the 'history that matters' to 'us' is therefore likely to remain always in question. A feminist engagement with history informed by intersectionality will require, at minimum, that multiple historical traumas be recognizable as inextricable from the identity of the nation. A particular historical trauma may be the focus of some specific analysis, but on my judgment, intersectional analysis contends that no one can take the position of the most foundational, once and for all.

In order to critically explore the potential of Adorno's thinking about Auschwitz for contemporary feminist analysis, in what follows I engage his work in the context of James' analysis of the Captive Maternal. Adorno's use of Auschwitz can be read as presenting the Holocaust as a singular event, as *the* paradigmatic historical violence. This illustrates one reason why Frankfurt School thinking may be difficult to use in contemporary feminist analysis that is concerned with the historical violence that may be more immediate to the lived experience of people who are neither white nor European. At stake therefore is whether Adorno's use of Auschwitz can be pluralized, whether his approach to accounting for this horror can be put on equal footing with other historical traumas. To explore this question, I turn to Joy James' essays "The Womb of Western Theory: Trauma, Time Theft, and the Captive Maternal" and "Political Trauma" in order to take stock of the concerns and conceptual vocabulary James uses to engage the trauma of capture in her work. I present a reading of the Captive Maternal that shows how it makes intelligible the raced and gendered dimensions of historical and contemporary white supremacy in the United States. With the concerns of James' work in mind, I turn to Theodor Adorno's analysis of Auschwitz in his 1965 lecture series *Metaphysics: Concepts and Problems*. I show that, for Adorno, the category Auschwitz is a sign of a metaphysical, moral rupture that has changed history. To Adorno, this trauma has engendered a condition of material guilt that encompasses everyone living after Auschwitz.

Finally, I explore the question of whether there are limitations in Adorno's approach that make it difficult to bring into conversation with James' conceptual framing. I situate James' analysis of Captive Maternals as one example of a project that thinks the specificity of race and gender at work in historical trauma. I suggest that it can thus help to establish some expectations for what makes a critical project useful for contemporary feminist theory. Thinking these two projects together suggests that Adorno's way of engaging metaphysical analysis needs to be critically thought through before it can be pluralized in the way that is called for by intersectional feminism. I conclude that James' approach, because it is race and gender attentive, focused on the agency of oppressed people, and expressly engages a diversity of activist-theorists, allows more easily for the kind of plurality necessary to thinking the 'history that matters to us.' I approach this engagement as someone who has learned much from each of these thinkers about how to think deeply and critically about the world, and offer, finally, a brief account of the implications of this work for figure-driven critical scholarship.

1   Captive Maternals

Joy James argues that the productive capacity of Black women and other "Captive Maternals" has been a crucial resource used to establish the prominence of Western theory and politics in the contemporary world. To think through James' critique, in this section I explicate the categories she develops to theoretically and politically confront the gendered power dynamics of enslavement and contemporary white supremacy: the *Captive Maternal* and its related concepts, the *Black Matrix*, the *Fulcrum*, and *Womb Theory*. These concepts have both theoretical and political stakes. In the realm of theory, they work to unpack a conceptual schema that has roots as far back as Aristotle's philosophy, and in this sense enact a far-ranging critique of the intellectual history of Western 'high' theory and culture. Politically, James uses these concepts to highlight specific instances of Black women's agency within and against institutionalized, patriarchal, capitalist, white supremacist power. Black women are not the only examples of Captive Maternals, but Black women's experience is of a primary interest for James' theorizing. I suggest that her use of this concept demonstrates one way to engage a founding historical trauma, U.S. slavery, informed by an intersectional analysis.[1]

On James' analysis, Captive Maternals can be "either biological females or those feminized into caretaking and consumption" (James 2016: 255). As caretakers, they are the people in society who do the necessary work of supporting life, and the caretaking of the Captive Maternal exceeds the labor of one's job to account for care for children, for homes, for partners, for the feelings of others and, ultimately, for the time of others. Historically, enslaved people and particularly, enslaved women, exemplify the situation of Captive Maternals. In the present, however, Captive Maternals are found throughout society and across the ideological and cultural spectrum, and can "work in and for governance, corporations, prisons, police, and the military" (James 2016: 258). The most common Captive Maternals are "those most vulnerable to violence, war, poverty, police, and captivity; those whose very existence enables the possessive empire that claims and dispossesses them" (James 2016: 255).

The terrible double-standard that is imposed on Captive Maternals is that their labor is a crucial component of the systems that simultaneously drain them. As James explains, "captive maternals manufacture time for others, providing respite, space, and quiet to think, while captives undertake the mundane chores and deprivations tied to survival of structure" (James 2021: 352). The work of Captive Maternals is absorbed by power systems and thereby strengthens and stabilizes social worlds and, more broadly, strengthened and stabilized the United States as it was historically developed. The generative

---

1 It should be noted that James might not necessarily call herself, at least primarily, an intersectional feminist. She articulates in her work that both feminism and intersectionality are terms that are easily coopted by dominant power, which is one of the reasons she develops her own conceptual vocabulary. For example, she writes: "I argue that leverage, rather than 'feminism' or 'intersectionality' or 'progressivism' might be a useful term for recognizing power and predation" (James 2016: 257). I do think that her work reflects the critical concerns that I introduced above as central to intersectional analyses. Her reasons for being wary of the term should, nonetheless, be accounted for.

power of Captive Maternals can be coopted through direct care to "consumer-captors" (James 2021: 352), but it can also be enacted through the act of caring for other Captive Maternals or for oppressed people more broadly. As James writes, "Paradoxically, the more captive maternals nurture, the more the recipients of their care are cushioned from and better able to tolerate bondage or emboldened to rebel against it" (James 2021: 345). James' reading of Assata Shakur illustrates this. In describing Shakur's work as a Captive Maternal, James includes Shakur's part in the community survival programs of the Black Panther Party, such as sickle-cell testing and free breakfast programs (James 2016: 254). This exemplifies the difficulty of the Captive Maternal as a member of a state that does not nurture them or their communities: care for each other not only helps each other to survive under oppression, it also props up and stabilizes the system harming them by helping make oppressed populations more resilient.

James argues that Western culture and theory has for hundreds of years normalized and naturalized the exploitation and trauma of Captive Maternals (James 2016: 259), and while this trauma should not necessarily be dwelled in, it absolutely should not be glossed over, as it is a structural component of the Captive Maternals' experience. In *The Language of Psychoanalysis*, Laplanche and Pontalis define trauma as "An event in the subject's life defined by its intensity, by the subject's incapacity to respond adequately to it, and by the upheaval and long-lasting effects that it brings about in the psychical organization. In economic terms, the trauma is characterised by an influx of excitations that is excessive by the standard of the subject's tolerance and capacity to master such excitations and work them out psychically" (Laplanche and Pontalis 1974: 465). Taking this psychoanalytic definition as a guide, chattel slavery can be understood as an historical trauma of U.S. American democracy in at least two ways. First, it is an historical atrocity that sits at the birth of the nation and so can be understood as a foundational trauma for the nation itself. Second, more existentially, the dynamic of captivity James analyzes is embodied in Captive Maternals who continue to live in this vicious cycle of productivity and drain.

A society does not literally have a psyche or a bodily identity, and one does not want to strain the metaphor. However, trauma seems an appropriate way to characterize the effects of the use of slavery to develop the United States as a democratic nation. There is a deep-seated tension between the ideals that have been formally articulated as foundational for the United States such as equality and liberty and the practice of chattel slavery; this fundamental contradiction is arguably one reason that the legacy of slavery remains unresolved to this day. It is an extreme violence, the enslavement of a human being, a violence that existentially rejects both the equality and liberty of enslaved people. Making this practice legal incorporates this violence into the bed-rock of the nation's founding. It seems legitimate to claim that this violence exceeds toleration, in particular if enslaved people are considered as part of the nation. Even if one were inclined to excuse the U.S. on a legal technicality (given that enslaved people were, by law, not citizens), the country remains bitterly divided to this day on whether or to what degree this violence has been 'worked out.' It therefore seems that this foundational violence exceeds the capacity of the nation to "respond adequately to it" and that the effects of this trauma have been, on the body of the nation, "long lasting." In this way, the logic of the Captive Maternal illuminates a gendered power dynamic that historically incorporated the trauma of enslavement into the development of U.S. American democracy.

Further, living Captive Maternals continue to be traumatized by racist social systems. Addressing Black Captive Maternals in the present, James writes, "the chit-chat of the little cuts and rat-like gnawing is the norm; they face verbal slander and intimidation, physical violence, domestic violence, rape and sexual assault, and contempt, policing in schools, jobs, society, and prisons, from every sector" (James 2016: 256). The intensity of these events is specific, although not exclusive, to Black women. Although Black women (and women in general) do experience incarceration and police violence, James notes that these are paradigmatic experiences for Black men. Similarly, Black men (and men in general) experience domestic abuse and sexual assault (and can experience all the things itemized as experiences of the Captive Maternal), yet these are paradigmatic of Black women's experiences. Further, the harm Black women experience is often inflicted in small, repeated doses of verbal or non-verbal disrespect. James characterizes these as little cuts to demonstrate how Black women's denigration in society can appear to be less than that of, for example, Black men because it can appear as less directly violent. However, this distinc-tion should be understood as one of kind, not of intensity: the incessant, daily experience of denigration and diminishment Black women often endure in white supremacist cultures is a traumatic continuation of historical racism. An implication is that the "intensity" of a potentially traumatic event will often be mediated by gender, race, and other aspects of social identity. When consider-ing what is an "intense" experience, one thus should ensure that one does not unconsciously regulate that category along gendered expectations. Doing so can occlude the difficult work a subject must go through to deal with, manage, or endure an intense experience of gendered assault or violence. Further, one of the ways the time of the Captive Maternal is stolen is through "the loss of leisure to recover from fatigue and violence" (James 2016: 280). If a gendered lens is not brought to understanding the situation of Captive Maternals, their role in stabilizing oppressive systems and the harms they endure while doing so can be rendered invisible. The ability to manage a trauma is thus deeply impacted by gendered experience.

However, it is important to James' thinking to analyze the Captive Maternals' role in society fundamentally in terms of their value, by what they *contribute*, both to the nation in general and, ultimately, to the potential for revolutionary action. The situation of the Captive Maternal thus needs to be understood in terms of what James calls the Black Matrix and the potential for a Fulcrum. James acknowledges that the repression of Black people does not always lead to resistance and that not all resistance is intrinsically transformational (James 2021: 349). However, as Western democracy stole from and traumatized Captive Maternals through slavery to develop the nation, also created was what James calls "the Black Matrix" (James 2016: 257). Black experience as a matrix is the medium or material through which trauma-inflicting democracy can be resisted or revolted against. It can form a "fulcrum" that grounds the leverage needed to shift oppressive structures, and "when that fulcrum originates in the Black Matrix, one is talking about a politics tethered to master/slave terror" (James 2016: 259). For Captive Maternals, this experience of terror is mediated by gender, and organized political work against this is usually accomplished by those most affected. When used to analyze the theoretical and political work of Black women, trauma is thus directly related to agency, and Black women "confront their subjugation with trauma and stolen time (like stolen lives) as central to political battles" (James 2016: 277). For example, Harriet Jacobs hid for years and then stole herself from slavery, then published the memoir *Incidents in the Life of a Slave Girl, Written by Herself*, producing through her lost time and the traumas she endured an indictment of the system of slavery (James 2016: 277). Mamie Till insisted that her son Emmett have an open casket funeral in 1955 so that the evidence that he was lynched would be on display (James 2021: 352–53). In this way, Till made her grief as a mother part of her broader struggle against the violent, racist systems that threaten Black lives. More recently, those who protested racist police violence, including Erica Garner protesting her father Eric's death by police officers (James 2016: 293–94), demonstrate the ongoing way in which trauma and political action are linked in the resistant work of Captive Maternals.

However, the rigor of such revolutionary work is occluded by what James calls Womb Theory. James argues, "In transitioning a colony through a republic into a representational democracy with imperial might, the emergent United States grew a womb, it took on the generative properties of the maternals it held captive" (James 2016: 256). This "womb-like captivity" (James

2016: 264) created the context for the generation of the Black Matrix. James reads Western Theory as Womb Theory in order to highlight the role the tradition of Western theory has played in legitimating the consumption of Captive Maternals for the sake of a predatory Western society. A Womb Theory is a philosophy or theoretical project that canonizes a hierarchy of rationality that privileges the thinking of free white men at the expense of other subjects. Such theories will usually attribute the superiority of free white men's thinking to nature, but James attributes it to their situation as a beneficiary of privilege maintained through the compulsory labor of Captive Maternals. For example, Aristotle's philosophy naturalized a hierarchy of humanity. Aristotle argued the human being is the rational animal, but also, that only free men are truly capable of exercising rationality. On his logic, women can recognize rational orders but cannot themselves think rationally, and slaves by their nature can neither recognize nor exercise the rational faculty. James' reading of Aristotle takes seriously how jarring it is to confront his casual acceptance that some humans are naturally superior to others. As she describes it, in Aristotle's philosophy,

> the capacity for consciousness to think critically and comprehensively is attributed only to those free from captivity and female identity. Slaves and females are told that they lack such intellectual capacity, and so are forewarned that, in a world dominated by humans, their tenuous links to "human" will be their demise in social and political life, if not an accelerant towards their biological death.
>
> JAMES 2016: 260

Naturalizing the inferior position of women and enslaved people dehumanizes oppressed people; this is one way that Western culture has normalized and obscured the theft and trauma that James argues are the hallmarks of the Captive Maternals' situation. Thinkers such as Aristotle developed a notion of humanity that legitimates the position in society of Captive Maternals not because they have been conquered but, more fundamentally, on grounds of their alleged "intellectual bankruptcy" (James 2016: 262). James argues that Womb Theory is a dominant thread within Western theory that persisted through the development of intellectual projects over time. As Western philosophers have built upon each other's work, theories of the human and of rationality that normalize racial and gendered hierarchies have persisted through this intellectual tradition and its canon.

While mainstream contemporary theorists would rarely endorse a theory of natural slavery such as Aristotle's, James argues that such theories will often retain biases concerning who counts as properly human and who is presumed to be a rational actor. In analyzing Womb Theory, James thus demonstrates how theory and philosophy are interwoven with politics in Western culture. The dominance of Womb Theory is one reason why the theoretical contributions of diverse thinkers are often discounted and why it remains difficult for the political demands of citizens who are not white men to be visible as reasonable or, at times, to be visible at all. However, in focusing on the revolutionary potential of Captive Maternal political theorizing and political action, James argues that "Captive Maternals are the antithesis to Womb Theory. Captive Maternals leverage a Black matrix to fracture the Western womb" (James 2016: 261). It is not that Captive Maternals are removed from Western society or cannot be part of Womb Theory; their situation is not pure. However, in exercising agency that resists captivity, it is possible for Captive Maternals to start the difficult process of reckoning with the legacy of racial trauma in the United States. Understanding the power dynamics that create and normalize their exploitative situation is an integral part of that process.

2   Auschwitz

I now turn to Adorno's invocations of *Auschwitz* to explore how he develops a theoretical comportment or frame for thinking characterized by complicity with historical traumatic violence, which Adorno names *guilt*. Auschwitz is not linked to the inception of the nation in the same way as chattel slavery (as it comes later in time), but on Adorno's analysis it relates directly to Western cultures and democracies. Returning to the psychoanalytic definition of trauma, I suggest that the Holocaust can also be read as an historical trauma. The violence of concentration camps is inarguably intense, as when Adorno uses the name *Auschwitz* he invokes the genocidal murder of almost six million European Jews during WWII, particularly as perpetrated through the mechanized cruelty and horror of the concentration camps. The magnitude of this trauma is such that Western nations have been unable to respond adequately to it, and in Adorno's analysis he explicates its long-lasting and systemic effects. That is, for Adorno, Auschwitz as an idea extends beyond that particular historical event to encompass "the world of torture which has continued to exist after Auschwitz" (Adorno 2002: 101), a world "which knows of things far worse than death and denies people the shot in the neck in order to torture them slowly to death" (Adorno 2002: 105). For Adorno, Auschwitz names a transition towards widespread dehumanization in the objective social, cultural, and political conditions of human existence. Adorno includes the use of the atom bomb and the Vietnam war as part of this "world of torture," and "Auschwitz" for Adorno operates as a sign that "culture has failed to its very core" (Adorno 2002: 118). The significance of this is that Auschwitz names for him a material change in the possibility of human experience as such, regardless of one's proximity to this particular event; Adorno stated, "there can be no one, whose organ of experience has not entirely atrophied, for whom the world *after* Auschwitz, that is, the world in which Auschwitz was possible, is the same world as it was before" (Adorno 2002: 104).

Adorno describes the objective social conditions that follow from Auschwitz as a "context of social guilt" (Adorno 2002: 108), a "hellish unity" (Adorno 2002: 104) that results in "total entrapment" (Adorno 2002: 126). He uses highly emotional language to sketch the scope of what he conceived of as a cultural failure, to gesture to the objective condition that *anyone* who lives in a world characterized by this guilt does so only under the condition that their life is lived at the expense of others, "that just by continuing to live one is taking away that possibility from someone else, to whom life has been denied; that one is stealing that person's life" (Adorno 2002: 113). The ubiquity and inescapable character of this guilt is *objective* on Adorno's analysis because its determination ultimately cannot be eradicated through subjective mechanisms. This irreducible quality of materiality is meant by Adorno to be a weight that people have to bear, which is why he goes on to discuss guilt as what ought to characterize experience 'after Auschwitz.' Adorno writes,

> Guilt reproduces itself in each of us—and what I am saying is addressed to us as subjects—since we cannot possibly remain fully conscious of this connection at every moment of our waking life. If we—each of us sitting here—knew at every moment what has happened to us and to what concatenations we owe our own existence, and how our own existence is interwoven with calamity, even if we have done nothing wrong, simply by having neglected, through fear, to help other people at a crucial moment, for example—a situation very familiar to me from the time of the Third Reich—if one were fully aware of all these things at every moment, one would really be unable to live. One is pushed, as it were, into forgetfulness, which is already a form of guilt. By failing to be aware at every moment of what threatens and what has happened, one also contributes to it; one resists it too little; and it can be repeated and reinstated at any moment.
>
> ADORNO 2002: 113

Adorno states quite directly that the magnitude of the horrors included under the name of Auschwitz, if present in our everyday lives, would make living impossible. Yet he presents a call to think the discontinuity between the magnitude of the loss and one's own psychic capabilities as part of a moral analysis. The violence and loss are too much to be taken up, and all that can easily be said is that there is a certain universality to the incapacity to respond "authentically" or totally to these historical events. Adorno's characterization of the role of violence in social conditions situates complicity with a world of torture, that is, guilt, as an objective condition of human existence, even when one is at a certain distance from violence itself. This is why Adorno insists on a metaphysical analysis, one that "is addressed to us as subjects," that should be taken up as a structural, not simply individual, determination. An individual personality practically requires the defense mechanisms that shut down such a realization of complicity, and this inability to grapple with the impact of this violence can thus be seen as existentially traumatic. The concept *guilt* expresses that a social subject bears a relationship to the violence undertaken to maintain the conditions of their social world. That is, guilt must be understood to mark an objective condition that has a relationship to, but is not reducible to, a psychological experience. It represents for him a relationship to a discontinuity between one's own, perhaps rather comfortable existence, and what happened. For Adorno, then, the category of subjectivity opens up an analysis of the relationship between the life one is able to live and the forces that craft the conditions for that life. This has potential moral ramifications, as it marks a way the subject can come to recognize and be accountable for the history of one's present.

Adorno asserts throughout the *Metaphysics* lectures that the philosophical legacy of metaphysical thinking in general is to ascribe meaning to life. He notes that the goal of what he calls old-style metaphysics is to "understand that which is" in order to be able to make positive, certain claims in the face of the enigmatic and chaotic (Adorno 2002: 104). While Adorno sees a strand of ideological thinking in this history, he also sees the history of metaphysics as containing the valuable project of reason confronting and grappling with irrationality. The historical context he tries to describe under the name Auschwitz, however, is one in which he asserts that faith in meaning is no longer possible, and anyone who tries to assert such faith acts inhumanly in the context of the victims of Auschwitz (Adorno 2002: 101). As I will explore below, on the terms of this argument, given the number of historical traumas that preceded Auschwitz, there perhaps never was any grounds for a metaphysical assertion of meaning. Nonetheless, Adorno takes up the specificity of his particular moment by claiming that to imply that there can be an overarching meaning to mechanized torture is immoral (Adorno 2002: 104).

If "old-style" metaphysics posits meaning in order to render experiences intelligible, and thus justifies existence, it is for Adorno the task of metaphysical critique to expose the parameters of thought that limit openness to change. On this thinking, if complete identification with victims is impossible for reasons of psychic health, and if redressing what has happened is impossible given both the overwhelming force behind the violence and distances of space and time, then critical reflection is the best hope for grappling with immorality. It may admittedly seem too difficult to confront the relation between oneself and such objectively determined oppressive social conditions. Frankly, Adorno's thought at times seems to imply a pessimism that borders on hopelessness. However, the hopeful moment in Adorno is that the forgetfulness that Adorno calls a form of guilt can be encountered by making the mechanisms that produce forgetfulness available to critical reflection while maintaining a somatically grounded moral commitment. Understanding the imbrications of historical, metaphysical, and somatic experience is essential because Adorno asserts that one cannot make a purely reasonable or rational argument about something like torture, especially under conditions of war. He states, "as soon as one attempts to provide a logical foundation for a proposition such as that one should not torture, one becomes embroiled in a bad infinity; and probably would even get the worst of the logical argument, whereas the truth in this proposition is precisely what falls outside such a dialectic" (Adorno 2002: 116). Instrumental reasoning can often provide a seemingly reasonable or logical argument in favor of harming others when faced with threats to security or future well-being. However, the truth of the proposition that one should not torture is for Adorno found in a physical aversion to causing pain which is, to him, an idea that cannot be captured in logic.

This is why Adorno asserts that "the true basis of morality is to be found in bodily feeling, in identification with unbearable pain" (Adorno 2002: 116). This is not itself a moral critique for Adorno, but rather marks its inauguration—this moment of physical identification is not produced by philosophical thought, but can be the non-cognitive spark that compels a serious and sustained resistant engagement with the world. The *significance* of historical trauma for ethical, social, and political analysis, if not its justificatory meaning, can only be attended to through the critique of any metaphysical positing and the recognition that the possibility of morality is imbricated with somatically-informed thinking. Without a metaphysical critique, materiality, and hence suffering, can be relegated to the status of an "extra-logical element" which is "conjured away by philosophy and rationalism" (Adorno 2002: 116). But in Adorno's view, this also conjures away the possibility of a moral response, as it is a physical aversion that informs the desire to alleviate suffering. For Adorno, the proper frame for a philosophical treatment of an historical trauma is one that can recognize the inevitability of one's guilt while engaging a morally and metaphysically informed resistance to the politics and culture that perpetuate violence.

3   Conclusion: Power Dynamics

My engagement here with James' work has at least four implications for understanding the need for feminist social theory that engages historical trauma. I propose that intersectionally informed feminist engagements with historical trauma should, first, not represent any one historical trauma as a singular, paradigmatic event; second, engage a raced and gendered attention to historical traumas and their contemporary impact; third, prioritize the agency and action (not just the subordination) of oppressed peoples, especially those most disempowered by Western democracies; and fourth, contest the ways that Western theory has diminished the theoretical contributions of diverse thinkers. In this final section, I reflect on Adorno's work in the context of these four expectations.

A counter-perspective to Adorno's engagement with Auschwitz as a singular event is offered by Charles Mills in *The Racial Contract*. The project of Mills' book is to re-introduce into the history of Western political philosophy a neglected account of the role of race in the theorization and actualization of traditional Western political systems. Mill's book defends the claim that "White Supremacy is the unnamed political system that has made the modern world what it is today" (Mills 1999: 1). In his final chapter, when he reflects on the larger ramifications of his theory of Racial Contract, he references Adorno's question of whether one can write poetry after Auschwitz. Mills notes:

> the despairing question of how there can be poetry after Auschwitz evokes the puzzled nonwhite reply of how there could have been poetry *before* Auschwitz, and *after* the killing fields in America, Africa, Asia. The standpoint of Native America, black Africa, colonial Asia, has always been aware that European civilization rests on extra-European barbarism, so that the Jewish Holocaust, the "Judeocide" (Mayer), is by no means a bolt from the blue, an unfathomable anomaly in the development of the West, but unique only in that it represents use of the Racial Contract against *Europeans*. I say this in no way to diminish its horror, of course, but to deny its *singularity*, to establish its conceptual identity with other

policies carried out by Europe in non-Europe for hundreds of years, but
using methods less efficient than those made possible by advanced mid-
twentieth century industrial society.

MILLS 1999: 102–3

It seems productive to maintain, as Mills also suggests, that there is something
politically and culturally significant about the mechanized torture of the Nazi
regimes. However, I follow Mills in being skeptical about the accuracy or the
efficacy of calling such a genocidal project new or singular. As Mills points out,
thinkers who engage with non-Anglo/a, non-European contexts have too-little
trouble pointing out other materially significant genocides perpetuated *by this
same political culture*. Mills shows that the Holocaust is an historical trauma,
but, despairingly, one of many.

Next, James' work calls for thinking the specificity of race and gender when
attending to historical traumas and their contemporary impact. Adorno's
philosophy engages guilt metaphysically in order to argue that the historical,
material impact of Auschwitz is inarguable. However, this runs the risk of leveling out all complicity with violence, as his use of metaphysical categories like
meaning and subject have not yet been thought through in terms of how social
identity affects how one comes to meaning and subjectivity. It might therefore
be more productive to maintain an awareness of the differential distribution of
social privileges along lines of gender, race, class, etc. when considering one's
relationship to an historical trauma. James exemplifies such awareness through
the analysis of the Captive Maternals whose trauma is articulated as specific to
gendered, racialized caretaking. This adds texture to the understanding of how
one experiences trauma.

This is related to my third implication, the stakes of focusing on the agency
and revolutionary potential of the actions of those people most subordinated
by Western democracies. Adorno's analysis of guilt takes as its standpoint the
position of the survivor of violence or the one who escaped it, and then, by
extension, those whose lives are supported by their position in the cultural
world that exists after Auschwitz. It is incredibly important to account for
complicity with historical violence; however, Adorno's account of guilt could
become overly paralyzing. This becomes noticeable when put in conversation
with James' analysis of the fulcrum, as her theory begins from a concern with
how even traumatic experience is a part of the Black Matrix that engenders
the agency of Captive Maternals and, potentially, revolutionary social change.
Their work thus seems to begin from different moments and from the point of
view of differently situated subjects. James' analysis can, perhaps, be understood as in the first instance a crisis of practice, as she is concerned with how

the actions of Captive Maternals are turned against them. Adorno's analysis can, perhaps, be understood as in the first instance a crisis of meaning, as he is concerned with how life can continue to be justified. Balancing action and meaning, agency and complicity, is extremely complicated. Further, this should not be accomplished in the abstract: each subject in a social analysis no doubt has some relationship to complicity with oppressive power as well as the potential for resistant or revolutionary action. The engagement between James' and Adorno's thinking reveals that both are important for how historical trauma is integrated into critique. The place one begins, in a problem of action or a problem of meaning, may be conditioned by where one stands in the social world as one begins to theorize.

Finally, for Adorno's work and, by implication, Frankfurt School thinking more generally, to be part of a gender and race attentive engagement with historical trauma, it must actively contest the way that Western theory has diminished the theoretical contributions of diverse thinkers. This needs to be accomplished in at least two ways: by reimagining who counts as a theorist and what makes work theoretically robust and also, by specifically engaging interlocuters and collaborators who come from the social groups most affected by the power dynamic one is unpacking. Although not focused on Adorno specifically, James' reading of Hannah Arendt and Michel Foucault is instructive here. She argues that these thinkers shared a historical world with theorists of color such as C.L.R. James and Frantz Fanon, yet that they did not seriously engage these thinkers (James 2016: 267–68). James writes, "Both Arendt and Foucault were primarily interested in how racism devastated Europeans; their eponymous theorist remains Aristotle's universal first-tier human" (James 2016: 268). This shows that thinkers who are concerned with political domination and who think about racism can end up with blind spots in their theorizing if they do not specifically engage with Black experiences and Black theorists and, more generally, with diverse experiences and theorists. Not doing so reinstitutes the idea that rationality and deliberative capacity is the appropriate provenance of free white men.

James' work accounts for how, historically, the United States became a nation through consuming the lives and labor of enslaved people, and demonstrates the logic of captivity that persists to this day in the current U.S. democracy. Adorno's work argues that the murder of almost 6 million Jewish people in concentration camps is a constitutive aspect of culture that continues to bear the guilt of this violence. Each of them works to understand the present as created, at least in part, by traumatic violence whose impact is felt in the contemporary present. While each is effective, I conclude that James' approach is more suited to the pluralization of traumas called for by feminist intersectional analyses.

I write as a feminist philosopher who has learned a tremendous amount from Adorno's texts about the logics of Western philosophy and the possibility of using rich conceptual thinking to work through emerging political problems. I hope I have done some justice here to the richness of his thinking, a full account of which well exceeds the scope of this chapter. But I am left with the impression that his will probably not be one of the first names I will think of if I were to reflect again on the question of this chapter: whose work on historical traumas can serve feminist philosophy theorizing today? Nonetheless, the Holocaust is an historical trauma relevant to feminist theory and, more generally, to a critical understanding of the contemporary world. Should one want to engage Adorno's work to think this through, I hope that I have offered here a starting point from which to begin a more thorough interrogation of his materialist, metaphysical engagement with Auschwitz.

This leads me to a final implication of my argument that is beyond the scope of the questions of history and trauma I focused on here, speaking more generally to questions of scholarship. It is not uncommon in my experience of academia that when one deeply learns from a thinker, one is called to advocate for them. However, this rumination on Adorno's work in the context of James' reminds me that one should take care with such advocacy. An attempt to deeply understand a thinker requires immersion in the conceptual world of their theory. This can too-easily turn into an endeavor to show how their work can encompass all experience, can be defended against all challenges. Adorno's philosophy, on my judgment, is incredibly generative and surprisingly prescient regarding, for example, developments in liberal capitalism and the ways that violence would come to be absorbed into the fabric of the world. To say that it is eloquent and significant does not require that it be presumed to account, as is, for any political trauma. Adorno presents a totalizing view of historical violence, and perhaps this should remain a moment in any engagement with slavery and genocide, as each inflicted unjustifiable suffering on victims who can never find justice. To grapple with genocide or captivity is to attempt to manage something unmanageable for the sake of a critique of the present and the hope for a better future. The violence called forth by the terms Auschwitz and Captive Maternals is so horrible that it cannot and should not be managed. And yet, effective methods for engaging in political dialogue and forming political movements require ways of making the relevance of history on the present both understood and felt. For this reason, feminist engagements with historical violence must expand what theory means in meaningful ways that engender plurality.

References

Adorno, Theodor W. 2002. *Metaphysics: Concept and Problems*. Stanford: Stanford University Press.

Crenshaw, Kimberlé. 1991. "Mapping the Margins: Intersectionality, Identity Politics, and Violence Against Women of Color." *Stanford Law Review* 43(6): 1241–99.

Davis, Angela Y. 1983. *Women, Race, and Class*. New York: Vintage.

James, Joy. 2016. "The Womb of Western Theory: Trauma, Time Theft, and the Captive Maternal." *Carceral Notebooks* 12: 44.

James, Joy. 2021. "Political Trauma." In *The Bloomsbury Handbook of 21st-Century Feminist Theory*, ed. Robin Truth Goodman. London: Bloomsbury Academic.

Laplanche, Jean, and Jean-Bertrand Pontalis. 1974. *The Language of Psycho-Analysis*. New York: W. W. Norton & Company.

Lorde, Audre. 2007. *Sister Outsider: Essays and Speeches*. Berkeley: Crossing Press.

Mills, Charles W. 1999. *The Racial Contract*. Ithaca: Cornell University Press.

CHAPTER 10

Beyond One-Dimensional Theory and Praxis

A Marcusean Alliance with Black Feminism

Nicole Yokum

Among early Frankfurt School theorists, Herbert Marcuse would seem to be a prime candidate for an alliance with Black Feminist theory and praxis, if only because of his mentorship of radical Black thinker and activist Angela Davis. Whereas Marcuse's early Frankfurt School peers didn't always exactly hit it off with student radicals – Adorno's (in)famous antagonism with the Students for a Democratic Society (SDS),[1] in the months leading up to his death, as a case in point – Marcuse's strong affinity with the student movement was never in question, his close relationship with Davis only confirming his deep commitment to their cause. In her autobiography, Davis vividly recalls her introduction to the formal study of philosophy under Marcuse's tutelage at Brandeis University: "stimulating weekly discussions" (Davis 1988: 135) between just the two of them, arranged at her initiative and not part of any official class. She also attests to the strong influence that Marcuse's activism, as an academic, had on her own development – through his involvement in conferences like "The Dialectics of Liberation," for example, and even in actions like stepping in to help pay bail for her friends when they found themselves in trouble. All of this was a reflection of Marcuse's broader investment in praxis that sustained a lively connection to the critical theory he was putting forth in works such as *Eros and Civilization* and *An Essay on Liberation*. Falling into step with Marcuse's model, Davis would go on to become both a successful academic and a figurehead of liberation herself, never forgetting the example that Marcuse had set for her of how to embrace both roles.

Indeed, Marcuse's belief that theory and praxis should be mutually informative, at least when historical circumstances allow, not only shaped his relationship to Davis, but also serves as a more general point of connection between Marcusean critical theory and Black Feminism. Black Feminist scholar, activist, and icon bell hooks maintains that feminist theories should be dually aimed at

---

1 Adorno's disdain for the German student movement – exemplified in his dealings with the Socialist German Student Union in the late '60s – came to a head when confrontations with protesting students in his lecture courses ultimately led him to cancel them in 1969.

understanding contemporary forms of interlocking oppression (the theoretical aspect of feminist work) *and* at opening up collective avenues of resistance (the practical side of things) (hooks 1991). This goal of a liberatory theory that is intimately linked with liberatory praxis resonates through the writing of other prominent Black Feminists as well – such as Patricia Hill Collins, who maintains that critical theory should give rise to praxis aiming to address the social problems that it diagnoses and attempts to explain. But the affinities between Marcuse and the Black Feminist tradition don't stop there. Another important conviction that they hold in common is the notion that the potential to initiate meaningful social change lives on among those who are most marginalized in society – those whose social positions can grant them access to a special perspective on structural oppression. In an *Essay on Liberation*, Marcuse departs from his earlier pessimism about the widespread one-dimensionality of modern society, now claiming that certain outsider populations have managed to resist the integration of thought and feeling into conformity with the modern industrial apparatus. Marcuse even suggests that one such population he has in mind is people of color in the United States. This coalesces with the key Black Feminist idea that Black women's multiply marginalized social positions offer them distinctive insights into interlocking systems of oppression, as well as the emotional motivation to resist. For Marcuse, alongside Black Feminists such as Audre Lorde, Myisha Cherry, and Brittney Cooper, righteous Black rage can be productively channeled into mounting a course of political action that might work to dismantle oppressive social hierarchies.

By elaborating on these links between Marcusean critical theory and Black Feminism in what follows, I strive to move beyond a "one-dimensional" approach to liberatory theory and praxis that fails to grapple with the question of how to sustain a lively interplay between the two so as to animate contemporary critical theory and struggle. The Black Feminist tradition, I maintain, evinces a longstanding commitment to producing theory that emerges out of and engages pressing social and political issues, and avoids getting mired in abstraction. This serves as a valuable corrective to forms of critical theory that, as Bernard Harcourt argues in *Critique and Praxis*, have "retreated" from activist to academic spaces, and from praxis to epistemology. At the same time, Marcuse's legacy as "a philosopher who urged participants in radical social movements to think more philosophically and more critically about the implications of their activism," as Davis puts it (Davis 2004: 44), remains fruitful for social justice movements, including those oriented by Black Feminist commitments. My contention, therefore, is that an alliance between Marcusean and Black Feminist critical theory might resuscitate strands of early Frankfurt School thought that meaningfully converge with Black Feminist efforts to address contemporary social problems surrounding racial injustice.

1   Theory and Liberatory Praxis

Marcuse and Adorno famously disagreed over the relationship between theory and praxis, and the question of whether praxis was actually possible for them in their contemporary contexts (Adorno, living in Germany in the late 1960s, leading up to his death in early August of 1969; and Marcuse, having emigrated to the United States). This difference in perspective comes to a head in the correspondence between them that began in February of 1969, when Adorno extended an offer for Marcuse to come and visit the Institute for Social Research in Frankfurt. Reaching out to his "old friend"[2] (Adorno and Marcuse 1999: 124) with an invitation, Adorno mentions that things in Frankfurt have been tense with the students. A group of socialist students from the SDS had recently "occupied a room in the Institute, and refused to leave," he recounts, forcing him to "call the police" (Adorno and Marcuse 1999: 124) – who had then issued arrests. Implying that the students' actions were regressive, Adorno proclaims the whole "situation" to be "dreadful in itself" (Adorno and Marcuse 1999: 124), evidently expecting Marcuse to commiserate, even feel bad for him. Instead – much to Adorno's chagrin – Marcuse stakes out a contrary stance to that of his friend, and essentially sides with the students. "[I]f the alternative is the police or the left-wing students," Marcuse announces in his reply, then – unless they were to directly threaten violence – he will always be "with the students" (Adorno and Marcuse 1999: 125).

Adorno's reproach of, as he sees it, the students' ill-fated efforts at resistance is informed by his conviction that praxis is still "blocked," as it was for him and Marcuse during the Holocaust. Given that "the transformation of the world" (by which he means the Communist Revolution) "failed," as he writes in *Negative Dialectics*, Adorno considers philosophy to have missed "the moment of its realization"; this means that theory and praxis have come apart such that praxis has been "delayed for the foreseeable future" (Adorno 2001: 15–16).[3] According to Adorno, then, even in 1969, one must still "recogniz[e] the objective impossibility" (Adorno and Marcuse 1999: 127) of 'breaking out' of the current political situation. He reminds Marcuse that, in their time, they had

---

2   Adorno signs this first letter "Your old friend, Theodor" (Adorno and Marcuse 1999: 124).

3   Page 3 of Introduction in digital edition: https://www.academia.edu/39707967/Negative _Dialectics.

both "withstood ... a much more dreadful situation – that of the murder of the Jews, without proceeding to praxis; simply because it was blocked" (Adorno and Marcuse 1999: 127) for them. The implication, here, is that, first, it should be obvious that nothing has substantially changed since then, so as to rejuvenate the possibility for praxis; and, second, if Adorno and Marcuse were, themselves, able to endure their own inability to act when it was so certain that meaningful praxis was impossible (even if this made them "cold," as Adorno suggests), then the students should be able to do the same. They should realize that occupying the Institute is surely futile, and that they're merely "grasp[ing] at repressive measures" (Adorno and Marcuse 1999: 124), as Adorno puts it, by disrupting lecture courses and staging heated confrontations with storied university professors.[4]

The nuance of Marcuse's contrasting stance is informative. For it's not as if Marcuse thinks that, thanks to the sds – and their counterparts in the U.S., among whom we could count Davis – we are on the verge of a revolution, and all of the blockages of the past have been cleared away. He readily admits to Adorno that *nobody* – not even the students themselves – believes their situation to be a "revolutionary one," or even a "pre-revolutionary one" (Adorno and Marcuse 1999: 125). And yet, he passionately disagrees as to whether this means that they cannot act. The present situation, he declares – regardless of how it compares to the one that he and Adorno had faced several decades earlier – is "so terrible, so suffocating and demeaning," that "one can bear it no longer, one is suffocating and one has to let some air in" (Adorno and Marcuse 1999: 125). One simply *must* do something, even if it's indisputable that revolution is not in the air; rebellion against the present social and political circumstances "forces a biological, physiological reaction," Marcuse avers (Adorno and Marcuse 1999: 125). And if he was ever cold, as Adorno claims, Marcuse attests that he is no longer able "to discover the 'cold streak' in himself" (Adorno and Marcuse 1999: 129) – whatever part of him may have been desensitized earlier has evidently been newly aroused, called to action by the very same global crises to which the protesting students are responding.

To be sure, much of Marcuse's oeuvre supplies confirmation of the position staked out in his letters to Adorno: that, regardless of what he had lived through, Marcuse never gave up on believing in the value of engaging in praxis – in resisting oppression on the practical level, not just the

---

4 In May of 1964, Adorno had taken legal action against students who had posted "Wanted" notices on campus featuring a selection of quotes from his work, encouraging anyone who agreed that "the discrepancy between analysis and action is unbearable" to contact him personally (Leslie 1999: 119–120).

theoretical (by analyzing it) – and perhaps even on the possibility of some kind of revolution. It is true that his 1964 classic, *One-Dimensional Man*, strikes a pessimistic note with its focus on the depth of the psychic and emotional conformity plaguing advanced industrialist subjects, and that it isn't entirely clear, in that text, how such subjects might alter or break free from this "mass society of blind conformity" (Wolin 2001: 168). However, in works that both pre-date, and especially those that post-date *One-Dimensional Man*, Marcuse comes out much more decidedly in favor of an endorsement of personal and political change: shifts in consciousness and revisions to the instinctual and emotional organization of the self that could map onto larger-scale efforts to re-envision the way that society is structured. *Eros and Civilization* of 1955 is well-known for Marcuse's creative re-interpretation of Freudian drive theory in the service of a speculative utopian vision; the "Political Preface" that he later added to it (in 1966) only emphasizes the overtly political ramifications of his view that domination is the true enemy of liberation, that aggression could be largely subordinated to the liberated life instincts, and that the battle for liberation must be waged on a "biological," instinctual level. "Today the fight for life, the fight for Eros" – "against Death" – "is the political fight" (Marcuse 1966: xxv), he declares. A few years later, in *An Essay on Liberation*, Marcuse explicitly stakes political hope in an idea at which he had hinted in *One-Dimensional Man*: that some segments of consumer capitalist society have managed to evade the full-scale social conditioning and psycho-affective one-dimensionality of which he is so critical. Specifically, he had initially suggested that "the outsiders and the poor, the unemployed and unemployable, [and] the persecuted colored races" (Marcuse 1964: 53) were among those who might be able to serve as pockets of resistance; by 1969, Marcuse is convinced that the "Great Refusal" – his label for "the protest against that which is" (Marcuse 1964: 63) – was taking hold in "a variety of forms" (Marcuse 1969: vii) (including both the Black Power and student movements).

The individual and social changes that Marcuse calls for in his political writings are an outgrowth of his theoretical work; *Eros and Civilization* is a great example of this. Bringing psychoanalysis to bear on his social critique in the tradition of the early Frankfurt School, Marcuse argues that, by introducing socio-historical specificity to Freud's theory of the instincts, we can reach a different conclusion than Freud did about the prospect of a non-repressive society (when Freud memorably claimed that repression is necessary for communal living, and that because of this, humans are destined to be unhappy[5]). "Marcuse's

---

5 Freud presents a grim picture of the prospect of human happiness in *Civilization and Its Discontents*, establishing his view that society must impose severe instinctual repression

strategy," as Whitebook captures it, is "to *historicize* psychoanalysis in order to combat Freud's skepticism about the possibility of radical change" (Whitebook 2004: 85). Marcuse maintains that the relationship that Freud sketches out between freedom and repression doesn't actually describe a universal truth about civilization; rather, Freud made a "generalization" about the way that human civilization(s) have thus far been organized, and mistook this historically specific empirical fact to disclose an unavoidable truth about the clash between Eros and Thanatos, the life and death instincts. Marcuse believes that he can open up a space for potential liberation by distinguishing between basic (unavoidable) and surplus (extra, unnecessary) repression, as well as between the reality and performance principles (where the performance principle is an historically specific, extra-repressive version of the reality principle). With the additional theoretical move of reinterpreting the hold of the death drive over the psyche as primarily a matter of imposed tension caused by scarcity (*Ananke*), Marcuse positions himself to propose an alternative vision of social and instinctual organization: one where – thanks to the level of technological advancement achieved by modern society – tension is relieved through the widespread reduction of scarcity, and the destructive impulses are effectively quelled. Strengthening Eros so that it becomes powerful enough to bind and mitigate the aggressive impulses also makes the latter possible. This requires a whole host of practical alterations to social institutions: reimagining work to replace alienated labor with libidinally satisfying, productive activities; and changing our expectations surrounding sexuality and intimate relationships to allow "pregenital polymorphous eroticism" (Marcuse 1966: 215) to flourish.

It is not hard to imagine how Marcuse's radical endorsement of a restructuring of the instincts, and, correspondingly, a major restructuring of capitalist society – a *political* stand for "free love," liberated sexuality, and, more generally, an overthrow of the logic of domination underlying social relations as they have historically been organized[6] – was appealing to young people in the '60s who were disillusioned with racism, capitalism, U.S. imperialism, and their parents' strict rules surrounding the outward expression of their erotic drives. Marcuse's intellectual prowess and esteemed position within the academy were also complemented by his visible activism, as he made many public political appearances. Indeed, not only were his books popular and widely

---

on its members because it is "perpetually threatened with disintegration" by our "primary mutual hostility" (Freud 1930: 69).

6   Marcuse writes that it is an "historical fact that civilization has progressed as organized *domination*" (Marcuse 1966: 34).

read in the '60s,[7] but Marcuse acquired a celebrity status as the so-called "father" of the New Left – according to David Held, he became "one of the most prominent (if not *the* most prominent) spokesmen and theoreticians of the Left" (Held 1980: 39). At UC San Diego, he was "constantly lecturing to packed audiences and directly involved in the anti-war movement and related New Left causes" (Held 1980: 13). This is the figure of Marcuse – scholar and revolutionary, a "Jagger, Lennon or Dylan" (Jeffries 2016: 310) with a philosophical pedigree – that left so deep of an impression on Davis. In response to her feeling of being drawn back to the U.S. to finish her PhD so that she could actively contribute to the racial justice movement there, Adorno advised her that her "desire to work directly in the radical movements of that period was akin to a media studies scholar deciding to become a radio technician" (Davis 2004: 8). Marcuse, contrastingly, taught her – and *showed* her – that she "didn't have to choose" (Davis 2004: 7) between her commitments to her studies on the one hand, and, on the other, to practical political action targeting "concrete social issues" (Davis 2004: 7).

Davis, herself, would go on to publish numerous texts on freedom and struggle that speak to her ongoing involvement, over the last six decades, with various progressive social causes – from Black liberation and Black Feminism to her advocacy for prison abolition, criminal justice reform, and opposition to the death penalty.[8] Like Marcuse, Davis has balanced her work as a scholar and university professor with consistent public speaking, lectures, and activism. And although she has not written extensively on the relationship between theory and practice, she counts herself as part of the tradition of Black Feminists[9] whose embrace of a close connection between them resonates with Marcuse's stance: that, at least when the present social and political context allows, theory and praxis should mutually inform one another – or, as he writes to Adorno, that it's "wrong to cling onto the difference abstractly in its previous form, when this has changed in a reality that embraces ... theory and practice" (Adorno and Marcuse 1999: 129). Notably, both bell hooks and sociologist

---

7 In "Marcuse's Legacies," Davis remarks on the irony "that the most well-known and most widely read thinker associated with the Frankfurt School thirty years ago became the least studied in the eighties and nineties, while Theodor Adorno, Max Horkheimer and Walter Benjamin are extensively studied in the contemporary era" (Davis 2004: 43).

8 Among them are *Women, Race, and Class*; *Women, Culture, and Politics*; *Blues Legacies and Black Feminism*; *Are Prisons Obsolete?*; and *Freedom is a Constant Struggle*.

9 Davis has contributed to Black Feminism through her publications, several of which focus on the history and legacy of Black Feminist thought and politics; she also formed an alliance of Black Feminists (with others, including Kimberlé Crenshaw) called the African American Agenda 2000.

Patricia Hill Collins, central figures in Black Feminist thought, have written on the importance of the interplay between Black Feminist theory and activism, conceiving of Black Feminism as a form of critical theory that implicitly takes up the Marcusean mantle of theory informing praxis.

hooks articulates a firm commitment to a "bond" (hooks 1991: 2) between theory and practice in her essay, "Theory as Liberatory Practice," as well as in her renowned first book (her first of many), *Feminist Theory: From Margin to Center*. Interestingly, whereas Marcuse found himself in the tricky position of trying to convince his Frankfurt School comrade, Adorno, that praxis was still possible, still meaningful, and still important, hooks describes the opposite situation: needing to convince Black people, especially Black women, that the production of theory goes hand-in-hand with effective activism. "Theory as Liberatory Practice" opens with a moving account of how hooks came to theory – by way of the need to make sense of her own childhood experiences of pain caused by sexism and racism – and thus links theorizing, from the outset, to the active process of healing. For her, then, in this particular sense, "no gap exists between theory and practice" (hooks 1991: 2) when we approach theorizing from lived experience, and the genuine need for "self-recovery" and "collective liberation" (hooks 1991: 2) from commonly damaging, oppressive forces. hooks goes on to argue that various factors have perpetuated a "false dichotomy between theory and practice" (hooks 1991: 5) in the context of feminism; the production and institutionalization of hegemonic feminist theory in hierarchically structured, predominantly white academic settings, for example – enabling those with access to power to appropriate the work of women of color in order to do a form of "theory" divorced from feminist struggle – has provoked the response of theory-trashing. Black women and others who found themselves marginalized in these spaces of theory production understandably became disillusioned with the gap created between theory and practice when those doing theory would reject the contributions of feminist practitioners whose thought they deemed "not theoretical enough" (hooks 1991: 4). However, by assuming the contrary stance that "all concrete action is ... more important than any theory written or spoken," hooks maintains, these feminists only "collude[d] with those whom they would oppose" (hooks 1991: 5), similarly promoting an unhelpful divide between theory and practice and the hierarchical valuation of one over the other. hooks attests to witnessing anti-intellectualism and the dismissal of theory in a number of settings in which she has found herself addressing Black liberation and Black Feminist issues.

hooks remained firm in her view, though, not only that theory is "a social practice" (hooks 1991: 5), and one whose production can be liberatory (hooks 1991: 7), but also that Black Feminists *must* participate in the creation of theory alongside their activist work because "we need new theories that can move us toward revolutionary struggle" (hooks 1991: 6). This conviction that theory and struggle belong together, and that the advancement of the feminist movement needs Black women's contributions to theory, comes through clearly in *Feminist Theory: From Margin to Center*. In her preface to the edition of the book released in 2015, "Seeing the Light," hooks writes of the sense in which feminist theory, beginning in the '60s and '70s, set out "to provide a revolutionary blueprint for the movement" (hooks 2015: xii); while some feminist scholarship focused on less immediately practical topics, such as recovering women's contributions to history, feminist theory aimed to supply a framework for understanding contemporary oppression that could "lead us in the direction of transforming patriarchal culture" (hooks 2015: xiii). Thus, theory, for hooks, is the necessary foundation for feminist struggle – the groundwork for political strategies and action – even if it does still take work to figure out how to translate theory into practice. hooks' investment in, first, producing an intersectional theory that accounts for the ways that gender, race, and class together shape female subjectivity; and, second, outlining "how this should concretely shape and inform feminist practice" (hooks 2015: xiii), inspired her to write *Feminist Theory: From Margin to Center*, she recounts. The book itself serves as an intervention of the type that she hopes to incite in feminist theory and practice: making contributions "from the margins" – that is, from social positions outside of the center of privilege occupied by historically hegemonic feminist theorists and practitioners – so that feminist theory, and the praxis that emerges from it, will be more expansive, inclusive, and complex, "serv[ing] to unify rather than to polarize" (hooks 2015: xviii). To be sure, hooks thinks that Black Feminists like herself have something "unique and valuable" (hooks 2015: 17) to offer, and should therefore move to the center of the production of feminist theory; but she also believes that this should entail creating theory that is broadly accessible to a wide audience,[10] to continue to avoid previous feminist hierarchies and the unnecessary gap between theory and practice.

Hill Collins concurs with hooks' assessment of the centrality, to Black Feminism, of the intimate connection between theory and praxis when she includes this relationship among her six "distinguishing features of Black feminist thought".[11] Hill Collins describes U.S. Black Feminism as featuring

---

10   hooks writes on page 9 of "Theory as Liberatory Practice" of her own "political decision" to use an accessible writing style in all of her work, and, on page 10, of her ongoing efforts to share her ideas by speaking in various settings beyond academia.

11   This is the title of the second chapter of Hill Collins' book, *Black Feminist Thought*.

"an ongoing dialogue whereby action and thought inform one another" (Hill Collins 2009: 34), and she specifically links this relationship between thought and practice to the status of Black Feminism as a "critical social theory" (Hill Collins 2009 [2000]: 35). For Hill Collins, what this means is that Black Feminism *theorizes* the social in order to serve its *active* "commitment to justice, for one's own group and for other groups" (Hill Collins 2009 [2000]: 35). Thus, the knowledge that is produced by Black Feminist thinkers can't simply be "knowledge for knowledge's sake" (Hill Collins 2009 [2000]: 35), as Hill Collins puts it; rather, it must serve the project of achieving social justice, which also suggests that it should be grounded in lived experience. Indeed, for Hill Collins, a key feature of the process through which "Black feminist practice requires Black feminist thought, and vice versa" (Hill Collins 2009 [2000]: 35), is the formulation of a special Black women's standpoint. Part of the purpose of generating thought specific to Black women is to articulate something like a self-defined standpoint that simultaneously encompasses a heterogeneity of experiences and finds enough commonalities among them to create consciousness of a collective identity. It is the resulting consciousness – achieved through collaboration and the hard work of collectively building insight – that, Hill Collins believes, "can foster Black women's activism" (Hill Collins 2009 [2000]: 33) and spark resistance.

This notion that Black women occupy a special standpoint, which lends them a distinctive perspective on society from their position at the intersection of race- and gender-based oppression, echoes hooks' idea that feminism would be well-served to take Black women's contributions from the margins and move it to the center of feminist analysis and praxis. Beyond Hill Collins' further elucidation of the role that the articulation of a Black Feminist standpoint might play in making the connection between Black Feminist theory and practice, though, a central theme of Black Feminism is, in fact, that Black women's standpoint is particularly valuable to liberatory movements. This overlaps with the tradition of celebrating Black women's justified anger at their experiences of social injustice – Black Feminists from Audre Lorde, several decades ago, through Brittney Cooper and Myisha Cherry today have identified the power of "eloquent" or "Lordean" rage to motivate political action aimed at transforming an unjust world. This brings us to another intriguing point of intersection between Marcuse and Black Feminism: the conviction that the righteous rage still to be found on the margins holds promise for social change.

2   A Standpoint from Which to Revolt: The Uses of Black Women's
       Distinctive Anger

Hill Collins introduces the idea that Black women possess a distinctive standpoint in a 1986 essay entitled "Learning from the Outsider Within: The Sociological Significance of Black Feminist Thought." Here, Hill Collins conceives of Black women's social position, historically (in the United States), as "outsiders within" insofar as they have often had "insider" access to white society – by performing domestic duties for white families, for example (cooking, cleaning, and child care) – at the same time as they will always remain "outsiders," never truly belonging to white families or society no matter how close they may get, or how intimate their familiarity with the inner workings of white social structures may be. Because of this "outsider within" status, Hill Collins argues, Black women can gain "a special standpoint on self, family, and society" (Hill Collins 1986: S14): a more comprehensive understanding of and perspective on social reality than those who are simply insiders, or those who would stay on the outside. She further notes that many Black female intellectuals draw on this "outsider within" knowledge in their work, citing hooks as an example – as hooks notably describes her own experience as one of "develop[ing] a particular way of seeing reality" by way of living "on the edge" of white society in childhood (hooks 2015: xvii). Black Feminist academics such as hooks, Hill Collins claims, can productively tap into their special standpoint "in producing distinctive analyses of race, class, and gender" (Hill Collins 1986: S15). She further implies that academia – not unlike mainstream white feminism, as we have already seen – replicates this same tension between welcoming Black women to the inside, while still insisting on keeping them marginalized.

In this original essay on Black women as "outsiders within," Hill Collins grounds her argument about the positive aspects of this special social status in the work of various classic sociologists, such as Georg Simmel. Analogous to the "outsider within," Simmel conceives of the "stranger" as having special insights into society that are not afforded to others, because people feel unusually comfortable confiding in them (perhaps because they think of the stranger as the "other," not fully human, in the same way that an upper-class white woman thinks of her Black maid) and because certain patterns tend to be more apparent to those who have a degree of distance from a situation. Simmel also crucially conceives of "objectivity" as involving a combination of nearness and remoteness. Beyond this sociological lineage justifying the significance of a particular Black women's standpoint, though – which becomes a Black *Feminist* standpoint through the process of politicization – Hill Collins's effort to claim Black women's supposed access to special knowledge about society is related, in the broader context of feminist thought, to feminist standpoint theory and so-called strong objectivity. Standpoint theory has its origins in connections drawn between Marxism and feminism by feminist scholars such as Dorothy Smith in the 1970s and Nancy Hartsock in the '80s; both were inspired by Marx to propose that, through everyday experience, women gain valuable knowledge of patriarchal society because of their subordinate position within it – knowledge that can serve as the basis for a trenchant social critique. Thus, standpoint theory calls attention to the Foucauldian idea that power relations shape knowledge production; where one is situated in social institutions and relationships, relative to centers of power, affects what one knows and how one knows it. Feminist philosopher Sandra Harding further developed the notion, resonant with Simmel's, that for objectivity to be "strong," it must be cognizant of the social location of those producing knowledge, and must include multiple perspectives; in fact, it should make an effort to move to the center the knowledge and experiences of historically marginalized social groups, such as women and people of color, because these perspectives have traditionally been left out of the development of "objective" truths.

Hill Collins brings further specificity in social location to her uptake of feminist standpoint theory to develop a Black Feminist standpoint theory, as her point seems to be that Black women's distinctive perspective on society is a result of their position at the intersection of race- and gender-based oppression. If we take her quintessential example, from the opening paragraph of "Learning from the Outsider Within," of Black women who perform domestic duties for white families, we see both race and gender at play in shaping experience: it is by virtue of their gender that these women are considered capable of fulfilling traditionally feminine and motherly tasks, and are therefore able to cultivate a certain intimacy with white society (even as being relegated to the home is a sign of gendered oppression); it is because of their race that they will never really be a part of the white family, but are being hired as servants to families of higher social (racial) status – while also needing to financially support and care for their own families back home. Later in the essay – in the course of presenting several key themes of Black Feminist thought (a preview of her later book) – Hill Collins attests to the "interlocking nature of oppression," asserting that Black women often have a "clearer view of their own subordination" than white women because they find themselves "at the intersection of multiple structures of domination" (Hill Collins 1986: S19). Her explanation for this is not that more oppression equals more knowledge, in a kind of additive view of the way that experience of various forms of structurally-based oppression leads to epistemological insight; rather, it's that Black women don't suffer the same illusions as white women with respect to their relationship to white male power, for they can't find comfort in their white privilege to balance out or cover over the pains associated with their gendered subordination. Being subject to oppression along the lines of gender and race (as well as, oftentimes, class) also enables Black Feminists to better understand the links among various systems of oppression, since they are all interconnected – a point made by Davis in *Women, Race, and Class*[12] – which sets up Black Feminists to potentially be more astute critical social theorists.

It's no accident that Hill Collins develops this core idea – about Black women having an epistemologically and politically useful experience of interlocking oppressions – in the direction of the cultivation of a distinctive Black Feminist standpoint not only in the context of a tradition of thinkers like Davis and hooks, but also at the same time that Crenshaw unofficially coins the term "intersectionality." In her now-classic 1991 essay "Mapping the Margins," Crenshaw, a lawyer and legal scholar, clarifies that her introduction of the term "intersectionality" is meant to pinpoint the way that Black women's experiences are shaped by race discrimination *in interaction* with gender discrimination; that is, as she puts it, "the intersection of racism and sexism factors into Black women's lives in ways that cannot be captured wholly by looking at the race and gender dimensions of those experiences separately" (Crenshaw 1991: 1244). This echoes Hill Collins' assertion that Black women are better poised to grasp the workings of overlapping oppressive structures than those who experience them singly; but Crenshaw also focuses quite extensively on the realm of "political intersectionality," calling attention to the way that feminist and antiracist politics have ironically often contributed to the marginalization of Black women by putting forth agendas that target either gendered or racial discrimination, while missing the intersection between the two. For example, antiracist politics aimed at racist misconceptions of domestic violence often prioritize "maintain[ing] the integrity of the community" (Crenshaw 1991: 1253) at the expense of recognizing the real social problem of the victimization of Black women within their own homes. At the same time, feminist attempts to assist women suffering from domestic violence often "elide or wholly disregard the particular intersectional needs of women of color" (Crenshaw 1991: 1262) by failing to take into account the way that racial and gender-based oppression uniquely come together in these women's experience. This is tied to a much

---

12   Davis writes critically of early women's rights leaders, for example, that they simply "did
      not suspect that the enslavement of Black people in the South, the economic exploitation
      of Northern workers and the social oppression of women might be systematically related"
      (Davis 1983: 66).

longer history of overt and implicit elision and exclusion of Black women from the mainstream feminist movement in the United States – a history well-documented by Davis in *Women, Race, and Class*.

What motivates many Black Feminists to intervene in antiracist and feminist politics, however – to stand up and fight the oppression they suffer at the intersection of race and gender (as well as other vectors of identity such as class, ability, and sexuality) – is not simply the rational understanding of systems of oppression that they may gain by virtue of their special social standpoint. They are also impelled by the emotions that their experiences of racism and sexism generate – more specifically, the distinctive anger that being personally subjected to injustice invokes in them. For contemporary antiracist philosopher Myisha Cherry, this "Lordean rage" – a particular form of righteous rage inspired by Black Feminist poet and writer Audre Lorde – importantly sets itself apart from other, more destructive varieties of rage[13] in ways that make it especially valuable for antiracist, and we might say feminist antiracist, struggle. Lordean rage is not only a response, specifically, to racism – to "racist actions, racist attitudes, and presumptions that arise out of those attitudes" (Cherry 2021a) – but it also crucially entails *metabolizing* emotion into action aimed precisely at addressing racial injustice. Although Cherry focuses exclusively on antiracism – not feminism – in defining Lordean rage, she does imagine historical Black Feminist icons Sojourner Truth and Ida B. Wells as having channeled Lordean rage in their own fights against racism and sexism. This nod to the intersectional foundation of Lordean rage more accurately reflects Lorde's own theorization of the power of rage, or anger, in her classic 1981 essay, "The Uses of Anger: Women Responding to Racism." Lorde's investigation focuses largely, but not exclusively, on the anger that Black women feel in response to racism that emerges in feminist contexts – for example, at a Women's Studies forum and in the women's movement. Her account of racism within feminism sets the stage for her broader claims that "[a]nger is loaded with information and energy," and that "[f]ocused with precision it can become a powerful source of energy serving progress and change" (Lorde 1984: 127).

Lorde's celebration of Black women's justified rage at injustice has reverberated through Black Feminism ever since. hooks expands on Lorde's discussion of the harmful silencing of Black women's rage in her book, *Killing*

---

13   Cherry argues that the other four kinds of rage – rogue rage, wipe rage, *ressentiment* rage, and narcissistic rage – are unproductive and can even be harmful. They "can obstruct racial justice and even perpetuate injustice," she claims, by aiming to harm others, demonstrating indifference to others' suffering, or reproducing oppressive behaviors (Cherry 2021b: 23).

Rage: Ending Racism;[14] in the contemporary context, it is not only Cherry who draws on this tradition for its philosophical and political implications, but also Brittney Cooper, whose popular 2018 book *Eloquent Rage: A Black Feminist Discovers Her Superpower*, calls upon Black women to get in touch with their (Lordean) righteous rage and to use it for progressive social change. "Black women have the right to be mad as hell" (Cooper 2018: 4), she writes in the book's opening chapter, "The Problem With Sass." "Black girl feminism is all the rage, and we need all the rage" (Cooper 2018: 5). Cooper cites Lorde as having taught her that "rage is a legitimate political emotion" (Cooper 2018: 5), though she explores throughout *Eloquent Rage* how her own process of claiming this Black girl's superpower – not only allowing herself to feel it without compunction, but 'focusing it with precision,' as Lorde advocates – has been messy and complicated. She describes her own struggles against the stereotype of the angry black woman (which often leads Black women to be dismissed out of turn), and her younger self's insistence that "feminism is white women's shit" (Cooper 2018: 10). Yet, having come through all of this, she maintains that the Lordean rage of Black Feminists is hugely valuable to a world that has consistently situated them at the intersection of systems of oppression – that "Black feminist rage can change this world" (Cooper 2018: 37). And she further suggests that, by focusing their rage in response to experiences of overlapping forms of discrimination, Black Feminists can achieve political victories that belong to everyone (Cooper 2018: 7). For Cooper, counter to what respectability politics will have us believe, it is the rage of Black women that can help to identify social problems, as it "expose[s] ... exactly what the system is made of" (Cooper 2018: 163); therefore, it is "a kind of power that America would do well to heed," because it can do "the necessary work of pushing American democracy forward" (Cooper 2018: 170).

Cooper's conviction in the power of Black Feminists' rage to locate instances of disrespect in the social world, to motivate struggles for justice, and to thereby propel social progress, maps onto third-generation Frankfurt School theorist Axel Honneth's focus on the "negative" emotions of the oppressed as his chosen "pre-theoretical resource for critique in everyday life" (Petherbridge 2011: 3), following the Frankfurt School commitment to constructing theory around a point of "immanent transcendence" (Zurn 2015: 16). But this also takes us back to Marcuse. In spite of the overwhelming pessimism of *One-Dimensional Man*, Marcuse suggests, there, that not everyone has

---

14   According to hooks, Black people generally learn to suppress their rage, because they learn early on that it can be "suicidal" (hooks 1995: 14) to "expres[s] it to the wrong white folks" (hooks 1995: 13).

fallen prey to one-dimensionality: a total conformism of thought and feeling with the advanced industrial apparatus that becomes widespread as subjects internalize the "false needs" associated with a materially comfortable, secure life, premised on structures of domination. Even if this society "is capable of "delivering the goods" on an increasingly large scale" (Marcuse 1964: xlvi) – as its "beneficial products," from indoor plumbing to mass transportation to widescreen TVs, become "available to more individuals in more social classes" (Marcuse 1964: 12) – there are hints, throughout the text, that "the goods" are still not on offer to everyone. Marcuse implies that the "inhuman existence" still found among various social groups, including "the persecuted colored races" (Marcuse 1964: 53), actually holds promise as a site of resistance to conformity.

And in *An Essay on Liberation* several years later, Marcuse stakes his claim that the "ghetto populations" are likely to "become the first mass basis of revolt" in the United States, specifically due to the U.S.'s inability to "indefinitely deliver its goods" (Marcuse 1969: vii). He explains that in traditional Marxian theory, it is, of course, the proletariat who are imagined to be "the historical agent of revolution" (Marcuse 1969: 16). However, the members of the working class, nowadays, have been fully inculcated into the capitalist order, right down to their thoughts and desires – they are the prime target for "a socially engineered arrest of consciousness" because false consciousness is crucial to their willingness to "happily" keep the system running (Marcuse 1969: 16). Even if a refusal of the current order is beyond them, though, the system of false needs reaches its limit in those populations who still come face-to-face with their own marginalized and dominated status on a daily basis. Those who are, in some way, deprived of the full panoply of luxuries of modern capitalism are also spared its false happy consciousness – the illusion that the psychic satisfaction, even euphoria that they gain from their appliances and fancy homes, signals that they are free. They have not bought into the system because they have not been given the chance; but this means that they have not been anaesthetized by it, either. Their unhappiness correctly assesses the state of their reality; they are not deluded about whether or not they are being dominated. They feel clearly the real sense in which they bear the brunt of the system's injustice and inequality.

3   Conclusion: Taking Marcuse and Feminism beyond One-Dimensionality

Marcuse never gave up on the possibility of meaningfully intervening in the current state of social and political affairs – no matter how apparently totalizing the "conquest of the unhappy consciousness" (Marcuse 1964: 56) among contemporary Western subjects, and how pessimistic of an outlook his peers' and even his own theoretical work often presented on the question of how to find a source of negativity in which to ground the potential for social change. This indicates that, in spite of his past experience of praxis being blocked, as Adorno would attest, Marcuse was still able to feel the urgency of those parts of the American population whose social position puts them in closer proximity to violence, death, and material scarcity. An accomplished scholar and activist himself, Marcuse nevertheless felt an emotional and political alliance with others in his social world – such as his radical students, among whom was included a young Angela Davis – in whom he vested hope for revolt. Those who could avoid the lure of the falsely "satisfying goods" of capitalism, he reckoned, still seemed able to "think, feel, and imagine for themselves" (Marcuse 1964: 50). This meant that they retained precious access to a critical perspective on interlocking systems of domination whose workings normally tended to be obscured by the widespread inculcation of false needs and desires – helping Marcuse to see beyond one-dimensionality.

Marcuse cautioned his students to be mindful of the complexity of translating theory into social transformation, Davis remembers (Davis 2019: v). But he saw potential for radical change in the special standpoint occupied by certain marginalized groups, and the nonconformist emotions associated with this clearer perspective on oppression – just as the Black Feminist tradition has long maintained that Black women's location at the intersection of multiple forms of oppression, and their distinctive outrage at the experience of injustice, can drive the process of liberation for everyone. hooks advises feminism to move Black women, in theory and practice, "from margin to center," and to thereby transcend the "one-dimensional perspective" (hooks 2015: 3) from which feminism has historically suffered. Scholars like Cooper take this a step further in suggesting that the eloquent rage of Black Feminists holds the keys to progressive social change for all. For Black Feminists as well as for Marcuse, then, "[t]he possibilities for revolutionary transformation are not exhausted" (Held 1980: 74) so long as Black women, as Cooper would say, are still "mad as hell" (Cooper 2018: 4).

References

Adorno, Theodor. 2001. *Negative Dialectics*. trans. Dennis Redmond. https://www .academia.edu/39707967/Negative_Dialectics.

Adorno, Theodor and Herbert Marcuse. 1999. "Correspondence on the German Student Movement." trans. Esther Leslie. *New Left Review* 233 (January): 123–136.

Cherry, Myisha. 2021a. "How Rage Can Battle Racism." *The Atlantic*, October 17.

Cherry, Myisha. 2021b. *The Case for Rage: Why Anger is Essential to Anti-Racist Struggle.* New York: Oxford University Press.

Cooper, Brittney. 2018. *Eloquent Rage: a Black Feminist Discovers Her Superpower.* New York: St. Martin's Press.

Crenshaw, Kimberlé. 1991. "Mapping the Margins: Intersectionality, Identity Politics, and Violence against Women of Color." *Stanford Law Review*, 43 (6) (July): 1241–1299.

Davis, Angela. 2019. "Foreword." Thorkelson, Nick. *Herbert Marcuse: Philosopher of Utopia. A Graphic Biography.* V–VI. San Francisco: City Lights Books.

Davis, Angela. 1988 [1974] *Angela Davis: an Autobiography.* New York: International Publishers.

Davis, Angela. 1983. *Women, Race, and Class.* New York: Vintage Books.

Davis, Angela Y. 1999. Blue's Legacies and Black Feminism: Gertrude "Ma" Rainey, Bessie Smith, and Billie Holiday. New York: Vintage Books.

Davis, Angela Y. 2016. *Freedom is a Constant Struggle: Ferguson, Palestine, and the Foundations of a Movement.* Chicago: Haymarket Books.

Davis, Angela Y. 2004. "Marcuse's Legacies." In *Herbert Marcuse: a Critical Reader.* eds. John Abromeit & W. Mark Cobb, 43–50. New York: Routledge.

Davis, Angela Y. 2003. *Are Prisons Obsolete?* New York: Seven Stories Press.

Davis, Angela Y. 1990. *Women, Culture, and Politics.* New York: Vintage Books.

Freud, Sigmund. 1961 [1930]. *Civilization and Its Discontents.* trans. and ed. James Strachey. New York: W. W. Norton & Company.

Harcourt, Bernard E. 2020. *Critique and Praxis.* New York: Columbia University Press.

Held, David. 1980 *Introduction to Critical Theory: Horkheimer to Habermas.* Berkeley: University of California Press.

Hill Collins, Patricia. 2009 [2000]. *Black Feminist Thought.* New York: Routledge Classics.

Hill Collins, Patricia. 1986. "Learning from the Outsider Within: the Sociological Significance of Black Feminist Thought." *Social Problems* 33 (6): S14–S32.

hooks, bell. 2015 [1984]. *Feminist Theory: from Margin to Center.* New York: Routledge.

hooks, bell. 1995. *Killing Rage: Ending Racism.* New York: Owl Books: Henry Holt and Company.

hooks, bell. 1991. "Theory as Liberatory Practice." *Yale Journal of Law and Feminism,* 4(1): 1–12.

Jeffries, Stuart. 2016. *Grand Hotel Abyss: Lives of the Frankfurt School.* Brooklyn: Verso.

Leslie, Esther. 1999. "Introduction to Adorno/Marcuse Correspondence on the German Student Movement." *New Left Review* 233 (January): 118–122.

Lorde, Audre. 1984. "The Uses of Anger: Women Responding to Racism." *Sister Outsider: Essays and Speeches by Audre Lorde.* New York: Ten Speed Press. 124–133.

Marcuse, Herbert. 1969. *An Essay on Liberation.* Boston: Beacon Press.

Marcuse, Herbert. 1966 [1955]. *Eros and Civilization.* Boston: Beacon Press.

Marcuse, Herbert. 1964. *One-Dimensional Man: Studies in the Ideology of Advanced Industrial Society.* Boston: Beacon Press.

Petherbridge, Danielle. 2011. "Introduction: Axel Honneth's Project of Critical Theory." In *Axel Honneth: Critical Essays (With a Reply by Axel Honneth)*, ed. Danielle Petherbridge, 1–30. Brill.

Whitebook, Joel. 2004 "The Marriage of Marx and Freud: Critical Theory and Psychoanalysis." *The Cambridge Companion to Critical Theory.* ed. Fred Rush. New York: Cambridge University Press.

Wolin, Richard. 2001. *Heidegger's Children: Hannah Arendt, Karl Lüwith, Hans Jonas, and Herbert Marcuse.* Princeton: Princeton University Press.

Zurn, Christopher F. 2015. *Axel Honneth: a Critical Theory of the Social.* Malden: Polity Press.

CHAPTER 11

Herbert Marcuse and Intersectional (Marxist) Feminism

Sergio Bedoya Cortés

1 Introduction[1]

Herbert Marcuse's theoretical commitment has an evident political component: the construction of a qualitatively distinct, different society. Under this theoretical-political assumption he devoted all his work; since the founding of Heideggerian Marxism, going through the reinterpretation of Hegelian philosophy due to the rise of fascism, the Marcusean approach to philosophy, politics, and psychoanalysis was mediated by his concern for subjective conditions, that is, for the achievement of the social conscience necessary for social transformation.

In this sense, and as a response to the economistic model based solely on the improvement of working conditions of the union struggles of the 20th century, Marcuse presented part of his analysis on the importance and influence that the student and sexual struggles of May 1968 had for the revolutionary and emancipatory processes at the Paris Conferences in 1974. However, this did not correspond to an isolated moment in his life but can be understood as a transcendental process in the conception of action and the political subject as a whole.

For Angela Davis (2005), Herbert Marcuse "w[as] more interested in exploring transformative oppositional possibilities than [his] colleagues Adorno and Horkheimer" (viii) and, in that sense, he "has been obscured by his historical role as political teacher and inspirer" (Habermas 2001: 234) with some scholars, focusing on him just as a Guru of May 68 and the Student Revolt, suggesting that Marcuse has been studied as an agitator but not as the social theorist that he was.

The search of the political subject for revolution was the principal commitment of Marcuse in his late decades and, in that sense, "Marcuse's interventions

1 This chapter was elaborated within the framework of the research project *Ontología política y del paisaje en América Latina* [*Political and landscape ontology in Latin America*] financed by the Universidad Libre de Colombia.

as a public intellectual helped to stimulate [debates] as [d]id the working class still have a revolutionary potential? What role could students play?" (Davis 2005: viii). This was evidenced, mainly, from the second half of the sixties of the last century, after finishing *One-Dimensional Man* and beginning to write *Repressive Tolerance*, where the thought of Marcuse began to turn towards a complementary search of the political subject of social transformation.

Marcuse, during the 1970s, discussed the role of the working class in contemporary capitalism and, in that sense, warned that "The working class [was] still the 'ontological' antagonist of capital, and the potentially revolutionary Subject: but it is a vastly expanded working class, which no longer corresponds directly to the Marxian proletariat" (Marcuse 1979: 20). With 'ontological', Marcuse understood that the historical role possessed by the proletariat would continue to be the fundamental role for emancipation. However, with the development of capitalism, the proletariat eclipsed its emancipatory capacity, as we will see below, despite the evident contradictions of the capitalist system. In Marcuse's thought:

> [T]he revolution itself will be an entirely different project than it was for Marx. One will have to contend with groups which were of no significance whatsoever to original Marxist theory; for example, the renowned marginal groups organized by students, oppressed racial and national minorities [and] women [...] [, but, in his historical understanding,] [t]hese are not substitute groups who are to become the new revolutionary subjects. They are [...] anticipatory groups that may function as catalysts, and no more than that.
> KELLNER 1984: 304

Thus, this chapter focuses on understanding how Marcuse's Marxism can be understood as one of the conceptual precursors of the *Intersectional Marxism* which authors such as Patricia Hill Collins, Claudia Jones, or Harold Cruse claim as a critical and emancipatory approach to women and gender oppression – not just within capitalism, but within the inhuman values of our civilization.

For this purpose, I would like to concentrate, first, on the concept of intersectionality in order to outline how we can understand the Marcusean understanding of the "agent of radical change" that fits with this tradition. Following this, I will outline how Marcuse finds in the Women's Liberation Movement the possibility of denying the principle of reality proper to the capitalist system. Thirdly, I will analyse the role that Marcuse's Marxist feminism plays in his new conception of socialism.

2   Intersectionality and Marxism or Intersectional Marxism

Intersectionality, as Bohrer (2019) explains, "is a term that [is] used in a whole variety of mobile ways and deployed to many different ends" (16). In this sense, intersectionality is understood as a theory that demonstrates that the various forms of discrimination do not work independently but rather interact within each other in specific geographical and temporal spaces (Rogers, Castree, and Kitchin 2013).

It is necessary to mention that thinking about intersectionality under a Marxist perspective, as Marcuse does, must take place within a historical and social framework; otherwise, the concept will become a source of post-modernism where Utopia is replaced by the "transform[ation of] the world by transforming its forms, space or language" (Jameson 1984: 61), instead of transforming the world "to create the material conditions for freedom and equality" (Marcuse 2014: 342). Marcuse understood that "as long as philosophy does not adopt the idea of a real transformation, the critique of reason stops at the status quo and becomes a critique of pure thought" (Marcuse 2009: 36). Thus, if intersectionality does not correspond to a specific historical and cultural context – if it is not based on the material conditions of humanity beyond forms and language – it just lays out an academic exercise that does not appeal to real human liberation and would culminate in the appropriation by the Establishment, that is, in ideology under Marxian terms. Therefore, under such an approach, oppression as "any unjust situation where, systematically [...] one group denies another group access to the resources of society" (Hill Collins 2000: 4) will not make any sense concerning socio-philosophical thought.

In that sense, in the 1920's "in the United States of America, there was a significant amount of overlap, discussion, and cross-pollination between the intersectional tradition and the Marxist tradition" (Bohrer 2019: 31). From many Afro-American scholars that understand that "race, gender, and class oppression were the fundamental causes of Black women's poverty" (Hill Collins 2000: 1), the analysis and identification of oppression is based not on the critique of pure thought but from a concrete historical framework that aims at the total-social transformation.

Capitalism, colonialism, racism, and sexism were factors that should be discussed, undoubtedly, not only in their nature of existence – that is, if they existed or not – since they were found in the reality of women, but rather they should be analysed under an exercise of critical reflection that would identify the dynamics of domination, exclusion, and their roots with the capitalist system. In that sense, the harassment of capitalism, which was expanding more around the globe and sought to expand its production model under legal standards, began to prohibit, in a certain way, long hours of work and child exploitation, and concentrated on obtaining cheaper labour from the inclusion of women in the formal and waged production process.

In this regard, many scholars, among whom Claudia Jones stands out, "reject[ed] a class-primary Marxist approach and androcentric notions of Blackness and Black liberation" (Bohrer 2001: 32) in order to develop theories of oppression that analyse the multidimensionality of exploitation and not only the different manifestations of subjugation on an economic basis, while some other "early black feminists' analyses by black women under capitalism clearly understood the uniquely cruel, interlocking oppressions experienced" (McDuffie 2011: 48). In any case, as we will see later, "the Marxist and the intersectional traditions share part of their histories [...] both traditions of theory being deeply committed to activism and street-level politics" (Bohrer 2019: 41) based on the total refusal of the current social, political, and cultural conditions.

In that sense, Claudia Jones "uses the term super[-]exploitation to conceptualize [the] «uniquely severe, persisten[t], and dehumanizing forms of capitalist exploitation» that referred to the way in which black women's labor is assumed" (Bohrer 2019: 48–49) in order to outline that although exploitation occurs from economic perspectives as Marx and Lenin had proposed, super-exploitation managed to structure the different forms or levels in which oppression was concatenated. The social division of labour, widely analysed by Marx and later developed under the imperial-colonial levels that Lenin had outlined, was also concentrated at micro levels that differentiated between genders and races since "the intuition of essence is misused to establish orders of value in which the relations of hierarchy and subordination required by the established order are derived from the 'essence' of man, of nationality, and of race" (Marcuse 2009: 32).

Thus, Marcuse concentrates his theory not on abstract individuals, but on the concrete/real humanity that is represented in the social, political, economic, and cultural situations experienced by men and women in their daily lives. Therefore, as John Abromeit explains, "Marcuse argues [...] that emancipatory social change cannot overshoot the objective possibilities that exist in a latent but unrealized state in the present historical situation. In this respect, Marcuse moves decisively beyond Heidegger, who dismisses the entire sphere of "ontic" history, and [...] insists that the entire history of the West has been misguided and that the slate needs to be wiped completely clean" (Marcuse 2005b: 185).

In that sense, emancipation processes must take place in an immanent way; that is, not by the product of external forces but by the contradictions of capitalism themselves. These contradictions have been realized within a historized ontic sphere that was distinguished from the contradictions inherently attributed to capitalism that Heidegger (Jansen 1989) interpreted as eternal since "nothing of the concrete material and cultural, none of these concrete social and political conditions that constitute history has any place in *Sein und Zeit*" (Jansen 1989: 102).

Thus, if the "[r]eality, where man's essence is determined, is the totality of the relations of production" (Marcuse 2009: 60), and the participation of women in this productive sphere has been carried out, the question of both emancipation and exploitation, under a Marxist perspective, will focus not only on the question of economic exploitation but also on its manifestations in other spheres of society, since, "in a repressive society one cannot speak of a genuine emancipation of women, because emancipation here never transcends the repression of the social order" (Marcuse 2014: 163).

In this way, "[t]he essence that the theory [of totality] attempts to conceptualize appeared first in the form of man's potentiality within a particular historical situation, in conflict with his immediate existence" (Marcuse 2009: 59), which led first, in the 19th century, to understanding the manifestation of exploitation only from the sphere of work. This interpretation, with time and due to the development of historical conditions, led to Marcuse's concentration on the Women's Liberation Movement – not only because of its political qualities which were able to create an environment of social mobilization that could generate an increase in class consciousness, but because the Movement was another response to the manifestations where exploitation had historically taken root.

Marcuse, asking himself about *The Failure of the New Left*, understood that "[t]he history of civilization is the history of male domination, of patriarchy [because w]omen's development has been determined and limited not only by the demands of the slave-owners, the feudal and bourgeois societies, but also and equally so by specifically male needs" (Marcuse, 2005a: 190). Thus, within this approach, it is understandable that theory, until today, has reproduced the dominant logic not only of the bourgeoisie but also of the patriarchy.[2] In that sense, if essence can be understood as the "totality of the social process as it is

---

2 In this regard, Hill-Collin (2002: 3) explains that "[t]he shadow obscuring this complex Black women's intellectual tradition is neither accidental nor benign. Suppressing the knowledge produced by any oppressed group makes it easier for dominant groups to rule because the seeming absence of dissent suggests that subordinate groups willingly collaborate in their own victimization".

organized in a particular historical epoch [...] [then,] every individual factor, considered as an isolated unit, is 'inessential', insofar as its 'essence' [...] can be grasped only in the light of its relation to the totality of the process" (Marcuse 2009: 51).

Therefore, either from the labour sphere – as orthodox Marxism does – or from the interpretation that was guided by the elimination of the concept of essence where the struggle is solely concentrated in individual emancipation – as postmodernism does – theory "succumbs to helpless relativism [...] promoting the very powers whose reactionary thought it wants to combat" (Marcuse 2009: 32) because both orthodox Marxism and postmodernism concentrate in human beings just as an isolated unit, just as a worker, just as a woman or just as a non-white individual. In this sense, Marcuse's effort to reconceptualize the concept of 'essence' in the light of the counter-hegemonic movements of the 1960s, focused not only on the search for a political subject capable of triggering the transformation of the existing reality but also, tried to develop a theory that moves "beyond appearance to essence and explain[s] its content as it appears to true consciousness" (Marcuse 2009: 62).

Thus, Marcuse saw in the Women's Liberation Movement and the Black and Brown populations the break of the appearance of domination. Marcuse (2009) understood that "[i]n the current historical period, the economy as the fundamental level has become 'essential' in such a way that all other levels have become its 'manifestations'" (51). Therefore, he continued to recognize himself as a Marxist by accepting that the domination of the capitalist system extended to the economic base – for which the proletariat would be the agent called upon for social transformation –, but, at the same time, he understood the multidimensionality of exploitation and its manifestations in a similar way to what other Marxist traditions have referred to as the superstructure.

In that sense, he comprehended that the 'manifestations' of exploitation "took on the appearance of a "natural" opposition: the opposition between innate qualities as the basis for a supposedly natural hierarchy, the domination of the masculine over the feminine" (Marcuse 2005a: 190). And, for this reason, in the search to build a qualitatively different society, under a new system of norms and values, it was necessary to recognize and understand the essence of domination from a feminine, feminist perspective.

Furthermore, "Marcuse sought a new revolutionary subject successively in non-integrated outsider minorities" (Kellner 1984: 280) since, within the framework of the social division of labour, the "technostructure of exploitation organizes a vast network of human instruments which produce and sustain a rich society" (Marcuse 1972: 14) abolishing "[t]he misery of unfulfilled vital needs [...] for the majority of the population; [while] outright poverty is "contained" among a minority (though a growing one) of the population" (Marcuse 1972: 19).

3   Marcuse and the Women's Liberation Movement

Marcuse, analysing the New Left, saw the Student Movement and Women's Liberation Movement as potential catalysts for a new class consciousness through denunciation that could overthrow capitalism. In that sense, the German philosopher specified that "women must become free to determine their own life, not as wife, not as mother, not as mistress, not as girlfriend, but as an individual human being" (Marcuse 1974: 288) inasmuch as "women are emancipated as labour power, as female labour power, but not as women" (Marcuse 2014: 31). Thus, Marcuse outlined that women's liberation is much deeper, much more radical, than the mere inclusion of women in the productive sphere, since "women in class society embody, embody in the most literal sense, the possibility of such a non-repressive reality principle" (Marcuse interview 1974, in Jansen 1989: 112) unlike the reality principle that has characterized Western civilization until now.

While postmodernism focused on women's liberation as a solely subjective experience within a specific historical and cultural context, Marcuse seeks to understand women's liberation as a part of Marxist/human liberation. Women's liberation is related not only to work and women's rights and freedoms, since these could take place within established society, but in terms of a free society where the rules of gender and class could be overturned.

The tension between the *sein bei sich* and *sein an sich*, the question of class consciousness, consists of what Marx and Marcuse called the subjective conditions and the objective conditions. In this sense, the objective conditions, such as the contradictions intrinsic to the economic, political, and cultural system, are dimensions that humanity cannot individually influence. Thus, the revolution becomes the axis that breaks through and transforms these objective conditions. The proletariat will always be a being in itself -*sein bei sich*-, that is, the exploited subject under this social system. However, as far as the subjective conditions are concerned, it is the consciousness of the subjects that determines the possibility of social transformation: the need for change can occur within the existing objective conditions -reform-, or it can be out outside these and seek total transformation -revolution (*sein an sich*).

In this sense, Marcuse observed that the objective conditions were sufficiently developed for the radical transformation of society due to social and economic situations of exploitation. However, the subjective conditions – people's awareness of exploitation and domination and their willingness/attitude to transform the conditions of exploitation – were not found sufficiently developed in order to begin the construction of a pre-revolutionary moment.[3]

Thus, Marcuse outlined a less diffuse way of achieving the radical transformation of Western society that focused on the construction and emancipation of consciousness: "the fact that the need for radical change must be rooted in the subjectivity of individuals themselves, in their intelligence and their passions, their drives and their goals [because, although] [...] in terms of political economy they may not be "forces of production", but for every human being they are decisive, [because] they constitute reality" (Marcuse 1978: 3–6). Accordingly, radical subjectivity means the emergence of self-consciousness that finds current economic and social conditions intolerable. The question is, however, how can we reject what is masked in the fetishism of merchandise, if consciousness is subordinated and rooted in material production?

Surplus consciousness, a form of consciousness that transcends material production processes, is "that free human [psychische] capacity which is no longer absorbed by the struggle for existence" (Marcuse 2014: 397). Surplus consciousness leads to forms of imagination, activities, and enjoyment that reveal the contradiction between the inhumanity of alienated work and the oppression of advanced industrial society but also generates the impulses of creativity and freedom proper to the realization of humanity by the other. As such, what should be translated into the work of radical subjectivity is the denotation of the impossibility of continuing to live under present conditions. It is the *Great Refusal*: it is a rejection of these conditions, but also the possibility of an orientation towards social transformation.

In this sense, the need for social change includes the class struggle, but it cannot be reduced to this. It is impossible to subsume all forms of oppression and manifestations of inhumanity in the advanced industrial society by the proletariat alone: the subjectivity of individuals tends to dissolve in class consciousness in the orthodox traditions, leaving aside all the different forms of refusals that can trigger rebellion. The revolution is thus deprived of an important prerequisite, namely the fact that a radical transformation must be conceptualized and analysed in terms of the subjectivity and the material conditions.

---

3 As I have mentioned before, for Marcuse the revolutionary subject is the proletariat. However, Women's Liberation Movements, students, and racial minorities constitute a proto-revolutionary subject due to the lack of revolutionary consciousness of the proletariat. Subjective struggles, in this sense, contribute to the genesis of revolutionary consciousness among the working class, but they will not constitute, by themselves, a force capable of transforming Western society.

People's imaginative capacity and their gender and race are also places where oppression unfolds, and since the contradictions of the current system – the objective conditions – are sufficiently developed, the role of subjective conditions is one of the main points to be developed in Marcuse's theory.

> The genesis of this Subject is a process which shatters the traditional framework of radical theory and practice. The ideas and goals of the cultural revolution have their foundation in the actual historical situation. They have a chance of becoming truly concrete, of affecting the whole if the rebels succeed in subjecting the new sensibility (the private, individual liberation) to the rigorous discipline of the mind.
>
> MARCUSE 1972: 131

With the 'rigorous discipline of the mind', Marcuse emphasizes what he already developed in *Eros & Civilization*; namely, that because "the pleasure principle comes into conflict with a harsh environment and after a series of disciplinary experiences, "the individual comes to the traumatic realization that full and painless gratification of his needs is impossible"" (E&C: 13 in Kellner 1999: 4). As a response to this symptomatic situation, Marcuse developed an evolving subjectivity that "is also embodied, gendered, oppositional, and struggles against domination, repression, and oppression" (Kellner 1999: 12). This "new subjectivity", produced as an antagonistic subjectivity of the reality principle, contains "needs, values, and aspirations that would be qualitatively different from subjectivity in one-dimensional society" (Kellner 1999: 13) that "can protect the [new] movement from the entertainment industry and the nut house, by channelling its energies into socially relevant manifestations" (Marcuse 1972: 131).

In this sense, faced with the temporary impossibility of the proletariat to develop and manifest itself as a truly revolutionary force (Marcuse 2017), new groups of people began to oppose the Establishment in new and different manners. "[T]he emancipation of sensibility [was] the common ground [of these groups]. [They] engender[ed] a new experience of a world violated by the requirements of the established society, and of the vital need for total transformation" (Marcuse 1972: 129) that approached the criticism of the capitalist system from unusual and conflictive places for orthodox Marxism.

The denunciations and rejections focused on national identities, happiness, public and quality education, sexual and gender liberation, and the preservation of nature – concerns that had always been rejected and displaced by orthodox/Soviet Marxism. Thus, in this sense, the emergence of these new groups also occurred as a response to the forms of domination present in the emancipatory processes that had taken place until the 1960s and that had been led by the former Soviet Union.

The Stalinist construction of Socialism was based on the Soviet "new rationality" that required the production process to develop within the framework of efficiency and performance of the established patterns, which allows us to understand Soviet Marxism as ambivalent: "on the one hand, it could be analysed as an ideology, as a tool of control and domination [...] while, on the other hand, it seemed like a revolutionary force that challenged the Advanced Industrial Society through the underprivileged" (Bedoya-Cortés 2023: 90). In this way, as Marcuse claimed, the Soviet population was incapable of developing the political consciousness necessary to carry out a political transformation. Instead, the Soviet consciousness led to the Soviet reality principle that, at one point, was possible to understand as a counterbalance to the capitalism principle of performativity, while, at the same time, it was simply recreating that principle as part of an economic competitiveness basis under the Soviet sign.

Thus, for Terry Maley (2017), Marcuse "is also very mindful of the fact that radical social change not only happens from the left or from below. [It] happens, also from above and from the right – to women, people of color, Indigenous populations, [and] the working classes in the global south and north" (x). Marcuse outlined that a truly radical opposition, in contemporary times, should concentrate on the feminist movement, organized militant students, and racial minorities[4] in conjunction with the working class, since only in this way could an organized movement be concentrated and configured with a true anti-capitalist potential.

However, the struggle was not only against the reality principle of capitalism; it was also a necessary opposition to the "Old Left Rationality" that, as I have explained before, restricted the transformative potentiality of the subaltern classes other than the proletariat by condemning them as "bourgeois children" (Marcuse 2005a: 43). It is in this sense, then, that Marcuse interprets the break from the communist parties of the New Left, that is, advocating for freer, less authoritarian forms of organization[5] and not only within the framework of

---

4   In this regard, Marcuse outlined that "the radical opposition is very much limited to minority groups. The liberation struggle of the blacks, as one of the minority groups, understands itself as being in the same anti-capitalist front with the student movement, the younger workers, the women [...] But this common need to fight back has not created unity in action, and there is no comprehensive organization that can guarantee even a minimally unified strategy" (Marcuse 2014: 215).

5   On the authoritarian form of the Soviet Union and its possible relationship with the role of women in a Soviet socialist society, Charles Reitz (2017) stated that for Marcuse "There can be

the construction of a different society but, in turn, in the pre-revolutionary and revolutionary process for the construction of a new society.

As Harold Cruse explains in his *The Crisis of the Negro Intellectual* "the communist parties of the period [did] not car[e] at all about racial equality, essentially lied about this commitment in order to lure unsuspecting black people into their organization on false pretenses" (Bohrer 2019: 44). However, the organizational processes of Black women in the United States were presented as "the most revolutionary segment of the U.S. working class, thereby challenging orthodox Marxist postulations that industrial (white male) workers represented the [revolutionary] vanguard" (McDuffie 2009: 34) – with which they challenged notions such as revolution or socialism that had been built by Stalinism and that were adapted to the principle of reality and performativity of the Soviet tradition.

4 A Broader and More Comprehensive Notion of Socialism

Socialism, as a notion or goal, has generated very different forms of understanding and conceptualization that, until today, are difficult to understand. Soviet Marxism, for example, understood socialism as a more advanced social stage that constituted the elimination of the domination of man by man; however, it resulted in new forms of dominance that gave it the character of being an authoritarian or totalitarian system.

In this way, in opposition to the different forms of exploitation and domination of the left and the right, and through the notion of a feminist socialism, Marcuse addresses the need to transform the smattering of socialism because he saw, even in Marx's notion of socialism, remnants of the performative principle of capitalism that would continue with the exploitation of man by man. For Marcuse, Marx found hope in technical-scientific development within the framework of the development of productive forces. Nevertheless, technical-scientific development led to the subordination of humanity to technology. Technique, by itself, "can promote authoritarianism as well as liberty" (Marcuse 2004: 41). In the framework of the advanced industrial society, "technological power tends to the concentration of economic power" (Marcuse 2004: 43): the

---

discrimination against women even under socialism [...] But the very goals of this [feminist] movement require changes of such enormity in the material as well as intellectual culture that they can be attained only by a change in the entire social system" (80).

Art und Weise[6] of gadgets and goods are determined by the large economic emporiums, and, while they reproduce the logic of capital, they affect the rationality that tends towards the freedom of those whom it serves.

Thus, this new technological rationality "is by no means confined to the subjects and objects of large[-]scale enterprises but characterizes the pervasive mode of thought and even the manifold forms of protest and rebellion" (Marcuse 2004: 44). Therefore, together with an alienated social, economic, and psychological climate, the possibility of change and transformation is diminished. Accepting this reality is the only apparent methodological principle – as if we were already in the kingdom of freedom.

In this sense, rather than only focusing on the reduction of the working day and the alienation of work within the context of the advanced industrial society (reform), the (new) notion of socialism must, in turn, be one in which life is understood as an end in itself, and the relationship between human beings is not understood as between objects, but as between equals. Therefore, the liberation of women, Black people, and Indigenous people can be viewed as a rejection of the establishment fundamentally woven into the socialist movement.

Thus, if we treat the oppression of the exploited as a consequence of the very premise of Western civilization contained within the capitalist system, rather than simply the functioning of capitalism, then the notion of socialism becomes a qualitatively different way of life than what has been established. For example, women's movements have been persecuted and oppressed by the patriarchal cultural systems and values present in the capitalist system that remained present after the transition from feudalism to capitalism. "The first great protest against the feudal hierarchy and the loyalties established in the feudal hierarchy, [was] with its specifically pernicious repression of the woman" (Marcuse 1974: 284).

However, since the establishment of the capitalist system, the role of women gradually changed. The technical-scientific development meant less use of natural force that had been historically attributed to men, which led to the inclusion of women in technical and professional tasks. All of this did not mean the weakening of male dominance in the sphere of work, nor did it mean female emancipation. On the contrary, this development "also enlarged the human base of exploitation and the surplus exploitation of the women as a housewife, mother, servant, in addition to her work in the process of production" (Marcuse 1974: 284), and also built the white chauvinist stereotype

---

6   Way, manner, and mode could be the translation of these words. However, "*Art und Weise*" expresses all the forms, modes, and properties that make particular objects particular but not general or universal.

of the Negro slave mother, "who was a traditional 'mammy' who puts the care of children and families of others above her own [...] [what worked] as a device of the imperialists to perpetuate the [...] ideology that Negro women are 'backward,' 'inferior,' and the 'natural slaves' of others" (Jones 1995: 111–112). Walter Benjamin accurately illustrates this phenomenon in his analysis of the Brechtian adaptation of Gorky's work *The Mother*, where he outlined how women were exploited in a tripartite way, namely, as a housewife, a proletarian, and as a "creator of new proletarians", that is, as a mother.

Something similar happens – as Patricia Hill Collins explains – with categories such as race and identity. These categories were deployed as forms of social classification of the populations present in the Americas as a distinctive element between the rulers and the ruled "homogenizing those who are subjected to racializing narratives, by reducing people to their racial identification" (Bohrer 2019: 245) that naturalized the social classes among races. In that sense, the process of exploitation resulted in "race and division of labour [that] were structurally associated and mutually reinforcing [...] a systematic racial division of labour [that] was imposed" (Quijano 2014: 781). The racial division of labour, as a form to support and develop capitalism, was established during the colonial and imperial periods and were the Indigenous and Black men and women who served as a free primary force for extracting natural resources or cultivating land within the framework of agricultural production (Du Bois 2007: 8; Mariátegui 2015: 15–47).

Thereby, if the social division of labour in the different modes of production is observed in-depth, it is possible to find a constant: housework, food preparation (Hill Collins, 2000: 45), reproductive labour[7] (Glenn 1992: 1), and the raising and procreation of slaves or proletarians were always tasks charged to women. In this sense, the sexual division of labour was a recurrent relationship within the different modes of production, and it can be understood under the genderization of work, that is, as the sexual division of (unpaid) work that is imposed on proletarian women, and not only as the sexual manifestation of oppression.

In the case of alienation, on the other hand, the subordination of Black men and women to the sphere of alienated labour to ensure subsistence is evident, either through specific and notable slavery mechanisms or through how Black men and women are presented in the production process: "We have pursued

---

7   "Reproductive labor", in Glenn's words, "includes activities such as purchasing household goods, preparing and serving food, laundering and repairing clothing, maintaining furnishings and appliances [and] socializing children" (Glen 1992: 1), tasks that were later incorporated into the paid productive sphere.

the shadow, they have obtained the substance; we have performed the labor, they have received the profits; we have planted the vines, they have eaten the fruits of them" (Stewart 1987: 59). This has generated, as Marcuse foresaw, the "capitalist co-optation of women's increasing role in the labor force" (Power 2013: 79), which has led, in any case, to the liberation of women that the most regressive and liberal-social democratic sectors had sought, namely, women's participation in the production process that has identified them not only in exploitation as women but also in exploitation as workers. Therefore, taking into account that "in the present situation, in view of the fact that the American working class is not a revolutionary class, [...] the radical political consciousness, is concentrated among minority non[-]integrated groups such as the students, such as the black and brown minorities, such as women and so on" (Marcuse 2014: 357). In this sense, the dispute for total liberation no longer focuses only on the freedom of humanity in subjective/identity terms, but it will focus on the liberation of humanity as the potentiality of the total and radical transformation of Western society.

The notion of total transformation, of total and radical denial of the norms and values of Western civilization, was not strictly developed by Marcuse, but rather was raised by André Breton through his Great Refusal, who "defended the total refusal of the institutions, values and way of life in bourgeois society" (Kellner 1984: 279). This was interpreted by Marcuse: "there can be no meaningful talk about social change unless the individuals themselves are liberated from capitalist needs and consciousness and possess 'radical needs' for thoroughgoing social change" (Kellner 1984: 279). Thus, if the rejection and confrontation were based on the total and radical denial of the social, political, and cultural standards typical of Western society, the revolution had to be considered under different normative and political parameters that surpass the system of norms and values not only of bourgeois society but of Western civilization.

Therefore, the question of emancipation is no longer a question of the liberation of women in terms of employability or amount of income, because the negation of all norms and values of Western civilization implies the negation of the sphere of work, the political and legal spheres and, with it, the rejection of the social division of labour where women and oppressed racial and national minorities are integrated into the production process. However, although the objective conditions are developed enough, the subjective conditions, the class consciousness, is not developed enough for revolution, and it is in this regard that Marcuse understood that "the revolution itself will be an entirely different project than it was for Marx. One will have to contend with groups which were of no significance whatsoever to original Marxist theory; for example, the renowned marginal groups organized by students, oppressed racial and national minorities, women" (Kellner 1984: 304) because these groups, unlike the gentrifying proletariat, contained a revolutionary potential that "might act as a "major catalyst" in future struggles" (Marcuse 2005a: 16).

In that sense, the only concrete way to derogate the dictatorship of capitalism is with an intersectional analysis and practice[8] that could interpret and organize the anger of the vast majority of these refusals against the reality principle of the advanced industrial society. The amalgamation of most refusals must be an anti-capitalist-Marxist movement (Marcuse 1974) in order to provide the opportunity to develop a new reality principle. The need for a movement is based on the fact that it cannot be assumed that "you could really change society without some organization, nor [...] to assume that in a free society no administration whatsoever would be necessary" (Marcuse 2014: 373), so that the mere individual disputes, or the spontaneous forms of rejection without an organized base, would be found "without definite goals" (Marcuse 2015: 51) where the conflicts between "anarchy and organization [...] suffused throughout the whole *commune movement*" (Marcuse 2014: 335). In that sense, Marcuse emphasizes the Socialist-Marxist-Organization in order to avoid the instrumentalization by ruling sectors of these refusals and, in turn, to eradicate the individualistic subjectivity typical of postmodern thought that can be solved only with the search that "these communes actually, though *temporarily*, become units of production that reconstruct not only personal affairs but also the common work" (Marcuse 2014: 335).

The individualistic principle, typical of the capitalist system and neoliberalism (Dardot & Laval 2013) is one of the characteristics that not only governs the economic system, but also life itself and the academic-political process typical of (political) philosophy, sociology, and political science. Some contemporary theories concentrate on the individuals, on the merely personal subjectivity for the emancipatory processes, and, in that sense, there arises the impossibility of the total transformation. Why the impossibility of the total transformation? The subjective conditions, as another place of domination, are connected in Marcuse's understanding to the objective conditions because "[t]he subjective conditions can be summed up under the title: «The

---

8 Marcuse (2005a), analysing Marx's eleventh Thesis on Feuerbach, explained that "Marx's famous thesis has been interpreted today as meaning that it is no longer necessary to understand and interpret the world [...] This is an idiotic interpretation because never has theory, never has the effort of thinking, of knowing what is going on and what can be done about it, been needed more than it is today. Today, more than ever before, there cannot possibly be any revolutionary practice without the theory guiding such practice" (152).

Consciousness of the Working Class and the Consciousness of the Ruling Class»" (Marcuse 2015: 13). Thus, the total transformation would become a partial transformation so that, if the "distress and neediness that appear in man's sensuousness are no more purely matters of cognition [...] as expressed in estranged labor, are purely economic" (Marcuse 2005a:100), then the transformation would be possible within the capitalist system and the bourgeois democracy, and the commitment to the transformation would be not revolutionary but reformist.

However, Marcuse comprehended, as a member of the *Institut für Sozialforschung*, that every political theory must be understood as a practical position of a specific class (Horkheimer 2002), but also that Philosophy can comprehend the world "in a more radical manner than any other science [...] The rationality of the «ought» as well as the «is». The «ought» and the «potential» not as moral or transcendental obligations but as «real» historical possibilities and imperatives!" (Marcuse and Kirsch 2016: 484). In that sense, Marcuse could not ignore the multidimensionality of oppression.

He did understand that women were exploited not only in the form of work and labour, but also under the historical gender roles forced upon women, either as mothers or as home-caregivers or housewives. Without those roles, capitalism both in its embryonic phase and in its subsequent development and consolidation could not have been constituted as a political, social, and economic system and, in turn, as a system of beliefs, norms, and values. Thus, if "conformist consciousness provides not only an imaginary compensation but also a real one [, and t]his militates against the rise of a radical character structure" (Marcuse 1992: 32), and if "[f]or all these reasons, today's rebellion becomes visible only in small groups which cut across social classes" (Marcuse 1992: 34) how can we configure a better favourable situation for the radical change both in the political and philosophical fields?

5   Conclusion

Marcuse presented, both in *Counterrevolution and Revolt* and in *An Essay on Liberation*, the conditions of possibility for transformation under the guise of being anti-capitalist forces – organized anti-capitalist forces that resemble the social movements of the second half of the twentieth century. Thus, it is possible to perceive that capitalism has discovered how to avoid, apparently, the singular class identity due to the increase in the always apparent purchasing power of the working classes, to which the rise of radical individualistic subjectivity has been added. However, it is due to the understanding that the identarian or subjective refusals, *along with the class condition*, the lack of a free human life, and also approaches to the notion of socialism as a qualitatively different society, that Marxist notions such as proletariat, emancipation, and party will take on contextual meaning; that is, they can be historicized in the light of the events that the 20th and 21st centuries have brought with them. In that sense, I would like to point towards two different conclusions that derive from Marcuse's perspective that I have tried to develop within this chapter.

Firstly, I would like to remark that Marcuse concentrates his analysis and critique on the real/concrete conditions of the inhumanity of capitalism. Therefore, the fight for human freedom is based neither in the appropriation of the surplus-value nor the exploitation of one over another, but rather must be understood as a fight for the development of the real human nature, the realization of those natural and social conditions that Marx presented in the *1844 Economic and Philosophical Manuscripts*. This is because capitalism, in the words of Kellner (1992), "neither allows for the full development of individuality, nor for the possibility of diverse, social and cooperative relationships. Instead, it promotes greed, competition, and asocial behavior" (43). Thus, if "essence is the totality of the social process as it is organized in a particular historical epoch" (Marcuse 2009: 51), and the process of integration of the vast majority of the population has tried to neglect the counter-hegemonic consciousness, Critical Theory should focus on the continuous and consistent analysis of new possibilities (Utopia).

In that sense, without abandoning the precepts of Marxism and socialism, Marcuse advocates the integration of the different subjectivities that he understood as the subjects capable of elaborating the conditions for the emergence of a pre-revolutionary situation. The result of this integration would lead the proletariat – the subject called to change society – to understand itself in a situation of alienation, oppression, and injustice, which would ultimately lead the collective consciousness to be a revolutionary consciousness. Therefore, Marcuse did not see in gender and racial struggles the potentiality of total transformation but foresaw that those refusals could act as triggers for the socialist rebellion.

Secondly, after understanding that the struggle for socialism is based on the necessity to realize true human nature, I would like to point out the necessity of an organized but intersubjectively Socialist-Marxist-Anti-Capitalist refusal in order to rescue the social initiatives and historical knowledge against the reality principle of capitalism based on communal principles of self-management and autogestion. In that sense, Marcuse bases his intersectional approach on Marxist-anti-capitalist opposition, since without it, feminist or racial refusals would focus on mere integration of women and minorities within the productive system – that is, supposed liberation as women, as Afro-Americans or as Indigenous rather than liberation as human beings.

Therefore, and in contrast to what was proposed by Claudia Jones, Marcuse finds the category of class to be the transversal axis for contemporary intersectionality because, as Douglas Kellner and Clayton Pierce specified, "repression impacts both genders, and women alone cannot overcome it. Marcuse explicitly supports all attempts [...] to expand an awareness of the conditions women face. Still Marcuse believes that the oppression of women, like that of blacks and Jews, may only be dismantled when social repression is dismantled as a whole" (Marcuse 2014: 163). In this way, Marcuse finds that the principle of intersectionality must be represented in what he called a "united front", where the manifestations of exploitation, as evidenced in the sexual and racial divisions of labour, mobilize the irruption of objective conditions in people's consciousness, thus generating the possibility for radical transformation.

References

Bedoya-Cortés, Sergio. 2023. "Movimientos Sociales, crítica y liberación: una aproximación desde la obra de Herbert Marcuse". In *La Escuela de Frankfurt: Crítica y Emancipación*, ed. S. Bedoya-Cortés, 85–113. Bogotá: Universidad Libre.

Bohrer, Ashley. 2019. *Marxism and Intersectionality*. Bielefeld: Transcript Verlag.

Dardot, Pierre, and Laval, Christian. 2013. *The New Way of the World: on Neoliberal Society*. London: Verso.

Davis, Angela. 2005. "Marcuse's Legacies". In *Collected Papers Volume III: the New Left and the 1960s*, H. Marcuse, vii–xiv. New York: Routledge.

Du Bois, William Edward Burghardt. 2007. *The Philadelphia Negro*. Oxford: Oxford University Press.

Glenn, Evelyn. 1992. "From Servitude to Service Work: Historical Continuities in the Racial Division of Paid Reproductive Labor". *Signs* 18: 1–43.

Habermas, Jürgen. 2001. "The Different Rhythms of Philosophy and Politics for Herbert Marcuse on his 100th Birthday". In *Collected Papers Volume II: Towards a Critical Theory of Society*, H. Marcuse, 233–238. New York: Routledge.

Hill Collins, Patricia. 2002. *Black Feminist Thought*. New York: Routledge.

Hill Collins, Patricia. 2000. "Gender, Black Feminism, and Black Political Economy". *The ANNALS of the American Academy of Political and Social Science* 568: 41–53.

Horkheimer, Max. 2002. *Critical Theory*. New York: Continuum.

Jameson, Fredric. 1984. *POSTMODERNISM, or, The Cultural Logic of Late Capitalism*. London: Verso.

Jansen, Peter-Erwin, Ed. 1989. *Befreiung Denken: ein politischer Imperativ: Materialien zu Herbert Marcuse*. Offenbach del Meno: Verlag 2000.

Jones, Claudia. 1995 "An End to the Neglect of the Problems of the Negro Woman! (1949)". in *Words of Fire: an Anthology of African-American Feminist Thought*, ed. B. Guy-Sheftall, 108–123. New York: The New Press.

Kellner, Douglas. 1984. *Herbert Marcuse and the crisis of Marxism*. London: MacMillan.

Kellner, Douglas. 1999. Marcuse and the Quest for Radical Subjectivity. *Social Thought and Research*, 22(1/2), 1–24.

Kellner, Douglas. 1992. "Commentaries on Ecology and the Critique of Modern Society". *Capitalism, Nature, Socialism: a Journal of Socialist Ecology* 3(3): 43–46.

Maley, Terry. 2017. "Introduction: Five New Lectures—in Context". In *Transvaluation of Values and Radical Social Change*, eds. P. Jansen, S. Surak and C. Reitz, vii–xxxiii. Toronto: International Herbert Marcuse Society.

Marcuse, Herbert. 1972. *Counterrevolution and Revolt*. Boston: Beacon Press.

Marcuse, Herbert. 1974. "Marxism and Feminism". *Women's Studies* 2(3): 279–288.

Marcuse, Herbert, 1978. *The Aesthetic Dimension*. Boston: Beacon Press.

Marcuse, Herbert. 1979. The Reification of the Proletariat. *Canadian Journal of Political and Social Theory*, 3(1), 20–23.

Marcuse, Herbert. 1992. "Ecology and the Critique of Modern Society". *Capitalism, Nature, Socialism: a Journal of Socialist Ecology* 3(3): 29–38.

Marcuse, Herbert. 2004. *Collected Papers Volume I: War, Technology and Fascism*. New York: Routledge.

Marcuse, Herbert. 2005a. *Collected Papers Volume III: the New Left and the 1960s*. New York: Routledge.

Marcuse, Herbert. 2005b. *Heideggerian Marxism*. Lincoln, Nebraska: University of Nebraska Press.

Marcuse, H. 2007. *One-Dimensional Man*. London: Routledge.

Marcuse, Herbert. 2009. *Negations*. London: May Fly Books.

Marcuse, Herbert. 2014. *Collected Papers Volume VI: Marxism, Revolution and Utopia*. New York: Routledge.

Marcuse, Herbert. 2015. *Paris Lectures at Vincennes University, 1974*. Maryland: International Herbert Marcuse Society.

Marcuse, Herbert. 2017. *Transvaluation of Values and Radical Social Change*. Toronto: International Herbert Marcuse Society.

Marcuse, Herbert, and Kirsch, Robert. 2016. "The Rationality of Philosophy", *New Political Science* 38(4): 476–484.

Mariátegui, José Carlos. 2015. *Siete ensayos de interpretación de la realidad peruana*. México D. F.: Cien de Iberoamérica.

McDuffie, Erik S. 2009. "'No Small Amount of Change Could Do': Esther Cooper Jackson and the Making of a Black Left Feminist". In *Want to Start a Revolution? Radical*

Women in the Black Freedom Struggle, eds. D. Gore, J. Theoharis, and K. Woodard, 25–46. New York: New York University Press.

McDuffie, Erik S. 2011. Sojourning for Freedom: Black Women, American Communism, and the Making of Black Left Feminism. Durham: Duke University Press.

Power, Nina. 2013. "Marcuse and Feminism Revisited". *Radical Philosophy Review 16*(1): 73–79.

Quijano, Aníbal. 2014. *Colonialidad del poder, eurocentrismo y América Latina*, in *Cuestiones y horizontes: de la dependencia histórico-estructural a la colonialidad/ descolonialidad del poder*, A. Quijano, 777–832. Buenos Aires: Clacso.

Reitz, Charles. 2017. "Recalling Herbert Marcuse: Critical Theory as Radical Socialism". In *Transvaluation of Values and Radical Social Change*, eds. P. Jansen, S. Surak and C. Reitz, 61–100. Toronto: International Herbert Marcuse Society.

Rogers, Alisdair, Castree, Noel, and Kitchin, Rob. 2013. *A Dictionary of Human Geography*. Oxford: Oxford University Press.

Stwart, Maria. 1987. Maria W. Stewart, America's First Black Woman Political Writer. Bloomington: Indiana University Press.

CHAPTER 12

Rethinking Astrology as Feminist Re-enchantment
A Reading of Adorno's "The Stars Down to Earth"

Jennifer L. Eagan

"The Stars Down to Earth" (1974) may be Adorno's strangest text. How can someone who exposed the deep and abiding problems with reason as deployed by the Enlightenment and authoritarian structures be so preoccupied with astrology? How can someone who deals with such high-stakes wrongs in the world and with much more impactful cultural constructions devote so much time to this small column in the *Los Angeles Times*? Perhaps this is why major commentaries on Adorno's work provide little or no treatment of this text. Drawing on Adorno's critique in this underexamined work, this chapter asserts other ways to look at astrology as a feminist way of re-enchanting the world and retrieving nature from the grasp of capitalism. Though Adorno's content analysis of the column is illuminating and his critique of astrology as part of the occult is perhaps understandable due to its role in the Third Reich and other right-wing movements (though that is not his focus in "Stars"), this work asserts another reading that focuses on astrology's potential to address the maladies of late capitalism. The purpose of this project is not to justify astrology, but to uncover and question the contradictions in Adorno's analysis. Despite the flaws in Adorno's treatment, which include drawing from one source, overstated claims, and contradictions, he generates some insights into the maladies of late capitalism, including a desire to reenchant experience that has been flattened by an obsession with daily life and getting ahead. In particular, I examine three curiosities in "The Stars Down to Earth": his treatment of women in the column and as readers of the column, the recuring and out of place appearances of jazz in this critique of astrology, and Adorno's use of psychoanalysis as his primary tool of analysis. Next, I examine the pathologies that astrology may address in light of Adorno's own notion of nature and the maladies of late capitalism: disenchantment and dissociation.

Countering Adorno's claim that astrology is necessarily right-wing in nature, I examine the recent advent of popular feminist/BIPOC (Black, Indigenous, and people of color)/Queer social movement-centered astrologers whose astrology claims to be liberatory and useful for connecting us more deeply to nature and to ourselves. Can this kind of astrology be a method through which to critique oppression and provide inspiration for a subversive, feminist, and liberatory leftist movement? I suggest that some works of recent astrologers may have that potential.

1   Adorno and Astrology

Astrology is the ancient and continuing practice of interpreting the motion of heavenly bodies relative to the earth as having some sort of influence or impact on affairs, most notably human affairs. In short, astrology asserts some version of the notion that there is a reflective and influential character between what is happening in the broader universe and the Earth, perhaps best summed up by the astrological adage "as above, so below." There are different historical lineages of astrology – Hellenistic, Roman, Vedic, Chinese, etc. – which have differing and overlapping features. Beyond this very general definition of astrology, it is difficult to know how to categorize the practice. Is it religious, spiritual, occult, pseudo-scientific, hermeneutic? If religious, is it necessarily pagan? These are difficult questions that astrologers and critics of astrology debate.[1]

In "The Stars Down to Earth," Adorno pursues two lines of inquiry that do not necessarily connect. First, he conducts a content analysis of Carroll Righter's *Los Angeles Times* astrology column published from 1952–1953. This compelling content analysis shows that the column has a conservative stance, feeds into a psychology of passivity that reflects a supplication to late capitalism and administered society, and may prime us for authoritarianism (Adorno 1974: 163–164). Adorno shows that the column is embedded with many biases that we associate with the U.S. in the 1950s – compliance with authority, the desire for upward mobility, and a contradictory desire for individualism and dependence on wage labor. Adorno's case for the conservativism of this column is bolstered by Righter's role as astrologer to Ronald Reagan (Lybarger 2015). Second, and beyond this particular analysis, Adorno makes more general claims about the nature of astrology and those who believe in it beyond his reading of the column. This leap from one contemporary column to a detailed and scathing indictment of all astrology is open to challenge and uncharacteristic of the usual subtlety and rigor of Adorno's philosophical work and cultural critique. Adorno's analysis of Righter's column is insightful,

---

1   For detailed discussions on the history of astrology and its relationship to cosmology and religion, see Campion 2009 (Vol. I & II) and Campion 2012. For a cross-cultural treatment of astrology, see Campion and Greenbaum (eds.) 2016, and for a contemporary psychological and archetypal treatment of astrology see Tarnas 2006.

but I take issue with his broader characterization of astrology. I examine each move in Adorno's work in turn.

Righter's column, like other astrological columns in newspapers, is based on the sun signs, divided into the twelve signs of the zodiac based on the birthday of the reader. This is a small and shallow sliver of astrology, and not representative of astrology as a larger practice. It is unclear if readers of the column took it at all seriously or only as a form of amusement. Perhaps an analysis of such columns only as a product of the culture industry and not as an article of occult belief would be more consistent with Adorno's past work. Regardless, Adorno assumes that the readers of the column take the horoscopes up as a belief system and not only as a form of entertainment, making astrology potentially different from other products of the culture industry. Though Adorno recognizes that "[t]he sharp division between alchemy and chemistry, between astrology and astronomy is a comparatively late achievement," he restricts his discussion to print, "pulp" astrological resources of his present day and generalizes from those (Adorno 1974: 50). In fact, Adorno mentions several astrological magazines but cites only one, *Forecast*, Winter Issue 1953, "Daily Advice for Virgo" (Adorno's sun sign, by the way) (Adorno 1974: 59). All other citations are from Righter's column in the LA *Times*. The received knowledge in the case of Righter's column expresses the dominion of an "abstract authority" – a boss that is both everywhere and nowhere with instructions on how one can win the game and climb the hierarchy with the right kind of specific knowledge, one who commands authority and is cold, distant, and inexplicable (Adorno 1974: 58).

As Adorno reads the column, its function seems to be to prime people to be functionaries of late capitalism. The horoscopes dole out advice, detached from the cosmos or any higher meaning beyond everyday functioning; there is no "as above" reference to the movement of the planets – only "so below" matters are addressed in the column. Signaled by the persistent phrase "business as usual," the content of the column is consistently about getting ahead at work, suppressing desires, and conforming to stay out of trouble and in the boss's good graces (Adorno 1974; 66). This received astrology functions like dreams for Freud, a normalizing function or coping mechanism that allows us to tolerate intolerable conditions demanded of us by civilization. However, unlike dreams which emerge from our own unconscious, the astrology of the column is a ready-made and received language that is not our own (Adorno 1974: 67). As in dreams, nonsense can seem to have its own interior logic that makes sense within its enclosed context. Adorno calls this feature of astrology "fictious reasonableness" (Adorno 1974: 68).

Righter appeals to the narcissism of the reader and the notion that one is the protagonist of one's own story while simultaneously appealing to anxiety, a recurring theme of threat, and the promise of relief from threat. The reader is attracted to the dream-like state of passivity, accepting their fate, and avoidant of activity that would chart their own course (Adorno 1974: 74). The reader hears the story of themselves: although they are subject to powerful others such as the powerful boss-father and other experts, they are assured of a happy ending if they play their cards right. This adherence to the status quo demands the renunciation of desires for the sake of the future or for "success" defined as pleasing the boss rather than oneself. If this strategy outlined in the horoscope fails, then it is the fault of the individual rather than the social situation. "They [the horoscopes] are indeed nothing but messages from the social status quo in the way it is conceived by the column. The over-all rule of the column is to enforce the requirements society makes on each individual so that it might 'function.' The more irrational the requirements, the more they call for irrational justifications" (Adorno 1974: 80). This leads Adorno to claim that astrology is an "ideology for dependence" (Adorno 1974: 155).

The requirements set out in the column aim to assuage and calm the neurotic subject that is presumed by Adorno to be the reader or target of the column. The reader is torn between contradictory aims: being virtuous versus getting what they want and indulging in pleasure. Like any product of late capitalism, the column has to take up these contradictory desires and try to satisfy both, taking a bi-phasic approach that accommodates both impulses (Adorno 1974: 89). For Adorno, astrology as transmitted by the column actually normalizes neurosis. "Defenses and behavioral patterns of this kind [bi-phasic] while actually neurotic are systematized and presented as normal and wholesome throughout the set-up of the column. As a matter of fact, this principle of organization permeates it to such an extent that most of the specific devices now to be analyzed can and will be presented within the framework of the bi-phasic approach" (Adorno 1974: 97). Conversely, it could be said that astrology normalizes the human tendency to attempt to see patterns in nature and to invest the material world with meaning, for better or worse. Adorno seems to be saying that there is a tipping point where we overinvest and overinterpret the meaning of nature such that our interpretations become the occult (Adorno 1974: 243–244). This bi-phasic approach structures the analysis along these bi-phasic themes: work and pleasure; adjustment and individuality; and ruggedness and dependence.

While all of Adorno's analysis of the column may be true, Adorno also writes about astrology more generally as a particularly troubling subset of occult practice. Astrology is a "pseudo-rationality," an irrationality embedded in a kind of rationality (Adorno 1974: 47). This sort of irrationality exploits a certain kind of "psychotic character" prone to "delusions" (Adorno 1974: 47). For Adorno, it is the political implications of intermingling the irrational and rational that creates the danger in astrology:

> It is in this spirit that we take up the study of astrology, not because we overrate its importance as a social phenomenon per se, nefarious though it is in various respects. Accordingly, the specific nature of our study is not a direct psychoanalysis of the occult, of the type initiated by Freud's famous essay "The Uncanny" and followed up by numerous scientific ventures, now collected by Dr. Devereux in *Psychoanalysis and The Occult*. We do not want to examine occult experiences or individual superstitious beliefs of any kind as expressions of the unconscious. In fact, the occult as such plays only a marginal role in systems such as organized astrology. Its sphere has little enough in common with that of the spiritualist who sees or hears ghosts or with telepathy.
>
> ADORNO 1974: 48

So, though more ostensibly normal than spiritualism, astrology exists in a "twilight zone" between reason and unconscious urges (Adorno 1974: 53), thinly veiled in an "authoritarian cloak" (Adorno 1974: 52). Adorno claims that its message is in the content itself, but then only examines a small fraction of the content. He claims without much knowledge of astrology beyond Righter's column that astrology in all its iterations is an "ideology of dependence."

According to Adorno, astrology is "secondary superstition" – a passive reception of advice wrapped in vague prediction that does not reveal the source of the methodology of the practice. Astrology as received consists of by-products accepted passively and second-hand and is not part of a tradition or practice that people are engaged in as a search for meaning. Astrology is in this sense, for Adorno, like any product of the culture industry. Though received passively, the transmission of culture industry products and what they do is complex, as Adorno notes in "How to Look at Television":

> When we speak of the multilayered structure of television shows, we are thinking of various superimposed layers with different degrees of manifestness or hiddenness that are utilized by mass culture as a technological means of 'handling' the audience. This was expressed felicitously by Leo Lowenthal when he coined the term 'psychoanalysis in reverse.' The implication is that somehow the psychoanalytic concept of a multilayered personality has been taken up by culture industry, and that the

concept is used in order to ensnare the consumer as completely as possible and in order to engage him psycho-dynamically in the service of
premeditated effects. A clear-cut division into allowed gratifications, forbidden gratifications, and recurrence of the forbidden gratifications in a
somewhat modified and deflected form is carried through.

ADORNO 1954: 166

Though the "handling" of the audience may be in effect for Righter's column,
astrology, unlike television, can also be a practice, an activity that individuals and groups engage in. In this sense, Adorno's insight that astrology is like
dreams is on point. Both dreams and astrology as practiced are creative acts
on the part of the subject rather than passively received cultural products.
They also both serve as coping mechanisms and through interpretative practice can be transformed into insights into the dilemma of the subject, at least
potentially.

In Adorno's claims about astrology generally, he does not directly connect
it to fascism or right-wing movements, but suggests that astrology as received
advice primes people to be especially subject to authority – or perhaps that
authoritarian personalities would be susceptible to the messages contained
therein. While astrology is seen as a "symptom of retrogression" in society like
other forms of propaganda, Adorno draws a link between astrology and psychosis – a link that he says we need to be careful about because it is overly
simplistic, but then abruptly makes (Adorno 1974: 165). How could astrology
have such an impact, and is this link between astrology, authoritarianism, and
even psychosis a necessary one?

This leads us squarely into methodological questions about Adorno's critique of the culture industry more broadly. What does astrology, as a mass cultural product, do to those exposed to it and how does it work? The mechanism
is not clear, as it is not clear in Adorno's analyses of other cultural products.
Despite this lack of mechanism, the message – intentional or unintentional,
reflective of society or intentionally driving us towards authoritarian capitula-
tion – of the analyses are compelling but perhaps oversimplified. As Morelock
describes the process, "Adorno's 'culture industry' model proposes a unidirectional flow of meaning. It is not from 'author' to audience per se, so much as
from system to audience, in other words from the interests of the ruling class
and the perpetuation of the present order, to the passive, more or less duped
audience" (2021: 397). If this is Adorno's model, then any cultural form will
transmit via the system of late capitalism, so there is nothing special about
astrology or the occult as a genre of transmission. The system will subsume
all mass culture. Surely there are more powerful objects of mass cultural

consumption than astrology, which is predominately consumed by women and consumed by a small number of people when compared to television or popular music. There are many questions that Adorno's methodology prompts us to ask. Do cultural products reflect or create desires? And how can we tell if they do anything at all? Do the subjects of capitalism already have the tendency towards totalitarianism built into their psyches regardless of what they consume? Do they develop this tendency over time from the environment that they are subjected to? Is this psyche changeable under different sets of conditions? Upon reading "Stars," it remains unclear how astrology as a broader practice is capable of having the effects of fostering dependence, conformity, and authoritarianism on a large scale.

One problem with Adorno's analyses of the cultural products of jazz and astrology is his painting with an enormously broad brush, his analysis focusing on a limited instantiation of the genre yet making general claims about the nature of the product as a whole and not admitting of any positive or liberatory potential – in part because his dismissal of the cultural form, his lack of curiosity, and his lack of depth of knowledge limit his scope.

2   Curiosities: Women, Jazz, and Psychoanalysis

There are so many curiosities about this out of character text. Though Adorno seems to talk about the occult more broadly, Adorno claims that astrology reveals more about society or is more troubling than other occult practices. Even given his analysis of the rational and irrational elements, it is difficult to see how astrology, in print horoscopes or beyond, is more powerful in ideological function than other religions or spiritual practices not considered to be "occult." One can imagine Adorno just being annoyed by the inanity and conservativism of Righter's column, and this text serving as an outlet for his frustration.

Could Righter's horoscopes just be like any mass-produced product of the time in the U.S. reflecting the conservatism of the early 1950s? Adorno draws such exaggerated conclusions from scant evidence that it is uncharacteristic of him as a thinker, and his reflections in "The Stars Down to Earth" do not quite resonate with his other works. Of particular curiosity about this text is the role of women as the readers of horoscopes, the recurrence of his critique of jazz, and the role of psychoanalysis in Adorno's analysis. Adorno presumes much about the readers of the column without evidence; there is no evidence that any readers take the claims of the column seriously, and he skims over the significance of the gendered presumptions built into the column and its implications – that women are the readers of the column without being directly addressed.

Adorno's treatment of women in "Stars" is out of character with his proto-feminist commitments in his other works, most notably *Dialectic of Enlightenment* (1944) and *Minima Moralia* (1944) (Duford 2007, Hewitt 2006). In a section of the text grappling with the column appealing to individualism on the one hand and the acknowledgement of prevailing outside forces on the other, Adorno describes who he imagines to be the readers of the horoscopes. "Thus precisely the kind of compulsive and isolated elderly women who must provide a good part of the astrological audience are often afraid of any contacts at all" (Adorno 1974: 109). He further characterizes the readers as "psychotic characters" out of touch with reality (Adorno 1974:109). Though seemingly addressed to men, the column according to Adorno appeals to a feminine stereotype, dependent and intellectually enfeebled by late capitalism (Adorno 1974: 162). Righter's depiction of women in the column is similarly dismissive. The role of the wife appears in the column as a conservative anchor, one who thwarts the desires of the imagined male ego-ideal (Adorno 1974:134–135). Many of the demands of the column seem to be directed towards the male reader, but as Adorno claims, are more suitably targeted towards women: " '[b]eing pleasant' [in the column] refers to the petty quarrels particularly characteristic of crankish women from the lower middle classes" (Adorno 1974: 109). The demand for supplication in the advice of the column is described by Adorno in gendered terms. "The net results of the practice furthered by the column is that conflicts should either be altogether avoided or settled by clever meekness – in fact, by a behavior reminiscent of that of the woman who wants to get the better of the man on whom she depends. By contrast there are no concrete references to autonomous and independent behavior" (Adorno 1974: 152). The demand for supplication in the face of authority and the degraded morality of playing the system to get one's way are both portrayed as women's behavior by Adorno, who suggests that the demands of late capitalism are feminizing men. These depictions of women and the feminine and masculine in "Stars" stand in contrast to Adorno's other work that is generally critical of the degradation of women and of dichotomous gendered stereotypes.

The most striking moment in the text is where Adorno has this significant insight: he presumes that the readers of the horoscopes are primarily women – yet the protagonist of Righter's horoscopes is clearly a man. Adorno makes this very significant observation and quickly moves on, chalking up this anomaly to the author of the horoscopes appealing to the vanity of his women readers or as a tacit acknowledgement of male identification, an expression of penis envy or wanting to be men in a patriarchal society (Adorno 1974: 83). As Adorno describes the ego ideal of the column, the imagined figure is male, young, a member of a church, a person with "gifts" but with education unspecified, a vice president or someone in middle management, conscious of their place in the hierarchy, someone with a weak ego engaged in the "pseudo-activity" of phony ambition (what we would today call "networking"), dependent on the system, and a compulsive rule-follower (Adorno 1974: 82). But according to Adorno, this is not the person who reads the column – yet this discrepancy does not strike Adorno as curious or as something to examine further. He even reiterates Righter's imagined addressee by referring to "he/him" (Adorno 1974: 89). Later in the text he writes: "It might be asked how the column's family policy [that the column is written for a male head of household] can be reconciled with our basic assumption that the real addressee is a middle-aged or elderly woman. To this it might be answered that the column, after it has set out to build up the image of a male addressee, has somehow to stick to its guns and follow up this idea with a fair amount of consistency. No fully satisfactory explanation, however, seems available" (Adorno 1974: 137). Between the thin explanation of appealing to women wanting to identify with men, and no explanation at all, Adorno glosses over this significant confusion in the column itself and in his analysis of its power as a cultural product.

Though Adorno claims that the sinister nature of the column is in its content, how can that content have an impact if the intended readers are women who are not represented as protagonists in the column? Adorno portrays the readers of Righter's column as women who sound like Freud's description of the superego as the spinster in the attic; yet, this column is supposed to appeal to them? Though Adorno is correct that astrology has been primarily marketed to and consumed by women, at least in the contemporary U.S., why would this column have the power to affect or pre-structure anyone's consciousness on a mass level? The advice of the column seems to point towards making adjustments that create a better fit to late capitalist society by being more extroverted, and yet more responsive to those in authority. However, this advice is more suited to the male ego-ideal of Righter's column than its actual readers – assuming those readers are indeed women. This advice is certainly not suitable for U.S. women in the early 1950s who are out of the flow of any sense of professional power. There is a certain nonsensical role for women in the column that is replicated in Adorno's analysis.

At several moments in the text, Adorno mentions jazz as an analogue to astrology. Both are guilty of "pseudo-individualization" and "semi-erudition," the same sort of seeming to be other than they really are. In referring to the formula of the column as appealing to everyone's desire to be special, yet appealing to the masses in a generic way, Adorno cites his own work "On Popular

Music" to define pseudo-individualization in footnote 10: "[b]y pseudo-individualization we mean endowing cultural mass production with a halo of free choice or open market on the basis of standardization itself" (Adorno 1974: 167). In emphasizing the passivity and dependence fostered by the column, Adorno claims that the "threat-help" pattern of the column is parallel to that found in "women's daytime serial and soap operas" which "generally follow the formula 'getting into trouble and out again,' a device which incidentally seems also to be valid for jazz which constantly employs and resolves some kind of 'jam'" (Adorno 1974: 75). Presumably this pattern is designed to assure us that everything will ultimately resolve and be OK, despite our powerlessness (Adorno 1974: 76).

I think there is an analogue with Fumi Okiji's critique in her book *Jazz as Critique: Adorno and Black Expression Revisited*. Okiji critiques Adorno for not understanding "the principles of structuration of jazz" (Okiji 2018: 12) and also not understanding, or even attempting to understand, the history of oppression and racism experienced by Black people in the U.S. "Is it really possible to mount an effective evaluation of jazz complicity without understanding the very particular relation black life has to America, democracy, and liberty?" (Okiji 2018: 22). Adorno covers his ignorance with silence on the topic, which is surprising given that his work on anti-Semitism and racism in other contexts is so sophisticated, particularly in *The Authoritarian Personality* (1950). Though some argue (see Robinson 1994, Daniel 1989-90) that Adorno's understanding of jazz is limited to the style labeled "jazz" as imported and appropriated in the Weimar Republic, in "On Jazz" Adorno is clearly talking about jazz as a musical form through the lens of his understanding (or misunderstanding) of it and he has to have understood the rootedness of those musical forms in Black culture. Even after his exposure to U.S. culture and presumably more familiarity with jazz music, Adorno did not revise his views on jazz. Similarly, Adorno gives a cursory treatment of astrology from the source of one column without the curiosity to explore astrology as a more complex practice with a complex history. Both jazz and astrology are more complex than Adorno presents them, and both are collaboratively practiced by subaltern people. Adorno's dismissiveness of, and lack of curiosity about, astrology as something consumed by women is perhaps similar to Adorno's treatment of jazz and his silence on anti-Black racism. Adorno does, however, associate astrology with racism as shallow ways of thinking that seem deeper than they are: "To him [the semi-erudite], astrology, just as other irrational creeds like racism, provides a shortcut by bringing the complex to a handy formula and offering at the same time the pleasant gratification that he who feels to be excluded from educational privileges nevertheless belongs to the minority of those who are 'in the know'"

(Adorno 1974: 61). However, Adorno gives astrology the most shallow of treatments and then makes sweeping claims about its shallowness, perhaps in a fashion similar to his treatment of jazz.

Though the conclusions drawn in "Stars" are akin to Adorno's work on authoritarianism and the culture industry, the primary lens that he uses to read Righter's column is psychoanalysis and is mostly independent of reference to his other cultural critiques. Though Adorno presents no evidence of how readers actually take up the horoscopes – a problem of his cultural analysis more broadly – Adorno claims that they are presented as though they are a "new father figure" to be obeyed to gain favor (Adorno 1974: 58). At other moments, Adorno talks about the column reinforcing a skewed function of the superego, providing a false sense of self as an executive in control while simultaneously infantilizing the reader with demands and imperatives (Adorno 1974: 114–117). However, this morality does not come from within or from an internalized parental voice, but is a morality externalized, alienated from the individual and in league with their desire to appear virtuous and to not get caught when fulfilling their desires (Adorno 1974: 120–121). For Adorno, astrology is a dream-like wish fulfillment that anesthetizes readers so that they can tolerate the intolerable and adjust to society as it is (Adorno 1974: 67). Its dream-like quality is reinforced by it being nonsense that seems to make sense only within its own context (Adorno 1974: 68). "Viewed psychoanalytically the interpretation of astrological ambition to present an apocryphal cult as scientific in order to assuage a bad conscience probably does not go deep enough. The ideal of security, the conquest of anxiety, seems to be involved. There exists a compulsive fear of committing an error, and as a correlate, a high gratification in being 'absolutely right' even if irreproachability may be obtained only by complete triviality and meaninglessness – philosophy reminiscent of the pedantry of the anal character" (Adorno 1974: 127). In this picture, the column seizes upon the basic desires and psychology of the reader and deforms them to worsen neurotic and anal tendencies while feeding a conventional, capitalist morality that appeals to the voracity of the id and the vanity of the ego.

Though a psychoanalytic lens is present in Adorno's other works, in "Stars" it takes center stage. But, given the narrowness of Adorno's analysis, is the column powerful enough to create these outcomes? Even if Adorno is right about the aims of the column, conscious or not, can it create effects in readers who may not take the content at all seriously? There are similar messages and mechanisms in traditional religions that are likely more powerful in creating the psychological picture Adorno paints. Psychoanalysis is further a curious methodology to use in the analysis of astrology since they have similar characteristics; both are pseudosciences without empirical grounding that create a language and an interpretive system which potentially gives us insights into individual identity and collective action.

For Adorno, psychoanalysis provides the language for the interpretation of astrology as expressing our damaged psychology and unspoken desires. Psychoanalysis is presented as a more rational approach to think through our predicament under late capitalism though it is, like astrology, another interpretive and pseudoscientific language. The legitimacy of psychoanalysis goes unquestioned and is not applied to himself as the person conducting the analysis. Though searching for insights, Adorno does not examine the source of his own frustrations or the sources of his own damaged perspective on jazz or on women in this text. While Adorno explores the ways that astrology can make us passive, he also provides some insights into the discontents that astrology seems to address.

3   Disenchantment and Dissociation

In seems clear from the reading above that astrology is not enough to create the passivity and authoritarian tendencies inherent in late capitalism, but why do people seemingly lose their capacity to act? Marx had an explanation in his account of alienation. Marx's account of alienation from self, nature, species being, and from others in the *Economic and Philosophic Manuscripts* rings true for labor today. "The alienation of the worker in his product means not only that his labor becomes an object, an external existence, but that it exists outside him, independently, as something alien to him, and that it becomes a power of its own confronting him. It means that the life which he has conferred on the object confronts him as something hostile and alien" (Marx 1844: 108). We lose our capacity to act by becoming disconnected from nature and from ourselves.

Nature for Adorno is the material substrate with which we have a mediated relationship. Unlike Marx, Adorno contends that we never have an unmediated relationship to nature. Nature cannot be fully reconciled in consciousness or fully known without mediation (Cook 2007: 50). Alienation from nature is the precursor to Horkheimer and Adorno's idea of disenchantment. Disenchantment, as a product of the Enlightenment, is the result of the natural and material world losing its mystery and unfixedness, becoming the object of science, explained by a certain narrow application of reason alone and no longer serving as a source of creativity. Speaking of the lack of creativity and intractability of Kant's pure reason, "[t]he mastery of nature draws the circle into which the criticism of pure reason banished thought" (Horkheimer &

Adorno 1944: 26). Nature is no longer a romantic source of meaning or inspiration, it is simply the set of mechanisms of the material world, wholly knowable and fully explained by a quantitative approach. Nothing more needs to be said or thought about nature. Alison Stone explains it this way:

> According to a familiar narrative, the emergence of modernity has involved a 'disenchantment' of nature. By disenchantment is meant: (1) that we have ceased to see nature as an inherently meaningful order; (2) that we have come to assume that nature is devoid of mystery, wholly accessible to our understanding; and (3) that we no longer find nature 'sacred', peopled by divine or demonic beings and worthy of reverence or dread.
>
> STONE 2006: 231

But this domination does not stop with the material world; the world of concepts and ideas is restricted within this narrow band of thought as well. "Ultimately, the Enlightenment consumed not just the symbols but their successors, universal concepts, and spared no remnant of metaphysics apart from the abstract fear of the collective from which it arose" (Horkheimer & Adorno 1944: 23). If a certain kind of reason dominates concepts as well, then the possibility for creativity goes with it. It seems that Horkheimer and Adorno attribute the desire for control of ideas to the fear of collective action, perhaps both political and economic. "It is not merely that domination is paid for by the alienation of men from the objects dominated: with the objectification of spirit, the very relations of men – even those of the individual to himself – were bewitched. The individual is reduced to the modal point of the conventional responses and modes of operation expected of him" (Horkheimer & Adorno 1944: 28). This is how humans are reduced, squeezed into a narrow band of rational thought, under conditions of the Enlightenment.

Rather than simply call for a re-enchantment of the natural world, as some environmental philosophers do, Horkheimer and Adorno recognize that appeals to nature as guides in social and economic relationships (think of gender, race, class) lead us to uphold the status quo in a way that is unchallengeable. They warn of a re-enchantment that takes place within the restrictive rationality of the Enlightenment, which put us under the spell of a naturalistic fallacy by way of excessive reverence for "human nature." Simply re-enchanting the natural world or the world of ideas will not work unless that re-enchantment is of a specific kind that does not fix nature in place and continue to insist on subsuming what we encounter in the natural or human worlds into fixed categories. As unpacked in the next section, astrology, as a practice, may have the potential to reconnect us to nature and to our individuality in ways that fuel the re-enchantment that breaks us out of a singular view of human nature and fixed state of the world.

According to Alison Stone, the dual themes of enchantment and disenchantment continue in Adorno's critique of reason. Adorno later identifies the narrow funnel of pure reason as "identity thinking," which subsumes all particulars under pre-explained categories and concepts so that nothing new can be found under the sun. By contrast, Adorno suggests that we should think in constellations. "Because thinking in constellations gives us only a sense of things in their specificity, it embodies an implicit acknowledgement that things cannot be fully understood in conceptual terms. *Negative Dialectics* thus implies that constellations 're-enchant' things: first, by making us aware that they are partly mysterious (in respect of their unique specificity, which cannot be conceptually understood), and, second, by giving us a sense that things in their uniqueness are meaningful" (Stone 2006: 242). Thinking in terms of constellations includes both theories and practices that break new ground, as well as artistic expressions of all sorts.

Working in tandem with disenchantment is the lack of connection to ourselves and the inability to experience ourselves. Adorno claims that the function of culture in the truest sense is to connect to ourselves, but that ready-made, prefabricated cultural products (like astrology, soap operas, and jazz) thwart our ability to experience ourselves as ourselves (Adorno 1944: 65). Psychoanalysis certainly gives us the notion that the self is a patchwork of pieces sown together from which we create a continuity of experience that makes sense to us, and that this synthesis of pieces that we are not fully aware of is the human condition. However, dissociation is a feature of this patchwork human consciousness when we cannot fully synthesize our experience in response to a certain reality. Interestingly, a clear and concise definition of dissociation is hard to come by, but piecing one together from various psychodynamic therapists, it is a feeling of being "not-me" or partially "not-me" and in some sense putting away or hiding features of ourselves in relation to others as a response to trauma, both big and small (Bromberg 2003, Stern 2010). Dissociation can be described as "detachment, depersonalization, and automatization" as exemplified by Radiohead's lyrics "This isn't me. This isn't happening" (Tucker 2003: 85), but in an interpersonal setting – having such an experience with someone else.

Distinguishing the normal from the pathological through the concept of dissociation is not so easy. Elizabeth Howell, a psychoanalytic practitioner, writes:

> [Dissociative Identity Disorder] is a prototype for the dissociative struc-
> ture of the mind. I am in agreement with Bromberg (1998, 2006) that this
> mental structure characterizes us all. Taking into account the inevita-
> bility of trauma, especially relational trauma, and the fact that dissocia-
> tion is a common aspect of trauma, how could it be otherwise? Many of
> today's clinicians are increasingly appreciative of a multiple-self view of
> the personality and the dissociative structure of the human mind. From
> this perspective, none of us is a singular unit, but rather a highly orga-
> nized aggregation of self-states that are internally dissociated to varying
> degrees and in varying ways.
>
> HOWELL 2011: xviii–xix

Dissociation is what happens to us when there is a collective trauma, a political trauma, that creates the shocking strangeness (Bromberg 2003: 13) that the
world is not what we thought it was and the people (and structures and institutions) that we rely on prove unreliable. This is how the moral self bifurcates,
due to our coping mechanisms making us numb to reality and obscuring our
part in shaping that reality.

In late capitalism, we are all currently operating within a sphere of severe
dissociation, where our experiences are disconnected from the reality we presume exists. On one level, this is not simply a temporary state of affairs, but
a permanent one, because that reality is perpetually shifting under foot, and
the people doing the experiencing are multiple in their perspectives and identities. This dissociation is compounded by narratives which separate us from
each other and dominant ideologies that prevail over new evidence (including
our own new experiences). Astrology is also a mediated relationship to nature;
a human interpretation that is reiterated and altered based on what appears to
us in the material world. This interpretation can steer in any direction, regressive or progressive, depending on our aims. Adorno rightly notes the tendency
in Righter's column to have us look at the mundane and our social status rather
than up at the stars themselves. Astrology narrativized and practiced in other
settings can have the effect of turning our attention to nature, our connection
to the universe, our role in creating the world, and ourselves as embodied.

4   Feminist/BIPOC/Queer Astrology

Despite the curiosities that stem from the short-sightedness in his analysis,
Adorno claims that astrology has a psychological function for people. Astrology
acknowledges the limitations of the social over individual aspirations and

affirms a desire for a certain dignity – that the individual matters within the social processes of which they have little control.

> Who wants to survive under present conditions is tempted to 'accept' such absurdities, like the verdict of the stars, rather than to penetrate them by thinking which means discomfort in many directions. In this respect, astrology is truly in harmony with a ubiquitous trend. In as much as the social system is the 'fate' of most individuals independent of their will and interest, it is projected upon the stars in order thus to obtain a higher degree of dignity and justification in which the individuals hope to participate themselves. At the same time, the idea that the stars, if one only reads them correctly, offer some advice mitigates the very same fear of the inexorability of social processes the stargazer himself creates.
>
> ADORNO 1974: 57–58

In this sense, astrology is a form of psychological self-defense, a reaction formation. In spite of the fact that I am subject to social and economic forces beyond my control that determine my destiny, I have cards to play in my own life. In addition to my individual claim to agency, nature writ large also has influence in the story of my life, and together these can override those broader social and economic forces. Though critical of astrology, Adorno did recognize this potential motivation for the belief in astrology as self-defense (Adorno 1974: 81). That motivation has fueled the development of a feminist astrology and the recent explosion of BIPOC and queer astrologers who are interested in progressive social change.

In the last several years, fueled by social media, astrology has seen a resurgence among the millennial generation (those born between 1981 and 1996). This new mode of astrological thinking has a decidedly feminist, queer, and leftist flavor. So, while Adorno may have evidence that Righter's column in the *LA Times* in the early 1950's has a right-wing and authoritarian bent, contemporary astrology seems to have an opposite political trajectory. In particular, the popularity of Chani Nicholas, whose book *You Were Born for This* (2020c) was a *New York Times* bestseller, seems to validate the desire for astrology with a leftist political flavor. Nicholas' astrological work, which also includes her online workshops, blog, social media feeds, and app have an overtly leftist, feminist, and queer message. She is the most famous of the many feminist, queer, and BIPOC astrologers who are using social media and connecting their content to progressive social movements. Other astrologers working in a similar vein include Alice Sparkly Kat, Diana Harper, Kirah Tabourn, and Renee Stills. These astrologers can trace their lineage through feminist astrologers like Demetra George (1986), Geraldine Hatch Hannon (1990), Lindsay River and Sally Gillespie (1987), and to writers on feminist spirituality like Starhawk (1979), Merlin Stone (1976), Monica Sjöö and Barbara Mor (1987), and Riane Eisler (1987). A common thread among these earlier feminist writers is recovering a history and sense of power from a distant past and using that spirituality to undo the patriarchy. The trend of left-leaning and feminist spiritual practices is a long one, and the contemporary astrologers inspiring social movements is part of a longer standing project within feminist movements.

The contemporary astrology created by feminist, BIPOC, and queer people differs from Adorno's profile of astrology in several ways. First, the demand that astrology be rational or scientific is absent. The fact that astrology is irrational and unprovable by scientific method is taken as true. When asked about skeptics of astrology in an interview, astrologer Chani Nicholas asserts that she does not care what they think, as it is not her job to convince people to engage with astrology. "I don't [care] – I love them [skeptics]! I don't think everyone should believe in astrology. I don't think everyone should use astrology. I think humans are diverse and we should have diverse ways of seeing ourselves and knowing ourselves. And God forbid everyone's on one thing!" (Nicholas, 2020b). The job of astrology in this view is not to convince or proselytize or to feign claims that astrology is a science. Within the context of her work questioning the origins and past aims of Western astrology, Alice Sparkly Kat says this: "Astrology is often compared to race. Both are exercises in imagination, pattern making, and the making of types. Both astrology and race are types of magical thinking and are not rational. Both astrology and race are social constructs and are rooted in the circulations of culture" (Kat 2021: 1). Though irrational, perhaps both race and astrology can be reframed and reconceived to recoup personal and political power by providing a standpoint through which to act, either through identity politics in the case of race or from a standpoint of connecting to nature in astrology.

The second difference between Adorno's account of astrology and contemporary astrology is the motivation for the engagement.[2] The contemporary aim is particularly opposed to conservatism and traditional seats of religious power. In a somewhat dismissive op-ed in *The New York Times*, David Brooks cites statistics on the current popularity of astrology among younger people. "According to a 2018 Pew poll, 29 percent of Americans say they believe in astrology. That's more than are members of mainline Protestant churches. This

---

2   I use the term "engagement" instead of "belief" since interest and use of astrology is distinct from a wholesale belief in a traditional sense.

surge in belief is primarily among the young. According to the National Science Foundation survey, 44 percent of 18- to 24-year-olds say that astrology is somewhat or very 'scientific.' Unsurprisingly, online horoscope sites are booming. Stella Bugbee, editor of *The Cut* told *The Atlantic* in 2017 the typical horoscope got 150 percent more traffic than it had the year before" (Brooks 2019). What Brooks gets right in the op-ed is the connection of astrology to other left-wing movements and practices, including the resistance witches who cast a hex on then Supreme Court nominee Brett Kavanaugh in 2018 and Brooke's much decried "wokeness," which those on the left frame as accountability for sexism, racism, and heterosexism. It seems that conservatives like Brooks are not enamored of the trends of contemporary astrology or the lack of appeal of traditional (conservative) religious authority, particularly Protestantism, the seat of right-wing political theology in the U.S.

The alternative to traditional religion is part of the appeal of astrology for the contemporary left.

> Since the dawn of colonial white-supremacist patriarchy, queer people have been vilified – in part through the enforcing of the gender binary. The violence of this philosophy has been proliferated by religious institutions like Christianity and Judaism that have allowed homophobic and transphobic violence to fester inside of their communities. For hundreds of years, queers have felt unwelcome in many traditional religious and spiritual settings. However, the search for meaning and ritual is ever-present for most humans.
>
> Practices like astrology have been appealing to the queer community in part because of its more inclusive and holistic look at human life. That isn't to say homophobia and transphobia aren't prevalent in astrological communities, but the practice [of astrology] itself is fairly accepting of us. [While] astrology isn't a religion, it connects us with something larger than ourselves without the politics that comes with institutionalized religion. It always comes down to being validated. We need accurate reflections of ourselves in order to heal and grow. When you grow up and out of a society that tells you that you are wrong, astrology becomes a system that affirms your essential nature.
>
> NICHOLAS 2020a

Beyond queer identity, the right-wing shift of Christianity in the U.S. has alienated people on the left, leaving them looking for other spiritual identities and communities that reflect their aims. "A lot of people, whether they're millennials or boomers, white or other, queer or cisnormal, have told me they were first attracted to astrology because it seems to offer a way to talk among ourselves about ourselves without having to address the trappings of identity. Rather than talking about ourselves within the typical categories of race, gender, and class, people want to build community around identities that feel authentic and close. Astrology fans want identity to be as complex as humanity" (Kat 2021: 9). The notion that astrology helps people feel "seen" in their particularity and as members in a community with similar aims is a consistent thread through contemporary astrology. As Kat suggests, perhaps this has the effect of increasing individuation rather than leveling it off as products of the culture industry tend to do in serving capitalism.

That is not to say that astrology is not potentially a part of the culture industry or cannot be used for right-wing ends. Contemporary astrology, for all of its memes, at its best is also an attempt to use astrology as a platform for action by seriously reckoning with a complicated past of which astrology itself is a part.

> In order to make astrology a more responsible cultural practice, we must understand how astrological meaning has been constructed within political economic history. We must understand what astrology has to do with courts, militaries, rule, and power – with capital, power, and labor. We must do this so we understand how it exists within neoliberalism, so we are able to make it our own again. A lot of people are surprised when I tell them astrology has lived longer as a right-wing practice than anything left-leaning. I don't understand why Adolph Hitler, J.P. Morgan, and Ronald Reagan all used astrology. This didn't happen because of the funny quirks of a few otherwise rather despicable men, nor is it a funny coincidence. It happens because due to the nature of astrology's lineage, like whiteness, it makes itself visible when certain sociopolitical relations are under threat.
>
> KAT 2021: 5–6

Skepticism about astrology itself and its role in the distant and recent past can be part of the practice. In this way, astrology is like critical theory, reading the patterns and signs of the past to create a different future, which starts with new language. This can take the form of encouraging people to channel Cancer season energy to take care of each other upon the overturning of Roe v. Wade (Kadlec 2022) or encouraging people to "REBEL AGAINST ALL SYSTEMS OF SUPREMACY" as a way to honor Aquarius season (Nicholas 2022). Predominately via social media, astrology can transmit supportive messages inspiring to the left while forming the basis for community.

Could astrology in this new register be a constructive coping mechanism for women and femmes under patriarchy? Could it perhaps be a way of claiming outsider status and resisting patriarchal views of nature? Astrology is anti-Enlightenment in the sense that it is against the domination of nature. The contemporary feminist/BIPOC/queer astrologers are trying to recoup something lost from an ancient practice and remake it differently. In reproducing something ancient they generate "the reproduction of our collective memory and the cultural symbols that give meaning to our life and nourish our struggles" (Federici 2019: 5). For Silvia Federici, this is the meaning of re-enchantment: "the possibility of recovering the power of collectively deciding our fate on this earth" (8). Astrology could be seen as a way of releasing our desire for domination over nature as well as the desire to control our own nature – to be in tune and in touch with the universe as a larger structure than the material world which has been co-opted by capitalism. "The separation of humankind from nature and the species's denial over its own nature is reflected as well in relations between human beings. Control over nature and self-control find political expression in forms of social domination: domination over 'primary nature' is reproduced in domination over 'second nature'" (Alway 1995: 34). As Alway makes the connection between the political control of nature and of the human world, astrology can provide a powerful counter narrative to break through that hegemony, even if some regard it as fake or flakey.

5   Conclusion

As Adorno claims, his analysis of astrology is a key, a code, a jumping off point to explore the symptoms of late capitalism (Adorno 1974: 153). In this, his aim succeeds. One of the most prominent attributes in Adorno's writings, and his gift to us, was in writing all of his thoughts down without holding back so that we can see the full measure of his thought. Though "The Stars Down to Earth" is a quirky and deeply flawed text, it provides ways of thinking about nature – both material nature and our own human natures – that resonate. This text is also a lesson in the precariousness of rationality and its limited usefulness as a weapon of critique. In using rationality as a weapon in this text, Adorno has shown us just how much we need to think in constellations to find meaning.

At the core of his philosophical work, Adorno is an anti-empiricist (Jay 1984: 50) because the world is already warped and broken by us so the truth cannot be found there. To address a world that has been fundamentally damaged, and our lives and perspectives along with it, one cannot rely on empirical method alone to get at the truth. A fractured reality requires a fractured methodology. Then, what do we need as tools to help us re-enchant the world? What should our relationship to nature be? How do we analyze past culture and create it anew knowing that we need something that mediates our connection to nature? We will need to continue to think in constellations that foster creativity in ways that may seem unreal, fantastic, utopian, and negative in Adorno's sense, negating the compelling world of the status quo to do the work we need to do to repair the damage done to nature and ourselves.

References

Adorno, Theodor W, Else Frenkel-Brunswik, Daniel J. Levinson, and R. Nevitt Sanford. 1950/ 2019. *The Authoritarian Personality*. New York: Verso.

Adorno, Theodor W. 1954/ 1991. "How to Look at Television" in *The Culture Industry: Selected Essays on Mass Culture*. J.M. Bernstein (ed.). New York: Routledge. 158–177.

Adorno, Theodor W. 1947/ 1974. *Minima Moralia: Reflections from Damaged Life*. Translated by E. F. N. Jephcott. New York: Verso.

Adorno, Theodor W. 1974/ 1994. *"The Stars Down to Earth" and Other Essays on the Irrational in Culture*. Edited by Stephen Crook. New York: Routledge.

Alway, Joan. 1995. *Critical Theory and Political Possibilities: Conceptions pf Emancipatory Politics in the Works of Horkheimer, Adorno, Marcuse, and Habermas*. Westport, CT: Greenwood Press.

Bromberg, Philip M. 2003. "One Need Not Be a House to Be Haunted: On Enactment, Dissociation, and the Dread of 'Not-M' – A Case Study." *Psychoanalytic Dialogues* 13, no. 5: 689–709.

Brooks, David. 2019. "The Age of Aquarius, All Over Again!" *New York Times*, June 10, 2019. https://www.nytimes.com/2019/06/10/opinion/astrology-occult-millennials.html.

Campion, Nicholas. 2012. *Astrology and Cosmology in the World's Religions*. New York: New York University Press.

Campion, Nicholas. 2009. *History of Western Astrology I: the Ancient World*. New York: Bloomsbury.

Campion, Nicholas. 2009. *History of Western Astrology II: the Medieval and Modern Worlds*. New York: Bloomsbury.

Campion, Nicholas and Dorian Geiseler Greenbaum (eds.). 2016. *Astrology in Time and Place: Cultural Questions in the History of Astrology*. Newcastle, UK: Cambridge Scholars Publishing.

Cook, Deborah. 2007. "Nature, Red in Tooth and Claw." *Continental Philosophy Review* 40: 49–72.

Daniel, Jaime Owen. 1989–90. "Introduction to Adorno's 'On Jazz.'" *Discourse*, 12, no. 1: 39–44.

Duford, Nathan. 2007. "Daughters of the Enlightenment: Reconstructing Adorno on Gender and Feminist Praxis" *Hypatia*, 32, no. 4 (Fall): 784–800.

Eisler, Riane. 1987. *The Chalice and The Blade: Our History, Our Future*. New York: HarperCollins.

Federici, Silvia. 2019. *Re-Enchanting the World: Feminism and the Politics of the Commons*. Oakland, CA: PM Press.

George, Demetra & Douglas Bloch. 1986/ 2003. *Asteroid Goddesses: the Mythology, Psychology, and Astrology of the Re-emerging Feminine*. Lake Worth, FL: Ibis Press.

Hanon, Geraldine Hatch. 1990. *Sacred Space: a Feminist Vision of Astrology*. Ithaca, NY: Firebrand Books.

Hewitt, Andrew. 2006. "A Feminine Dialectic of Enlightenment?" In *Feminist Interpretations of Adorno*, edited by Renée Heberlee, 69–96. University Park: Pennsylvania State University Press.

Horkheimer, Max. & Adorno Theodor W. 1944/ 1993. *Dialectic of Enlightenment*. Translated by John Cumming. New York: Continuum.

Howell, Elizabeth F. 2011. *Understanding and Treating Dissociative Identity Disorder: a Relational Approach*. New York: Routledge.

Jay, Martin. 1984. *Adorno*. Cambridge, MA: Harvard University Press.

Kadlec, Jeanna. 2022 "The new moon in cancer for writers." *Substack*, June 29, https://jeannakadlec.substack.com/p/the-new-moon-in-cancer-for-writers-c49.

Kat, Alice Sparkly. 2021. *Post-Colonial Astrology: Reading the Planets through Capital, Power, and Labor*. Berkeley, CA: North Atlantic Books.

Lybarger, Jeremy. 2015. "Ronald Reagan's Black Magic Man." *Guernica Magazine*, January 26, 2015. https://www.guernicamag.com/jeremy-lybarger-ronald-reagans-black-magic-man/.

Marx, Karl. 1844/ 1964. "Estranged Labor." In *The Economic and Philosophic Manuscripts of 1844*. Translated by M. Milligan, 106–119. New York: International Publishers.

Morelock, Jeremiah. 2021. "Siegfried Kracauer and the Interpretation of Films" in *How to Critique Authoritarian Populism: Methodologies of the Frankfurt School* (Morelock, ed.) Leiden, ND: Brill. 391–411.

Nicholas, Chani. "Welcome to Aquarius Season," Instagram, January 19, 2022. https://www.instagram.com/p/CY75GnNrCYT/.

Nicholas, Chani. 2020a. "Chani Nicholas is Queering Astrology One Meme at a Time." Interview by Marina Wantanabe. *Bitch Magazine*, January 7, 2020. https://www.bitchmedia.org/article/bitch-interview/chani-nicholas-queering-astrology.

Nicholas, Chani. 2020b. "The Existential Lure of Astrology" Interview by Nayomi Reghay. *Vox*, January 20, 2020. https://www.vox.com/identities/2020/1/20/21070974/chani-nicholas-astrology.

Nicholas, Chani. 2020c. *You Were Born for This: Astrology for Radical Self-Acceptance.* New York: Harper Collins.

Okiji, Fumi. 2018. *Jazz as Critique: Adorno and Black Expression Revisited.* Stanford, CA: Stanford University Press.

River, Lindsay and Sally Gillespie. 1987. *The Knot of Time: Astrology and Female Experience.* London: The Women's Press.

Robinson, J. Bradford. 1994. "The Jazz Essays of Theodor Adorno: Some Thoughts on Jazz Reception in Weimar Germany" *Popular Music*, 13, no. 1: 1–25.

Sjöö, Monica and Barbara. Mor. 1987. *The Great Cosmic Mother: Rediscovering the Religion of the Earth.* San Francisco: Harper & Row.

Starhawk. 1979. *The Spiral Dance: a Rebirth of the Ancient Religion of the Great Goddess.* San Francisco: Harper & Row.

Stern, Donnel B. 2010. *Partners in Thought: Working with Unformulated Experience, Dissociation and Enactment.* New York: Routledge.

Stone, Alison. 2006. "Adorno and the Disenchantment of Nature" *Philosophy and Social Criticism*, 32:2. 231–253.

Stone, Merlin. 1976. *When God Was a Woman.* New York: Harcourt.

Tarnas, Richard. 2006. *Cosmos and Psyche: Intimations of a New World View.* New York: Viking.

Tucker, Shawn. 2003. "The Aesthetics of Dissociation: Radiohead's 'How to Disappear Completely' and Jasper John's Device Paintings." *Soundings: an Interdisciplinary Journal* 96, no. 1: 85–98.

PART 4

Socialized Nature: Essential Categorical Questions in Science

∴

CHAPTER 13

Negative Dialectics and the Force of Matter

Theodor W. Adorno and Karen Barad: towards a New-Material Feminism for Thinking Contemporary Crises

Simon Reiners

Critical social theory, at least since Marx, is based on the consistently materialistic conviction that Being (as social existence) determines consciousness. However, the configuration of the world is not seen as ontologically, naturalistically given, but as having become in historical-practical processes. Accordingly, the justification of social practices is replaced by the description of the historical-practical becoming of an ensemble of relations through practices and the consideration of the material surroundings of the reproduction of activities. Indispensably linked to this is the description of the structures that are at a specific historical moment responsible for the distribution and possibility of suffering and happiness (Horkheimer 1988a: 105). Marx's historical-materialism, for instance, examined these structures in what he described as the transition from bourgeois society to human society during the mid-19th century (Marx and Engels 2010: 5). About eighty years later, for Max Horkheimer, social theory of his day was necessarily an economic theory. An economic theory of society reveals how the distribution of wealth through economic forces enables and obstructs happiness. This displays the central task of critical-historical materialism. It is and has been to give an account of historically grown relations of one time towards the goal of overcoming the inscribed power relations.

Nowadays, the boundaries of what Marx describes as 'human society' and the socio-economic relations that Horkheimer examined have shifted. In times of climate crises and rapid (bio-)technologization, relations are transforming significantly. According to feminist theorists such as Judith Butler and Donna Haraway, this affects the boundaries of public and private as much as those between human and machine or human and nature (Butler 1993; Haraway 2016). Hence, there has been a renewed interest in matter and materiality in recent decades, which is assembled under the term 'New Materialism' (Coole and Frost 2010; Dolphijn and van der Tuin 2012). With reference to current insights from natural science and technology studies, theorists have endeavored to no longer include matter as merely passive material of human action (e.g., Barad 2007; Bennett 2010). They argue that the focus on discourse and culture alone leads to an impoverished understanding of contemporary relations (e.g., Habermas 2003; 2005; Vogel 2015).

It may come as a surprise that the emphasis on the naturalness of humans comes into question for feminist theories. After all, moving away from naturalisms by reference to the linguistic turn and Poststructuralism has been enormously productive for analyzing power, knowledge, subjectivation, and thereby the dissolution of sex and gender (e.g., Butler 1990, Fraser 1989; Scott 1989). However, the developments, which often appear under the term 'Anthropocene', revoke the relevance of materiality, not as the Other of discourse, but as part of anti-essentialist meaning generation (Grusin 2017: viii). Donna Haraway calls this "material-semiotic" (Haraway 2016: 23) and Karen Barad "material-discursive" (Barad 2007: 141).

From the 1970s on, the movement of so-called Ecofeminism pointed out a homology in the construction of femininity and naturalness as passive, regarded as in need of control against dominant, active masculinity. The Ecofeminist theorists identify a connection between ecological exploitation with an exploitation of the female body as a reproductive organism. In both cases, the oppression is evaluated as the result of patriarchy (e.g., Griffin 1978).

The position of Ecofeminism is criticized by today's "Anthropocene Feminism" (Grusin 2017: x) because Ecofeminism itself codifies the dualism of male/female, human/natural. More recent feminist theories, which continue to link women's emancipation with liberation from the domination of nature, see this less as a naturalistic struggle to valorize the other side of such dualisms. Instead, theories from the very diverse spectrum of so-called New-Material Feminisms argue for abolishing these dualisms altogether. In doing so, they point to interconnectedness, interdependence, and responsibility rather than to supposedly natural differences (see Alaimo and Hekman 2008).[1] These non-dualistic positions strive toward growing and living together on a damaged planet without placing human life at the center.

Taking into account these developments of materialist theory originating from recent feminist thought, it can be surprising that the Critical Theory of the Frankfurt School has hardly been confronted with them so far.[2] I argue that

---

1   This is not to be confused with Marxist-Feminism. Marxist-Feminists are more concerned with highlighting how capitalism and private property support the oppression of women rather than deconstructing the socio-material construction of the female and non-human body. (e.g., Federici 2020).

2   For texts on the relation between Haraway and Adorno see Becker-Schmidt (2002); Gransee (1998), and more recently between Adorno and Bennett Rudolph (2019). How this controversy can be omitted is shown most recently in Stögner and Colligs (2022).

the Frankfurt School as critical-historical materialism that describes current (power) relations in order to overcome them has lost its vocabulary to give an account of these contemporary developments. The discourse about these changes is far advanced in the New-Material Feminisms.

Following this, my comprehensive question is: *What kind of materialist perspective does a Critical Theory in the legacy of the Frankfurt School need, in order to live up to the claim of historical materialism?*

That is, what perspective does Critical Theory need to be able to think and describe the changing material relations during times of climate crises and rapid (bio-)technologization. How can contemporary crises be grasped, described, and finally transformed? Such historical materialism would have to escape all scientistic and essentialist reductionism to follow the claim of Critical versus traditional theory (Horkheimer 1988b). At the same time, however, such a perspective would have to offer the possibility of seeing matter as less passively involved in the production of meaning and ensembles of world relations (Coole and Frost 2010).

In the early phase of the Frankfurt School, there is still a certain amount of attention to the significance of nature for social conflicts. In particular, in the *Dialectic of Enlightenment* by Horkheimer and Adorno, they strive for a critical reflection of the natural in relation to reason.

Adorno systematically advances this basic assumption in the *Negative Dialectics*. He strives to describe a materialism that takes the reciprocal mediation of subject and object as the systematic starting point of critical reflection (Adorno 1973: 193). Having said this, New-Material Feminist theorist Karen Barad, based on findings from quantum physics, sees herself in the position of providing a non-essentialist understanding of meaning-generating matter. The concept she derives from this she calls 'agential realism' (Barad 2007). She attempts to show the extent to which subject and object are not enclosed, predetermined entities but rather mutually constitutive (ibid.: 139).

The particular position of Adorno in the Frankfurt School, who still dares to ask the question about the mediation of matter to mind and language, and the non-essentialist elements in Barad's materialism, allow attempting a rapprochement between the Frankfurt School and New-Material Feminism. However, even if, at first, it seems that there are possible overlaps in the two positions, they cannot be easily brought together. Adorno's focus on the rational, enlightened subject, for example, breaks with Barad's posthumanism. Likewise, the respective handling of reality as dialectically mediated versus agentially-objectively given, as well as finally the view on critique and transformation as negative dialectical or performative close themselves to a mere synthesis.

I will therefore, firstly, compare the concepts of materiality, subject, and praxis in the theories of Theodor W. Adorno, as representative of the early Frankfurt School, and Karen Barad as representative of New-Material Feminism. Secondly, I will show homologies but moreover the significant difference between these perspectives. Thirdly, I provide a more profound study of current materialistic (crisis-)phenomena by bringing these two perspectives into conversation. I aim to observe more precisely whether such a collective reading of Adorno and Barad can make visible a non-essentialist materialism; one that can open the view on the material practices of the present that bear *responsibility* for the distribution of happiness and suffering – in the time of the not-so-human Anthropocene.

We are trained to only see the immediate promises of progress, power, and profits. Very particular human means to such ends are for example radioactivity and chemicals.[3] They however leave traces on our human bodies and landscapes alike. They shape planetary times. To see them differently shows the multiple stories that progress, power, and profit entail. How human is the Anthropocene? Who decides what lives and what is disposable? What perspective do we need to see and answer those challenges? "The storm of the Anthropocene itself swoops us off the ladder into the waves of the more than human sea" (Tsing et al. 2017: G9).

1   Materiality, Subject and Praxis

1.1   *Adorno – the Negativity of Materiality*
Together with Kant and Hegel, Adorno shares the conviction that there is an irreducible difference between thinking and being, concept and non-conceptual, subject and object, or spirit (Geist) and matter (Sommer 2016: 201). He argues that the difficult task of philosophy is to "unlock the non-conceptual mediated by the concept and mediated by self-criticism of concepts" (Adorno 2014: 112; transl. SR) – that is: to identify. According to Hegel, this process, as a

---

3 Radioactivity and chemicals are two very present and pressing examples to show the Janus-face of technological progress and the critical changes of the planet. Radioactivity is used to relieve human life from the exhaustion of resources for providing energy. Its disposal, however, changes the life on the planet into an unthinkable future. Chemicals are necessary tools to shape modern human life, development and health. However, these substances are a major part of the exceeding of planetary boundaries, and the effects of most of the 350.000 so far known chemicals is not yet understood. Many other examples could be stressed to that account.

dialectical one, ultimately merges into the subject, which wholly appropriates the object. With reference to Kant's 'thing-in-itself', Adorno counters Hegel that the complete renunciation of referring to a *something* (ein Etwas) outside of thinking ultimately identifies only itself with itself and thus becomes tautological. Knowledge that is pure identification of particulars through general terms makes the thing (die Sache) disappear (Adorno 1973: 184). A previously set irrevocable difference of subject and object disappears in Hegel (ultimately also in Kant) in favor of the omnipotence of the subject.

Adorno, with negative dialectics against Hegelian dialectics, wants to hold on to the task of philosophy to emphasize the Other of thinking *as* Other of thinking (ibid.: 9). Because thinking as identifying obstructs the view of the Other of the subject, this Other can never appear positively for Adorno, but always only as the limit of thinking in thinking itself, hence negatively. This dialectical movement is most evident in the "object's preponderance" (ibid.: 183).

With the object's preponderance, subject is not simply exchanged for object. Adorno wants to express the valorization of the object side via a reciprocal relationship in mediation (Thyen 1989: 209). To this end, he refers to the doubling of both object and subject: on the one hand, *object* is to be understood as that which is withdrawn from but necessary for thinking as an in-itself (O_1). On the other hand, however, object as a concrete object is only mediated by a thinking subject for-us (O_2). Whereas *subject* is always only mediated by the object that it thinks (S_1). However, it does not thereby dissolve itself towards the object since something must think something (S_2). "In truth, the subject is never quite the subject, and the object never quite the object" (Adorno 1973: 175). Thus, as soon as either one appears in consciousness both are not in-themselves, but only become what they are through the other (subject or object). This leads Adorno to abolish the rigid separation of ontology and epistemology since only through recognition do both subject and object co-constitutively become. Nevertheless, they must be thought of as independent of each other, as in O_1 and S_2 (Sommer 2016: 252). The object's preponderance now expresses the importance of what is heterogeneous to the subject for the mediation of the subject: "An object can be conceived only by a subject but always remains something other than the subject, whereas a subject by its very nature is from the outset an object as well. Not even as an idea can we conceive a subject that is not an object, but we can conceive an object that is not a subject" (Adorno 1973: 183). Accordingly, the difference of subject and object is neither absolute (as in the realist sense) nor dissolved (as in the idealist sense) nor 'symmetrical' (or equivalent) but relational amid mutual constitution.

It is only through the examination of the object's preponderance that it is possible to understand what mediation implies and what that, which is not given in the mind, plays for the mind. Adorno's transition to materialism thus results from an immanent critique of idealism and hence of the subject's capacity to synthesize (Sommer 2016: 251). Adorno, though, rejects empiricism's notion of encountering something realistically given by abandoning the subject's epistemological position. Depersonalization of cognition also becomes meaningless. Adorno consequently continues to hold on to the subject as the Archimedean point of philosophy. The question is only how the subject becomes the point of realization of its own incapacity.

This is where Adorno has to introduce the concept of non-identity. For him, the non-identical is precisely not just the ontological determination of that which does not dissolve in thought, such as Kant's thing-in-itself. Non-identity is a mode of cognition, namely the reference to the objection against the absoluteness of the subject and reference to the relevance of that which is not absorbed in thinking (Thyen 1989: 202). The concept of non-identity thus provides the answer to the question of what a materialism is that does not want to set a fundamental determination of matter against the spirit: matter remains *ex negativo* as a counter-concept to spirit, as its undialectical moment that does not make it possible for thought to reach reconciliation: "Viewed from outside, that which in reflecting upon the mind appears specifically as not mental, as an object, is material" (Adorno 1973: 193).

At the same time, however, the material moment is an effective, affective or, one is already tempted to say, forceful carrier of information, making it possible for the subject to realize its limits. Thereby, Adorno also answers the question of how this reflection on the singularity, historicity, and contingency of boundaries becomes possible for the subject. The material occurs very concretely in the subject through somatic moments. Here, in body and suffering, subject and object are directly connected (ibid.: 204). Since, according to Adorno, physical pain is not absorbed in discourse and thus refers to a surplus that, on the one hand, demands to enter philosophy and, on the other hand, ethically demands to pass: "Woe speaks: Go" (ibid.: 203). Experience, not cognition, makes it possible for the subject to become aware of its own temporality and becoming (ibid.: 29). The smallest trace of suffering, Adorno argues, exposes the lies of identitarian philosophy which tried to abandon materiality from claims to knowledge. The specific material moment in this case allows a minimum of such knowledge as "negative knowledge" (ibid.: 405) – that it could be otherwise. This happens to be a thought that identitarian philosophy necessarily attempted to suppress and that converges with critique as a way to praxis (ibid.: 203).

Negative dialectics is thus the claim to the recognition of the material, but unseizable moment of the object and its effects on the subject: The ability to experience this non-identity of the subject puts the latter in the position to step into distance from itself, to reflect on its subjectivation and to develop practices of resistance as a mode for transformation. According to Adorno, however, it remains impossible to capture this experience (linguistically) so that the material actually remains the Other of thought (ibid.: 207). Once language would apprehend experience it loses its materiality and merges entirely into discourse. However, as long as materiality remains the Other of thought, practical subjectivity leaves its exceptional position, gets involved with what is not itself, and is thus at its own limit.

1.2   *Barad – Materiality as Becoming*

Karen Barad takes a unique position in New-Material Feminist perspectives on matter as efficacious, contingent, and relational, and the critique of the ontological priority of the subject (Coole and Frost 2010). She moves on the borders to the often-criticized return to essentialist positions of nature and matter (Lettow 2017: 116). As a quantum physicist and with her reference to Niels Bohr's scientific work on measurements, Barad attempts to show the extent to which subject and object are not pre-given entities but mutually constitutive. Such a non-essentialist feminist reading of 'agential realism', as Barad calls her project, could be explored, subsequent to Adorno's understanding of materiality.

The starting point is Barad's inclusion of the concept of apparatuses. It aims for a materialism without a fundamental determination of the meaning of matter before its production. Following Bohr, apparatuses still refer directly to an arrangement of measuring instruments that bring forth what is measured. Barad, with Foucault and beyond, extends this concept in a direction according to which apparatuses are an arrangement of material-discursive practices, which, however, not only bring forth what is sayable, thinkable, doable, like in dispositifs, but also draw in stable reality, objective entities, and differences in the first place (Barad 2007: 165f.; Hoppe and Lemke 2015: 6). Hence, the hyphen between material and discursive is meant to indicate their entanglement. Neither side possesses an ontological primacy, but the difference between matter and discourse is itself only mutually constitutive.

Only indeterminacy can be quasi-ontologically fundamental. Barad re-reads the philosophical concept of phenomena: "[P]henomena are the ontological inseparability/entanglement [...]. Phenomena are constitutive of reality" (Barad 2007: 139f.). Phenomena thus describe the ontologically primary inseparability between interacting components of reality. They are the non-dualistic whole of relations without relata (ibid.: 128).

In order to understand how differences – or things – can appear within phenomena, Barad introduces the neologism 'intra-action'. This is meant to describe the equiprimordiality (Gleichursprünglichkeit) and reciprocal constitution of objects and subjects within phenomena, in contrast to 'interaction' that takes place between antecedent entities or relations (ibid.: 33). Intraaction is how individual material entities acquire meaning (come to matter) without necessarily being understood as separate from others and supratemporal. There are ongoing processes of materialization "out of nothingness" (Barad 2012a: 7).

Finally, Barad uses the term 'agential cuts' to denote what can be conceived as a subject-object difference at a given spatial and temporal moment through certain material-discursive intra-actions, but without abolishing their fundamental reciprocal condition. Agential cuts are always found within phenomena rather than denoting something outside them. Only by remaining connected subject and object, or object and object, are some*thing*. At this point, Barad's double use of the concept of matter now reveals itself.

On the one hand, she uses the term 'matter' when speaking of objects and subjects as produced by intra-actions (Barad 2007: 810). The question of their genealogy thus comes to the fore. On the other hand, the concept of matter stands for the absolutely indeterminate and thus absolute opposite of subject and object. Matter, similar to Adorno, is without image (bilderlos) instead of being a determinate substance, and at the same time, the open basis for further determinations. As a result, the intra-actively generated bodies always point beyond themselves to an 'it-could-also-be-otherwise' and thus to excluded potentialities. "The reconfiguration of the world continues without end. [...] Boundaries do not sit still" (Barad 2007: 170f.).

This shows how Barad connects to Butler's concept of performativity rather than concepts of representation: Through the procedurality of repeated citation or performance, Butler argues, specific materializations of bodies are brought forth in real terms in regulative practices. They thus demand that the historicity of bodies be taken seriously. At the same time, Butler expects that this shift in the level of description will provide an alternative perspective on possibilities of transformation as permanently drawn boundaries become unstable (Butler 1993: 191f.). Barad aims to transcend Butler's performativity through a posthuman perspective, viewing practice as multiform, non-rational, and materially-discursively rather than only discursively situated. Barad's posthumanism thus does not consist in valorizing the non-human of the human/ non-human dualism, as is often the case in posthumanist positions (Lettow 2017: 116). On the contrary, she wants to enable the overcoming of this dualism (Barad 2007: 151). Posthuman performativity thus concludes by referring to the material-discursive practices of bringing forth and progressively trans-forming world relations without speaking of substantial actors. If reality is a situational-spatio-temporal realm of constant processes, this also opens up for resignification of bodies.

2   Provisional Evaluation

At this juncture, it can be shown how Barad's New-Material Feminism is found in classical historical-materialist terms and finally may be relocated in Adorno's specific version of materiality. That being determines consciousness initially also means that what counts as human at a given time in history is itself a product of the dialectic of nature (Cotter 2016: 173). Posthuman per-formativity makes clear that Barad is precisely concerned at its core with the historicity and genealogy of materializations of reality and thus also of con-sciousness. Moreover, according to Barad, practices of viewing, knowing, and measuring are – following Marx' third Feuerbach-thesis – practices of bringing up the observed (Barad 2012a: 8; Marx and Engels 2010: 4).

However, deviating from Marx, Barad does not presuppose the separation of the cognizing and the cognized. Adorno, too against Marx, does not consider it possible that through the pure cognition of production practices, the possibil-ities are given to step out of one's position, and that thereby means for change are already available (Adorno 1973: 91). All that remains is the recognition of the interconnectedness with processes of constituting the differences between subjects and objects. In Adorno's and likewise Barad's theory, however, the dualism of subject and object is not abolished but shifted: to the critique of the identifying, adequate representational capacity of the world as the apparent basis of cognition. Instead, ontology and epistemology merge, making cogni-tion intelligible in the first place as a process of bringing forth real dualisms.

In conclusion, Barad's and Adorno's concepts of matter, subject, and praxis overlap in the conceptions of "the absence of images" (ibid.: 207) (Bilderlosigkeit) and phenomena. Matter does not constitute the object of cognition. It is the radical difference of that which continuously eludes iden-tifying thought (Adorno) as well as agential cuts (Barad) and yet constitutes their necessary foundation (Hoppe and Lemke 2015: 11; Schmidt 1983: 27). In this way, materialism points to the insufficiency of cognition of the Being-of-the-world: In one case for the speaking subject, in the other case for intelligible bodies in the world. In this manner, matter gains force as the Other of what is, insofar as it provides the impetus for negative dialectic and intra-action. It follows for the subject that thinking or knowing denotes the infinite task for a praxis of self-transgression: *self-transgression* because it is not within the capacity of thinkers and knowers to grasp and change the non-conceptual or phenomena. Materialism in Adorno's and Barad's understanding does not allow to envision the Other of what is; an *infinite task* because the experience of non-identity and intra-actions urge for transgression. For Adorno it is the force of somatic experience, such as suffering, that demands practices of over-coming: "Woe speaks: Go" (Adorno 1973: 203). Posthuman performativity per se is a force to praxis. Neither shows a direction nor aims for that task.

However, such an assessment of Barad's materialism must already show that it is not absorbed in a simple identification with Adorno's position. Agential cuts in phenomena point beyond themselves, can make losses visible, and make it possible to ask what conditions are necessary for such an "other-ness" (Meißner 2016: 4). Matter then is that which also provides the possibility of opening up to the indeterminate, instead of being pure negation of what exists. This movement goes beyond Adorno's absence of images.

3   Considerations

So far, I have shown in which aspects overlappings can be found in the think-ing of Barad and Adorno. However, it would be a hasty conclusion to draw simple analogies and to declare agential realism a renewed form of negative dialectics. To avoid this, I will first show how Barad's agential realism leaves the potential of a critical, negative dialectic unredeemed. Second, I will highlight how Adorno's negative dialectical materialism cannot be simply merged with a New-Material Feminism like Barad's.

3.1   *Barad's Apparatus*
Adorno's negative dialectical critique of conceptualization amounts to point-ing to the subject's precarious access to knowledge (Sommer 2016: 26). Barad's critique of knowledge practices also aims at the inadmissible affirmation of relations as natural, without therefore opposing anything objective or stable. However, Barad loses the possibility of a negative dialectical standpoint that reduces itself to self-criticism: Writing necessarily presupposes a difference between what is written about and those who write it. Hence, the question Barad has to answer to is, how she herself is part of an apparatus that produces world and effect relations – through (her) writing? On the one hand, such a critical reflection is missing in her ahistorical, quasi-authoritarian affirmation of a specific interpretation of quantum physics. On the other hand, it turns phenomena into 'true' ontology instead of drawing ex-negativo the connection

between ontology and epistemology from the failure of substance ontological theories. Dynamics of becoming are 'quasi-natural' in agential realism. Barad would thus have to ask how quantum physics itself is intra-actively produced, interwoven, and engendering; how Barad herself is part of an apparatus (Meißner 2016: 4). Since it lacks this level of reflection, it also escapes the possibility of reflecting on the relations of domination involved, which is a significant aim of the Frankfurt School.

3.2   Potence of the Subject

A crucial aspect for Adorno is the analysis of the subject's incapacity (Menke 2008: 189). Barad likewise decentered the humanistic subject. Nevertheless, her work does not focus on the conditions of impossibility. Agential realism creates matter through the notions of apparatus and phenomenon to the "meta-subject" (Lettow 2017: 112) that is successfully creative through intra-action. Co-constitutive intra-action becomes the positive endowment of difference, rather than looking to the non-identical of mediation that destroys the subject's superiority. In contrast, for Barad, critical reflection on what it means to possess and execute power is lost in the omnipotence of a meta-subject that is self-identical. Self-identity leaves no room for non-identity or difference as spaces of experience of an "Otherwise".

3.3   Contingency and Critique

The risk of losing the ground for critical potential for change by referring to the ontological contingency of real conditions initially affects both Barad and Adorno. However, Adorno remains faithful to the claim to experience modes of domination and coercion in their historicity. For Adorno, recognizing this domination and coercion is at least still possible through the experience of suffering, which cannot be rejected but is a claim for overcoming it (Adorno 1997: 18). Barad's shortcoming in this regard lies in the depersonalization of cognition and the complete abandonment of subject and object separation prior to mutual determination. Insofar as reality constitution depends on conditions (Braunmühl 2017: 6), the idea of a "free flow of being and becoming" (Cotter 2016: 176) runs the risk of obscuring and solidifying relations, since no perspective on conditions under which they became is possible. Karen Barad's agential realism thus apparently falls short of critical potentials to envision real existing coercion and suffering.

But concerns can also be raised against Adorno's materialism. A perspective of a New-Material Feminism calls for thinking his position further. Above all, the focus needs to be laid upon his insistence, albeit critical reflection, on the

necessary assumption of Kant's dualistic two worlds of noumenal and phe-
nomenal things.

3.3.1   Two Worlds: Subject

The core idea of Barad's posthumanism is to abolish the separation of human
subject and non-human object (Barad 2007: 136 fn. 6). The 'force of matter',
as Barad understands it in anti-substantial terms, is the exposure of the false
image of rational, powerful subjects and the end of the question of adequate
representation of the passive material in the subject.

   Negative dialectics is also a critique of this capacity of the subject, directed
against the Enlightenment (Menke 2008: 195): the non-identical reminds
thought of the impossibility of mediation. Adorno, however, does not ask
whether and by what means this subject *is*, but only how *able* it is. All force
to change thus remains with the subject, for instance, by reflecting on emancipatory potentials of language (Hogh 2015: 63f.). The subject remains pre-
constitutive and only its sorts of capacities are in question. The problem is not
one of reality, but of realization. Accordingly, Adorno remains attached to the
ideal of the Enlightenment subject through language critique as the starting
point of the dilemma and the site of liberation.

   A genealogical critique to which Barad's posthumanism amounts, dispenses
entirely with the quasi-metaphysics of a noumenal world. Moreover, on this
path critique can finally dispense with the recourse to a 'true' transcendent
liberated 'Dasein' and remain purely immanent.

3.3.2   Two Worlds: Object

Starting from Bohr's quantum physicist's understanding, realism means for
Barad the farewell to the hope for unmediated access to the world and the reconciliation of the different. For this hope necessarily hinges on the transcendental assumption of the existence of an objective, stable (noumenal) world
(Barad 2007: 128).

   Adorno's critique of language as a critique of knowledge is based on the
premise of a non-residual mediability of the world. The associated mode of
critique of a precedence of the object is based on the assumption of an object
that lies outside the subject: "Not even as an idea can we conceive a subject
that is not an object, but we can conceive an object that is not a subject"
(Adorno 1973: 183) – O_1. However, the principle of mimesis, for example, as
an attempt at unmediated access to the object O_1, or even the concept of first
nature as a boundary concept of cognition cannot do without the hypothetical

antithesis of a noumenal world. Adorno's theory becomes self-contradictory at this point: even the pure idea of first nature must, from this point of view, be a second nature that has become historical. Otherwise, Adorno would fall behind his critique of identifying thought (Schmid Noerr 1991: 48f.). But what then are the two worlds that still allow for a critique of it? In contrast, the question must be how matter can exist that is not to be grasped from the subject's point of view – not even as a non-conceptual Other.

3.3.3 Motion Rather than Hope

Negative dialectics and performativity share the protest against what is. Both ask what it means to become something and thus to possess identity. The difference, however, lies predominantly in the description of the possibilities that would lead to disidentification and resignification and thus overcoming solidifying (language) practices.

Negative dialectics as a method against identification relies on the sheer force of negation. Its critique of not entirely successful mediation of opposites enables representational critique, but this does not detach itself from the mode of representation but rather exhibits the conditions of its impossible success (Sommer 2016: 216). The pure force of negation must consequently leave Adorno aporetic and with powerless hope or fortune (for the addendum) since he cannot design countermodels (Adorno 1973: 365; 381).

Performativity also relies on the force of negation. It differs, however, in that it does not deduce this from the failure of representation, but from a critique of representational thinking per se. For what is, is not how it is represented but how it is consistently practiced. Performativity refers directly to the processual and productive dimension of diverse intra-active practices of materialization. It can thus also point to possibilities of a resignifying opening without at the same time having to determine what should be different and how. The constitutive exclusions that arise through iterative citationality or intra-action are necessary for reproduction, gain relevance, and as a result, permanently drawn boundaries become unstable (Butler 1990; Barad 2007: 208). Barad's posthumanist performativity also extends the totality of language practice to include the irritating force of matter – as a practice rather than substance. The impossibility of representation can be understood as a possibility. It is precisely the questioning of the conditions of this impossibility that becomes possible and enables iterative intra-action to overcome what exists. This overcoming becomes active instead of relying on hope and fortune, though it lacks the domination-critical dimension of hope.

4   Possibilities

At this point, this chapter could be closed. I may have shown that neither Barad
nor Adorno embrace a naïve realism and develop a materialism concerned
with practices of emergence but cancel each other out. Instead of such a classical and destructive consideration of the Frankfurt School and New-Material
Feminism, I will attempt a different kind of reading, by reading both theories
together. Bringing them into conversation will not mean to simply tot up both
positions but to look at how they mutually exceed their potentials.

Instead of focusing on identity or differences as before, I want to observe the
overlaps between Adorno and Barad that transcend their perspectives.[4] To this
end, I will ask what potential is inherent in Adorno's materialism but can be
perceived and exposed not from his perspective but from the New-Materialist
Feminist view of posthuman performativity. This *superimposition* of Adorno
works back on Barad's agential realism and makes it possible to go beyond
Barad's weak points as well.

4.1   *Immanence as Position*
To think with Adorno's materialism is both to *recognize* that the material world
as we can perceive it is socially mediated, and to be able to *experience* that
it is not absorbed in it. To think from here beyond this holds the empowerment to see the multiplicity of dimensions beyond the humanistic, idealistic,
rational subject. These make possible a perspective on practices beyond, but
not without, the subject. Adorno can convincingly demonstrate that thinking
must always start from a subject. It is a necessary assumption if one is not to
look at the world in a standpoint-transcendent way. This makes it possible to
look beyond the subject. For Adorno, as for Barad, the subject is the product
of relations with and in nature – however, it can potentially detach itself from
this position and open up to what is not quite itself through the experience of
being otherwise.

The separation into 'two worlds' that is still to be assumed for Adorno can be
transferred here if he transcends himself through agential realism: The subject
does not recognize itself but experiences itself as incapable and dependent
on a world that apparently exists independently of it. A posthumanism with

---

4   This way of bringing theories into conversation resembles Deleuze's philosophical meth-
     ode of observing inter-ference between different ideas. For example: the multiple overlays
     between Lewis Carroll and Plato in *Logic of Sense* (Deleuze 2015). Haraway calls this method
     of "mapping of interference, not of replication, reflection, or reproduction" *diffraction*
     (Haraway 1992: 304).

Adorno would then be to read this assumption as subjects experiencing their not-always-being-so. However, since this starts from the subject and can only be described from its point of view, the subject must be assumed as a real agential cut in a phenomenon. Here it stands in immanent relational difference to the world of the sensible and not in demarcation to the object as a transcendent thing-in-itself. Thus, the concrete individual, always stuck in these two poles of dualism, would also not be Barad's 'meta-subject' as phenomenon. Conversely, this interference makes it comprehensible how Barad can write from the situated and immanent position of a first-person: Another position is neither conceivable nor necessary.

4.2   *Bodies and Language*

Furthermore, materiality – as the Other that is, being at the same time mediated into the subject and part of the subject – is already laid out in Adorno's concept of the 'body'. The body is the starting point of experience and critique. To consider this view from the body more precisely as the endpoint of his aporetic materialism allows seeing further beyond it a way to understand materiality as multiplicity instead of stopping at absence of speech through absence of an image. Adorno's 'termination' meets Barad's understanding of materiality and goes beyond itself: language as the central object of analysis must here disappear behind the body. For the subject, in order to open up to posthumanism and to have a view of more than itself, must experience – not comprehend – itself as an agential cut. Its own materiality as body is the information carrier to this experience (Thyen 1989: 218). Accordingly, corporeality, and not first language, would be the measure of a self-critique in the sense of a self-location/distinction as not quite different. Experience forms the medium. As an instrument for cognition, language can neither be the place nor the medium of self-disidentification and acceptance of the subject as spatial and temporal instead of absolute. Language is itself part of the agential cut.

Thinking Adorno through a New-Material Feminist lens here as well would thus also mean to go beyond the potentials of language which may exceed indentitarian thinking, such as constellations, equivocation, or emphatic words (Hogh 2015: 115f.). This lens makes it possible to see the role of materiality as part of and before language and not only in or as a result of language. Following Adorno, there are experiences that the subject can make as an agential cut, which are not absorbed in language. Thus, a philosophy that wants and needs to comprehend its time is dependent on real bodily experiences rather than cognition, which always implies identifying language.

According to Adorno, these are experiences of suffering and happiness that cannot be made comprehensible. Matter also has a direct weight here (Adorno

1973: 201). In these places, matter appears forceful (wirk-mächtig) as the not-quite-Other of the subject, as relationally different but indeterminately direct. And not as a substantial given, but as the part of the phenomenon with which the subject is interwoven, but from which it is nevertheless different as an agential cut. To speak with the vocabulary of New-Materialism, matter is consequently not neutral for understanding a situation of subject and object in its time/phenomenon. The "experience of being shaken" (Wilford 2008: 418) by the force that the not-so-subjective exerts on the subject enables a posthumanist perspective on Adorno's materialism in Barad's sense – as a suspension of the dualism of passive and active, without in turn positing the non-human as the absolute.

4.3   Negation and Resignification

The effects of a new-materialistic view of Adorno can become even clearer when it encounters his core concept of non-identity. The non-identical is the forceful reference to that which is not available to the cognizing subject. However, this does not preclude its real experiencability, not by grasping it as a concrete object, but by grasping that there is something that denies access (Sommer 2016: 252). This does not lie in representation – on this, Barad and Adorno agree – but in the negation of what is essentialistic. The reference is thus not to a concrete object, but, again new-materialistically speaking, to the force of matter to negate and thus always to resignify. For through negation, and here it goes beyond Adorno again, there is always also the reference to an 'ability', an opening up to a world of which we are, and which can thus change for us and with us, allowing for new weight: "in the continual reopening and unsettling of what might yet be, of what was, and what comes to be" (Barad 2010: 251). The reference to this ability is already inherent as potential in Adorno's concept of non-identity and the experience of negation, but it only becomes visible through meeting with Barad's understanding of performativity.

Via Adorno, this was meant to clarify the relevance of body and non-identity for (an-)Other thinking. This thinking, even if posthumanistic, since it drives the subject beyond itself, must start from a subject that experiences the force of matter as its not-quite-Other and thus makes the possibility of opening phenomena possible. With this, however, the subject now shows itself not first and foremost in its inability to represent – where it ended with Adorno – but as the key to the possibility of bringing about manifold dynamics. Neither without nor solely through the subject are new cuts inscribed in the world. However, if a materialist philosophy is further concerned with the possibilities for cognition, and thus with transcending real disproportions and iniquitousness, it must first be concerned with understanding possibilities that allow such

spaces for resignifications in the first place. This requires a subject that understands its Being as part of that phenomenon and thus of material-discursive
practices – Being as Becoming. The immediacy of matter is thereby precisely
not the endpoint, but opening, surplus, and endless process in which the subject participates. Matter continues without essence in thought. Materialism
remains infinite.

4.4   Normativity and Transformation

This diffraction works back on Barad and creates exceedings of her position as
well: what does it mean to think feminist posthumanism, the dissolution of passive and active, from the subject to make available the possibility of resolving
phenomena and thus material-discursive practices? Arguably, Barad possesses
an unspoken normative claim, which consists in considering the overcoming
of dualisms desirable and giving 'us' (co-)responsibility for it. Barad cannot
justify this normativity from her position itself since she wants the falsity of
dualisms to be described only empirically. She cannot say how we actively
influence material-discursive practices and their displacement (Braunmühl
2017: 4). To think from the subject, however, would be to think our responsibility for stabilizing and irritating practices (in Barad's sense). To observe this
becomes the task of social sciences: to investigate our part in specific apparatuses. Social sciences then keep their claim that the socially situated subject
must not be thought away from the phenomenon but must be understood in
its relational difference. Nevertheless, social sciences become obliged to look
beyond themselves to ecological rather than purely economic relations in a
broad sense. They should investigate specific relational arrangements in a
specific (social) apparatus that bears responsibility for certain exclusions, but
without claiming to map reality as a whole (Meißner 2016: 24f.). To apply this
to the examples stressed at the beginning: How do humans apply chemicals
in mastery of nature, of living and death? How do chemicals co-constitutively
change our landscapes, bodies, and our human understanding of time?

In a more abstract sense this mode of doing social sciences could also apply
to Adorno's focus on language as a material-discursive practice that effects specific, but not all, exclusions and differences in that specific phenomenon we
call 'present'.

Now, however, Barad can only say in superimposition with Adorno that the
overcoming of individual apparatuses and the opening to resignification is necessary (in a normative sense as well) – namely, if the agential cuts and the production of exclusions can be determined as 'wrong' – without simultaneously
providing the reference to a determinable 'right'. Dualisms, Adorno argues,
are not only empirically false, but necessarily entail hierarchies, privileges,

suffering, and exclusions (Adorno 1973: 364). Barad's lack of a social theory can hence be supplemented. What can then be attacked with Barad are practices of knowledge as practices of bringing forth dualisms by genealogically grasping them as part of an apparatus and providing possibilities to surpass them. Power and domination asymmetries as necessarily inscribed in any form of mediation of dualisms become surmountable, up to this point, however, only insofar as the world is a permanent process of becoming. No active subject can yet be seen, except Barad's problematic omnipotent 'meta-subject'.

According to Barad, unlike Adorno, knowledge and practice are not subject-specific. They are part of intra-actions, which first produce what counts as subject and what counts as object, hence acts of knowing and doing. Intra-action could be viewed from the subject, however, if the repercussion of Adorno's perspective on subjects as agential cuts calls forth Barad's own apparatus. This view makes 'our' responsibility to the apparatus concretely visible in which a) participation in material-discursive practices of reproduction and b) spaces to surpass them become visible. Neither Adorno nor Barad themselves can provide the final step towards productive overcoming. Because we are neither entirely alone, nor necessarily and independently of apparatuses that (re-)produce agential cuts, we must continue to embrace this project of surpassing them. Every agential cut entails power relations and domination as the core of specific knowledge practices. Knowledge is always 'political' insofar as it produces intelligibility and response-ability (Barad) or suffering and social exclusions (Adorno). Since we are always part of those practices that are responsible for these exclusions, there can be no fortunity (Glücken) of transformation through, but also not without us. If we are not before their intra-active generation, we are now – because we want to understand, and to understand means to change (Marx and Engels 2010: 5).

Though no concrete practices of transformation are described here, the task of "making available new possibilities" (Meißner 2016: 29) follows from this perspective, as we are able to experience the falseness of structures – empirical as well as normative. It is the force of matter as a working of 'exteriority within' – us that points to such a 'being able'. Accordingly, the question posed to materialism is not simply the description of relations, but, through the experience of their not-being-so, also the question of the possibilities of their openness. Thus, materialism is not the pure negation of describeability. But rather is materialism the question of which conditions make it possible or impossible to understand ourselves as part of a world of which we are, without negating from the beginning that there is such a subject. For it is the humanistic subject, in Adorno as well as in Barad, that attempts to understand its 'Being-of-the-world' and thereby problematize familiar ways of coping with disproportions.

The unavailability and, at the same time, necessary condition of the non-human, experienced through non-identity, can make other responses possible than immanent critique without becoming externalist. This is the core of the superimposition of a feminist posthuman performativity and phenomena with the experience of non-identity and corporeality of the Critical Theory of Adorno.

5   Closure – Materialism Infinite

To think New-Material Feminism from the non-identical of the seemingly self-sufficient subject makes it possible for agential realism to understand apparatuses as always problematic and permeated by societal power asymmetries without releasing them from their fundamental contingency. The question now turns to our response-ability for possible transformations because that is the only question we can ask without overestimating our capacities. Goals, practices, and problems are more than human because we are of and with the world we are trying to understand.

The implications for a new, albeit critical-historical, materialism that is able to cope with changed realities are manifold. However, some aspects can be named. It must be about describing possibilities and impossibilities for the insight of being part of a contingent apparatus. This is to be able to make the experience of relational difference and thereby, if to recognize also means to change, at least to open new spaces of possibility. Thinking of the present as a task of philosophy does not consist in transferring an Other into one's own (our language, for instance). Instead, the recognition of relationality is the core of thinking the present. If ever practices in their multiplicity are to be considered transformative, then the question is only to what extent they make possible or undermine that perspective and experience.

Such materialism does not require a final certainty about how we are, how the world is, what validity overlaps from it, how it ought to be and how to get there. This knowledge remains impossible. The point is rather to attack this knowledge process itself as always already part of these relations: 'Western' rationality must be taken seriously as a real agential, praxeological-historical cut in the phenomenon 'world'. It causes exclusions, hierarchies, and suffering, qua its real existence. And yet, this present must be read not as a stable whole but as contingent, conditioned by material-discursive practices. Only such a perspective opens a view upon contemporary relations and entailed crises that go beyond solemn human means – as relational. Thus, even if we are incapable of comprehending and unable to succeed, we must take up the infinitely abandoned task of reading the present for what these constitutive, material-discursive practices are that close off the space of the possibility of another becoming. This is a task, which therefore cannot succeed through our solemn actions as human subjects, but also cannot succeed without us.

We do not simply condition the present – as, for example, controversial descriptions of the crises of the present want to grasp by the concept of the so-called 'Anthropocene' as the result of human mastery of nature. This overestimates the capacities of the human subject alone. But to see relationality enables us to view problems differently than through ongoing mastery of nature in hubris. To understand and change the powerful and long-lasting effects of radioactivity, chemicals and many other examples that made modern human life what it is, needs the perspective of the knowing, human subject. This position however is always already beyond such subjectivity. Contrariwise it is not radioactivity or chemicals that could be described as forceful actors, like other new-material theories describe (e.g., Bennett 2010). Relations do not sit still and hence cannot be finally grasped and identified. Only matter as anti-essentialist, but relational, can exceed trained subjects' perspective. Materialism remains infinite.

At the same time, this does not have to abandon the responsibility that the omnipotent, rational subject shares. We might still understand ourselves as such subjects. Thus, we are part of material-discursive apparatuses that keep the space of possibilities limited by our knowledge practices and can hence take part in transformation. To finally know the means to this is an infinite, impossible, but indispensable task of thinking in a world of which we are, and which does not stand still. A perspective of forceful and affective matter that, nonetheless, remains anti-essentialist and further does not neglect the position of the knowing subject, allows for a critical-materialist perspective towards contemporary relations at stake. Such a position enriched through New-Material Feminist insides allows a Critical Theory in the legacy of the early Frankfurt School to describe and thereby critique present phenomena such as rapid (bio)technologization and the pressing issue of the climate crisis.

References

Adorno, Theodor W. 1973. *Negative Dialectics*. Trans. by E. B. Ashton. New York: Continuum.
Adorno, Theodor W. 1997. *Minima Moralia. Reflexionen aus dem beschädigten Leben.* Frankfurt: Suhrkamp.

Adorno, Theodor W. 2014. *Vorlesung über Negative Dialektik.* Frankfurt am Main: Suhrkamp.

Alaimo, Stacy and Hekman, S. 2008. *Material Feminisms.* Bloomington: Indiana University Press.

Barad, Karen. 2007. *Meeting the Universe Halfway. Quantum Physics and the Entanglement of Matter and Meaning.* Durham & London: Duke University Press.

Barad, Karen. 2010. "Quantum Entanglements and Hauntological Relations of Inheritance. Dis/continuities, SpaceTime Enfoldings, and Justice-to-Come." In *Derrida Today* l3 (2), 240–68. Edinburgh: Edinburgh University Press.

Barad, Karen. 2012a. "On Touching. The Inhuman That Therefore I am." In *differences: a Journal of Feminist Cultural Studies* 25 (3), 206–223. Durham & London: Duke University Press.

Becker-Schmidt, Regina. 2002. „Erkenntniskritik, Wissenschaftskritik, Gesellschaftskritik. Positionen von Donna Haraway und Theodor W. Adorno kontrovers diskutiert." In *IWM Working Paper* 1. Vienna.

Bennett, Jane. 2010. *Vibrant Matter. A Political Ecology of Things.* Durham&London: Duke University Press.

Braunmühl, Caroline. 2017. "Beyond Hierarchical Oppositions. A Feminist Critique of Karen Barad's Agential Realism." In *Feminist Theory* 19 (2), 1–18. Thousand Oaks: SAGE.

Butler, Judith. 1990. *Gender Trouble. Feminism and the Subversion of Identity.* New York: Routledge.

Butler, Judith. 1993. *Bodies that Matter. On the Discursive Limits of 'Sex'.* New York: Routledge.

Coole, Diana and Frost, S. 2010. "Introducing the New Materialism." In *New Materialisms. Ontology, Agency, and Politics,* eds. D. Coole and S. Frost, 1–43. Durham&London: Duke University Press.

Cotter, Jennifer. 2016. "New Materialism and the Labor Theory of Value." In *Minnesota Review* 87, 171–181. Durham&London: Duke University Press.

Deleuze, Gilles. 2015. *Logic of Sense.* Trans. by C. Boundas. London: Bloomsbury.

Dolphijn, Rick and van der Tuin, I. 2012. *New Materialism. Interviews and Cartographies.* Ann Arbor: Open Humanities Press.

Federici, Silvia. 2020. *Beyond the Periphery of the Skin Rethinking, Remaking, and Reclaiming the Body in Contemporary Capitalism.* Oakland: PM Press.

Fraser, Nancy. 1989. *Unruly Practices. Power, Discourse and Gender in Contemporary Social Theory.* Minneapolis: University of Minnesota Press.

Gransee, Carmen. 1998. „Grenz-Bestimmungen. Erkenntniskritische Anmerkungen zum Naturbegriff bei Donna Haraway." In *Kurskorrekturen. Feminismus zwischen kritischer Theorie und Postmoderne,* ed. G. Knapp, 126–125. Frankfurt am Main: Campus.

Griffin, Susan. 1978. *Woman and Nature. The Roaring Inside Her*. New York: Harper & Row.

Grusin, Richard. 2017. *Anthropocene Feminism*. Minneapolis: University of Minnesota Press.

Habermas, Jürgen. 2003. *The Future of Human Nature*. Cambridge: Polity Press.

Habermas, Jürgen. 2005. *Zwischen Naturalismus und Religion. Philosophische Aufsätze*. Frankfurt am Main: Suhrkamp.

Haraway, Donna J. (1992). "The Promises of monsters: a regenerative politics for inappropriate/d others". In *Cultural Studies* 1, 295–337. New York: Routledge.

Haraway, Donna J. 2016. "A Cyborg Manifesto. Science, Technology, and Socialist-Feminism in the Late Twentieth Century." In *Manifestly Haraway*, ed. Donna Haraway, 3–90. Minneapolis: Minnesota University Press.

Hogh, Philip. 2015. *Kommunikation und Ausdruck. Sprachphilosophie nach Adorno*. Weilerswist: Velbrück.

Hoppe, Katharina and Lemke, T. 2015. „Die Macht der Materie. Grundlagen und Grenzen des agentiellen Realismus von Karen Barad." In *Soziale Welt* 66 (3), 260–280. Baden-Baden: Nomos.

Horkheimer, Max. 1988a. *Gesammelte Schriften Band 3*. Frankfurt am Main: Fischer.

Horkheimer, Max, 1988b. *Gesammelte Schriften Band 4*. Frankfurt am Main: Fischer.

Lettow, Susanne. 2017. "Turning the Turn. New Materialism, Historical Materialism and Critical Theory." In *Thesis Eleven* 140, 106–121. Thousand Oaks: SAGE.

Marx, Karl, and Friedrich, E. 2010. *Marx and Engels Collected Works. Volume 5. 1845–1887*. Trans. by C. Dutt. London: Lawrence & Wishart.

Meißner, Hannah. 2016. "Conversing with the Unexpected. Towards a Feminist Ethics of Knowing." In *Rhizomes. Cultural Studies in Emerging Knowledge* 30. BGSU.

Menke, Christoph. 2008. „Subjektivität und Gelingen. Derrida und Adorno." In *Derrida und Adorno. Zur Aktualität von Dekonstruktion und Frankfurter Schule*, eds. E. Waniek and E. Vogt, 189–206. Wien: Turia + Kant.

Rudolph, Matthias. 2019. "Ein ontologischer Kurzschluss. Jane Bennetts 'Vital Materialism' im Lichte von Theodor W. Adornos Ontologiekritik." In *Zeitschrift für kritische Theorie* 25, (48/49), 81–100. Spring: zu Klampen.

Schmid Noerr, Gunzelin. 1991. „Ein nicht-naturalistischer Begriff zweiter Natur." In *Die Unnatürlichkeit der Natur. Über Sozialität der Natur und Natürlichkeit des Sozialen*, eds. G. Schmid Noerr and M. Lutz-Bachmann, 44–55. Frankfurt am Main: Nexus.

Schmidt, Alfred. 1983. „Begriff des Materialismus bei Adorno." In *Adorno-Konferenz 1983*, eds. L. Friedeburg and J. Habermas, 14–31. Frankfurt am Main: Suhrkamp.

Scott, Joan W. 1989. *Gender and the Politics of History*. New York: Columbia University Press.

Sommer, Marc N. 2016. *Das Konzept einer negativen Dialektik. Adorno und Hegel*. Tübingen: Mohr Siebek.

Stögner, Karin and Colligs A. 2022. *Kritische Theorie und Feminismus*. Berlin: Suhrkamp.

Thyen, Anke. 1989. *Negative Dialektik und Erfahrung. Zur Rationalität des Nichtidentischen bei Adorno*. Frankfurt am Main: Suhrkamp.

Tsing, Anna and Gan, E., Swanson, H., Burbandt, N. (2017). "Introduction: Haunted Landscapes of the Anthropocene." In *Arts of Living on a Damaged Planet*, eds. A. Tsing, E. Gan, H. Swanson, N. Burbandt, G1–G14. Minneapolis: University of Minnesota Press.

Vogel, Steven. 2015. *Thinking Like a Mall. Environmental Philosophy after the End of Nature*. Cambridge: The MIT Press.

Wilford, Justin. 2008. "Towards a Morality of Materiality. Adorno and the Primacy of the Object." In *Space and Culture* 11, 409–421. Thousand Oaks: SAGE.

CHAPTER 14

Theorizing beyond the Man

The Frankfurt School and Post-humanist Feminism

Mario Mikhail

The relation between feminism and the early Frankfurt School is highly problematic and widely misunderstood. The early Frankfurt School's ideas regarding gender, women, and sexuality may seem unsystematic and scattered; however, this is due to their unconventional approach to feminist issues. This chapter argues that in the work of the early Frankfurt School theorists there are recurrent themes that correspond with post-humanist feminism. The thought of Theodor Adorno, Max Horkheimer, Herbert Marcuse, and Walter Benjamin, despite their variations and differences, entailed a post-gendered and a post-humanist non-hierarchical politics that encompassed humans, non-humans, animals, and technology. This chapter traces the ideas of the domination over nature and its interconnection with patriarchy in the writings of Adorno, Horkheimer, and Marcuse. Their ideas aimed to destabilize the anthropocentrism of modernity and critique the heteropatriarchal domination over nature and marginalized humans. They expressed affinity with non-humans and envisioned a non-instrumental relation between nature and humans. Moreover, by bringing Benjamin to the discussion, this chapter will exemplify how technology can contribute to and facilitate this post-humanist/post-gendered egalitarian sociopolitical conception. Finally, this article demonstrates the connections between the theories of the early Frankfurt School and the post-humanist feminist thinking of Donna Haraway and Rosi Braidotti.

1   Introduction

The early Frankfurt School theorists are not generally regarded as feminist thinkers. Most gender analysts do not return to their writing looking for feminist insights. Issues related to feminism and gender were not the central focus of the early Frankfurt studies. However, that does not negate the fact that there is a presence of gender-related analytical pieces in their thought. They were neither disinterested in gender nor did they belittle gender's importance. The location of feminist and gender related issues in their writings needs a reconsideration. This study will revisit the thought of Theodor Adorno, Max Horkheimer, Herbert Marcuse, and Walter Benjamin to analyze their philosophical reflections from a post-humanist approach. The chapter argues that their theoretical contributions regarding women, gender, sexuality, nature, and technology constitute key themes in the post-humanist feminist approach to politics. That does not mean that early Frankfurt theorists had a unitary approach, because there are indeed differences among them. However, there are broad motifs shared in their thought. This chapter is going to explore the feminist and queer motifs in their thought and their linkage with the domination over nature and other earthly creatures. This chapter also explores the meditative role of technological innovation, particularly in the reflections of Walter Benjamin. This analytical approach is going to identify the post-humanist feminist themes in their philosophy. By doing so, the chapter is going to reinterpret the thought of the early Frankfurt theorists through the lens of post-humanist feminist theory which transgresses the civilization/nature divide and advocates for a post-gendered/post-human paradigm devoid of anthropocentrism.

There are several interpretations regarding the position of gender and feminism in the writings of the early Frankfurt School. However, the works of the early Frankfurt School theorists have been a target of feminist criticisms. The work of the early Frankfurt School theorists is widely criticized for its absence of women to a large extent; for example, some scholars claim that the early Frankfurt theorists marginalized women, instrumentalized women, and reinforced gender stereotypes in their analysis (Bauer 1999: 102–103; Hewitt 1992: 168–170; Taylor 2012: 79–80). However, this analysis lacks a proper understanding regarding the early Frankfurt Schools' thought and their definitions of femininity. It should be noted that whenever the early Frankfurt School theorists mention femininity, they do not refer to any essentialist notions regarding women. Furthermore, the lack of focus on women is not a result of neglect. This notion should be understood as an aspect of a different analysis that transcends all essentialist notions about women and the centrality of gender altogether, as will be discussed later.

2   With Women contra Femininity

Although the issues related to feminism are not formulated in a systematic manner in the work of the early Frankfurt theorists, such issues are not neglected. First, Adorno and Horkheimer's reading of Marquis de Sade's Juliette is vital to consider. Juliette embodies the joy of destroying civilization using the weapons of civilization itself, i.e., reason and logic (Adorno & Horkheimer 2002 [1947]: 74–76). "'This boldness, stridently proclaimed by Nietzsche, has also taken hold of Juliette. "Live dangerously" is her message, too: "Dare henceforth to do anything without fear"'" (Adorno & Horkheimer 2002 [1947]: 77). Juliette subverted her traditional gender role by embracing the masculine tools of civilization, in order to destroy patriarchal structures (Duford 2017: 788–789). This aligns with Adorno and Horkheimer's conception of gender as a mythic construction utilized for domination (Duford 2017: 788). While they criticized Juliette's approach of embracing tools of domination, this analysis remains particularly vital because it manifests a key element in their thought regarding gender. They regarded gender roles as artificial structures that can be performed by anyone. Juliette performed a masculine role for the purpose of destroying patriarchy. Accordingly, this analysis of masculinity demonstrates that it can be subversively performed by women, and that masculinity is not something exclusive to men.

In *Minima Moralia*, Adorno provides additional insights regarding women in modern society. According to Adorno, the feminine character is the product of the masculine society (Adorno 2005 [1951]: 95). It is "the negative imprint of domination" (Adorno 2005 [1951]: 95). Adorno states that the bourgeois conceptions about the feminine character, just like nature, are scars of the "social mutilation" (Adorno 2005 [1951]: 95). The naturalness of femininity is a bourgeois delusion. The naturalness of feminine characteristics is a manifestation of the masculine bourgeoisie society which fabricated fake natures for the purpose of domination (Adorno 2005 [1951]). Adorno's treatment of Nietzsche's statement on women elucidates this fabrication. Nietzsche infamously proclaimed that a whip is needed whenever meeting women. Adorno, however, detected the flaw in Nietzsche's advice; Nietzsche was mistaken in associating femininity with women, because the notion of femininity that Nietzsche despised is in reality an "effect of the whip" (Adorno 2005 [1951]: 96). The conformist character of the feminine is a fabrication of this masculine violence (Adorno 2005 [1951]: 96). Adorno ends this aphorism by stating that "The liberation of nature would be to abolish its self-fabrication. Glorification of the feminine character implies the humiliation of all who bear it" (Adorno 2005 [1951]: 96). In these passages, a clearer understanding of women and gender in Adorno's thought can be identified. The feminine is a product of masculine domination, not a natural category in any form. The docility of femininity has been constructed and naturalized by the intense violence of the masculinity of bourgeois society. Thus, femininity is constructed artificially and so can be subverted. Furthermore, the liberation of women and nature are interconnected; this is a recurrent theme that is going to be discussed in depth later.

From these writings, it becomes apparent that Adorno and Horkheimer did not neglect gender and issues related to feminism. The disruption of traditional gender roles, the domination of heteropatriarchy over women, and the avocation of difference reflect not only a feminist critical attitude, but also a queer approach (Duford 2017). Revealing the delusions of naturalized gender identities and recognizing gender characteristics as social fabrications may open up possibilities of subversive gender identities which suggests a sense of queerness. Adorno's and Horkheimer's approach to gender was rather radical.

On the other hand, feminism is clearly visible in the thought of Marcuse, although it was not the central focus of his work. Marcuse shared Adorno and Horkheimer's understanding that the feminine is not biological, but rather a product of social conditioning (Marcuse 1974b: 280). However, Marcuse believed that the feminine characteristics (e.g., tenderness and nonviolence) that were attributed to women by the patriarchal society constitute an antithesis to masculine domination and exploitation (Marcuse 1974b: 283). Although Marcuse affirmed the feminine characteristics, he was far from naturalizing them. Marcuse believed that these artificial characteristics can be utilized as a foundation for a liberated society. This approach remains debatable. However, Marcuse shared Adorno's and Horkheimer's insights regarding patriarchal domination over women and the unnaturalness of the feminine.

Sexuality was the main focus of Marcuse's book *Eros and Civilization*. According to Marcuse, sexuality has been organized to be subjugated to the performance principle in a process he termed surplus repression. This process desexualized the body; moreover, human sexuality became centralized in the genitalia, and it became contained within monogamous relations to redirect the human libido towards procreation, not pleasure (Marcuse 1974a [1955]: 38–48). He advocated for an emancipated mode of sexuality – polymorphous perversity – to resexualize the whole body once more (Marcuse 1974a [1955]: 209–211). Polymorphous perversity emancipates sexuality from the performance principle, procreation, and the primacy of genital gratification. This process in turn makes pleasure the goal of sexuality (Marcuse 1974a [1955]: 49–52). Here, Marcuse was critical of heteronormative monogamous sexuality. Marcuse also offered an alternative model of sexuality to counter the traditional heteronormative sexuality which subjugates sexuality to the capitalist system.

On the other hand, the analysis of gender and sexuality in the writings of Walter Benjamin was more subtle. Benjamin is probably the least common among the early Frankfurt School theorists whom scholars return to looking for insights regarding feminist issues. Some feminist scholars regarded Benjamin's writings as problematic (Chow 1989; Wolff 1985). However, Chisholm noticed a sense of queerness in his writings by his subversion of traditional gender roles and procreative sexuality (Chisholm 2002; Chisholm 2009: 252–253). Benjamin described lesbian love as "pure" because it is liberated from pregnancy and the family (Chisholm 2002: 28). As Chisholm (2009) notices, the subversiveness of Benjamin's thought is exemplified in his linguistic and allegorical uses of the categories of sexuality/eros/gender as lenses to analyze the social and cultural phenomena of modernity.

In Benjamin's (2006b) reading of Baudelaire, he explains the shifts in gender identities caused by the new conditions of labor.

> During the nineteenth century, women were for the first time used in large numbers in the production process outside the home. This was done for the most part in a primitive way, by employing them in factories. As a result, masculine traits were bound to appear in these women eventually. These were caused, in particular, by the distorting influence of factory work. Higher forms of production, as well as the political struggle per se, fostered masculine characteristics of a more refined nature ... The masculinization of woman was in keeping with this, so Baudelaire approved of the process. At the same time, however, he sought to free it from economic bondage.
>
> 58

It appears, yet again similar to Adorno, Horkheimer, and Marcuse, that Benjamin regards gendered traits as a result of social processes. As Benjamin explains, the sociopolitical developments of capitalism reconfigured gender identities and influenced women to adopt masculine qualities. This implies that for Benjamin neither masculinity nor femininity are natural, and gender attributes change with sociopolitical currents. It is also worth noting that Benjamin attributed this subversion specifically to the technology of the factory and the new means of production. This specifically technological aspect will be discussed later as it relates to Benjamin's overall philosophy. Thus, similar to Adorno's, Horkheimer's, and Marcuse's works, Benjamin's writings are penetrated by queerness.

3   Nature, Gender, and Post-humanism

Most attempts to understand gender in the thought of the early Frankfurt theorists utilizing most of the prevailing feminist theories would eventually lead to severe analytical errors and would fail to properly understand the early Frankfurt School's treatment of gender. If most feminist theories locate gender as the core of their analysis, the early Frankfurt School theorists consider gender as a piece within a bigger picture that combines nature, humanity, and technology. Thus, examining nature in the thought of the early Frankfurt School thinkers is fundamental to understanding their conceptions regarding feminist issues.

According to Adorno and Horkheimer (2002 [1947]), rationality has come to dominate extra-human nature and humans – and has denied the fact that human beings are in actuality a part of this nature – for the sake of domination. According to the logic of the Enlightenment, whether it is nature or society, every aspect of life can be quantified and reduced to calculations. Furthermore, the rationale of domination and the manipulation of nature has been extended to reach humanity in capitalist societies. For Adorno and Horkheimer, blind domination over nature has taken hold over every aspect of the world, including humanity itself.

The presence of non-humans is present throughout the writings of the early Frankfurt School thinkers. Adorno and Horkheimer (2002 [1947]) noted that reason has subjugated animals to several forms of terror under the pretense of man's superiority (Adorno & Horkheimer 2002 [1947]: 203–204). Adorno (2005) argues that genuine progress is not concerned with dominating nature; on the contrary, "progress means: to step out of the magic spell, even out of the spell of progress that is itself nature, in that humanity becomes aware of its own inbred nature and brings to a halt the domination it exacts upon nature and through which domination by nature continues. It could be said that progress occurs where it ends" (150). Thus, for Adorno the main condition for emancipation is that humanity realizes its true place in the world as a part of nature, and this necessitates the termination of man's terror inflicted upon nature.

When Adorno and Horkheimer discussed the domination over nature, they referred to women as another object of domination by man. Adorno and Horkheimer located a link between the domination over nature and the domination over women. Man has considered woman closer to nature, denying women individuality and subjecting them to the same brutal domination as a 'species' in nature (Adorno & Horkheimer 2002 [1947]: 87–88). As discussed above, in *Minima Moralia*, Adorno explored the connection between the domination over women on the one hand and nature on the other hand. He also associated the liberation of nature with the liberation of women from the heteropatriarchal rational violence inflicted on the world. In a passage from *Dialectic of Enlightenment*, Adorno and Horkheimer (2002 [1947]) noticed the fundamental link between the subjugation of women and non-humans.

For the being endowed with reason, however, concern for the unreason-
ing animal is idle. Western civilization has left that to women. They have
no autonomous share in the capabilities which gave rise to this civilization. The man must go out into hostile life, must act and strive. The
woman is not a subject. She does not produce but looks after the produc-
ers, a living monument to the long-vanished time of the self-sufficient
household. The division of labor imposed on her by the man was unfa-
vorable. She became an embodiment of biological function, an image of
nature, in the suppression of which this civilization's claim to glory lay. To
dominate nature boundlessly, to turn the cosmos into an endless hunting
ground, has been the dream of millennia. It shaped the idea of man in
a male society. It was the purpose of reason, on which man prided himself. Woman was smaller and weaker, between her and man there was a
difference she could not overcome, a difference set by nature, the most
shaming, degrading agency possible within the male society. When domination of nature is the true goal, biological inferiority remains the ultimate stigma, the weakness imprinted by nature, the mark which invites
violence.

> 206

In this passage Adorno and Horkheimer realized a linkage between the domination over nature and women. Women were naturalized and reduced to mere
biological functions which transformed them into natural objects. The reason
of patriarchy engraved biological inferiority on women. The fabricated natural
weakness rendered women objects of domination. This patriarchal reason has
made the care of non-reasonable weak creatures (i.e., animals) a concern for
women who seemingly resemble them. Women and animals were subjugated
to the same epistemological violence which fabricated their attributes and
dominated their existence.

Marcuse was also interested in the animal question. Marcuse noted that
the advancement of civilization was linked with the mastery over and the
exploitation of nature, animals, and humans (Marcuse 1974b: 52). He criticized
the violence inflicted upon animals in modern industrial society (Marcuse
2002 [1964]: 242; Marcuse 1972: 68). However, while he regarded the call for
universal vegetarianism or the use of synthetic food as too early, he believed
that a genuinely liberated society is not possible without the reduction of
the cruelty of man inflicted upon animals (Marcuse 1972: 68). It seems that
Marcuse regarded the ideal society as a society devoid of any exploitation of
animals, including their consumption as food. Here, Marcuse's thought lays the
foundation for a radical form of vegetarianism which transforms the politics

of human-animal relations towards a politics of liberation (Young 2016: 547–548). It is important to note that the ideal for Marcuse is a vegetarian world in which animals are not consumed by humans. Thus, he referred to the idea of synthetic food which is a technological innovation that will result in the end of animal suffering. By stating this, Marcuse indicated the role of technology in a utopian future without domination and exploitation. However, the role of technology is more prevalent in Benjamin's philosophy.

Walter Benjamin's reflections were rather fragmented; nonetheless, a rough orientation can be deduced. According to Benjamin, bourgeois society has transformed nature by commodifying sexuality and the female body (Chisholm 2002: 27). Benjamin argues that bourgeois culture transformed intimacy and women into objects that are mass-produced. One of the manifestations of this process of commodification is the "prostitution of the metropolis" (Benjamin 1985: 40). Benjamin considers nature similar to fashion, in the sense that nature changes with time (Benjamin 2004). The natural flow of the being is composed of sexuality and spirit (Benjamin 2004). Benjamin shared similar insights with his colleagues regarding nature and women. He also emphasized that nature is not static. This is vital to consider since Benjamin allocated segments of his writings to a futuristic conception of nature that involves technology.

Benjamin (2006a) makes a distinction between first technology and second technology. First technology aims to assert mastery over nature while second technology "aims rather at an interplay between nature and humanity" (107). The ruling class's lust for profit transformed technology into a tool of bloodshed; nonetheless, technology still stands as the means of liberation (Benjamin 2004). Second technology is associated with play and endless experimentation (Benjamin 2006a). Film in particular possesses the widest "space for play" (Benjamin 2006a: 127). Technology potentially allows humanity to form a collective body that incorporates humans, animals, plants, and non-living matter in a process of "annihilation and fulfillment" (Benjamin 2004: 395). Moreover, according to Benjamin, modern technology has also subverted the traditional gender division of labor and the gender stereotypes that were attached to this process (Geulen 1996: 163). Benjamin had an appreciation for the figure of Mickey Mouse because it disrupted the hierarchy between humans and animals (Mourenza 2015: 41). The figure of Mickey Mouse in Benjamin's thought represents a posthumanist figure which blurs the lines between animals, humans, technology, and nature through the technological medium of film (Mourenza 2015: 45). It is also worth mentioning that the word 'Maus' in German is feminine. The frequent use of this word by Benjamin manifests the sexual ambiguity of the character (Hansen 2012: 331).

Benjamin (2004) reworks the technology-nature relation and turns it on its head in a motion destructive to several repressive categories such as hetero-normativity, family, and nationalism by stating:

> The mastery of nature (so the imperialists teach) is the purpose of all technology. But who would trust a cane wielder who proclaimed the mastery of children by adults to be the purpose of education? Is not education, above all, the indispensable ordering of the relationship between generations and therefore mastery (if we are to use this term) of that relationship and not of children? And likewise technology is the mastery of not nature but of the relation between nature and man. Men as a species completed their development thousands of years ago; but mankind as a species is just beginning his. In technology, a physis is being organized through which mankind's contact with the cosmos takes a new and different form from that which it had in nations and families.
>
> 487

This line of thought is imperative to consider. Benjamin advocated a unity between living organisms. Benjamin seems to have the clearest vision among the early Frankfurt School thinkers regarding an egalitarian sociopolitical model that combines nature and humans – the same paradigm that is subtly but persistently flowing throughout the writings of Adorno, Horkheimer, and Marcuse.

Throughout the writings of the early Frankfurt School theorists there is a demonstration of a common suffering that humans, animals, and nature share. The early Frankfurt School thinkers' correlation between the suffering of humans and animals indicates a notion of equality. Equating the suffering of humans with non-humans lays the foundation for egalitarianism between humans and non-humans. The association between the suffering of humans and non-humans indicates that they are equal with almost the same degree of importance in the cosmos. Thus, the early Frankfurt thinker's conceptions of emancipation included both humans and non-humans (nature and animals). The reference and use of the term "nature" (and not just 'animals') by the early Frankfurt School thinkers may indicate that they perceived even non-living natural entities as entities also deserving of the alleviation of suffering equal to other living creatures i.e., humans and animals.

Benjamin, however, realized that technology will perform a fundamental role in achieving this aim. Benjamin saw that technology can disrupt not only gender stereotypes but also the boundaries between nature and civilization. Second, technology specifically is the means to resurrect a collective

techno-body consisting of humans, animals, plants, and possibly other entities. The experimental disposition of second technology gives rise to a room
for play full of potentialities. It is rather hard to make a claim about the place
of gender in Benjamin's vision. However, Benjamin realized that technology
indeed disturbs gender stereotypes. Moreover, Benjamin's language is penetrated by gender non-conforming and subversive allegorical constructions.
These elements can be an indication that Benjamin's techno collective body is
post-gendered, or, in a more conservative reading of those elements, that gender is not vital or central in Benjamin's futurist emancipated body. Whether
Benjamin consciously post-gendered his futuristic cosmos or unconsciously
deemphasized gender, both movements function to fulfill the same goal, which
is the abolition of gender or the gradual withering away of gender.

Adorno's, Horkheimer's, Marcuse's, and Benjamin's analyses with respect to
gender may appear confusing, obscure, and unrelated at first. However, their
respective analyses demonstrate an underlying theme in their thought. Before
addressing this theme in depth, the theory of post-humanist feminism has to
be examined.

4   Forging the Post-humanist Link

Post-humanist feminism questions the centrality of man in the world.
According to Rosi Braidotti, the hegemonic model that dominates the rational
Western civilization rests on the superiority of the species of human beings
which is most especially articulated in the rational, heterosexual, masculine,
and white family man (Braidotti 2017: 21–23). This epistemic violence naturalized other earthly beings such as women and Indigenous peoples as sexually
and racially inferior (Braidotti 2017: 23–24). The process of othering has prior-
itized certain ideals – e.g., whiteness and masculinity – while characteristics
that contradicted this ideal were constructed as deviant or monstrous – e.g.,
non-masculine, non-white (Braidotti 2009: 526). The same underlying logic that
constructed gendered and racial others has created the human-animal divide
in which humans are rendered dominant (Braidotti 2009: 526). Posthumanist
feminism rejects this anthropocentrism and calls for an alternative which
entails a "human-nonhuman continuum, which is consolidated by pervasive
technological mediation" (Braidotti 2017: 26). The results of this approach
are political and socially tremendous. The previously naturalized "others" are
empowered by this critical queer, ecological, anti-racial, and postcolonial attitude, and other earthly creatures such as plants, animals, cells, insects, and
bacteria are brought into the field of politics (Braidotti 2017: 26). Braidotti also

calls for a sexuality beyond the binary divisions of genders starting from the principles of polymorphous perversity, i.e., playfulness and nonprocreation (Braidotti 2017: 36–39). Sexuality is a force that has been constricted with gender binaries; however, the polymorphous perverse character of emancipated sexuality transgresses the binary structures of gender (Braidotti 2017: 36–37). Post-humanist feminism celebrates sexed bodies that transcend heteronormative sexuality and gender binaries, which promotes the actualization of the post-humanist approach (Braidotti 2017: 38). As Braidotti (2017) writes "sexuality beyond gender is the epistemological, but also political, side of contemporary vitalist neomaterialism. It consolidates a feminist genealogy that includes creative deterritorializations, intensive and hybrid cross-fertilizations and generative encounters with multiple human and nonhuman others. The counteractualization of the virtual sexualities – of the bodies without organs that we have not been able to sustain as yet – is a posthuman feminist political praxis" (39).

Another important feminist post-humanist scholar is Donna Haraway. Haraway introduced the cyborg as a post-humanist figure. Haraway described the post-humanist figure of the cyborg as a "hybrid of machine and organism" (Haraway 2006: 117). Haraway writes "The cyborg is a creature in a post-gender world; it has no truck with bisexuality, pre-oedipal symbiosis, unalienated labor, or other seductions to organic wholeness through a final appropriation of all the powers of the parts into a higher unity" (Haraway 2006: 118). The figure of the cyborg transgresses all boundaries between humans, animals, organisms, and technology (Haraway 2006: 119–122). According to Haraway (2006), the myth of the cyborg is a hybrid between animals, humans, and machine which was made possible through technological hybridization. The cyborg dissolves the distinction between nature and culture. Along the nature-culture dissolution, other fabricated differences also get abolished such as categories of gender and race. In that sense, post-humanist feminism can be understood as an approach which aims to destabilize not only gender but the place of humanity itself in the world (Haraway 2006: 119). Moreover, Haraway asserted the perverse and intimate aspects of the cyborg: "The cyborg is resolutely committed to partiality, irony, intimacy, and perversity. It is oppositional, utopian, and completely without innocence" (119).

This radical feminist theoretical model is vital to rethink the thought of the early Frankfurt School theorists and how feminism, sexuality, and nature can be grouped together in a coherent manner to properly rethink their writings. There are clear resemblances between post-humanist feminism and the early Frankfurt School theorists' thought.

There are key themes in the thought of Adorno, Horkheimer, Marcuse, and Benjamin that can be deduced. First, is the reality of the feminine character as a product of a historical masculine conditioning. The characteristics associated with women are not a result of a natural process but an effect of heteropatriarchal domination. Another key theme present in the early Frankfurt School's thought is that human sexuality is partially constructed by the structures of heteropatriarchal domination which transformed sexuality into an instrument to serve capitalism. This heteropatriarchal/capitalist domination limited the perversity and the emancipatory potentials of human sexuality. Another key motif is the domination of nature by the forces of modernity and capitalism. Frankfurt School theorists expressed a deep association and affinity with non-human creatures. They sympathized with the suffering of non-humans and called for the termination of this cruelty in a utopian future, including some sort of unity between all organisms. Furthermore, they located a fundamental connection between the domination over nature and marginalized humans – particularly women – by the instrumental reason of the heteropatriarchal domination of modernity. Finally, Benjamin, and to a lesser extent Marcuse, believed that technological innovations could fruitfully disrupt the boundaries of nature and humanity, or at least end the violence inflicted upon non-human creatures towards the realization of an egalitarian world between all species.

These key motifs can be loosely identified as exemplary of what is commonly referred to today as post-humanist feminism. As noted above, the issues of gender, sexuality, and queerness were not at the center of the early Frankfurt School's thought. Nonetheless, the early Frankfurt School thinkers did explore these topics and they offered profound insights regarding them. However, the early Frankfurt thinkers were not systematic in their treatment of such topics. These ideas were fragmented throughout their writings, but they were repeated several times. It is unlikely that the constant recurrence of these ideas was a result of randomness. The early Frankfurt School disturbed the binary divisions of gender and revealed its fabrication by heteropatriarchy. Moreover, the early Frankfurt School theorists endorsed queer sexuality and queer gender identities to liberate humanity from the forces of heteropatriarchy. By focusing on the suffering of animals and their relation to the suffering of marginalized humans, the early Frankfurt School theorists transformed the position of human suffering – which is traditionally located at the center of analyses – and rendered it as a part of an earthly suffering inflicted upon all marginalized creatures by modernity and capitalism. The utopian ideal involves the end of all forms of suffering and violence inflicted upon all marginalized creatures with possible mediation via technology. Here, the early Frankfurt School's approach to gender can be understood. This may also explain the absence of a coherent or systematic approach to gender and feminist issues. This technique could possibly be a piece of a grand theoretical schema which aimed to destroy the anthropocentric approach to politics and the reallocation of the position of humanity from the center to a part of a greater whole. The totality they envisioned includes all living creatures and even non-living worldly entities. Thus, the fragmentation of the topics of nature, women, and technology in the early Frankfurt School's thought can be understood within this context.

Although the early Frankfurt School did not formulate a coherent theory for a post-humanist alternative, their writings nevertheless demonstrate key ideas exemplified by contemporary scholars of post-humanist feminism like Haraway and Braidotti who call for a critical post-humanist feminist alternative that transcends the borders of nature, humanity, and technology. Reconsidering the early Frankfurt School thinkers' writings through this lens makes available a different interpretation of their thought.

The early Frankfurt thinkers regarded different worldly entities as equals. The critique of the common suffering of different living creatures, especially marginalized humans (women in particular) and animals inflicted upon them by the violence of the heteropatriarchy of modernity is a pervasive theme throughout their writings. The post-humanist tactics employed by the early Frankfurt School theorists included the following aspects: firstly, the destruction of naturalized gender categories. Secondly, the call for an emancipated sexuality and gender identities accompanied by the revitalization of play/perversity. Thirdly, the call for a futuristic world which rests upon the principles of solidarity and equality between living creatures with the possible aid of technology in a paradigm that disrupts the demarcation between nature and humanity. The early Frankfurt School theorists erected the foundations for a post-humanist feminist philosophy, even if they were not coherently organized in their system of thought.

5   Conclusion

The investigation of feminist issues in the thought of the early Frankfurt School is not a simple task. The depth of the early Frankfurt School's approach to feminism, gender, and sexuality may be obscure at first; however, after a careful investigation through this analysis, the scattered and fragmented presence of these issues in their writing becomes apparent. In the system of thought of the early Frankfurt School thinkers there is a profoundly radical theme lurking underneath. The early Frankfurt approach aimed to reveal and destroy the fabrications of binary gender identities to reach queer potentialities. This recurrent motif in their writings aimed to transgress all boundaries in the natural and non-natural world. They abolished the anthropocentrism of man which is fundamentally centered around the heteropatriarchal domination which subjugated marginalized humans (especially women) and non-humans to its monstrous violence. They envisioned a utopian future in which both humans and non-humans can live together equally in a world where cruelty and exploitation are absent. For Benjamin, and to a lesser extent Marcuse, technology will perform a vital role in achieving this future. This procedure entails the birth of a totality of techno-organism. This techno-organismic body is a rhythmic interplay between humanity, nature, and technology which overcomes the bourgeois atrocities of mastery and domination.

This radical attitude towards humanity and nature predicated post-humanist feminist thought. The key motifs articulated by post-humanist feminist scholars such as Braidotti and Haraway are found in the thought of Adorno, Horkheimer, Marcuse, and Benjamin. The destruction of the centrality of man, abolishing the demarcation between humanity and other creatures in the world, and liberating marginalized humans and animals from the instrumental reason of heteropatriarchy were the underlying themes in their thought, despite the variations in their philosophical reflections.

References

Adorno, Theodor W. 2005. *Critical Models: Interventions and Catchwords*. New York: Columbia University Press.

Adorno, Theodor, and Horkheimer, Max. 2002 [1947]. *Dialectic of Enlightenment*. Stanford: Stanford University Press.

Adorno, Theodor. 2005 [1951]. *Minima Moralia*, London: Verso.

Bauer, Karin. 1999. *Adorno's Nietzschean Narratives Critiques of Ideology, Readings of Wagner*. Albany, NY: State University of New York Press.

Benjamin, Walter, 2004. *Walter Benjamin: Selected Writings, 1: 1913–1926*. Marcus Bullock & Michael Jennings, eds., Cambridge, Massachusetts: Belknap Press of Harvard University Press.

Benjamin, Walter, 2006a. *Walter Benjamin: Selected Writings, 3: 1935–1938*. Howard Eiland & Michael Jennings, eds., Cambridge, Massachusetts: Belknap Press of Harvard University Press.

Benjamin, Walter, 2006b. Walter Benjamin: *Selected Writings, 4: 1938–1940*. Howard Eiland & Michael Jennings, eds., Cambridge, Massachusetts: Belknap Press of Harvard University Press.

Benjamin, Walter. 1985. "Central Park." *New German Critique* (34), 32–58.

Braidotti, Rosi. 2009. Animals, Anomalies, and Inorganic Others. *PMLA/Publications of the Modern Language Association of America*, 124(2), 526–532.

Braidotti, Rosi. 2017. "Four Theses on posthuman Feminism." In *Anthropocene Feminism*, edited by Richard Grusin. Minneapolis: University of Minnesota Press.

Chisholm, Dianne. 2002. "A Queer Return to Walter Benjamin." *Journal of Urban History* 29, no. 1: 25–38.

Chisholm, Dianne. 2009. "Benjamin's Gender, Sex, and Eros." In *A Companion to the Works of Walter Benjamin*, edited by Rolf J. Goebel. Rochester, NY: Camden House.

Chow, R., 1989. "Walter Benjamin's Love Affair with Death." *New German Critique* (48), p.63–86.

Duford, Nathan. 2017. "Daughters of the Enlightenment: Reconstructing Adorno on Gender and Feminist Praxis." *Hypatia* 32, no. 4: 784–800.

Geulen, Eva. 1996. "Toward a Genealogy of Gender in Walter Benjamin's Writing." *The German Quarterly* 69, no. 2: 161.

Hansen, Miriam Bratu. 2012. *Cinema and Experience: Siegfried Kracauer, Walter Benjamin, and Theodor W. Adorno.* Berkeley: University of California Press.

Haraway, Donna. 2006. "A Cyborg Manifesto: Science, Technology, and Socialist Feminism in the Late 20th Century." In *The International Handbook of Virtual Learning Environments*, edited by Weiss Joël. Dordrecht: Springer.

Hewitt, Andrew. 1992. "A Feminine Dialectic of Enlightenment? Horkheimer and Adorno Revisited." *New German Critique*, no. 56: 143.

Marcuse, Herbert. 1972. *Counterrevolution and Revolt.* Boston: Beacon Press.

Marcuse, Herbert. 1974a [1955]. *Eros and Civilization.* Boston: Beacon Press.

Marcuse, Herbert. 1974b. "Marxism and Feminism." *Women's Studies: an Interdisciplinary Journal* 2, no. 3: 279–288.

Marcuse, Herbert. 2002 [1964]. *One-Dimensional Man.* London: Routledge.

Mourenza, Daniel. 2015. "On Some Posthuman Motifs in Walter Benjamin: Mickey Mouse, Barbarism and Technological Innervation." *Cinema: Journal of Philosophy and the Moving Image.* (7), 28–47.

Taylor, B. 2012. "Enlightenment and the Uses of Woman." *History Workshop Journal* 74, no. 1: 79–87.

Wolff, J., 1985. "The Invisible Flâneuse. Women and the Literature of Modernity." *Theory, Culture and Society*, 2(3), pp.37–46.

Young, Katherine E. 2016. "Herbert's Herbivore: One-Dimensional Society and the Possibility of Radical Vegetarianism." *New Political Science* 38, no. 4: 547–60.

CHAPTER 15

The New Man Is a Woman

Marcuse and the Question of the New Anthropology

Cristian Arão

The relationship between Critical Theory and feminist thought is usually thought through the post-Habermasian perspective. It is the ideas of philosophers such as Nancy Fraser, Iris Young, and Seyla Benhabib that are commonly invoked to address issues of gender and the oppression of women. However, feminism was already an important issue at the beginning of the Frankfurt School. Herbert Marcuse, influenced by thinkers like Angela Davis and movements like the Women's Liberation Movement, has developed an intriguing approach to the feminist struggle and the issue of women under capitalism. Based on the idea developed by Davis that femininity represents an antithesis of the capitalist *ethos*, Marcuse proposes that society should feminize itself to build a less violent, brutish, and selfish world.

1   Performance Principle

During the 20th century, many thinkers set out to think about how post-capitalist human beings should be. This new man would need to be qualitatively different from the subjective construction of capitalism, embodying values opposite to those of the bourgeois individual. The discussion on this new anthropology involved the participation of important political references of this century, such as Frantz Fanon and Che Guevara. Herbert Marcuse also participated in this discussion by stating that post-capitalist man must embody the antithesis of the performance principle.

The performance principle means the mentality and *ethos* of the advanced industrial society; it is the way of life that sustains capitalism. This concept arises from the concept of the reality principle coined by Freud; according to the psychoanalyst, at the dawn of humanity, the reality principle replaced the pleasure principle through the need to relinquish momentary pleasure. Under the pleasure principle, one lived in an animalistic way; it is only with the establishment of the reality principle that the human being truly emerges. However, this renunciation, which marked the birth of humanity, does not completely distance human beings from pleasure. This moment is marked by postponement and a certain modification of pleasure rather than by abandonment. In this way, the pleasure principle is not incompatible with the reality principle.

The performance principle, on the other hand, according to Marcuse, is a historical form of the reality principle and is irreconcilable with the pleasure principle, because under the performance principle, there is a surplus repression, that is, a demand for renunciation that goes beyond what is necessary. We need to work, but it is not necessary that we spend most of our lives working, nor that work activity be synonymous with obedience and suffering. With the performance principle, the demand for renunciation in favor of productivism is accentuated, hence the ideas of love of labor and praise of sacrifice; the virtuous individual, in this context, is the selfless individual who neither seeks nor gives in to pleasures.

In favor of the need for performance, in addition to sacrifice, individualism, brutalization, and violence also appear as important characteristics. Brutalization, however, should not be understood as an absence of any kind of reasoning. Logical capacity must be refined, but only to follow imposed standards. The subject of capitalism must know how to make calculations and have the technical knowledge to better serve the world of value production. Its logic and knowledge must be, therefore, framed and at the service of what is necessary for production.

On the other hand, using the mind for reflections of other types that do not respond directly to what is useful for the market results in accusations of uselessness and daydreaming. Consequently, people become more and more brutish and ignorant about their reality, as the rewarded attitudes are the departure from reflection on the world and the training of reason for the world of labor.

In this scenario, the model is the active individual, who is not so concerned about the whys, but who knows a lot about the "how to do its"; it is the person who recognizes his/her place on the production line, responds masterfully to the commands given, and who lets his/her performance be less affected by factors external to the work.

With this brutalization, a lot of sensitivity is also lost and, consequently, the concern with care is also reduced. In the world of "every man for himself" where other people are seen more as competitors than as possible collaborators, the Other becomes more and more an obstacle to be overcome.

2   "New Anthropology" and Theory of Instincts

To address how the values of the performance principle are not repeated in a post-capitalist society, Marcuse uses an Aristotelian concept. For Aristotle, in *Nicomachean Ethics*, the individual creates a "second nature" by repeating certain behaviors, such that it becomes a disposition to keep repeating them. According to Marcuse, "'Second nature' [...] is not changed automatically by the establishment of new social institutions. There can be discrimination against women even under socialism" (Marcuse 2005: 166). This means that the creation of a non-repressive way of life does not depend only on a change in material bases; it is also essential to change consciousness, so that the values of the performance principle do not repeat themselves. Thus, for the emergence of new anthropology based on a rejection of the values of capitalism, other transformations are needed beyond taking over the means of production.

The concern with the non-repetition of the capitalist way of life in a future society was a recurrent issue in the 20th century in various socialist circles. Considering that there are no eternal and immutable qualities present in human beings and that the subject is constituted from the social reality, there has been much debate about why countries that have gone through revolutions made in the name of socialism maintain ways of life that are very similar to the capitalist *ethos*.

Marcuse, analyzing the USSR, concludes that the morality of Soviet communism was not very different from the principles of the capitalist system, because it was also based on the performance principle. For this and other reasons, Marcuse considered that the dimension of subjectivity was neglected by the Marxism of his time, and for this reason, he began a project to investigate the relationship between psychology and social transformations. And in his endeavor, he will seek answers in Freudian psychoanalysis; this research started in 1945 has as its first product the work *Eros and Civilization* – and later Freud's thought continued to accompany Marcuse throughout his work.

The concept "Eros", present in the title of the work, refers to Freud's theory of the instincts. Eros is the life instinct and its antagonist, Thanatos, is the death instinct. These two concepts arise in the final phase of the instinct theory. According to the psychoanalyst: "Of all the slowly developed parts of analytic theory, the theory of the instincts is the one that has felt its way the most painfully forward. And yet that theory was also indispensable to the whole structure that something had to be put in its place" (Freud 1962: 64). It is not our place to develop this groping done until the final stage of this theory; however, it is important to emphasize this to understand how Freud was concerned with the theme.

To the psychoanalyst, these instincts are forces that are present in the border zone between the physical and the psychical, and that impel the individual in some direction. Eros (the instinct of life) is what leads the individual to create bonds in the sense of self-preservation. The term in question commonly refers to sexuality, however, this concept encompasses a much larger dimension; the sexual dimension is just one of the facets of Eros, which also corresponds to everything that has a constructive character – of bringing together and maintaining units in larger groups. On the other hand, Thanatos (the death instinct) has a destructive and aggressive character. Its purpose is to reduce tensions to return to an inorganic state. According to Freud:

> Starting from speculations on the beginning of life and from biological parallels, I drew the conclusion that, besides the instinct to preserve living substance and to join it into ever larger units, there must exist another, contrary instinct seeking to dissolve those units and to bring them back to their primaeval, inorganic state. That is to say, as well as Eros there was an instinct of death. The phenomena of life could be explained from the concurrent or mutually opposing action of these two instincts. It was not easy, however, to demonstrate the activities of this supposed death instinct. The manifestations of Eros were conspicuous and noisy enough. It might be assumed that the death instinct operated silently within the organism towards its dissolution, but that, of course, was no proof. A more fruitful idea was that a portion of the instinct is diverted towards the external world and comes to light as an instinct of aggressiveness and destructiveness. In this way the instinct itself could be pressed into the service of Eros, in that the organism was destroying some other thing, whether animate or inanimate, instead of destroying its own self. Conversely, any restriction of this aggressiveness directed outwards would be bound to increase the self-destruction, which is in any case proceeding. At the same time one can suspect from this example that the two kinds of instinct seldom-perhaps never-appear in isolation from each other, but are alloyed with each other in varying and very different proportions and so become unrecognizable to our judgement. In sadism, long since known to us as a component instinct of sexuality, we should have before us a particularly strong alloy of this kind between trends of love and the destructive instinct; while its counterpart, masochism, would be a union between destructiveness directed inwards and sexuality -a union which makes what is otherwise an imperceptible trend into a conspicuous and tangible one.

>   FREUD 1962: 66

Thus, the relationship of antagonistic instincts does not occur at a distance, but always in close proximity, shaping and altering both. Freud saw the existence of a force that would guide people to love and union, but he also saw another side of the human being. A side that delights in violence and aggression, that rejoices in the suffering of others, and sometimes even in its own suffering. The author did not have to deal with much resistance to the acceptance of Eros by his contemporaries; on the other hand, accepting the existence of a dark side in human beings was difficult even for Freud himself. Ironically, the author states: "For 'little children do not like it' when there is talk of the inborn human inclination to 'badness', to aggressiveness and destructiveness, and so to cruelty as well" (Freud 1962: 67).

On the last page of *Civilization and its Discontents*, Freud, after developing his theory on the primordial instincts in civilization, rehearses an analysis of the social situation and writes how Eros and Thanatos would be present.

> The fateful question for the human species seems to me to be whether and to what extent their cultural development will succeed in mastering the disturbance of their communal life by the human instinct of aggression and self-destruction. It may be that in this respect precisely the present time deserves a special interest. Men have gained control over the forces of nature to such an extent that with their help they would have no difficulty in exterminating one another to the last man. They know this, and hence comes a large part of their current unrest, their unhappiness and their mood of anxiety. And now it is to be expected that the other of the two 'Heavenly Powers', eternal Eros, will make an effort to assert himself in the struggle with his equally immortal adversary. But who can foresee with what success and with what result?
>
> FREUD 1962: 92

Therefore, the death instinct would be responsible for aggressiveness, self-destruction, and renunciation in human culture, and in Freudian thought, the solution to these ills would fall under the responsibility of Eros. In the endless struggle of the two primordial forces, the life instinct would be at a disadvantage and should become more powerful than the death instinct. This abstract and almost theological discourse gains practical resonance in Marcuse's work. Eros' struggle against Thanatos is seen as a political problem.

In this scenario, the Marcusean perspective is defending life in the struggle against death so that a new reality principle – and with it a new subject – can emerge; an individual who is free from the feeling of guilt and capable of realizing all the potential of the life instinct. Thus, creating new anthropology is not a theoretical activity, but a theoretical and practical effort to think about and carry out a new conception of the human being.

> What is at stake is the idea of a new theory of man, not only as theory but also as a way of existence: the genesis and development of a vital need for freedom and of the vital needs of freedom- of a freedom no longer based on and limited by scarcity and the necessity of alienated labor. The development of qualitatively new human needs appears as a biological necessity; they are needs in a very biological sense. For among a great part of the manipulated population in the developed capitalist countries the need for freedom does not or no longer exists as a vital, necessary need. Along with these vital needs the new theory of man also implies the genesis of a new morality as the heir and the negation of the Judeo-Christian morality which up to now has characterized the history of Western civilization.
>
> MARCUSE 2014: 251

In creating his theory of the new anthropology, Marcuse did not work only with psychoanalytic concepts. To deal with the self-creation of this new man, the author also uses the concept of "human nature" developed by the young Marx, which, according to the Frankfurtian, had its value minimized by the Marxism of his time. According to him:

> In the treatment of human nature, Marxism shows a similar tendency to minimize the role of the natural basis in social change-a tendency which contrasts sharply with the earlier writings of Marx. To be sure, "human nature" would be different under socialism to the degree to which men and women would, for the first time in history, develop and fulfill their own needs and faculties in association with each other. But this change is to come about almost as a by-product of the new socialist institutions. Marxist emphasis on the development of political consciousness shows little concern with the roots of liberation in individuals, i.e., with the roots of social relationships there where individuals most directly and profoundly experience their world and themselves: in their sensibility, in their instinctual needs.
>
> MARCUSE 1972: 62

Marcuse rescues *The Economic and Philosophical Manuscripts of 1844* to discuss how the question of human nature was largely neglected until then. Marx, reflecting on the concept of being human, thought of human nature as something historical and changeable. The philosophy of the young Marx seems to indicate a radical sensibility. "Marx speaks of the 'complete emancipation of all human senses and qualities' as the feature of socialism [...] This means the emergence of a new type of man" (Marcuse 1972: 64). Thus, a change in the relationship between man and nature (exterior and interior) would entail the transformation of man himself.

> "Emancipation of the senses" implies that the senses become "practical" in the reconstruction of society, that they generate new (socialist) relationships between man and man, man and things, man and nature. But the senses become also "sources" of a new (socialist) rationality: freed from that of exploitation. The emancipated senses would repel the instrumentalist rationality of capitalism while preserving and developing its achievements.
>
> MARCUSE 1972: 64

The emancipation of the senses here indicates the liberation from the training of sensibility performed under the performance principle. "In the name of increasing profit and decreasing expenses, the division of labor causes those on the production line to lose themselves in the process, reducing their intellectual and motor functions to focus on carrying out their daily task" (Arão 2019: 173).

In this way, the emancipation of the senses appears as an antithesis of instrumental reason and brutalization. The sensible is only of interest to the performance principle if it can be quantified, calculated, and controlled. Therefore, the *ethos* that should replace the capitalist way of life and allow the emergence of the socialist "new man" should have antithetical qualities to brutality and insensitivity. This represents a perspective linked to sensitivity, but also receptivity and care. Such characteristics would represent the overcoming of the performance principle.

3 Femininity as Antithesis of the Performance Principle

Angela Davis, in an essay entitled *Woman and Capitalism*, argues that it is femininity that represents this antithesis to the performance principle. According to Davis, the fact that women have historically become more linked to the family and with the responsibility for domestic care has kept them largely outside the world of social production (Davis 2000: 163) and consequently kept them from being made them not so integrated to the capitalist way of life vis-à-vis men.

The capitalist mode of production unleashes the condition for the historical supersession of the sexually based division of labor. The universal equivalence of labor-power conceptually implies the release of the woman from her naturally infused roles in labor. This potentiality, needless to say, could not become more than an abstract promise of equal exploitation. Capitalism could not even proclaim for women this rudimentary egalitarianism. Instead, it transmuted a more or less naturally conditioned oppression into an oppression whose content became thoroughly socio-historical. It was only then that women were effectively exiled from the sphere of social production – or permitted, at most, a tangential role. Their containment within the family became, not a natural necessity, but rather a peculiarly societal phenomenon. It is therefore only in bourgeois society that the oppression of women assumes a decisive social dimension and function.

DAVIS 2000: 160

In view of this, Davis proposes a positive look at femininity. It may be possible to extract something good from the non-integration of women in the world of alienated labor because this femininity has developed throughout history with characteristics linked to care and sensitivity. However, this perception of positive aspects linked to the idea of femininity was already controversial at the time Davis wrote the text in question in the early 1970s. According to her:

In efforts to debunk the myth of the woman as an exclusively emotional being, an equally abstract position has been too often assumed. The abstract negation of "femininity" is embraced; attempts are made to demonstrate that women can be as non-emotional, reality-affirming and dominating as men are alleged to be. The model, however, is usually a concealed "masculine" one.

DAVIS 2000: 166

Therefore, to renounce the role of an emotional and sensitive being, part of the feminist movement considered it important to abandon the idea of femininity. Davis, on the other hand, believed in the revolutionary potential of the qualities that were historically bequeathed to women because the purpose of the feminist movement, for her, is not the adequacy of women to the capitalist system, but the contribution to its overcoming. In this sense, there is no reason for women to fight to be as embedded in the performance principle as men.

Marcuse had contact with this text by Angela Davis before it was published (possibly still in 1971) and he dialogues with its contents first in

Counter-Revolution and Revolt in 1972 and later in a conference called Marxism and Feminism in 1974. In the lecture and the book, Marcuse applies the concepts developed in *Eros and Civilization* to deal with how the feminist struggle can contribute to a change of consciousness in the society. In this context, Marcuse highlights more specifically the importance of the Women's Liberation Movement. According to him, this movement is "perhaps the most important and potentially the most radical political movement that we have" (Marcuse 2005: 165).

Thus, under the influence of the Women's Liberation Movement, Angela Davis and, possibly other feminist thinkers, Marcuse proposes a change in the concept of socialism and calls it "feminist socialism". This adjective "feminist", as with "female" or "feminine" in Marcuse's work, designates a series of characteristics and values that would oppose the characteristics and values of the established society, which would be masculine. This happens because, for the author, in the development of patriarchal civilization, masculine values are the dominant ones – these are the values that sustain capitalism.

Marcuse, then, finds in the work of Angela Davis a guide for the idea of new anthropology. Continuing the thought elaborated by her, he defends the argument that society must be feminized. In this way, ending patriarchy becomes, for him, as important as taking over the means of production.

4 Feminist Socialism

Regarding this proposal of "feminizing" society, that is, creating another "second nature" that is not linked to the performance principle, Marcuse is concerned to highlight two extremely important things. 1) The female society is not a matriarchal society. 2) Despite denying values such as virility, the Marcusean proposal does not end in a conformist and cowardly passivity. Although the idea is to create a female society, Marcuse does not propose that it be a society governed by women. This is not a revolution in which women take power; what is proposed is not an inversion in the sense that women are the rulers, but that the values of the feminine guide society, including "feminizing" men

> would be a female society. In this sense, it has nothing to do with matriarchy of any sort; the image of the woman as mother is itself repressive; it transforms a biological fact into an ethical and cultural value and thus it supports and justifies her social repression. At stake is rather the ascent of Eros over aggression, in men and women; and this means, in a male-dominated civilization, the "feminization" of the male. It would

express the decisive change in the instinctual structure: the weakening of primary aggressiveness which, by a combination of biological and social factors, has governed the patriarchal culture.

MARCUSE 1972: 75

Marcuse, starting from the positive idea of femininity presented by Angela Davis, contends that the most important thing is that masculinity be transformed and acquire feminine characteristics. Reworking the arguments elaborated by Davis in *Woman and Capitalism*, he affirms that throughout the civilizing process, the values of the performance principle were established with a close relationship to the ideal of what is masculine. In this way, women remain on the margins of this *ethos*.

> These female qualities may well be socially determined by the development of capitalism. The process is truly dialectical. Although the reduction of the concrete individual faculties to abstract labor power established an abstract equality between men and women (equality before the machine), this abstraction was less complete in the case of women. They were employed in the material process of production to a lesser extent than men. Women were fully employed in the household, the family, which was supposed to be the sphere of realization for the bourgeois individual. However, this sphere was isolated from the productive process and thus contributed to the women's mutilation. And yet, this isolation (separation) from the alienated work world of capitalism enabled the woman to remain less brutalized by the Performance Principle, to remain closer to her sensibility: more human than men.
>
> MARCUSE 1972: 77

For Marcuse, the fact that many women were relatively removed from the world of alienated labor, protected them, in a way, from the moral norms of capitalism; this also as enabled the feminine to be more linked to Eros, that is, to the values of aggregation and conservation of human life. As a result, the image of women is generally associated with care.

However, this second nature does not correspond to an absence of aggressiveness or conformity. Revolution, for Marcuse, is a violent process, and denying violence is not only unnatural (because the human being has a death instinct as well as a life instinct), but also counterproductive, as no major change occurs without the need for a fight. According to the philosopher:

Far from fostering submissiveness and weakness, in this reconstruction the feminine characteristics would activate aggressive energy against domination and exploitation. They would operate as needs and eventual goals in the socialist organization of production, in the social division of labor, in the setting of priorities once scarcity has been conquered. And thus, entering the reconstruction of society as a whole, the feminine characteristics would cease to be specifically feminine, to the degree to which they would be universalized in socialist culture, material and intellectual.

MARCUSE 2005: 170

In this sense, the philosopher proposes a distinction between "aggression" and "surplus-aggression", as was done with "repression" and "surplus-repression". "The surplus-aggression of the male is socially conditioned" (Marcuse 1972: 77). For Marcuse, aggressiveness is natural for the human being and is not a problem in itself. Its transformation into surplus-aggression creates a culture of aggressiveness linked to the male figure. In the same way that surplus-aggression is harmful, so too is over-passivity, for pusillanimity only leads to conformism. Thus, an aggressiveness that militates in favor of social transformation is necessary.

Primary aggressiveness would persist, as it would in any form of society, but it may well lose the specifically masculine quality of domination and exploitation. Technical progress, the chief vehicle of productive aggressiveness, would be freed from its capitalist features and channeled into the destruction of the ugly destructiveness of capitalism.

MARCUSE 2005: 170–171

Note, therefore, that, although there is a criticism of the culture of aggressiveness, violence cannot be ruled out either. Violence that aims to end surplus-aggression is necessary, and this is necessary because social transformations are the result of journeys of struggle. The figure that Marcuse refers to in order to illustrate this idea is Delacroix's painting, *Liberty Leading the People*.

In this sense too, the woman holds the promise of liberation. It is the woman who, in Delacroix' painting, holding the flag of the revolution, leads the people on the barricades. She wears no uniform; her breasts are bare, and her beautiful face shows no trace of violence. But she has a rifle in her hand-for the end of violence is still to be fought for.

MARCUSE 1972: 78

The apparent contradiction in the idea of fighting for the end of violence is resolved through the distinction between aggression and surplus-aggression. This means that revolutionary violence is not part of the way of life but a tool that channels the death instinct to fight various forms of oppression. We find an example of this idea beyond the artistic dimension in the Zapatista movement, which engages in a kind of pacifist guerrilla war and wields rifles to assert a voice.

> The existence of the Zapatistas as the Ejército Zapatista de Liberación Nacional (EZLN) (the Zapatista Army of National Liberation) is one important example: they are not armed in a way that would allow them to win a full military confrontation with the Mexican army, but they are armed sufficiently for it to make it unattractive for the Mexican army to intervene with direct military force. However, 'unattractive' here cannot be understood in purely military terms, in terms of violence against violence. What makes military intervention 'unattractive' for the Mexican army is not just the armed violence that the Zapatistas could oppose to the army's violence, but above all the strength of the social connections that the Zapatistas have woven both with their own communities and with the wider community in Mexico and beyond.
>
> HOLLOWAY 2002: 238

5   Androgynia

Thus, the qualities of femininity, for Marcuse, would construct a reality principle different from the performance principle. They would, therefore, be the way out from productivism and surplus-aggression. "In this context, the liberation of the woman would indeed appear as the antithesis to the Performance Principle, would indeed appear as the revolutionary function of the female in the reconstruction of society" (Marcuse 2005: 170). Finalizing his exposition on the importance of the struggle of women in *Counter-Revolution and Revolt*, the author makes an analogy with the classic passage in which Marx considers the proletariat as the gravediggers of capitalism. "Here too the historical process is dialectical: the patriarchal society has created a female image, a female counter-force, which may still become one of the gravediggers of patriarchal society" (Marcuse 1972: 72). Paraphrasing the author of *Das Kapital*, Marcuse compares the formation of the proletariat in capitalism with the formation of the feminine in patriarchy.

This perspective, however, has suffered several criticisms. In 1978, when interviewing Marcuse, Briton Bryan Magee stated that many people considered the division of male and female values to be sexist. In response, the Critical Theorist expounds that this classification of genres is a product of society, and however much it was created on oppressive grounds, there is no reason not to use it.

Such a theoretical position is in line with other themes in Marcuse's works, including technology, for example. Marcuse understands that the technologies were created based on exploitation at work, but that doesn't mean we should stop using them. We must appropriate technology in order to direct it towards the ends of human emancipation.

It is not possible to deny that gender roles exist and are present in our reality. From there, what Marcuse does is to understand that patriarchy, by keeping many women away from the world of waged work and simultaneously making women responsible for reproductive and emotional care, ended up fostering an axiology antithetical to the performance principle and, therefore, may unintentionally create a risk to the perpetuation of patriarchy and capitalism.

However, this is not about defending the assertion that women are feminine. For Marcuse, the important movement is the feminization of man. This means that men need to be guided by the gradual abandonment of qualities linked to the performance principle, and recognize the importance of values such as passivity, tolerance, and care. Hence a kind of androgyny may arise. From the moment that men acquire feminine characteristics, the boundaries that mark gender divisions loosen.

> I think there are good reasons for calling this image of socialist society feminist socialism: the woman would have achieved full economic, political, and cultural equality in the all-round development of her faculties, and over and above this equality, social as well as personal relationships would be permeated with the receptive sensitivity which, under male domination, was largely concentrated in the woman: the masculine-feminine antithesis would then have been transformed into a synthesis – the legendary idea of androgynism.
>
> MARCUSE 2005: 171

In this way, it can be noted that even though Marcuse works with concepts such as masculinity and femininity, the conclusion of his proposal is to overcome the contradiction of genders with the emergence of a synthesis. This synthesis, however, does not keep the characteristics of the feminine and the masculine equally. In this dialectical process, surplus-aggression, brutishness, surplus-repression, and other elements of the performance principle must give way to a culture of care, life instinct, and constructive aggressiveness.

This kind of gender dissolution, however, does not aim to end all differences between men and women in order to make them completely equal. According to Marcuse:

> no degree of androgynous fusion could ever abolish the natural differences between male and female as individuals. All joy, and all sorrow are rooted in this difference, in this relation to the other, of whom you want to become part, and who you want to become part of yourself, and who never can and never will become such a part of yourself. Feminist socialism would thus continue to be riddled with conflicts arising from this condition, the ineradicable conflicts of needs and values, but the androgynous character of society might gradually diminish the violence and humiliation in the resolution of these conflicts.
>
> MARCUSE 2005: 171

It is important to note that the idea is not to create a monotonous (one-tone) society. As much as the feminine qualities spread through society they do not reach all people in the same way, nor is this process something that will happen by decree. Thus, even in feminist socialism, it is not possible to eradicate all inequalities, prejudices, and subjugations in a single stroke. However, the expected trend is that over time conflicts will attenuate.

It can be seen, therefore, that, although Marcuse draws upon the concept of femininity, his concern is much more with masculinity. Recognizing the positive characteristics of the feminine elaborated by Angela Davis, he proposes that men should take for themselves attributes that are normally expected to be present in women.

6   Marcuse and Feminism

Thus, it is clear that, for Marcuse, a member of the first generation of the Frankfurt School, gender issues play a fundamental role. However, in the case of Critical Theory, this is not where the first analyzes of the oppression of women by men appear. If, like Marcuse, we consider that Critical Theory also comes from Marxism,[1] we find observations on these issues of gender in Marx's

---

1   "Let me make one further observation in conclusion. I have alread indicated that if Critical Theory, which remains indebted to Marx, does not wish to stop at merely improving the

own work. It is possible to find analyzes on this theme even in the manuscripts that make up the book *The German Ideology*. In them, Marx argues that the first moment in which the division of labor appears in history is with the emergence of the family, which originally operated as a kind of slavery regime where women and children were submissive to men.

> The division of labour in which all these contradictions are implicit, and which in its turn is based on the natural division of labour in the family and the separation of society into individual families opposed to one another, simultaneously implies the distribution, and indeed the unequal distribution, both quantitative and qualitative, of labour and its products, hence property: the nucleus, the first form of which lies in the family, where wife and children are the slaves of the husband. This latent slavery in the family, though still very crude, is the first form of property, but even at this stage it corresponds perfectly to the definition of modern economists, who call it the power of disposing of the labour-power of others. Division of labour and private property are, after all, identical expressions: in the one the same thing is affirmed with reference to activity as is affirmed in the other with reference to the product of the activity.
>
> MARX AND ENGELS 1998: 51–52

Marx will return to this question in his maturity with his ethnological studies, based on the work of the anthropologist Lewis H. Morgan. Even though Marx did not complete his studies on the subject, nor has he left any work on the issue, Engels took on the responsibility of continuing the project and produced *The Origin of the Family, Private Property and the State*.

Based on the research developed by Marx, Engels, investigating the role of monogamy, concludes that the monogamous relationship constitutes the first class oppression with the subjugation of women by men (Engels 2004: 73). Thus, it is noted that inequality between genders and the concern with the problem of women's oppression are themes that were present at the beginning of Critical Theory. Marcuse, in *Counter-Revolution and Revolt*, reminds us that, for Marxist theory, the exploitation of one gender over the other is the primary oppression, even though part of Marxism has not been committed to this issue.

It is precisely because of the attention to this problem and the commitment and connection with the feminist movements that Marcuse has even come to

---

existing state of affairs, it must accommodate within itself the extreme possibilities for freedom that have been only crudely indicated". (Marcuse 2014: 254).

be called an "honorary woman"[2] by feminists. Today, even though his ideas no longer directly influence social movements,[3] nor is he one of the most read philosophers, much of what he wrote and defended politically remains valid today, and arguably even more necessary than ever.

Concerning feminism more specifically, it is important to bring out the possible relationship of the critical theorist with Carol Gilligan's ethics of care. According to Tammy A. Shel (2009), in *The Dialectic of Tolerance and Intolerance in the Ethics of Caring*, in Marcuse's philosophy, something close to what is proposed by Gilligan can be found. According to Gilligan, there are two moral perspectives: one male and one female; the male view would be the default while the female would be on the fringes (Gilligan, 1985). Gilligan proposes, then, something similar to the Frankfurt School philosopher, when he proposes an ethics of care based on feminine values.

Concluding his approach to the importance of feminism in his Marxism and Feminism conference, Marcuse, in a confessional tone, raises an extremely important issue for the theme: the relationship between public and private ethics. Perhaps today, in the second decade of the 21st century, we can see more clearly that personal relationships are influenced by how society is organized, and therefore, that many personal problems are also political issues. The male chauvinism suffered by a woman at home or work, for example, is an intimate issue, but not only; it is also a problem of political order because the patriarchal moment is the manifestation of the patriarchal society. Thus, shame, fear, and the feeling of guilt that can arise from a male chauvinist act, although they are personal feelings, are the result of political conflicts.

However, this is not a fully accepted issue today, let alone was it in the 1970s. A considerable part of the liberal perspective tends to consider the private sphere as something independent, as if each relationship were a microcosm unto itself and not part of society. On this question, possibly echoing the ideas of authors such as Carol Hanisch (2021), who in 1969 argued that the personal is political, Marcuse argues that the oppression of women must end first at home.[4] In this way, Marcuse brings gender equality guidelines to everyday life, because there cannot be an egalitarian society when a woman is still submissive in her own home.

---

2 As reported by Angela Davis in the documentary *Herbert's Hippopotamus: Marcuse and Revolution in Paradise*: https://www.youtube.com/watch?v=gbzhmMDFcFQ.

3 In Brazil, Marcuse is much more a straw man used by the far right than a thinker considered by the left.

4 "The liberation of women begins at home, before it can enter society at large" (Marcuse 2005: 172).

7   Final Considerations

In this way, the relevance of feminist thought and the issue of women's oppression for Marcuse's thought is noted. The idea of female society is the culmination of the project to build the new anthropology that appears as an antithesis to the values of the performance principle. While this new *ethos* represents tolerance and passivity, it in no way encourages permissiveness and self-indulgence. Aggressiveness still exists and must be directed towards the destruction of the old society so that a new one can emerge.

The conclusion of the revolutionary process would then be the creation of a second nature based on the legacy of feminine values. Such values would reconcile humanity with sensitivity to allow a more harmonious coexistence and this would create another type of reality principle. Just as the performance principle is a historical form with the characteristics of surplus-repression and surplus-aggression, the new historical nature would allow human beings to live without unnecessary repression and violence.

The subject of this new world was commonly called in the last century the "new man" because it was still much more common to use the word "man" to refer to humanity. Thus, in Marcuse's work, as in many others, the expression "new man" appears as a synonym for "new anthropology" or "new humanity".

So, curiously when looking for the "new man", that is, this kind of figure that represents the denial of the *ethos* of capitalism, Marcuse finds the image of the woman, because femininity is the antithesis of the performance principle. It is up to man to feminize himself to abandon the culture of brutalization, violence, and the death instinct.

References

Arão, Cristian. 2019. "A Liberdade Como Essência Humana: o Problema do Sujeito no Jovem Marx". *Revista Ideação* 39, no. 1: 167–177. https://doi.org/10.13102/ideac.v1i39 .4583.

Davis, Angela. 2000. "Woman and Capitalism: Dialectics of Oppression and Liberation". In *The Black Feminist Reader*, eds. Joy James and T. Denean Sharpley-Whiting, 146–182. New Jersey: Blackwell.

Engels, Friedrich. 2004 [1884]. *The Origin of the Family, Private Property and the State*. Chippendale, NSW: Resistance Books.

Freud, Sigmund. 1962 [1929]. *Civilization and its Discontents*. New York: Norton & Company.

Gilligan, Carol. 1985. *In a Different Voice: Women's Conceptions of Self and Morality*. New Brunswick, NJ: Rutgers University Press.

Hanisch, Carol. 2021. "The Personal is Political" In *Women's Liberation! Feminist Writings that Inspired a Revolution*, eds. Alix Kates Shulman and Honor Moore, 82–85. New York: Library of America.

Holloway, John. 2002. *Change the World Without Taking Power*. London: Pluto Press.

Marcuse, Herbert. 1972. *Counter-Revolution and Revolt*. Boston: Beacon Press.

Marcuse, Herbert. 2014. *Marxism, Revolution and Utopia*. ed. Douglas Kellner and Clayton Pierce, New York: Routledge.

Marcuse, Herbert. 2005. *The New Left and the 1960's*. ed. Douglas Kellner, New York: Routledge.

Marx, Karl and Engels, Friedrich. 1998 [1932]. *The German Ideology*. New York: Prometheus Book.

Shel, Tammy, A. 2009. "The Dialectic of Tolerance and Intolerance in the Ethics of Caring" In *Marcuse's Challenge to Education*, eds. Douglas Kellner, Tyson Lewis, Clayton Pierce, and K. Daniel Cho, 117–131. Lanhan: Rowman &Littlefield.

CHAPTER 16

Reification and Forgetting

Thinking the Domination of Nature and of Women with and against Adorno

Lea Gekle

1   Introduction

Adorno conceptualizes social theory as producing critical knowledge about society by confronting the empirical realm (Adorno 1977: 120). Central to Adorno's analysis of social reality is his understanding of reification, which describes a social interaction where humans relate to each other not as subjects but as objects. Even though it is definitely not the center of his interests, the oppression of women under capitalism appears in a certain number of Adorno's texts. In the *Dialectic of Enlightenment* as well as *Minima Moralia* the domination of women appears as structurally linked to domination of nature and expresses itself as a specific form of reification.

Feminist scholarship has been, since at least the late 80s, interested in Adorno's analysis of women's oppression.[1] Within this field, several authors focus on Adorno's effort to think a connection between the domination of nature and women in late capitalist societies (i.e., Jagentowicz Mills 1991; Mills 1987; King 1998; Plumwood 1993). In the last couple of years these debates have regained interest, especially in France, and several works about the possible and impossible connections between feminist theory and Adorno's social theory have been published (Ferrarese 2021, Naït Ahmed 2019a; 2019b; Guillibert 2020; Wezel 2020; Vuillerod 2021). Some of these authors (Guillibert 2020; Wezel 2020; Vuillerod 2021) think about the possible proximity of eco-feminist thought and Adorno's reflections on domination of nature and women. The aim of this chapter is to carve out the usefulness of Adorno's concept of reification and domination of nature in order to criticize essentialist tendencies in

---

1 The debate about the possible connections between Adorno's thought and feminist philosophy are getting more vivid since the beginning of 2000. Without being exhaustive, one can quote some more general studies about Adorno and male domination (Ferrarese 2021; Naït Ahmed 2019a; 2019b; Ferrarese et al. 2020; Heberle 2006; Becker-Schmidt 2004a; 2004b; Dayan-Herzbrun, Gabriel, et Varikas 2004; O'Neill 1999; Lee 2005).

(eco)feminist thought, while stating at the same time that Adorno's thinking can and needs to be criticized by feminist approaches.[2]

Through an analysis of Ynestra King's article "The Ecology Feminism and the Feminism of Ecology," my first step is to point out a fundamental problem one has to confront while thinking about domination of women as an expression of domination of nature: the question of the historicity of forms of domination and their social mediation. Her article is important not only because it is "one of the first ecofeminist articles" – as Jagentowicz Mills highlights (1991: 170) – but also because it openly refers to Adorno's concept of reification as forgetting.[3] I use King's approach as a theoretical launching pad in order to reveal, in a second step, Adorno's conception of a historically determined understanding of domination of nature and women. Whereas he proposes a conceptual framework in order to think about the socially mediated concept of nature and therefore steps out of an essentialist understanding of the domination of nature and women, Adorno's analysis of women's oppression is symptomatic for (at least) *two* problematic tendencies one finds in his work. The first concerns the historical determination of (male) domination. The second deals with the difficulty Adorno presents in theorizing individual agency.[4] Several authors, (i.e., Becker-Schmidt 2004a; 2004b; Naït Ahmed 2019a; 2019b) highlight the insufficiency of Adorno's studies of the "female character." Whereas I agree with their analysis of the insufficiency of the sociological analysis Adorno proposes concerning women's oppression, I confront his analysis of

---

2   Concerning the discussion about possible connections between eco-feminism and Critical Theory see: (Jagentowicz Mills 1991; Mills 1987; King 1998; Guillibert 2020; Wezel 2020; Plumwood 1993). This task, trying to analyze the social role of women without reassigning them to the very same social role is a fundamental question in feminism. See i.e., Hewitt 2006; Hache 2016. The eco-feminist movement has been criticized very severely (Biehl 1991) as proposing an essentialist approach as an answer to male domination. For attempts to think an anti-essentialist eco-feminism, see: Gaard 2011; Mellor 1994; Hache 2016; Salleh 1991.

3   I am not alone in analyzing King's relationship to Critical Theory and, especially, Adorno. Jagentowicz Mills studies King's approach as well. Whereas she is focusing on a critique of King regarding the question of the self-determination of women's body, I underline the problem of the ahistoricity of her concept of domination of women and nature. Paul Guillibert (2020) also analyses Jagentowicz Mills' critique of King's approach but highlights Mills critique concerning a romantic understanding of nature in King's text. He tries to think about the "revolt of nature" in Adorno's and Horkheimer's *Dialectic of Enlightenment* and Carolyn Merchant's *The Death of Nature*.

4   Most of the secondary literature agrees on this point: Adorno produces an image of women as objects rather than subjects (Ferrarese 2021; Wezel 2020; Naït Ahmed 2019a; 2019b; Becker-Schmidt 2004a; 2004b; Geulen 1996; Ziege 2004). Other approaches, for example by Duford (2017), try nonetheless to carve out a political potential in Adorno's analysis and critique of patriarchy.

the social role of women in late capitalist societies with Maria Mies' studies on "housewifization" (Mies 2014) and the dualism of production and reproduction. I argue for a historically informed theoretical approach which thinks about the division of labour and the reproduction-production dualism within contemporary society. This allows a concrete analysis of female subjectivation in a materialist framework without neglecting a larger historical horizon. It also makes it possible to think of contemporary forms of oppression as having a longer history than simply the recent history of capital, without stepping out of a historically specific analysis. The confrontation with these different strands of feminist thought allows me also to critically interrogate, in a more general sense, Adorno's conception of critical social theory, highlighting its potential as well as some of its problems.[5]

2   Women, Nature, and the De-historization of Domination

2.1   *The Dualism between Nature and Society*

Despite the heterogeneous positions, one can identify two aspects which most eco-feminist approaches have in common. Emilie Hache highlights in her French anthology of eco-feminist texts that the movement deduces a political, scientific, and spiritual program from its diagnosis about patriarchal capitalism and the social conception of an inferiority of nature and women (Hache 2016: 19–20). Patriarchal society is understood to be based on two fundamental dualisms; namely, the distinction between nature and society (Griffin 1981; Daly 1990) and the distinction between production and reproduction.[6] Hache argues that these dualisms are accompanied by a normative judgement on what belongs to nature and is therefore devalued, and what belongs to culture and is therefore valued (Hache 2016: 20). The production-reproduction dualism as the social process which organizes social life presents itself as a descriptive temporal relation. This is to say that under a certain social organization it establishes a normative relation by defining production as prior to reproduction (Salleh 2003: 65).

For my purpose, Ynestra King's approach to formulate a critique of these dualisms is interesting. She uses Adorno's and Horkheimer's definition of

---

5   In this chapter, I try to carve out Adorno's position about domination of nature and women. Even though, of course, I will have to relate to the co-authored *Dialectic of Enlightenment*, I will focus on Adorno's studies on reification of women.

6   Ariel Salleh highlights the large sense of reproduction: «biological process, economic relations and cultural practice » (Salleh 2003: 64).

reification in order to develop her own theory of reification, and shows in her article "The Ecology of Feminism and Feminism of Ecology" that ecology and feminism must be thought of in relation to one another. She writes:

> All human beings are natural beings. That may seem like an obvious fact, yet we live in a culture that is founded on the repudiation and domination of nature. This has a special significance for women because, in patriarchal thought, women are believed to be closer to nature than men. This gives women a particular stake in ending the domination of nature – in healing the alienation between human and nonhuman nature.
>
> KING 1998: 429

In King's argument, a first step consists in pointing out the "naturality" of human beings. Despite our "natural origins," our contemporary relationship to nature is defined by a progressive distancing from it. The distancing expresses a relation of domination. Humanity relates to nature while objectifying it; women, being considered as close to nature, are therefore objectified too. Thus, Western societies are "founded on the domination of nature." King uses the reified image of women in capitalist society against itself. Her political and theoretical strategy consists in considering that the particular position of women within patriarchal society gives them also a status particularly capable to fight for "human as well as non-human nature." Here, then, it is not a matter of a primary essentialism, which considers the category "woman" as a fixed, biological category, but rather a political strategy that makes of the essentialization of women by patriarchy a political weapon.[7] Two points are nonetheless highly problematic. The first one, elaborated by Patricia Jagentowicz Mills in her article "Feminism and Ecology: On the Domination of Nature," is that King's strategic reaffirmation of femininity does not introduce a category which allows critical distance to it, and therefore potentially reproduces the reified image (Jagentowicz Mills 1991: 171).[8] Secondly, and this point is linked to the first one, using such big categories as "women" and "nature" de-historicizes their domination. Ecofeminists like Ariel Salleh do indeed consider this enlarging of the analytical framework as enriching. In contrast to certain Marxist analysis

---

7   The debate about the strategic use of essentialism is vivid. See i.e., Spivak (2006: 284). For a critique of it see: (Biehl 1991; Butler 2006).

8   Jagentowicz Mills interrogates King's lack of conceptual precision (1991: 172) and highlights that this lack is highly problematic when it comes to "reproductive freedom" because it assigns women as having a specific form of responsibility *for* reproduction and nature (1991: 170–172).

which deduces contemporary forms of oppression and exploitation from the place the subjects have within the organization of production, Salleh highlights eco-feminists' capacity to "[ask] whether there are not yet deeper causal structures, general processes and particular contingencies, formative of older gender innocent Marxist understandings" (Salleh 2003: 64).

This might be the aim of King's elaboration but it seems to me that she cannot enlarge the scope of the analysis without de-historicizing it. Reducing the question of domination to a one-dimensional "origin" of domination de-historicizes her approach. Male domination is explained simply as the forgetting of this apparent primary dependency on nature. No doubt, of course, that there is a dependency on nature, but in transforming it to a general, primary dependency, one cannot understand the specificity of the "metabolism" (Marx) between nature and society under capitalism. It simply pretends that there would be a "first nature," untouched by the logics of capital and that the recovery of this forgotten "first nature" leads us to step out of the contemporary configuration of nature and society. This means, firstly, as Jagentowicz Mills highlights, not only a potentially problematic understanding of "nature" as necessarily good (Jagentowicz Mills, 1991: 163). Secondly, it means a "forgetting" of a non-socially mediated relationship between human and nature which itself presupposes that a world without a socially determined relationship between those two would be possible. This second point interests me here, because Adorno criticizes these kind of nature conceptions: For him nature and naturality are always socially mediated. This is why reification is defined in the *Dialectic of Enlightenment* as the forgetting of nature as a social relation – in a double sense. The first concerns the apparent naturality of the state of society. Society tends to be considered as natural and unchangeable rather than historically grown; here forgetting means to forget the historicity of what appears "natural." The second sense concerns the appropriation and exploitation of nature and its resources under capitalism. Forgetting about nature and its destruction is one of the necessary conditions for the existence of a capitalist mode of production (Horkheimer and Adorno 2002: 190–191).

We have now seen that the question of reification and forgetting is central to both the first generation of the Frankfurt School and to Ynestra King. Even though King's work refers openly to the *Dialectic of Enlightenment*, it involves a "forgetting" of nature which is problematic because she refers to a social function as a biological one.

2.2   *The Recovery of First Nature and the Loss of Historicity*

Whereas Jagentowicz Mills is right in highlighting and problematizing the injunction in King's work to "'reconcile with nature'" (Jagentowicz Mills

1991: 172), I stress that King turns the concept of reification, which is supposed to show the historical anchorage of a specific social relation, into a trans-historical and essentializing category. She writes:

> The process of objectification, of the making of women and nature into "others" to be appropriated and dominated, is based on a profound for-getting by men. They forget that they were born of women, were depen-dent on women in their early helpless years, and are dependent on nonhuman nature all their lives, which allows first for objectification and then for domination. "The loss of memory is a transcendental condition for science. All objectification is a forgetting".
>
> KING 1998: 432

While King quotes Horkheimer and Adorno's famous phrase from the *Dialectic of Enlightenment* on reification as forgetting, she gives a different meaning to forgetting.[9] Forgetting is, by King, described as a forgetting of a supposedly primary connection between mother and child. She then understands the pro-cess of entering civilization as an ongoing forgetting of this naturalness of this first dependency. However, this historical process is not analyzed in detail and highlights a fundamental problem with King's approach to her concept of reifi-cation. While presenting the nature/culture dualism as a structural process for our Western societies, reification is eternalized and does not receive a concrete historical determination.

King reduces the reproduction-production dualism to a forgetting of the 'biological' dependence of men on women and therefore simply proposes a reversal of it, rather than a way to step out of this dualism (Jagentowicz Mills 1991: 170–1). And it is here that a primary type of essentialism appears – because she thinks "women" as a "natural group" (Wittig 1992: 9). To think of women's oppression solely via the biological function of childbirth means to produce a biological identity that considers the domination of nature to be identical to the domination of the biological identity of childbirth. This gesture then reproduces the idea that childbirth is *the* essential function of

---

9 In her study on Adorno and care (Ferrarese 2021), Ferrarese highlights the connection between « forgetting » and reification. She proposes to understand « forgetting » as more a « political category than a cognitive » (Ferrarese 2021: 49–50). In her analysis of the differ-ent forms of "reification as forgetting," she quotes one which is of particular interest for us, the one Adorno mentions in his lecture Introduction to Sociology. Here, Adorno shows that "reification as forgetting" means to forget about the historical becoming of our social reality (Ferrarese 2021: 53–54).

women in society. Of course, the reproduction of society depends on reproduction of humankind, but reproduction is not the "essence" of women.
Reducing women to motherhood means also to presuppose motherhood as
an evident and natural bond. Furthermore, defining childbirth and motherhood as an initial relationship between men and women does not explain
how this childbirth is socially organized, nor does it explain that the reduction of femininity to the capacity to give birth is problematic, as it is an essentialist definition of female identity.[10]

3   Domination of Nature and Women in Adorno and Horkheimer

3.1   *Domination of Nature and Progress*
Despite the proximity of some of the analyses of this specific ecofeminist[11]
approach and first generation of Critical Theory, I stress that the thinkers from
Frankfurt can be read as being able to bring a fruitful critique to the question
of the historicity of patriarchal domination thanks to their conception of a
socially mediated relationship between nature and society. I will point out that
Adorno and Horkheimer's analysis of the domination of nature tries to link a
historically determined analysis of the transformation of reason and its consequences to the relationship between humanity and nature.

In the segment *Le prix du progrès* of the *Dialectic of Enlightenment*, the
authors link self-preservation, scientific progress, the domination of nature,
and instrumental reason (Horkheimer and Adorno 2002: 190–191). They analyze Pierre Flourens' criticism of the use of chloroform to anesthetize his
patients. Following experiments on animals, he finds that chloroform is a
"'deception'" of consciousness rather than a real hindrance to our "'capacity
of feeling'" (Horkheimer and Adorno 2002: 190). We will feel pain perfectly
well, but the inability to remember pain after the operation will not allow us
to object to this type of anesthesia. Not remembering pain does not mean not
having felt pain.[12] While analyizing the same passage, Estelle Ferrarese highlights that the "forgetting of suffering" is not only a question which concerns
ourselves but also one which concerns the "others" (Ferrarese 2021: 52). On

---

10   Jagentowicz Mill asks about the limitation an essentialist understanding of childbirth
      implies for "reproductive freedom" (Jagentowicz Mill 1991: 170).
11   Ecofeminism is a heterogeneous movement. Often criticized for its essentialism, cer-
      tain ecofeminist authors try to develop a non-essentialist ecofeminism (i.e., Gaard 2011;
      Salleh 2003).
12   See also Ferrarese's analysis of this paragraph (Ferrarese 2021: 49–55).

the one hand, the 'price of progress', the price of self-preservation – because medical progress remains in the continuity of self-preservation – is then that of the domination of the other, of nature, and is based on the objectification and instrumentalization of the other, in this case the animals on which the first tests were carried out. On the other hand, this instrumentalization of animals by humans falls back on humans and turns into a domination of humans by humans as they instrumentalize themselves in a similar way as the animals they had used to progress in medicine. Anesthesia as forgetting pain becomes in Adorno and Horkheimer the metaphor of reification. Reification means forgetting the pain inflicted on what has been constituted as the "other" by instrumental reason, without being able to extract oneself from this relationship of domination and finding oneself as well as an actor and a victim of this domination.

Forgetting is also forgetting our historicity. The principle of domination lies in instrumental reason. Humanity, which tries to "learn from nature [...] how to use it to dominate wholly both it and human beings" (Horkheimer et Adorno 2002: 2) produces in the instrumental approach to nature its own domination, because in the principle of instrumental reason lies a way of dominating the environment and others. The promise of the *Aufklärung*, namely human progress as liberation, transforms progress into technical progress and therefore into domination. Thus, progress is measured as progress in the domination of nature.

A first sense of reification as forgetting can then be identified: Forgetting our historicity would also mean to forget that the price for technical progress is forgetting our dependence on nature. While forgetting the dependence we integrate the principle of an inner and outer, of a "subjective" and "objective" un-freedom. Adorno stresses in his lectures on *History and Freedom* that the contemporary society expresses a double form of un-freedom. The objective un-freedom in capitalist society is the fact that we have to sell our labor in order to survive. The subjective un-freedom is the socio-psychological consequence of the capitalist way of production. This un-freedom as produced by the capitalist organization of society is at the same time what produces its apparent dynamic (Adorno, 2006: 3–4). This is why, in the writings of the Frankfurters, domination of nature and humanity tends to become the philosophical motor of world history (Horkheimer and Adorno 2002: 186).

Domination of nature is the substantial motor for historical development, not as a general motor for history but for the historical developments under capitalism. Adorno tries to think the recent technical developments of capital in the framework of a progressing domination of nature and enlarges the scope of his analysis.[13]

Whereas King links domination of nature and women by referring to the forgetting of a biological dependency, Adorno and Horkheimer stress in the *Dialectic of Enlightenment* that forgetting is the necessary condition for technical progress – that carries in itself the gesture of domination. Even though Adorno and Horkheimer try to broaden the concept of domination, as well as to produce a historically determined analysis of domination, I stress that the analysis of women's oppression in late capitalist society brings their approach into difficulties. Therefore, I will analyze the two definitions the authors make of reification. The first one defines, as already stated, reification as forgetting, whereas the second relates much more closely to Lukács, in the sense that it expresses a specific form of intersubjectivity. This comparison will allow me to analyze the tension between a general historical motor of domination and the necessity for a historically determined analysis of domination and its consequences for Adorno's conception of women's oppression in late capitalist society.[14]

3.2   *Forgetting, Reification and Stigma*

The philosophical objective of the *Dialectic of Enlightenment* is the understanding of the contemporary forms of domination in the economy and in culture, paying specific attention to the domination of nature. For Adorno and Horkheimer, as for King, however, women are particularly exposed to domination because they are considered, by the patriarchy, as being closer to nature than men. Therefore, Adorno describes women as the scar [*Wundmal*] of society.[15] 'Wundmal', in German, has, as it appears, more meanings than the English translation 'scar' suggests. It means "wound" but also "stigma."[16]

---

13   Becker-Schmidt proposes an interesting analysis of the difference between Marx's social theory and Adorno's attempt to enlarge the scope of historical materialist research while integrating different aspects of the social world (analysis of the state, the administered world, and the culture industry) in his analysis (2004b: 79).

14   The debate about the historicity of Adorno's concept of domination is quite vivid. Paul Guillibert (Guillibert 2020: 87, 90) stresses that Adorno has an ahistorical conception of domination, whereas Jean-Baptiste Vuillerod (Vuillerod 2021) more recently maintains that Adorno's analysis of domination is always linked to the theoretical desire to understand contemporary domination (Vuillerod 2021: 96–7).

15   This passage has been very often commented on by feminist scholarship. See i.e. (Ferrarese 2021: 69f; Wezel 2020: 69–73).

16   Of course, this also opens a possible interpretation which establish a link between scar, bleeding, and menstruation.

Here, "Wundmal" means not only a social mark of disgrace written in the body. "Wundmal" also focuses on the idea that it is a hurt place – but that the skin grows back over it and covers it. If reification is forgetting, then women are bearing the scars of this forgetting and are the reminder of domination of nature (Wezel 2020: 70–71).

Women are, in Adorno's analysis of patriarchal society, the 'representatives of nature' and therefore the living memory of domination.[17] Adorno and Horkheimer write in the *Dialectic of Enlightenment*

> As a representative of nature, woman in bourgeois society has become an enigma of irresistibility and powerlessness. Thus she reflects back the vain lie of power, which substitutes the mastery over nature for reconciliation with it.
>
> HORKHEIMER AND ADORNO 2002: 56

Here, as in eco-feminism, there is a connection between nature and "woman," but the authors are clear that this is a social role assigned to women. Women are described as an "enigma." As such, they represent irrationality and the incomprehensible and find themselves therefore excluded from the rationalized world without really being outside of it. The problem here is the romanticization of women. By stating that society produces women as the other by simply describing the ways in which they are put outside of society, Adorno and Horkheimer try to "value" this otherness. And therefore, they stay, as Becker-Schmidt highlights, within the logic of the identical and the other (Becker-Schmidt 2004a: 71). Here lies indeed a certain ambiguity: Adorno and Horkheimer seem to think that in the social role of the excluded and the "other" lies a critical potential, but while stating this potential they trap her again in the category of the "other" and underestimate the ways in which women are produced as the other. The relationship between women and men, in a society that mystifies its relationship to nature, becomes "irresistible" at the same time that women are considered "powerless." As "scars," women recall the injury and history of domination. They reveal the myth Enlightenment tells of itself; the freedom and equality proposed by the latter is dismantled as a lie: The scarification points out the process of forgetting the injury caused by patriarchy.

---

17   For an analysis of the process of « de-naturalization and re-naturalization » in Adorno's work concerning women, see Naït Ahmed 2019a.

Rather than to point to their critical potential and to something which does not reproduce the assigned identity, Adorno reassigns women not to an essence but to a social role (Wezel 2020: 71–72).

I have already exposed the first aspect of reification as forgetting. This first aspect thinks the forgetting of the historicity of social relations as a condition for the foundation of Western progress on the domination of nature. The second aspect of reification is connected to the first one and is supposed to link to history of domination with the materialist analysis of domination under capitalism. Adorno relies heavily on Lukács' analysis of reification, which considers the main form of social interaction to be the one which happens in the sphere of the exchange of commodities. In Lukács' theory of reification, human beings do not relate to each other as humans but as things. Reification is then a form of social relation produced by capitalism which objectifies human beings (Lukács 1971: 83–4).

Here lies both the potentially productive and the problematic aspect. If it is true, as i.e. Eva-Maria Ziege (but also (Schneider: 2019)) states, that Adorno uses the category of commodity fetishism in order to think a new "'social cement'" (Ziege 2004: 12), he ascribes a special position of women in society.[18] Adorno thinks the integration of women in society, on the one hand, via the bourgeois contract of marriage. The contract of marriage is the legal instauration of an unjust exchange, highlight Adorno and Horkheimer in the *Dialectic of Enlightenment*. It not only objectifies women but also excludes them systematically of from being subject *à part entière*. Women are integrated in male society, while being constituted as the object of an unjust exchange (Horkheimer and Adorno 2002: 56). On the other hand, women's position within the capitalist society has been defined by their "exclusion from production" (Ziege 2004: 14), therefore they "had, as Ziege writes, developed particular traits of the bourgeois, even if they were different from those of the bourgeois man" (Ziege 2004: 14).[19]

Namely the latter aspect which seems to describe women as "agents of commodity" (Ziege 2004: 18) has often been criticized by feminist scholarship. I adhere to the readings which stresses that the lapse into a problematic understanding of women's oppression in Adorno lies in a not sufficiently, historically elaborated understanding of reification and domination (Becker-Schmidt 2004a: 65, 2004b: 78–9, Naït Ahmed 2019a: 21). With the help of some feminist authors, I show that the process of reification developed by Adorno, which

---

18   I am quoiting the online version of Ziege's article.
19   The direct citations of Ziege are personal translations of the author.

helps to criticize a primary form of essentialism, needs itself a historization and stronger confrontation in order to maintain its critical capacity.

This first aspect is linked to a second problematic aspect that lies in a tension one finds in Adorno's way to think the exemplarity of the condition of women while only reflecting partially on what the condition could carry as emancipatory potential (Becker-Schmidt 2004a; Naït Ahmed 2019a). This tension has been widely discussed in the feminist scholarship about Adorno (i.e., Becker-Schmidt 2004a, 2004b; Hewitt 2006, Duford 2017). These authors suggest, broadly speaking, that one finds in Adorno's studies on reification and women a critical potential. But one finds, as well, his tendency to attribute little capacity for critical action to individuals due to the "context of total delusion" [totaler Verblendungszusammenhang] and which paints a picture of women as particularly exposed to the mechanisms of domination. I will read the existence of these two, mutually exclusive positions, as a tension one finds in Adorno. This tension lies, and here I join Becker-Schmidt's position, in a lack of a precise analysis of the social role women have in capitalist society. I will stress that feminist theory offers indeed a useful tool to think what Becker-Schmidt calls the "double socialization" [doppelte Vergesellschaftung] of women (Becker-Schmidt 2004a: 86), which means to think about the integration of women in the labour-market as well as in the reproductive sphere.

In the last part of this chapter, I show, with recourse to Maria Mies' work *Patriarchy and accumulation on a world scale. Women in the international division of labour,* how one could think an approach linking a precise contemporary analysis with a historically informed theory about the reproduction-production dualism in Western societies. The problem I am trying to resolve can be resumed as the following: While I showed that King's eco-feminism enlarges the categories in which one can think about male domination by trying to overcome the nature-society dualism as well as the reproduction-production dualism, she de-historizes and essentializes her approach because she does not propose a precise analysis of contemporary forms of women's oppression. Adorno and Horkheimer's approach to reification and analysis of the social imbrications of our concept of nature seems here an important critique because it allows them to criticize domination in a specific social configuration. I showed that nonetheless, women's oppression points systematically to a tension in their concept of domination and how to think the concrete expressions of male domination. Here, I will show how another feminist approach can resolve this problem. Using Maria Mies' account on social division of labour,[20] I highlight that she can think about the social division of labor and a possible overcoming of the reproduction-production dualism within contemporary society. This allows a concrete analysis of female subjectivation in a materialist framework without neglecting a larger historical horizon and helps to think about contemporary forms of oppression as having simultaneously a specific historical configuration as well as a longer history than only the recent history of capital.

4   Reification and Social Role

4.1   *Considering Female Reification as a Difficulty for Critical Theory*
The core of Adorno's social theory lies in his conception of the fetish character of the commodity and of reification. Adorno deduces domination in culture, history, and gender from the extension of the principle of the fetish character of commodities and proposes a a critical interrogation of the relationship between philosophy and sociology. When Becker-Schmidt highlights that he does not seriously take into account the "double socialization" of women, then this is also a critique of Adorno's social theory. Modern capitalist society socially integrates women as well as via the necessity of wage-labour but also via reproductive work. I think that this is linked to Adorno's concept of reification and brings the aim of his critical social theory into difficulties. The lack of an analysis of the social roles of women within capitalist production becomes particularly clear when one thinks about his conception of women as "objects" in *Minima Moralia.*

Adorno describes here the reification of women in the patriarchal society of late capitalism. One of the main and not wrong arguments of Adorno is that that emancipation of women in the 1930s and 1940s was articulated around work. He stresses that the integration of women in the labour-market did not contribute to the emancipation of women, but on the contrary, maintains the state of reification.

---

20   I have stated the problematic conception of King's conception of nature and maternity. Maria Mies' work has recently been criticized for the same "mythologiz[ing] femininity" (Hester 2018: 38). Hester mainly refers to Mies' essay "Mother Earth" which was published in 2015. She highlights its difficulties to "challenge [...] hegemonic gender roles." (Hester 2018: 39). Whereas I agree with this critique, I refer to Mies' earlier work on housewifization because it challenges in a productive way reductionist approaches to the question of social divisions of labour.

Yet, equally the continued existence of traditional society has warped the emancipation of women. Few things are as symptomatic of the decay of the workers' movement as its failure to notice this. The admittance of women to every conceivable supervised activity conceals continuing dehumanization. In big business they remain what they were in the family, objects. We should think not only of their miserable working-day, and of their home-life senselessly clinging to self-contained conditions of domestic labour in the midst of an industrial world, but also of themselves. Willingly, without any countervailing impulse, they reflect and identify themselves with domination. Instead of solving the question of women's oppression, male society has so extended its own principle that the victims are no longer able to even pose the question.

ADORNO 2005: 92

One can easily point to two problems that feminist approaches may address. First: that women are reified is one thing; that they are reified in the same way in domestic and in "big business" work seems dubious. Second: that women are 'voluntary' in their domination (more voluntary than others) seems hard to hold on to as an idea. Even though Nathan Duford highlights in his article that this passage must be understood as a critique of the belief that women's emancipation would be realized once they could, in the same way as men, integrate the wage labour market (2017: 795), I stress that Adorno's statement in *Minima Moralia* underlines also the problematic aspects of his analysis.[21] Thinking about women only to the extent to which they are objectified prevents Adorno from posing the question of the ways in which they are integrated in society. Here I stress that the "victims" have been able to "raise the question," in a more precise way than Adorno. Confronting Adorno's lack of empirical analysis about the integration of women in late capitalist society with feminist approaches on the question, I will stress that social theory needs to be able to take into account these questions, if it wants to be a critical theory of society.

Maria Mies' *Patriarchy and accumulation on a world scale. Women in the international division of labour* analyzes historically the devalorization of the productivity of women and tries to show how the "housewifization" has been a historical process starting with the domination of nature by men and the conceptualization of production as prior to reproduction. Mies shows how

---

21   Ferrarese (2021: 68) describes this integration of women trough labour as the "ruse of domination".

"housewifization" is a historical process within capitalist society and a specific form of appropriation of a kind of work which is generally attributed to women. Showing the historicity of this process states that domestic labour is constitutional for the functioning and maintaining of capitalist production. She analyzes the process in the following way:

> The housewifization of women, however, had not only the objective of ensuring that there were enough workers and soldiers for capital and the state. The creation of housework and the housewife as an agent of consumption became a very important strategy in the late nineteenth and early twentieth centuries. By that time not only had the household been discovered as an important market for a whole range of new gadgets and items, but also scientific home-management had become a new ideology for the further domestication of women. Not only was the housewife called on to reduce the labour power costs, she was also mobilized to use her energies to create new needs.
>
> MIES 2014: 106

Women in this analysis are not simply objects, but very important subjects in the production and reproduction of capitalist society. And even though Adorno might have stressed that they are indeed 'very important subjects in the production and reproduction of capitalist society', he would have highlighted the fact that their objectivation resides in the fact of not recognizing themselves as victims and agents. Here I think, Mies' empirical study has indeed a denaturalizing effect. She states something very similar to Adorno when she says that women are also "creator of new needs" and "agents of consumption." But because she also highlights the other side of the social role of women – that in the "housewifization" lies an interest of capital in "reducing labour power costs" – her analysis is more precise and therefore opens up to "potentialities" which Adorno might not see. These potentialities lie in the fact that an understanding of one's own specific integration in society potentially creates a common ground where organization is possible – and the feminist movements which have arisen from it and are still arising show this to be true.

Clearly leaving behind a Marxist definition of productivity and labor, Mies accords a triple sense of "productivity" to the sphere of reproduction. The first sense concerns the biological reproduction of humankind as instruments for capital. The second sense concerns the development of new needs and markets which come along with the "domestication of women," and the third sense, which is openly mentioned here, is the production of new cultural products.

I think that Mies' empirical study about the process of "housewifization" challenges Adorno's conceptualization of his social theory.

In Adorno's writings and teachings about the relationship between sociology and philosophy, he argues that philosophy can neither claim universal validity nor be situated outside empirical knowledge about the world. Sociology provides philosophy with empirical material. The latter, on the other hand, makes it possible to analyze the epistemological presuppositions of sociology (Adorno 1977: 130–1). If this is Adorno's approach, it demonstrates that, at least in the *Dialectic of Enlightenment* and *Minima Moralia*, there is a difficulty in accounting for the "empirical material" sociology provides. Adorno's analysis of women's positions lacks this dialogue with empirical knowledge that his social theory is supposed to produce.

The tension one finds in Adorno's works between his historically too unspecific conception of domination and the importance for historically determined analyses of contemporary domination troubles his analysis of female reification. Constructivist approaches in feminism share the diagnosis of society without succumbing to a stereotypical image of women. The use of empirical knowledge about female socialization in feminist thought can bridge the gap Adorno eventually fails to bridge: analyzing reification of women as an expression of domination under capitalism without reducing women to their role as "objects."

5   Conclusion

This chapter thinks – via the modus of a triple critique – about the relevance of Adorno's social theory for thinking domination of women and nature in late capitalist societies. The aim of this chapter has been to develop a constructive criticism of Adorno, in order to bridge a gap between approaches which are trying to enlarge the scope of analysis of women's oppression and the ones analyzing female oppression within the mode of production. It is therefore also a critique of feminist approaches which reduce female subjectivation to their apparent proximity to nature, or those who reduce it simply to a question of their place within the mode of production.

Analyzing the relationship between domination of nature and women allows indeed a questioning of the structural link between the domination of nature and women in Western societies. Nonetheless, two problems appeared: I have tried to show with the eco-feminist Ynestra King and her direct reference to reification as forgetting that she does produce an ahistorical conception of domination of women and nature. Trying to highlight the difference in

Adorno's concept of reification, I have carved out how Adorno shows on the one hand that the historical motor of capitalist society is domination of nature and therefore proposes a historically determined analysis of the nature-society dualism. On the other hand, I've also shown that the historic determination of women's oppression does indeed bring Adorno to difficulties. Adorno's attempt to think about the social role of women and domination of nature within capitalism via the prism of reification is indeed a fruitful attempt to criticize essentialist approaches which think an ahistorical and unmediated (i.e., not socially mediated) connection between women and nature because it allows Adorno to maintain two strands: the analysis of a historical becoming of women's oppression as well as its historic specificity. Here, I eventually also demonstrated that this tension found in Adorno's and Horkheimer's *Dialectic of Enlightenment* re-appears in Adorno's *Minima Moralia* and needs to be addressed as a problem for his social theory. While relying on Becker-Schmidt's critique of Adorno's lack of a sociological analysis of female socialization and under the recourse to different feminist authors (i.e., Ferrarese 2021, Naït Ahmed 2019a, 2019b), I stressed that female experience of domination remains a serious problem for Adorno's own conceptualization of social theory. Using eco-feminist approaches to the question of domestic labour, I showed how Adorno does not evoke a sufficiently precise sociological analysis of women in society. In other words, my interrogations about the relationship of reification brought me to conceive Adorno's approach to reification as very productive for a critique of essentialism. But I also tried to carve out a tension one finds in Adorno's work; only under a critical backdrop to feminist authors analyzing in an empirically more precise way the reification and integration of women in late capitalist society, can one use Adorno's larger conception of a social theory in order to think about contemporary forms of social domination.

References

Adorno, Theodor W. March 1977. "Actuality of Philosophy." *Telos* March 20, 1977, vol. 1977 no. 31.

Adorno, Theodor W. 2005. *Minima Moralia: Reflections on a Damaged Life*. Radical Thinkers. London; New York: Verso.

Adorno, Theodor W. 2006. *History and Freedom: Lectures 1964–1965*. Cambridge: Polity Press.

Becker-Schmidt, Regina. 2004a. "Adorno kritisieren – und dabei von ihm lernen. Von der Bedeutung seiner Theorie für die Geschlechterforschung". In *Die Lebendigkeit der kritischen Gesellschaftstheorie: Dokumentation der Arbeitstagung aus Anlass des 100. Geburtstages von Theodor W. Adorno, 4.-6. Juli 2003 an der Johann Wolfgang Goethe-Universität, Frankfurt am Main,* edited by Andreas Gruschka and Ulrich Oevermann, Originalausg, 65–95. Wetzlar: Büchse der Pandora.

Becker-Schmidt, Regina. 2004b. "Adornos Gesellschaftstheorie. Anstoß für feministische Kritik und Herausforderung zum Weiterdenken". In *Theodor W. Adorno: Philosoph des beschädigten Lebens,* édité par Moshe Zuckermann, 61–82. Conferences: Tagungsbände des Minerva Instituts für deutsche Geschichte Universität Tel Aviv, Bd. 3. Göttingen: Wallstein Verlag.

Biehl, Janet. 1991. *Rethinking Ecofeminist Politics.* Boston: South End Press.

Butler, Judith. 2006. *Gender Trouble: Feminism and the Subversion of Identity.* Routledge classics. New York: Routledge.

Daly, Mary. 1990. *Gyn/ecology: the Metaethics of Radical Feminism.* Boston: Beacon Press.

Dayan-Herzbrun, Sonia, Nicole Gabriel, and Éléni Varikas, ed. 2004. *Adorno critique de la domination une lecture féministe.* Paris: Kimé.

Duford, Nathan. Fall 2017. "Daughters of the Enlightenment: Reconstructing Adorno on Genderand Feminist Praxis." *Hypatia* vol. 32, no. 4. https.//doi.org/10.1111/hypa.12360.

Ferrarese, Estelle. 2021. *The fragility of concern for others: Adorno and the ethics of care.* Edinburgh: Edinburgh University Press.

Ferrarese, Estelle, Salima Naït-Ahmed, Frank Müller, Alexandra Richter, and Éliette Pinel, 2020. "Politique de la non-identité". *Trajectoires,* n° Hors série n°4.

Gaard, Greta. 2011. "Ecofeminism Revisited: Rejecting Essentialism and Re-Placing Species in a Material Feminist Environmentalism". *Feminist Formations* 23 (2): 26–53.

Geulen, Eva. 1996. "Toward a Genealogy of Gender in Walter Benjamin's Writing". *The German Quarterly,* Vol. 69, N° 2, Spring 1996, Wiley edition.

Griffin, Susan. 1981. *Woman and Nature: the Roaring inside Her.* 4. pr. Harper Colophon Books. New York: Harper&Row.

Guillibert, Paul. 2020. "Natures en révolte. L'histoire écoféministe et la critique de la raison instrumentale". In *Retour vers la nature? questions féministes,* edited by Katia Genel, Jean-Baptiste Vuillerod and Lucie Wezel. Lormont: Le Bord de l'eau.

Hache, Émilie, ed. 2016. *Reclaim: recueil de textes écoféministes.* Sorcières. Paris: Cambourakis.

Heberle, Renée, ed. 2006. *Feminist Interpretations of Theodor Adorno.* Re-reading the Canon. University Park, PA: Pennsylvania State University Press.

Hester, Helen. 2018. *Xenofeminism.* Cambridge. Polity Press.

Hewitt, Andrew. 2006. "A Feminine Dialectic of Enlightenment". In *Feminist Interpretations of Theodor Adorno,* edited by Renée Heberle, 69–96. Re-reading the Canon. University Park, PA: Pennsylvania State University Press.

Horkheimer, Max and Theodor W. Adorno. 2002. *Dialectic of Enlightenment: Philosophical Fragments.* Cultural Memory in the Present. Stanford, CA: Stanford University Press.

Jagentowicz Mills, Patricia. 1991. "Feminism and Ecology: on the Domination of Nature". *Hypatia* 6 (1): 162–78. https://doi.org/10.1111/j.1527-2001.1991.tb00215.x.

King, Ynestra. 1998. "Toward an Ecological Feminism and a Feminist Ecology". In *Debating the Earth: the Environmental Politics Reader*, edited by John S. Dryzek and David Schlosberg, 429–37. Oxford [England]; New York: Oxford University Press.

Lee, Lisa Yun. 2005. *Dialectics of the Body: Corporeality in the Philosophy of T.W. Adorno*. New York: Routledge.

Lukács, György. 1971. *History and Class Consciousness: Studies in Marxist Dialectics*. Cambridge, MA: MIT Press.

Mellor, Mary. 1994. "Varieties of Ecofeminism". *Capitalism Nature Socialism* 5 (4): 117–25 https://doi.org/10.1080/10455759409358615.

Mies, Maria. 2014. *Patriarchy and Accumulation on a World Scale: Women in the International Division of Labour*. Critique, Influence, Change 06. London: Zed Books.

Mills, Patricia Jagentowicz. 1987. *Woman, Nature, and Psyche*. New Haven: Yale University Press.

Naït Ahmed, Salima. 2019a. "De la « dénaturalisation » à la « renaturalisation » des femmes: Nature et réification chez Adorno". *Trajectoires*, n° 12 (février). https://doi .org/10.4000/trajectoires.3157.

Naït Ahmed, Salima. 2019b. "Adorno und die Kritik der weiblichen Lebensformen". *Recherches germaniques*, n° 49 (décembre): 151–61. https://doi.org/10.4000/rg.2748.

O'Neill, Maggie. 1999. "Adorno and Women: Negative Dialectics, Kulturkritik and Unintentional Truth". In *Adorno, Culture, and Feminism*, edited by Maggie O'Neill, 21–40. London; Thousand Oaks, CA: SAGE Publications.

Plumwood, Val. 1993. *Feminism and the Mastery of Nature*. Opening out. London; New York: Routledge.

Salleh, Ariel. 1991. "Essentialism and Ecofeminism". *Arena*, n° 94: 167–73.

Salleh, Ariel. 2003. "Ecofeminism as Sociology". *Capitalism Nature Socialism* 14 (1): 61–74. https://doi.org/10.1080/10455750308565514.

Schneider, Christian. 2019. "Die Wunde Freud". In *Adorno Handbuch*, édité par Richard Klein, Johann Kreuzer, et Stefan Müller-Doohm. Stuttgart: J.B. Metzler.

Spivak, Gayatri Chakravorty. 2006. *In Other Worlds: Essays in Cultural Politics*. New York: Routledge, Taylor & Francis Group.

Vuillerod, Jean-Baptiste. 2021. *Theodor W. Adorno: La domination de la nature*.

Wezel, Lucie. 2020. "La cicatrice du féminin". In *Retour vers la nature? questions féministes*, edited by Katia Genel, Jean-Baptiste Vuillerod and Lucie Wezel, 61–76. Lormont: Le Bord de l'eau.

Wittig, Monique. 1992. "One Is Not Born a Woman". In *The Straight Mind and Other Essays*, 9–20. Boston: Beacon Press.

Ziege, Eva-Maria. 2004. "La critique du "féminin" chez T.W. Adorno et dans la première théorie critique". *Adorno critique de la domination: Une lecture féministe* 2004/2 (2): 1–31.

CHAPTER 17

About Mules, Divas, and Other *Specifically Feminine* Characteristics

Imaculada Kangussu and Nathalia N. Barroso

Dignity is a woman in peace.
Unknown Author

∵

Herbert Marcuse has dialogued intensely and meaningfully with issues of gender and feminism.[1] His well-known article about "Marxism and Feminism" (1974) was republished more than three decades later in *differences: A Journal of Feminist Cultural Studies* (2006). The seal of Frankfurt School's Critical Theory, its main characteristic – the entanglement between the materialist theory of Marx and the psychological theories of Freud – is very evident in this text. It is also present in lectures and interviews that Marcuse has done on feminism over the decade of the 1970s, and now seems to be even more significative than then, as we will see.

Here, we would like to consider Marcuse's feminist perspectives exploring three points, which are interlaced: the so-called (1) *specifically feminine* characteristics, (2) the unequal equality of exploitation, and (3) the radical political potential of feminism for *human* liberation. For the first two points, we deal with Marcuse's writings; for the last, we turn to Angela Davis as well. Together, Marcuse and Davis can wake up new hopes. Both critical theorists and activists make it clear how social and cultural transformations have happened when women have appealed to the aesthetic dimension – music in our case study – as a sort of ally capable of providing a trench in dark times – as now.

---

1 A first and briefer version of this article was presented on October 11, 2019, at University of California Santa Barbara, in the panel "The Radical Thought of Angela Davis and Herbert Marcuse" with Arnold Farr and Andrew Lamas. We would like, again, to thank them for the invitation. We would also like to thank our first reader of the new version, Christine Payne, for her comments and for giving us some words and expressions that we could not find.

1   Specifically Feminine

Marcuse concludes his article "Marxism and Feminism" (1974) by stating that "we men have to pay for the sins of a patriarchal civilization and its tyranny of power" (Marcuse 1974: 288). At the beginning of this text, Marcuse contends that the "Women's Movement is perhaps the most important and most radical political movement that we have" (1974: 279). The Women's Liberation Movement has originated and operated within patriarchal civilization and under "patriarchal civilization, women have been subjected to a specific kind of repression" (1974: 280). Woman "came to be regarded as inferior, as weaker, mainly as a support for, or as the adjunct to man, as sexual object, as tool of reproduction" (1974: 283). In a lecture delivered in February 1972, Marcuse observed that, despite this situation, women created the feminist movement "which could propel a decisive transformation of the entire material and intellectual culture, could reduce repression, and provide the psychological, instinctual foundation for a less aggressive Reality Principle" (Marcuse 2001a: 198–9).

Marcuse considers that the goals of feminism go far beyond capitalist borders, "namely into regions which can never be attained within a capitalist framework, nor within the framework of any class society" (1974: 281). The liberation of women is considered necessary to "the transition to a better society for men and women" (Marcuse 1974: 288). And the radical potential of the feminist movement depends on "the liberation and ascent of *specifically feminine* characteristics on a social scale" (Marcuse 1974: 282), which could help to build a "*qualitatively* different society" since they would imply a subversion of values. The *specifically feminine* characteristics are "receptivity, sensitivity, non-violence, tenderness, and so on" (Marcuse 1974: 283). These qualities are necessary for "making life an end in itself, for the development of the sense and the intellect for the pacification of aggressiveness, the enjoyment of being, for the emancipation of the sense and the intellect from the rationality of domination: creative receptivity versus repressive productivity" (Marcuse 1974: 286) – and aesthetic feelings versus instrumental rationality. The *specifically feminine* characteristics could channel aggressiveness into "the destruction of the ugly destructiveness of capitalism" (Marcuse 1974: 286).

The statement concerning "*specifically feminine* characteristics", has provoked protests among feminists. Delicately, Wendy Brown sees a sort of "quaintness" in this statement (Brown 2006: 1). In a two-day conversation held in July 1977 in Pontresina, Switzerland, published as "Images of femininity",[2] Silvia Bovenschen and Marianne Schuller established a deep discussion, bordering on confrontation, with Marcuse. To make a long story short, their charge was that the postulation of *specifically feminine* characteristics denotes a sexist and traditional male point of view implicit first, in the attribution of specific characteristics to women in general, and second, in the fact that these *specifically feminine* attributes have been considered on a global scale as a sort of minor series of sensible qualities, like "receptivity, sensitivity, non-violence, tenderness, and so on" (Marcuse 1974: 283). Marcuse considers that the feminine potential to transform society is not only a result of the Women's Liberation Movement; it is also present in these qualities that have been considered 'minor' because they are 'feminine' and because women has been considered inferior, weaker.

Marcuse responded to the "accusations" saying that even though 'receptivity', 'softness', and other female characteristics could be considered synonyms of submission – because they are indeed fruits of social exclusion – he considers them the opposite; he considers them as a Great Refusal against destructive productivity and against the aggressions demanded by the performance principle. His second argument is that the *specifically feminine* characteristics are not natural or part of a metaphysical feminine essence but an historical phenomenon. The radical potential of feminism for Marcuse is not a result of the 'natural' capacities of women, for the *specifically feminine* characteristics are not a biological fact but rather a sort of second nature developed through history. The confrontation of male reason and female sensibility is a cultural situation, and behind it is hidden the social necessity of harmony and consonance between them. This does not mean that men should become irrational, nor that women should turn themselves into walking brains. The solution is not to substitute reason for sensibility but to reconcile them in a non-hierarchical relationship – as has already been proposed by Schiller's *Letters on the Aesthetic Education*, Marcuse remembers (1966: 182).

At the very beginning of the second day of conversations, Marcuse observes that the emancipation of women implies the emancipation of men – and so society's emancipation. This is an historical possibility: because the patriarchal society is in a phase in its "development" that requires reiterated and renewed destruction and exploitation, radical modifications become necessary not only in the modes of production but also in the interior of the subjects.

---

2   See Marcuse, Bovenschen & Shuller 1978: 65ss. For different points of views about the "specifically feminine characteristics", and better comprehension of this Marcusean statement, see Steuernagel 1994: 89–105, Power 2013: 73–80, and Love 2017: 118–131.

What does this mean concretely? Silvia Bovenschen and Marianne Schuller wanted to know (so do we). Marcuse explains that women's liberation means more than equal rights. It means preference for values and necessities different from the ones that rule the existent production relations. The *specifically feminine* necessities and qualities contradict the capitalist values and its mode of production. The *specifically feminine* characteristics that women have had to repress to act like men could be emancipatory. Developing themselves hidden in the margins of the Big World, *specifically feminine* characteristics become resilient qualities, Marcuse thinks. The aim of the Women's Movement, as he understands it, is not the complete equivalence with men the way they are. The goal is a transformation in the ways of seeing gender differences so that the resilient qualities – once considered as *specifically feminine* characteristics – can be considered as human characteristics.

In an emancipated society, specifically feminine characteristics would be universal "so that they were no longer specifically "feminine" at all but would characterize all culture" (Power 2013: 79). In other words, the abandonment of patriarchal and capitalist values would undermine the specific masculine characteristics, overcome the stereotypes of gender normativity, and the hierarchical differences between feminine and masculine characteristics.

Before the conversation in Pontresina, in a text written around 1972–73, but only published in 2001, Marcuse had explained his statement about the *specifically feminine* characteristics and insisted on its political potential:

> *Women's Liberation Movement* is of the utmost importance – precisely to the degree to which it becomes a *political* movement. The negation of the values and goals of the male-dominated patriarchal society is also the negation of the values and goals of capitalism – and this on the physiological, instinctual level of the individual. I have been accused of succumbing to the "male-chauvinist" image of the woman by attributing to her specific qualities which are actually socially determined (tenderness, softness, etc.). Now it seems to me meaningless to separate in this way socially determined and physiological ("natural") qualities: in the historical development, the former sink into physiology and become "second nature". In any case, these female qualities have become a *fact*, and as factual, they can be put to political, social use. To suppress them because they are historically determined would be sacrificing to the male Establishment.
>
> 2001: 182

2   Unequal Equality of Exploitation

Because of its dynamics and its potential to transcend a merely reformist framework, in "The Radical Transformation of Norms, Needs, and Values",[3] Marcuse considers the Women's Liberation Movement as an "example of new forces in the fight against the old world" (2017: 57), since it has the potential of that transformation of values that could construct a qualitatively different society by refusing the male standard, i.e., the norm by which all else has been measured. "The very process of civilization was male-dominated, patriarchal, which determined not only according to the requires of slave, feudal, and capitalist society (as were men!), but also according to the needs of men *as male*: male-female *became* masculine-feminine" (Marcuse 2017: 57).

> While as object of exploitation, as embodiment of abstract labor power, women were increasingly employed in the process of material production (unequal equality of exploitation!), they were also to embody the qualities of gratification, care, feeling, which could not be displayed in the world of capitalism without undermining its repressive foundation, namely, the function of human relationships as relationships of things: exchange values.
>
> 2017: 58

Even though exploitation is primarily determined on the basis that some must sell their labor-power, and considerations of gender and race come after, Marcuse observes in "The Radical Transformation of Norms, Needs, and Values", that sexism and racism have been used in the construction of hierarchies inside the labor market. And even if exploitation occurs "equally" to all laborers, and gives place to a non-hierarchical relation, feminist theories have shown that equal treatment (in labor exploitation) can lead to inequalities because the privileged model of deliberation ignores the historical inequalities created by contingent gender and social conditions.[4] A concern with formal

---

3 Marcuse did not title this lecture presented on March 3, 1977, in St. Louis. The title was selected by the editors of the book. In the copy of the lecture discovered recently in the Frankfurt Marcuse Archive, it is written – in a handwritten note added by Marcuse just after the date – "Incomplete!" Here we quote the text without "correcting" it. Words in *italics* are the ones underscored by Marcuse in his original text.

4 On the topic of the necessity of considering existent differences between social positions and situations in the fights for equality, see Fraser 1986, and Benhabib 1992.

legal equality must consider human necessities that are attributed primarily to women, like aid to maternity, to elders, and child-care, for example.

As we have seen, the *specifically feminine* characteristics are historical, the fruit of "thousands of years" of social exclusion. The problem is that, since the norms which determine the inclusion have been the male ones, to challenge their exclusion, women are required to behave like men, to show they are equal to men. Because rationality has historically been considered masculine, women are constructed as "feminine" with distinct characteristics and capacities. In other words, women have been forced to move to a "feminine" universe and conform themselves to patterns and expectations they did not establish. And to allow the equal treatment in exploitation, the realm of femininity has been separated from the process of production. "'Femininity' was supposed to be a quality of the household of domestic care, of sexual relations. But this 'private sector' too remained part of patriarchal hierarchy, in work as well as pleasure: exploitation". (Marcuse 2017: 58). Firmly institutionalized, the division of human qualities into feminine and masculine has been reproduced from generation to generation of class societies, Marcuse considers. This sexist division has led to the assumption of antagonist social conditions as if they were a natural relation of opposites, or a relation between natural opposites. Marcuse illustrates the situation with a list of "inherent *antithesis of qualities*" (2017: 58):

Male		Female
productivity	means	receptivity
aggressiveness	means	non-violence
competitive striving	means	gratification
rationality	means	sensitivity

The question is that "at a time when the aggressiveness and brutality of the male-dominated society attains a peak of destructiveness, it is no longer 'compensated' by a development of the productive forces and a rational mastery of nature" (Marcuse 2017: 58). So, the necessary struggle against the socially imposed male domination is a struggle for justice on all levels of society. In an emancipatory transformation, Marcuse considers that:

The negation of male domination would *invalidate* the *attribution* of feminine qualities to the *woman as such*, and instead: make these qualities creative and receptive in the society *as a whole*: in the social organization of labor, in work and leisure, in the male as well as the female. The liberation of *women* would then also be the liberation of *men* – who are also in need of it!

2017: 59

The movement that guides the Marcusean approach to feminist liberation movements can be seen in a temporal manner: first, in history (for "thousands of years of social conditioning"), women stayed inside the house in the margins of the public life, while men went to the outside world to get the material stuff necessary for survival. In such an excluded position, women developed the so-called *specifically feminine* characteristics, which assume the form of a quasi-nature, of a second nature. In a second historical moment, women and men were considered equal: not as human beings but as beasts or working machines. Women's second nature is petrified evidence of the price paid – by humanity – for social progress. The historical *specifically feminine* characteristics have resisted the equalization of women and men when they have been transformed into mere labor-force and have survived as a second nature even in the capitalist market world. Marcuse considers that these resilient *specifically feminine* characteristics shall overcome specifically gendered associations and become *human* characteristics.

Feminism is still the spectre that haunts the capitalist world. Its goal is a qualitatively different society: a change not of replacing one system of domination by another, masculine by feminine, reason by sensibility, "but as the 'leap' into a qualitatively different stage of history, of civilization, *where human beings, in solidarity, develop their own needs and faculties*" (Marcuse 2017: 60).

It is possible to hear echoes of this position in the words of Angela Davis (a former student of Marcuse): "We are still faced with the challenge of understanding the complex ways race, class, gender, sexuality, nation, and ability are intertwined – but also how we moved beyond these categories of understanding the interrelationships of ideas and process that seems separated and unrelated" (Davis 2016: 4). Davis highlights that feminism does not belong to a specific group, to anyone in particular. It is not an exclusionary phenomenon, and increasingly there are men who are involved in groups like *Men against Rape*, *Alternative Masculinities*, *Against Domestic Violence*, for example. A "slogan 'Women's Right are Human Rights' began to emerge in the aftermath of an amazing conference that took place in 1985 in Nairobi, Kenya" (Davis 2016: 96). More than an approach embraced by women, feminism "has to be an approach embraced by people of all genders" (Davis 2016: 47–8). It serves as an emblem of larger struggles for freedom.

3   Mules Carry the Weight

Despite the consideration of feminism as a sort of concrete universal for struggles for freedom – by herself and by Marcuse – Davis highlights some phenomena that can find rescue in the Marcusean concept of specifically *feminine*
characteristics. In a brief text of 2017, after presenting the idea that Black people – who were not given freedom but had to struggle for that freedom – should
be the universal measure of citizenship, "Black people should be the measure
of humanity", Davis asks: "What happens if we imagine Black women as the
measure of humanity?" She goes on asking: "Zora Neale Hurston reminded us
that Black woman is the mule of the world. What if the mules of the world
become the very height of humanity? This is the question that has been posed
by the uprising of young people today" (2017: x). Can we consider the mules of
the world a *specific* characterisation of the *feminine*?

Angela Davis is referring to Zora Neale Hurston's 1937 novel, *Their Eyes Were
Watching God*, where Nanny, the grandmother of the heroine Janie Crawford,
warns her granddaughter that "de nigger woman is de mule uh de world so
fur as Ah can see. An been prayni fuh it tuh be different wid you" (Hurston
1999: 14). As it can be noticed, Hurston's character's observation is, at the same
time, a mourning on Black women's plight, an affirmation of their strength,
and a desire that things could be different. Intellectuals who work on Black
feminism examining the intersections between race, class, and gender have
employed and developed Hurston's "mule" metaphor.[5] The point seems to
be: "if the mules of the world become the very height of humanity" it changes
the frame through which we perceive reality and creates a sort of new ontology; a new ontology in the sense that human characterization (what makes
humans human) will be located in the realization of the essential jobs for living and for surviving – and for keeping things clean.

This position challenges the values adopted by philosophy since Classical
Greece, when material work was considered inferior to intellectual, spiritual
pursuits. If the mules of the world become the human being's pattern, that
means that the intelligibility matrix – from which we understand, and judge,
and construct the reality we share – will have it focus on the smallest of the
small, the lowest of the low. The desire for transformation in this direction –
that can already be perceived in *Their Eyes Were Watching God* – makes up a
new ontology.

---

5   See Patton 2010, Parks 2010, and Beauboeuf-Lafontant 2009.

Up to now, the history that still runs has been the history of winners. In the development of civilization, it is possible to notice a blindness towards the ones who work on the bottom. It is paramount to rearrange the perspective of the gaze. Instead of modeling the way of life, behaviors, values, affections, emotions, mesmerized by the dominant classes – that is, looking up and adopting the paradigm, and following blindly the symbolic structure established by the ones who rule – if we want to understand the mechanism of socially established structure, it is necessary to shift the direction of the eyes and adopt very new perspectives.

It is important to remember that what human beings have in common and share universally is fragility and vulnerability: of bodies, minds, and the human condition itself. We need nature and we need each other. The historical problem is that, in trying to look away from the signs of precariousness, humanity has learned to disregard the most basic, roughest, and urgent jobs, those which are most immediately necessary for human survival – the daily life-sustaining jobs. This movement of disregarding and forgetting feeds a kind of class unconsciousness and helps to spread the feeling that capital is more important than work.

In such a situation it is necessary to see that civilization depends on the people who clean the shit. Their work forms the basis of every good, of every commodity, every piece of merchandise. Some keep clean hands, while someone else does the dirty job and is considered ontologically inferior – and is kept out of the historical scene.

The important point that Davis proposes is that when the smallest is the measure of humanity, everyone is considered, everybody is inside, nobody is out of the game. Because the dominant class will either recognize itself as an oppressor over the dominated ones or will turn a blind eye on this fact to avoid seeing itself as such, Black women can play the role once attributed to the "proletariat", in the sense that they are the only group able to see society, i.e., leaving none outside. Just as the proletariat was once considered the only class that could have a class consciousness – since the dominant class had to forge an illusionist self-image not to admit its direct or indirect oppression against the proletarians – this role now can be played by working class Black women.

The existing social reality implies the non-knowledge, the blindness of its participants. It is supported by a false consciousness. The strengthening of a real consciousness implies, instead of the pseudo identification with the winners, the perception that the universal condition shared by humanity is its vulnerability. The question is: how to shift the focus from the usual way of seeing, desiring, dreaming? How to transform the symbolic structure, to reconfigure values, to create new modes of symbolization? According to Davis, who found her statement in a novel, art can radically alter the lives that we live and transform collective sensibility. Art can transform our ways of thinking and of feeling: "the most remarkable aspect is the way which it transforms the most horrid forms of suffering into beauty and joy" (Davis 2019).

To establish a distinct paradigm, to change the symbolic frame through which reality is perceived as such, Davis proposes that Black women should be the measure of humanity, since the Black Radical Tradition, overcoming racial identity, "can certainly be described as a salient historical manifestation of the Great Refusal. This tradition has been embraced not only by people of African descent, but also by those who eschew assimilation into oppressive structures and support the liberation of all people" (Davis 2017: viii).

If the mules of the world were the measure of humanity, everyone would be considered, everybody would be inside. *It is precisely those who are in the lowest – or without a – place within the social whole that stand for the universal dimension of the society. This perception implies a radical transformation in the entire social edifice.*

In this millennium, there have been multiple insurrections, disruptions, and environmental catastrophes on a planetary scale; nevertheless, they have not yet produced a radical change in the dominant paradigm. In order to survive, even people who have not embraced them are forced to follow behavior patterns fixed by the system. The question is how to shake it. In *Blues Legacies and Black Feminism: Gertrude "Ma" Rainey, Bessie Smith, and Billie Holiday* (1998), Angela Davis makes it clear how the named Black women have shaken the paradigmatic notions of genre and class through the blues. Blues music has been a powerful vehicle for Black women to express desires and share personal experiences that are, more than singular, common ones. Through lyrics that portray their personal sexuality and needs, "coupled with a refusal to be mistreated", Black women show feelings, with which other women readily identify themselves. The songs create an emotional common expression concerning facts and emotions that used to be experienced alone and, most of the time, in shame. The blues lyrics made possible a shared moment in which feminine feelings and thoughts, once forbidden to find their proper space in the world ruled by white males, can finally be experienced. Expressed desires are thus incorporated – they have a body in the songs – even though it is not yet possible to fulfill them. Notwithstanding that their expression happens in the aesthetic dimension, somehow it is in this dimension that the forbidden desires are lightened and become visible – or hearable, at least.

4   Blues Divas

In *Blues Legacies and Black Feminism,* Davis presents the blues as the first Black artistic manifestation after the end of slavery. The female blues configures the ways that Black women have found to denunciate abuses and make their voices heard – it was born as a power of change and of affirming a new model of society. The blues, Davis writes, "articulated a new valuation of individual emotional needs and desires. The birth of the blues was aesthetic evidence of new psychosocial realities within the black population" (Davis 1998: 5).

Blues is an expression of Black women that affirms the necessity for union whose bases are beyond gender and include race and class. The blues also creates the possibility of allowing others to recognize that they too belong to the "non-place". In Davis' words, "what I wanted to know more about was the way their work addressed urgent social issues and helped to shape collective modes of black consciousness" (Davis 1998: XIV). She pointed to the blues as a rich territory for an examination of the way intersectionality presents itself, since aesthetic representations concerning gender and sexuality politics, in the blues, are always intertwined with representations of race and class.

The women's blues songs have female narrators and singers who are not entirely subservient to male desire. Simultaneously, they represent the autonomy of women and the refusal to be mistreated by their lovers and bosses. Blues singers challenged the main ideological assumptions about women's place and the notion that their lives should be reduced to the domestic sphere. Sexuality is a recurring theme in such songs: it is presented as the domain in which major changes occur when comparing the lives of enslaved and free Black people. The expression of sexuality in the Blues ladies' songs is considered by Davis as important evidence of transformations occurring in the lives of Black women. It highlights the possibility of Black women choosing sexual partners These transformations are important because they are signs of more sexual freedom. Since slavery, freedom had been the focus of the redemption songs. Like the songs sung by Black people during slavery, the Classic Female Blues expressed a collective desire not only for individual desires but also for collective freedom.

Blues marks a new appreciation of "subjectivity", of individual emotional needs and desires. The blues singers inaugurated a new way of living, a sort of autonomous cultural policy created by them. That policy made possible the rise of a new way of thinking, which has been the best way, according to Davis, for Black women to emerge and occupy the historical agenda of the Black Feminist Movement in the U.S. "The liberation of women begins at home, before it can enter society at large" (Marcuse 1974: 288). In other words, there is an emphasis on subjectivity, which is considered the first step for social change. The blues' Black singers embodied and expressed their own desire of autonomy. Their desire echoes universal desires: of women's liberation and, beyond this, the universal desire of being free. In some blues song, singular feelings might reveal themselves as universal and transhistorical ones.

The realism of the blues is permeated by many layers of complex and profound meanings. Even though most of the lyrics deal with the emotional and sexual matters that are associated with a specific historical reality, in not a few of them there are complex and more universal statements that transcend the particularities of the singers and take the form of denunciations of a common condition of Black women.

Although the socioeconomic and political reality of the first decades of the 20th century did not allow women to assert themselves as political subjects with their full rights assured, the blues singers overcame these restrictions, and their songs expressed that they did not agree with standards of femininity and behavior that were imposed. Blues songs challenged the persistence of the dominant notions of women's subordination. They drew parallels between male desire and female desire without one standing out, without making women inferior. The songs often expressed the pursuit of happiness, which was often associated with the accomplishment of a sexual desire:

> Even as they may have shed tears, they found the courage to lift their heads and fight back, asserting their right to be respected not as appendages or victims of men, but as truly independent human beings with vividly articulate sexual desires. Blues women provide emphatic examples of black female independence.
>
> 1998: 20

Through blues, problems are removed from isolated individual experiences and restructured as community-shared issues. The female characters evoked by blues songs did not fit the normative models of abuse and victims of violence. The female characters were usually independent women who wanted to end the abuse suffered, women who did not think twice before wielding guns against the men who abused them. "Women's blues, specifically, celebrated and valorized black working-class life while simultaneously contesting patriarchal assumptions about women's place both in the dominant culture and within African-American communities" (Davis 1998: 120).

Blues allowed women to develop a way to recognize themselves as living beings, and it also permitted the creation of a new social consciousness about being a Black woman. Furthermore, it made possible – and even provoked – the emergence of a new consciousness in Black working-class communities. Some of the songs presented pedagogical features when dealing with themes such as domestic violence and romantic difficulties. The songs featured women sharing their personal experiences to make explicit the politics that shaped their lives and the lives of many Black women in the first decades of the 20th century. Blues singers can be given credit for the dissemination of feminist attitudes towards male supremacy, and, more important, they are also responsible for recognizing the social character of personal experience.

Davis points out that for a protest to gain political character it is necessary to define an organized political structure that will act as a channel whereby individual complaints are transformed into collective protest.

> The blues as a genre marked a point in African-American historical development when black communities seemed open to all sorts of new possibilities. It was a musical form whose implied celebration of exploration and transformation held a special meaning for African-American women. It offered them the possibility of challenging the social norms governing women's place within the community and within the society at large.
>
> 1998: 74

When expressed through aesthetic forms, a protest is rarely a direct call to an action, but the critical aesthetic representation of a social problem is understood as a powerful constituent for social and political acts. Therefore, blues as a form and aesthetic phenomenon must be understood as a form that attests to and registers a lack of reality and the attainable possibilities of social transformation. Davis presents art as an incentive for a critical attitude, as long as it can incite its audience to perceive and challenge imposed social conditions. But art alone cannot prepare the ground for political changes. Together with art, a mass movement, preferably popular, must occur to encourage the emergence of critical attitudes. "When the blues "name" the problems the community wants to overcome, they help create the emotional conditions for protest, but do not and could not, of themselves constitute social protest" (Davis 1998: 113).

The Blues is presented as an individual expression of collectivity; there are songs that focus on the listener's interior but insist on the resignification outside of Black lives. The aesthetic of blues is an aesthetic of self-awareness, which does not relegate anyone or any kind of behavior of the mules of the world and other marginalized groups to a minor place. The Blues has a socializing character, in the sense that it makes people aware of their individual emotional experiences by realizing that others have the same feelings. Blues create a collective character that increases the possibility of affirmation, recognition, and resistance:

> The blues aesthetic is an aesthetic of self-consciousness, after all. But, in a less obvious sense, the defense of the blues proposed by the classical blues artists I am exploring – Gertrude "Ma" Rainey and Bessie Smith – has profound feminist implications. For in defending as well as in performing the blues, they were establishing it as a genre that belonged as much to women as to men. They were also implicitly defining the blues as a site where women could articulate and communicate their protests against male dominance.
>
> 1998: 127–8

Art has its own language in which it enunciates truths that would not be accessible to everyday language, and music can present a new narrative, a new possibility to expression. The song "Menina Pretinha", for example, written by the eleven-year-old Brazilian rapper MC Soffia, presents to young girls – and not only to them – a possibility of loving their natural hair when she sings: "My hair is not stiff/ It is curly and very beautiful". The musical expression of personal feelings that denies ongoing patterns can be liberating. "We take seriously the old feminist adage that 'personal is political'" (Davis 2016: 104). It not only means that personal experiences have political implications, "but that our interior lives, our emotional lives are very much informed by ideology" (Davis 2016: 142).

5   Musical Interlude

Since the beginning, music has played a fundamental role in the Black radical tradition. "And the Black radical tradition is related not simply to Black people but to all people who are struggling for freedom. It is emblematic of larger struggles for freedom" (Davis 2016: 39). According to Angela Davis, "it is a tradition that can be claimed by people everywhere. Regardless of race, regardless of nationality, regardless of geographical location" (2016: 112). The very title of her book, *Freedom is a Constant Struggle*, is the title of a popular song of the Mississippi Civil Rights Movement:

> They say that freedom is a constant struggle.
> They say that freedom is a constant struggle.
> They say that freedom is a constant struggle.

O Lord, we've struggled so long.
We must be free; we must be free.

In *The Souls of Black Folk* (1903) of W.E.B. Du Bois, a bar of song stands at the beginning of each chapter on the top of the page. "They that walked in darkness sang songs in the olden days – Sorrow Songs – for they were weary at heart" (Du Bois 2012: 212). According to Du Bois, the Sorrow Songs are "some echo of haunting melody from the only American music which welled up from the black souls in the dark past" (2012: 6). In these songs, slaves gave rhythm and voice to their repressed and painful feelings. "Such a message is naturally veiled, and half articulate", writes Du Bois, "the music is distinctly sorrowful [...] it gropes toward some unseen power" (2012: 217–8). Du Bois highlights that there is hope under the mournful weeping of the slave songs with verses like "My soul wants something that's new, that's new", and that:

> Through all the sorrow of the Sorrow Songs there breathes a hope – a Faith in the ultimate justice of things. The minor cadences of despair change often to triumph and calm confidence. Sometimes it is faith in life, sometimes it is faith in death, sometimes assurance of boundless justice. But whichever it is, the meaning is always clear: that sometime, somewhere, men will judge men by their souls and not by their skins. Is such hope justified?
>
> 2012: 221–2

Even though its realization is not yet possible, the desire is true – and it is incorporated, it gets a body in the songs. Notwithstanding that its expression happens in the aesthetic dimension, somehow it is in this dimension that the forbidden desire is lightened and becomes visible – or hearable, at least.

The freedom songs were considered by Martin Luther King Jr. as an important part of the meetings in Birmingham. "These songs bind us together, give us courage together, help us to march together" (King 2000: 65). King considered the songs the soul and the anthems of the movement, which bind people together and give them courage. "They are more than just incarnations of clever phrases designed to invigorate a campaign; they are as old as the history of the Negro in America", King writes. "We sing the freedom songs today for the same reason the slaves sang them, because we too are in bondage and the songs add hope to our determination that 'We shall overcome, Black and White together, we shall overcome someday'" (2000: 64). King considers "We shall overcome" as the battle hymn of the Civil Rights Movement.

In the fight against racism (and sexism, as well), music has created a shared moment in which the feelings and thoughts that could not find their proper space in the so-called real world could be experienced. Performed in a communal context, the songs have created self-confidence and invigorated self-respect "To have certain spaces by means of performance can provide a view of a different sense of who you are: you are human as opposed to being a commodity. You are human as opposed to being an object. You are human as opposed to be(ing) manipulated" (West 2014: 49). Cornel West continues by saying, "During slavery we could keep the Black tradition alive by lifting our voices – music was fundamental in sustaining Black dignity and sanity" (2014: 74).

West reveals that Black radical leaders had different tastes: Du Bois loved Spirituals, Sorrow Songs, and distanced himself from blues and jazz; Martin Luther King Jr. liked gospels and was suspicious of funk. And Malcolm X is always tied to the underdogs, always looking at the world from below:

> The way he spoke had a swing to it, had a rhythm to it; it was a call and response with the audience that you get with jazz musicians. And he was the blues, the sense of catastrophe, the sense of emergency, the sense of urgency, the sense of needing to get it out, to cry out, to shout, somehow allowed that fire inside of his bones to be expressed with power and vision. He never lost that. He never, ever lost that.
>
> 2014: 119

West insists: "music has really been the fundamental means by which Black people have been able to preserve sanity and dignity and, at our best, integrity" (2014:116).

Music can both protest against the given social relations and, at the same time, transcend them in an experience which is different from ordinary ones. Music can be revolutionary – subversive of perception and understanding – when it breaks through the prevailing and petrified social reality and opens a liberating horizon of change. In *The Aesthetic Dimension*, Marcuse considers that music, as a mode of art, can "explode the given reality in the name of a truth normally denied or even unheard [...] the truth of art lies in its power to break the monopoly of established reality (i.e., of those who established it) to *define* what is *real*" (1978: 7; 9).

Black music is a good example of how things can change through the aesthetic dimension. It has not only created solid communities between Black people, but it was powerful enough to make white guys surrender to it, even in the tough times of segregation. Jazz melody and rhythm imposed new feelings, new ways of thinking, and living as well.

The blacks take over some of the most sublime and sublimated concepts of Western civilization, desublimate them, and redefine them. For
example, the "soul" (in its essence lily-white ever since Plato) the traditional seat of everything that is truly tender, deep, immortal [...] has
been desublimated and in its transubstantiation migrated to the Negro
culture: they are soul brothers; the soul is black, violent, orgiastic; it is
no longer in Beethoven, Schubert, but in the blues, in jazz, in rock'n'roll.

MARCUSE 1969: 35–6

6   Critical Feminist Theory

In a talk (Lower Plaza, Friday, Oct. 24, 1969) in defense of academic freedom
and of Angela Davis as the student's representative, Marcuse said:

Angela Davis was the ideal victim of repression. She is black, she is militant, she is a Communist, she is highly intelligent, and she is pretty [...]
The fight for Angela is, in the last analysis, a fight for you [...] It is a fight
for you, for us, I would like to think, who can no longer tolerate, who get
sick in the stomach to see the richest society in the world live on the
economy of death, live on the economy of planned obsolescence and
pollution which we cannot tolerate any longer.

1969: 2

For Marcuse, "the absolute need" of breaking out of the whole administered
world "could become the driving force of a historical practice, the effective
cause of qualitative change" (1991: 255). This "absolute need" might perhaps
work as a material force based on a drive that is present in outsiders and intellectuals. In Marcuse's words:

Underneath the conservative popular base is the substratum of the outcasts and outsiders, the exploited and persecuted of other races and
other colors, the unemployed and the unemployable. They exist outside
the democratic process; their life is the most immediate and the most
real need for ending intolerable conditions and institutions. Thus their
opposition is revolutionary even if their consciousness is not. Their opposition hits the system from without and is therefore not deflected by the
system; it is an elementary force which violates the rules of the game
and, in doing so, reveals it as a rigged game. When they get together and
go out into the streets, without arms, without protection, in order to ask

for the most primitive civil rights, they know that they face dogs, stones, and bombs, jail, concentration camps, even death. Their force is behind every political demonstration for the victims of law and order. The fact that they start refusing to play the game may be the fact which marks the beginning of the end of a period [...] the chance is that, in this period, the historical extremes may meet again: the most advanced consciousness of humanity and its most exploited force.

> 1991: 256-7

This perhaps means a meeting between intellectuals (we?) and "the mules of the world" (we)? The fact is that while the mules of the world – and their essential work – are ignored, the winners present themselves as the ideal measure materialized in a human life. Adopting this measure implies to look only up, and to leave down in darkness, out of the historical scene, in an ob-scene zone, the part of humanity that carries the weight of the hard material work. To change the glance and to regard the mules of the world as "the very height of humanity" can turn alienation into awareness. Perhaps Marcuse is noticing the recognition of harsh realities as a launching pad towards decreasing said realities as such.

The Women's Liberation Movement has opened a new dimension of change, a subversion of the system of needs, desires, and satisfactions. In his reflections on feminism, Marcuse reiterates a point that can be seen as fundamental in his philosophy at least since *Eros and Civilization* (published in 1955): the necessity of changing the human agents of change "prior to the revolution, *within* the established structure, changing the future *subjects* if change = *change at the roots!*" (2017: 59).

In *Counterrevolution and Revolt*, more explicitly, Marcuse adverts that if individuals are to build a qualitatively different society, they must change themselves in their very instincts and sensibilities. In his words: "the emancipation of the senses must accompany the emancipation of consciousness, thus involving the totality of human existence" (1972: 74). The decisive change in the instinctual structure, according to Marcuse, should be "the weaking of primary aggressiveness which has governed the patriarchal culture" (1972: 75).

In this book, aesthetics and feminine needs are seen as subversive forces, capable of counteracting the dominating male aggressiveness that has shaped "the social and natural universe".

The faculty of being "receptive", "passive", is a precondition of freedom: it is the ability of seeing things in their own right, to experience the joy enclosed in them, the erotic energy of nature – an energy which is there to be liberated [...] This receptivity is itself the soil of creation: it is opposed, not to productivity, but to *destructive* productivity.

1972: 74

Marcuse observes that destructive productivity has been the "more conspicuous feature" of the "male principle", which has been the ruling force of symbolic structures. So, an emancipated society would definitely be a feminine society. That has nothing to do with matriarchy: "the image of the woman as mother is itself repressive; it transforms a biological fact into an ethical and cultural value and thus it supports and justifies her social repression. At stake is rather the ascent of Eros, in men *and* women" (1972: 75). In a male dominated civilization, this means the feminization (Marcuse writes "femalization") of men. This would be a radical change in the instinctive as well as in the symbolic structure: "the weaking of primary aggressiveness which, by combination of biological and social factors, has governed the patriarchal culture" (1972: 75).

Neither women nor men are free within the established structure. On the assembly line the dehumanization of men is as deep as that of women. But the liberation of women is more sweeping than that of men since the repression of women has been reinforced by the argument of biological constitution. So, feminism is a radical transforming force because it transcends the entire cultural and social organization. "The movement becomes radical to the degree to which it aims, not only at equality within the job and value structure of the *established* society (which would be the equality of dehumanization) but rather at a change in the structure itself" (1972: 75).

According to Marcuse, the historical alienation of women – in the sense of exclusion from the public sphere – enables them to remain less brutalized and closer to their sensibility: "more human than man". "The historical process is dialectical: the patriarchal society has created a female image, a female counter-force, which may still become one of the gravediggers of patriarchal society. In this sense too, the woman holds the promise of liberation" (1972: 78).

Now, we think it is necessary to expand and amplify the concept of "gender" – by showing its importance in each and every part of the symbolic structure we are in, and also by considering non-binary, broader, and boundless meanings for it. Because the concept of gender is embedded in a range of political, social, and cultural formations, Angela Davis has already highlighted that:

Radical feminism, or radical antiracist feminism are important in the sense that they have affected the way especially young people think about social justice struggles today. That we cannot assume that it is possible to be victorious in any movement as long as we don't consider how gender figures in it, how gender and sexuality and class and nationality figure into those struggles.

2006: 47

We would like to finish this chapter with a sort of critical conclusion: "feminism involves a consciousness of capitalism". In Angela Davis' words:

> It must involve a consciousness of capitalism, and racism, and colonialism, and post colonialities, and ability, and more genders than we can even imagine, and more sexualities than we ever thought we could name. Feminism has helped us not only to recognize a range of connections among discourses, and institutions, and identities, and ideologies that we often tend to consider separately. But it has also helped us to develop epistemological and organizing strategies that take us beyond the categories "woman" and "gender" [...] Feminism insists on methods of thought and action that urge us to think about things together that appear to be separate.
>
> 2016: 104

References

Beauboeuf-Lafontant, Tamara. 2009. *Behind the Mask of the Strong Black Woman: Voice and Embodiment of a Costly Performance*. Philadelphia: Temple University Press.

Benhabib, Seyla. 1992. *Situating the Self. Gender, Community and Postmodernism in Contemporary Ethics*. New York: Routledge.

Brown, Wendy. 2006. "Feminist Theory and the Frankfurt School: Introduction". *differences: a Journal of Feminist Cultural Studies* 17(1).

Davis, Angela Y. 1998. *Blues Legacies and Black Feminism: Gertrude "Ma" Rainey, Bessie Smith and Billie Holiday*. New York: Vintage.

Davis, Angela Y. 2016. *Freedom is a Constant Struggle*. Chicago: Haymarket Books.

Davis, Angela Y. 2017. "Foreword" in *The Great Refusal. Herbert Marcuse And Contemporary Social Movements,* eds. Lamas, Andrew T., Wolfson, Todd and Funke, Peter. Philadelphia: Temple University Press.

Davis, Angela Y. 2019. "Angela Davis on Toni Morrison: Her words have radically altered the lives that we live" YouTube. Democracy Now! https://www.youtube.com /watch?v=JqQCbOHEGP8.

Du Bois, W.E.B. 2012 [1903]. *The Souls of Black Folk*. New York: Signet Classic.

Fraser, Nancy. 1986. "Toward a Discourse of Ethic of Solidarity". *Praxis International* 5(4).

Hurston, Zora Neale. 1999. *Their Eyes Were Watching God*. New York: Perennial Classics.

King Jr., Martin Luther. 2000. "New Day in Birmingham". In *Why We Can't Wait*. New York: Signet Classics.

Love, Heather. 2017. "Queer Critique, Queer Refusal" in *The Great Refusal. Herbert Marcuse and Contemporary Social Movements*, eds. Andrew T. Lamas, Todd Wolfson, and Peter N. Funke Philadelphia: Temple University Press. 118–131.

Marcuse, Herbert. 1955. *Eros and Civilization. A Philosophical Inquiry into Freud*. Boston: Beacon Press.

Marcuse, Herbert. 1969. *An Essay on Liberation*. Boston: Beacon Press.

Marcuse, Herbert. 1972. *Counter-Revolution and Revolt*. Boston: Beacon Press.

Marcuse, Herbert. 1974. "Marxism and Feminism". *Women's Studies* 2(1): 279–288. Republished in 2006. "Marxism and Feminism". *differences: a Journal of Feminist Cultural Studies* 17(1): 147–157.

Marcuse, Herbert. 1978. *The Aesthetic Dimension. Toward a Critique of Marxist Aesthetic*. Boston: Beacon Press.

Marcuse, Herbert. 1991. *One-dimensional Man*. London: Routledge.

Marcuse, Herbert. 2001. "The Historical Fate of Bourgeois Democracy". In *Towards a Critical Theory of Society. Collected Papers of Herbert Marcuse. Volume 2*, ed. Douglas Kellner. London and New York: Routledge.

Marcuse, Herbert. 2001a. "A Revolution in Values". In *Towards a Critical Theory of Society. Collected Papers of Herbert Marcuse. Volume 2*, ed. Douglas Kellner. London and New York: Routledge.

Marcuse, Herbert. 2017. "The Radical Transformation of Norms, Needs, and Values". In *Transvaluation of Values and Radical Social Change – Five New Lectures*, eds. Peter-Ervin Jansen, Sarah Surak and Charles Reitz. International Herbert Marcuse Society.

Marcuse, Herbert & Bovenschen, Silvia & Shuller, Marianne. 1978. "Weiblichkeitsbilder". In *Gespräche mit Herbert Marcuse*, eds. Jürgen Habermas and Silvia Bovenschen. Frankfurt: Suhrkamp.

Parks, Sheri. 2010. *Fierce Angels: the Strong Black Woman in American Life and Culture*. New York: Random House.

Patton, Stacey. 2010. "Mules of the World" accessed at: https://www.wcwonline.org/WRB-Issues/the-mules-of-the-world.

Power, Nina. 2013. "Marcuse and Feminism Revisited". *Radical Philosophy Review* 16(1).

Steuernagel, Trudy. 1994. "Marcuse, the Women's Movement, and Women's Studies". In *Marcuse: from the New Left to the Next Left*, eds. John Bokina, and Timothy J. Lukes. University of Kansas Press. 89–105.

West, Cornel. 2014. *Black Prophetic Fire*. Boston: Beacon Press.

Index